Tyrants

A History of Power, Injustice, and Terror

WALLER R. NEWELL

CAMBRIDGE
UNIVERSITY PRESS

CAMBRIDGE
UNIVERSITY PRESS

32 Avenue of the Americas, New York NY 10013-2473, USA

Cambridge University Press is part of the University of Cambridge.

It furthers the University's mission by disseminating knowledge in the pursuit of education, learning, and research at the highest international levels of excellence.

www.cambridge.org
Information on this title: www.cambridge.org/9781107083059

© Waller R. Newell 2016

First published 2016

Printed in the United States of America

A catalog record for this publication is available from the British Library.

Library of Congress Cataloging in Publication Data
Names: Newell, Waller R., author.
Title: Tyrants : a history of power, injustice, and terror / Waller R. Newell.
Description: New York, NY : Cambridge University Press, 2016. |
Includes bibliographical references and index.
Identifiers: LCCN 2015046853 | ISBN 9781107083059 (hardback)
Subjects: LCSH: Despotism.
Classification: LCC JC381.N44 2016 | DDC 321.909–dc23
LC record available at http://lccn.loc.gov/2015046853

ISBN 978-1-107-08305-9 Hardback

Contents

Preface

When Russian President Vladimir Putin orchestrated an invasion of the Crimea, in violation of the territorial integrity of Ukraine to which the Russian government itself had been a signatory, U.S. Secretary of State John Kerry remarked in some bewilderment that Putin, with his aggressive militarism, seemed like a figure out of "the nineteenth century."

If you agree with that, you should probably stop reading this book right now. After all, won't the progress of history take care of retrograde adventurers like Putin? He can't be more than a brief detour on our way to the spread of democracy around the world and the end of aggression.

If, on the other hand, you believe, like me, that Vladimir Putin is a figure from *every* century, then read on. Because this is a book about how and why tyranny is a permanent feature on the human landscape. It's about the kind of tyrannical governments that have existed throughout history and still do today – some since ancient times, some specifically connected to the modern age. It follows the strange career of tyranny from its origins in ancient Greece and Rome to the state-building despots who brought Europe out of feudalism into the modern age. Finally, it explains the totalitarian tyrannies that began with the Jacobin Terror of 1793 and continued through the Bolsheviks, Nazis, Chairman Mao, the Khmer Rouge, and today's Jihadists.

This book is also about the often twisted psychological makeup of tyrants, including those who aspire to become tyrants, namely terrorists. For terrorists, as we'll see, are tyrants in waiting, and tyrannies, once established, continue to terrorize their captive subjects. Finally, it's about the ways in which tyrants can attract rapt and devoted followers to carry out their murderous agenda.

If you find these topics interesting – and above all, necessary for informed citizens who want to protect and promote democracy – then this book is for you. It's not about every form of injustice of which man is capable. Its focus is mainly on the West. But it is based on the belief that tyranny is a permanent alternative in human affairs and in explaining political action.

The progress of history, if that has actually taken place, has plainly not gotten rid of tyranny. The genocidal horrors of the last century's totalitarianism are surely proof of that, along with today's aspirants to a worldwide Caliphate, such as ISIS. Believing in the progress of history may actually, as we'll see, contribute to the spread of tyranny itself. Not only because it lulls us into thinking that tyranny is fading away, but because all of the worst totalitarian regimes, after all, have claimed that they were on the *side* of history, bringing a better world for us all in the future through mass murder and conquest in the present.

Across the world today, we are witnessing both a heroic struggle for democracy and the disturbing strength of tyrannical regimes and movements. Whether it is the Syrian civil war, Putin's aggression, or the threat of ISIS, democracy and tyranny often appear to be in a dead heat. While American forces are now engaged against Jihadism in Iraq, self-identified Muslim terrorists inspired by our enemies there conduct brutal attacks on America's own soil. Why is this happening now? How should the West respond? What are the lessons of history?

The spirit of free self-government has triumphed over tyranny again and again, from Marathon and Salamis to Waterloo, Dunkirk, D-Day, Solidarity, and Operation Desert Storm, but democracies seem to undergo periodic bouts of amnesia, unable to identify tyranny for what it is.

I hope this book will help provide a cure for that amnesia. Democracy is a better idea than tyranny on every level, and in a fair fight it almost never loses. But to defend that idea and make it successful, we need to be aware of its greatest and most resilient enemy – tyranny.

Acknowledgments

A year as Visiting Fellow in Humanistic Studies at the Beverley Rogers, Carol C. Harter Black Mountain Institute, the University of Nevada Las Vegas gave me the opportunity to complete this book free of my normal academic duties, for which I am most grateful. A public lecture for the Black Mountain Institute gave me the opportunity to preview Part Three of this book before an appreciative audience. Thanks are due as well to the Heritage Foundation, and particularly to David Azerad and Arthur Milikh, for enabling me to present the overall themes of the book at a public lecture in Washington, and to explore them further in an essay for their journal *First Principles*.

A long-standing group of former teachers and current colleagues, all friends as well, and from many walks of life besides the academic, has sustained me throughout this book, as it has through my earlier books. Even when I don't see them for a while, I frequently imagine them reacting to what I write and hope they approve. They include, in no special order, Thomas and Lorraine Pangle, Harvey Mansfield, Lynette Mitchell, Charles Fairbanks, Robert Goldberg, Leah Bradshaw, Catherine and Michael Zuckert, Peter Ahrensdorf, Stephen Smith, Norman and Karen Doidge, Gary Clewley, Paul Rahe, Clifford Orwin, Ryan Balot, Barry Strauss, George Jonas, Gerald Owen, Robert Sibley, Ken Green, Mark Lutz, David Fott, along with my Carleton colleagues Tom Darby, Farhang Rajaee, and Geoffrey Kellow, and former students of mine who are making their way into the academic world, including Alex Duff and Matthew Post.

Finally, I owe deep thanks to my editor, Robert Dreesen, for his unstinting support, encouragement, and wise suggestions for improving this book as it came into being. And, as always, thanks to my wife Jacqueline for her matchless editing skills, erudition, and advice – really my collaborator.

Introduction: The Strange Career of Tyranny

High above the island of Capri, overlooking the Bay of Naples, stand the ruins of the Roman Emperor Tiberius' summer villa. It's a two-hour hike up a winding narrow roadway to the top, and when you finally make it, the vistas are stunning. Even more impressive, however, is the villa itself, really a gargantuan palace that, even in its fragmented condition, creates a powerful impression of majesty, might, and fear. Vaulted paths lead you through a winding labyrinth of chambers, until you emerge on what would have been a shaded, colonnaded terrace onto which the main rooms of the palace opened – a terrace that was an entire mile in length, capturing and funneling the breezes off the Bay. Here the Emperor, his family, and his entourage would have relaxed in the shaded cool. Even higher up, and the crown of the whole site, is a huge circular platform where Tiberius received delegations from his throne. Preserved intact because a Christian church was built there, with the entire Bay of Naples and the Neapolitan coast as its backdrop, standing there you truly feel you are on the top of the world – on top, in fact, of Mount Olympus. Not coincidentally, the villa was called The Villa of Jupiter, and trembling officials and ambassadors brought into the Emperor's presence in the clouds must truly have felt they were in the presence of the King of the Gods. It was a calculated effect. And Tiberius was fully capable of a god's capricious wrath. It was said that when someone displeased him (and that didn't take much), he would order him thrown off there and then, plunging to his death in the rocky surf far below.

The Roman Empire was in many ways the greatest state the world has ever known. Most historians would agree that it was well into the modern era before Europe even approached its architectural sophistication and city planning. But the greatness of Rome was based on a thinly disguised tyranny. The Emperor was the apex of all power, the source of all strength, patronage, and honor. The famous Roman roads spanning the world from Scotland to Jordan; the cities with their beautiful forums, baths, theaters, central heating, and water systems, appearing as if air-lifted to their locales stretching from Syria to Spain; the fearsome legions, plausibly described as the greatest killing machine in history until Hitler's Wehrmacht – all flowed from the will and obeyed every command of one absolute master. Created by Augustus Caesar, predecessor of the gloomy Tiberius, the office of Emperor was a masterpiece of propaganda and manipulation, whereby a tyrant was sheathed in modest constitutional garb as merely the "first citizen" of an allegedly self-governing republic, his title originally meaning nothing more than a "field commander" hailed by his troops. But everyone knew the truth. By the end of the first century AD, the emperor was being addressed as *Dominus et Deus* – lord of all mankind, with the absolute power of life and death akin to that of a master over his slaves, a living god. A famous architect foolish enough to have criticized the young Emperor Hadrian's amateur blueprint for a temple met with execution for "insulting the Emperor's majesty." And Hadrian was one of the so-called Good Emperors.

Here is a powerful and disturbing theme that this book will explore: Can tyranny ever be a constructive or beneficial force? The dilemma is an age-old one. Alexander the Great, Augustus Caesar, Constantine the Great, Charlemagne – it could be argued that all brought about greater power and prosperity for their peoples, or at least a restoration of peace and order after long intervals of civil war and strife, through their imperial will, including through supreme ambition, usurpation, war, and murder. But it's an especially acute dilemma for an age like ours that regards democracy as the *only* justifiable form of government. We're taught that tyranny cannot go together with man's progress toward greater freedom and equality. We're taught that the modern age represents, since the Renaissance, the Age of Reason and the Enlightenment, mankind's steady march away from feudal oppression and ignorance toward open and free societies. What was once called the Whig theory of history, no longer fashionable among academic historians but still widely believed in the English-speaking nations, argued that English history beginning with Magna Carta was a steady, largely peaceable progression toward ever greater individual liberty, rights, and constitutional limits on arbitrary power, especially the power of kings, culminating in the Glorious Revolution of 1689, precursor to the American Revolution of 1776.

But what about the contribution of the Tudors to this evolution? Henry VII, Henry VIII, and Elizabeth I ruled with iron-fisted absolutism, Machiavellian duplicity, and concentration of all power in the monarch's hands that was unknown in previous English history. A cringing Parliament agreed that any proclamation of Henry VIII had the force of law. The detention, torture, and execution, often without trial, of suspected political or religious enemies was widespread (and modern – it had rarely taken place in the so-called Dark Ages). In bringing the Reformation to England, Henry cut a swath of destruction through the Old Church leaving entire cathedrals and monasteries in ruins as if from a twentieth-century bombing raid. Yet by the end of the Tudor era, the basis had been laid for England's transformation from a minor and backward realm into one of the strongest military and economic powers in Europe, its reach already extending to the New World. Just as with the Roman Empire, it looks, from the case of England, as if autocracy might sometimes be an indispensable ingredient for the rise to greatness, even the rise to freedom and prosperity, of a people. And Henry VIII was only one of a succession of modernizing, state-building tyrants. Napoleon, Stalin, Hitler, and Mao were all to come, and in each case, their monstrous aggressiveness, bottomless craving for prestige, and absolute autocratic authority helped bring about needed economic, military, and technical advancements for their peoples, though at the cost of wars or genocide that consumed millions of lives.

This is our theme – the strange career of tyranny as both the oppressor of liberty and the builder of civilizations, a short history of its past and where it lives today. As we'll see, tyranny is not just about institutions, but also about personalities – outsized, sometimes charismatic, sometimes amusing, always fascinating and frightening. Even today, we cannot escape their importance, for good or for ill, in state building; in laying the groundwork for greater stability, power, and prosperity; and sometimes even for eventual democratic self-government. And we especially cannot escape the uncomfortable but unavoidable question of whether there are better and worse varieties of tyranny available in the world of international relations – whether there is a lesser of evils among the kinds of nondemocratic authority we support, for instance in the revolutions that have been unfolding in the Muslim world since the Arab Spring. Mubarak or Morsi? Assad or the Muslim Brotherhood? Or to state the opposition more generally – military dictatorship or Islamist extremism? Authoritarianism or totalitarianism? In some situations, there may be no third way. As we'll see in this book, this, too, is a dilemma with a very long pedigree, one that I will argue can give us some important guidance today in promoting a maximum net gain for the forces of democracy over the forces of oppression.

THE THREE FACES OF TYRANNY

I'm going to argue in this book that there are three main types of tyranny that emerge from the history of the West (and not only the West). They are not absolutely distinct from one another, but they do stand out as separate kinds. The first is what I call "garden-variety" tyrants, at once the oldest and still the most familiar from our own world. These are basically men who dispose of an entire country and society as if it were their personal property, exploiting it for their own pleasure and profit and to advance their own clan and cronies. As Aristotle put it, they rule as "masters" over a country as if it were their own private "household." It's not inconceivable that such a ruler can benefit his country – he can be a vigorous leader in war, and help expand the economy. But at the end of the day, it's all about and his and his family's profit and pleasure. As the cynical Sophist Thrasymachus in Plato's *Republic* says, if the tyrant fattens up his flock of human sheep, it's only to make them more profitable for eventual slaughter. These tyrants often (although not always) descend into titanic excesses of hedonism and cruelty, since they are awash in purloined wealth and unrestrained by law. Examples from history of garden-variety tyrants abound, ranging from Hiero I of Syracuse to the Emperor Nero, General Franco of Spain, the Somozas of Nicaragua, Papa Doc Duvalier, and, until recently, Mubarak of Egypt.

The second type is the tyrant as reformer. These are men who are indeed driven to possess supreme honor and wealth, and power unconstrained by law or democracy. But they are not mere hedonists or profit seekers. They really want to improve their society and people through the constructive exercise of their untrammeled authority. Examples include Alexander the Great, Julius Caesar, the Tudors, "enlightened despots" such as Louis XIV, Frederick the Great, Napoleon, and Kemal Ataturk. Whereas nobody in his right mind could have anything but moral contempt for garden-variety tyrants like Nero, sots of greed and witless excess, reforming tyrants present a more complex challenge, because they often attract large followings of admiring clients and subjects who sincerely believe they are doing what's best for the common good. Frequently, they are not perceived as tyrants but as champions of the common people. Not only do they bring victory and independence to their peoples through war, but reforming tyrants embark on large-scale projects of public improvement in the realms of urban renewal, law, sanitation, education, and closing the economic gap between the rich and the poor. Although hardly immune to a monopoly on public honor and the camouflage of usurped legitimate titles, they want much, much more than to be a mere clan chieftain or khan fattening himself off his subjects. They want nothing less than to impose order on a chaotic world for the benefit of mankind, with eternal fame as their reward, an impulse that emerged early on with aspiring world-scale tyrants like Nebuchadnezzar or the Pharaohs of Egypt. In their personal lives, they are often ascetic or at least restrained, employ violence for concrete aims rather than whimsical cruelty, and are willing to endure the same hardships as their soldiers.

The third type of tyranny is millenarian. These rulers are neither content to be mere garden-variety tyrants, gluttons, and exploiters, nor even to be reforming tyrants who make constructive improvements. They are driven by the impulse to impose a millenarian blueprint that will bring about a society of the future in which the individual will be submerged in the collective and all privilege and alienation will forever be eradicated. Their league includes Robespierre, Stalin, Hitler, Chairman Mao, Pol Pot, and today's Jihadists. The gruesome paradox of their revolution is that the coming world of perfect harmony of tomorrow will require prodigious excesses of mass murder, warfare, and genocide in the present. I term it "utopian genocide" driven by ideas that kill. Because of their connection to the psychology of terrorism, I will say more about them later in this Introduction. For now, let's bear in mind that, while garden-variety and reforming tyrants have existed throughout human history from earliest times to the present, millenarian tyrants are strictly modern, with no precedents before the Jacobin Terror of 1793. Some see them as a secularized version of religious apocalypticism comparable to the Cathars or Anabaptists, but for reasons I'll get to later in the book, I don't believe that comparison holds up. Millenarian tyrants certainly do things for their countries that overlap with the reforming-tyrant type – Stalin and Hitler both contributed to their respective countries' economic and technological modernization. They are capable behind closed doors of some of the twisted excesses of the garden-variety tyrant, but, at bottom, their goal is "beyond politics" – they want to destroy today's world in order to bring about the nirvana of "communism," "the thousand-year Reich" or "the world-wide Caliphate."

Before we get too far into the strange career of tyranny, I should stress that everything about the topic of tyranny, no matter which category, is controversial and inevitably in the eye of the beholder, to a degree. Thomas Hobbes' jaundiced observation that we call someone a tyrant if he gores our ox and a statesman if he helps us out contains a grain of truth. Some of history's major tyrants from Caesar to Hitler were widely admired and widely loathed. Merely to suggest examples, as I have done, of the three faces of tyranny could be challenged. Many Spaniards idolized Franco. Ask a Turk what he thinks of Ataturk and you'll likely get a very different answer than if you ask an Armenian or Greek. My purpose here is not to abandon making a moral judgment against tyranny but, on the contrary, to make that judgment more precise by understanding the wide variety among tyrannies and the different kinds of peril they pose to free self-government.

THE ANCIENT AND MODERN UNDERSTANDINGS OF TYRANNY

In order to see why millenarian tyranny is uniquely modern, first appearing in the Jacobin Terror of 1793, we need to broaden our scope to look at some major shifts between ancient and modern philosophy, morality, culture, and our understanding of history and psychology. I will explore these in detail in the rest of the book, but let's start with an over-view.

In general, tyranny was viewed rather differently in ancient and modern times by those who observed and thought about political and social life. Plato's take is best known from his famous denunciation of the tyrant in the *Republic* as a man ruled by his passions, oppressive and suspicious, a populist demagogue who mirrors the very worst excesses of democratic hedonism and stirs up the resentment of the mob against their aristocratic betters. Not only individuals, but entire countries could be tyrants – as Pericles famously reminded the democracy of Athens in his *Funeral Oration*, they were a "tyrant city" in the eyes of their coerced "allies." But as I've already observed, the Greeks also recognized that tyrants could play a constructive role in taking over from more legitimate but less effective governments, and Plato himself in the *Laws* envisions a young tyrant with a "passion for rule" who is guided by a wise counselor to found a just society. The theme of the young prince guided away from overweening ambition toward civic virtue by a philosophic mentor echoes down through antiquity and the Renaissance from Cicero's *Dream of Scipio* (though as we'll see, in real life Cicero didn't do too well in this mentoring role with the young Octavian Caesar) to Erasmus' *Education of a Christian Prince*. Over all, the ancients taught, the cure for tyrannical impulses lay in forming a virtuous character through an education in moderation and prudence.

The great critique of the ancient approach begins in the Renaissance with Machiavelli's classic manual on power-seeking, *The Prince*. Machiavelli argues that a successful ruler must be the source of his *own* prudent judgment, not dependent on a counselor (who, after all, might take his state away from him!). But that means a radical change in the meaning of political prudence. For how can the prince be the source of his own prudence unless he liberates himself from the old-fashioned constraints of ancient moral philosophy and Christian piety? The new prince can be the source of his own prudence only if his prudence flows from his *will*. The most successful princes, Machiavelli teaches, do no less than "master Fortuna" – that is, they re-shape the world according to their own blueprint. Moreover, a bold and hot-blooded youth will have better luck at this than a man-made prematurely old and cautious by traditional morality. For the ancient Greek moralists and their Christian successors, virtue meant accommodating yourself to the natural order. Machiavelli opens up the intoxicating prospect that a prince can conquer nature and increase the power and prosperity both of himself and his subjects. Although Machiavelli gives some notoriously frank advice to princes or aspiring princes on how to remove opponents through treachery and assassination, we should remember that he is not advocating tyranny for its own sake, especially the kind of witless hedonistic excess and whimsical cruelty denounced by Plato, and exemplified in real life by the likes of Nero or Caligula. For Machiavelli, princely ambition and ruthlessness are justified only insofar as they bring increased security, wealth and greatness to the prince's people. Even healthy republics occasionally need such vigorous and domineering personalities as their leading statesmen, to prevent the people from becoming idle, greedy, and lax, hence vulnerable to demagogues.

For Machiavelli, it's not so much a matter of promoting a moderate character to guard against the temptation of tyranny, as it had been for the ancients, but of finding the right *method* for the prince's self-controlled, disciplined, and rational application of power for real-world success from which all will benefit. As we'll see, the rise of modern state-building despots like Henry VIII and of English and American commercial republicanism both flow from Machiavelli's pragmatic and this-worldly teachings. The rise of modernity to which Machiavelli's writings give birth is reflected in the millenarian overtone of his language when he writes that, in freeing statecraft from the distortions of classical and Christian morality, he is opening up a new world: "I have decided to take a path as yet untrodden by anyone," the theoretical equivalent of the recent discovery of the New World, which will eventually provide the blank canvas for the unfolding of what Alexander Hamilton termed "the new science of politics," the creation of Machiavelli and his successors such as Montesquieu. Machiavelli believed that Republican Rome was the greatest state that had ever existed, and that its greatness could be reenacted by modern man. For the American Founders, the New World would be the site of nothing less than a New Rome, a "New Order of the Ages."

Machiavelli's summons to the conquest of nature by methodically ruthless princes certainly expands the scope of political power beyond anything envisioned by the ancients. Moreover, while ancient world-conquerors like Alexander the Great or Julius Caesar aimed to impose on their subjects the aristocratic pattern of Greco-Roman culture (those cookie-cutter cities with their forums, gymnasiums, and theaters stretching from Bath to Leptis Magna), Machiavelli is frankly more populist and pro-democratic in encouraging princes to ally themselves with the common people and help them prosper economically. He prefers the solid, unambitious decency of "the people" to the ineradicable arrogance of "the nobles." Still, at the end of the day, Machiavelli is a rationalist, not a full-blown millenarian. His populism is dry-eyed and utilitarian. He believes that people universally want "security and well-being," and that a pragmatic statecraft can be forged that will bring this about. In terms of our three categories of tyranny, the Machiavellian Prince is in the category of the reforming tyrant.

Only with Rousseau does the full-blown millenarian tyrant emerge in the cultural imagination of Europe, translated into reality by the Jacobins – the return to an alleged Golden Age through revolutionary violence and genocide, the origins of totalitarianism in the romanticization of the "the People" and their return to "Year One." The French Revolution began in 1789 as a Lockean revolution patterned on the Glorious and American revolutions, led by students of the Enlightenment like Lafayette and Talleyrand, bent on establishing the rights of man, limited government, and economic opportunity. In 1793, the Jacobins, led by Robespierre, turned it into a Rousseauan revolution, bent on returning to an alleged Golden Age of pure collective equality without private possessions or individual self-interest, to be achieved through the destruction of the aristocracy and bourgeoisie and anyone else who was loyal to them, aspired to their status, or shared their values. This was history's first millenarian tyranny. After Robespierre, the league of millenarian tyrants includes Stalin, Hitler, Chairman Mao, Pol Pot, and today's Jihadists. Later in this book, I'll explore Rousseau's influence and how the French Revolution differed from the Glorious and American revolutions in its apocalyptic terror, utopian aims, and frightening personalities. For now, by way of introduction, I want to explore millenarian tyranny through a contemporary portal. For Americans today, the millenarian variety of tyranny is most immediately encountered, I believe, in the context of terrorism, because terrorists, as I'm about to argue, are millenarian tyrants in waiting.

TYRANTS IN WAITING: TERRORISM AND THE
RIGHTEOUS ANGER OF YOUNG MEN

In considering the creed of the terrorist, we have to keep in mind that tyranny is not just a variety of government but a category of human psychology, an especially dark, disturbing, and intriguing one. And we especially have to consider the connection between the tyrannical impulse and the righteous anger of young men. There's a powerful stereotype, both from fiction and real events, that pictures the tyrant as a bitter, narrow-minded, and soulless old man keeping down the young and the idealistic, secretly envious of their passion for life and for justice – General Pinochet, Gabriel Garcia Marquez' *The Autumn of the Patriarch*, the Emperor Palpatine in *Star Wars*. Though this is a part of the truth, it's also the case that many of history's most famous and notorious tyrants were relatively young. Indeed, going back to Homer's *Iliad*, the very longing for heroism and nobility itself can harbor the potential for tyranny, rooted in anger over perceived slights to one's dignity and a ferocious longing for triumph and revenge. Achilles detests his elder, Agamemnon, King of Kings among the Greeks and regards him as a tyrant. But Achilles, as the poem goes on to show, is fully capable of tyrannical behavior himself. Achilles needs to be reformed, and Plato's *Republic* is, in many ways, a parents' guide to preventing your troubled teen from turning out like him.

This reinforces an observation common to ancient and modern writers on statecraft, one that Machiavelli would endorse as much as Plato: Potential tyrants and great statesmen or leading citizens may share some of the *same* dark traits of aggressiveness and a lust for honor. The problem is how to tell them apart beforehand, especially since the potential tyrant may appear in the guise of the liberator or hero. Think of the young Abraham Lincoln's Lyceum speech, in which, recalling such members of "the tribe of the eagle" as Alexander, Caesar, and Napoleon, he toyed with whether greater glory came to the man who saved the republic or overthrew it. His own career provided him with the answer to that existential dilemma, to his country's everlasting benefit. But we are not always so fortunate with the ambitious in our midst. Despite the differences between ancient and modern tyranny, I will argue in this book, if there is a cure for tyrannical longings, it must be through the kind of appeal made by Plato to young men to prefer civic virtue and the satisfaction of a well-ordered character. Education is the answer. That's as true now as it was in the past, especially given the appeal of Jihadism to young men.

This requires that we think about how terrorists are tyrants in waiting and often turn into them. The Boston Marathon killings, the horrific gutting of the young British soldier outside his barracks, the beheading in Oklahoma by a convert to Islam, the slaughter of the Charlie Hebdo cartoonists by a French cell of Al Qaeda – these and many other grisly episodes should prompt us to reconsider the role that righteous anger in young men plays in extremist politics. Usually we are told that terrorist acts, while reprehensible, can be traced to "root causes," that such acts are born of despair over lack of economic opportunity and the peaceful benefits of a pluralist secular society. This doctrine was reaffirmed in then-candidate Barack Obama's first major foreign policy speech, *The War We Need to Win*, and it has been hauled out every time a terrorist attack occurs on American soil. Yet, in almost all these cases, the terrorists were already living in a secular pluralist society and capable of enjoying its benefits. So how can poverty and lack of opportunity be the "root cause"?

The tremendous power of this *idee fixe* goes back to the very beginning of modernity in the Age of Reason and the Enlightenment. Thinkers including Hobbes and Voltaire argued that tyrannical ambition, military strife, and civil war were caused by denying human beings their basic right to pursue their own material self-interest. Once they enjoyed the balm of security and well-being, the sources of aggression and conflict would melt away, leaving us free, as Voltaire encouraged, to "cultivate our garden." Hobbes was particularly critical of the way in which ancient philosophers, headed up by Aristotle, encouraged young men to believe themselves capable of achieving great, noble, and heroic deeds that would benefit everyone and give them an immortal reputation. And this brings us back to terrorism in the present.

What if terrorism had little if anything to do with economic deprivation or lack of individual opportunity? What if it were rooted in the capacity of young men for righteous zeal, anger, and indignation, harnessed in the service of what they fervently believe to be a righteous, even divine mission to bring justice to the world? Homer's *Iliad* begins with the rage of Achilles – that is the key to understanding the great issues of war and peace. Achilles believes the gods are on his side, and if the gods are not, he is willing to shake his fist even at them. Plato and the other ancient thinkers try to redirect this anger away from tyrannical ambition and fanatical extremism to the spirited service of the common good under a republic of laws.

Righteous anger, it seems to me, is where we should start in attempting to understand terrorism and addressing its psychological deformities, including its potential for developing into tyranny. Recent studies suggest that male traits of aggressiveness, competitiveness, and honor seeking may be biologically hardwired, rather than learned behavior. Studies also show that young men are one of the chief causes of violence, political or otherwise, in all societies. These studies usually conclude with the need to reform the characters of young men, habituating them to give up their overly self-assertive, judgmental stands and become more tolerant and peaceful. But what if the bellicose capacities of young men were summoned into existence by the perception of justice and injustice, the conviction that injustice has to be fought and justice upheld? I would argue that these perceptions exist in every society of which we have any knowledge. The point is not to try to get rid of righteous indignation, therefore, but to convert it to the service of a view of justice that is sane and reasonable.

Hobbes understood that many young men begin as Achilles. They want honor from serving what they perceive to be a noble cause. While he thought this passion could be tamed by material well-being, he did not think it could ever be entirely eradicated. The social contract would always have to be on guard against the wolves prowling its dark perimeters. Since then, however, there has been a tendency to think that the entire world has become like that social contract or is on the verge of becoming so, if only we could extend the benefits of prosperity to those who still cling to aberrant passions of righteous zeal. And yet reality contradicts this belief every day, whether it be in Paris, Copenhagen, Moore, Oklahoma, or Iraq.

As I've observed, in the romanticization of revolution, revolutionaries are often portrayed as young idealists fighting the grip on power and privilege of rigid old men. In reality, as the history of revolutions from the Jacobins to the present amply demonstrates, young revolutionaries aim precisely to establish a state where they will have absolute power to force others into a collectivist straitjacket. That's why terrorists are often tyrants in waiting, and why tyrannies terrorize their own populations while often supporting new terrorists abroad (think of the Iranian Islamic Republic). Their contempt for what they perceive as the bloated softness and weakness of modern society is translated into a demand that the masses be purified of their corrupt material pleasures, a kind of monasticism imposed on an entire society. (Sergey Nechaev's classic statement of the terrorist's creed was revealingly entitled *Catechism of the Revolutionist*). That indignation toward the sloth of the masses, that desire for a totalitarian collective purged of its frivolity and laxity is what drives many of the young men who believe they are waging Jihad. The ideology of Jihadism, a sedulous blend of pseudo-religious messianism hitched to the service of a totalitarian utopia, only increases the dangerous appeal of this distorted kind of idealism.

As this book will explore, the passion for justice born of righteous anger, with its call for the wholesale destruction and reconstruction of existence, is at the psychological core of revolutionary politics. Anger over the feeling that one has been treated unjustly – oppressed, insulted, slighted, overlooked – is common to all people. Few act violently on that sense of righteous indignation, content to seethe inwardly, and fewer still carry that vengeance through to the attempted destruction of the world around them and its replacement with a new order that will enshrine their own supremacy. This book deals with that exclusive club and how an unbridled and destructive passion for justice is the engine of modern radical extremism.

In just about every case of a millenarian tyrant, we find a shattering experience in early life – failure to achieve a respectable career, distant or oppressive parents, shame and disgrace over the family name, a feeling of being excluded by the upper class – that drove these young men to bring everything down in flames in order to avenge themselves for these injustices and insults, a vengeance now extended from the original cruel or neglectful authority figure who treated them so slightingly (sometimes without being aware of it) to entire social forces and classes – "the bourgeoisie," "the reactionaries," "the aristos," "the Jews." Hence, if Hitler had succeeded in getting into art school, or if Lenin's brother had not been executed for being a subversive, if Mao had not felt looked down on as a student for his peasant origins, Germany, Russia, and China might well have been spared the million-fold suffering brought about by their supremacy. The ideological visions of Bolshevism, Nazism, and Maoism are, to be sure, indispensable for understanding their success and appeal, and we'll examine them in detail when we turn to millenarian tyranny in Part Three. But the righteous anger and aggressiveness of the Leader is the crucible in which those totalitarian fantasies are forged and imposed on reality with indomitable will-power.

Another thing that distinguishes millenarian tyrants from mere assassins and rank-and-file terrorist cadres is their megalomaniacal conviction that they are not merely political outsiders driven by a passion for vengeance and justice, but great "thinkers" or "artists" whose genius has been overlooked, but whose visions will someday govern every facet of everyone else's life every moment of the day. Hitler fancied himself a great artist gone to waste due to his sacrifices for the German people. Lenin's dreary harangues and vicious diatribes were dressed up in an indigestible mish-mash of pseudo-Marxist dialectics. Stalin told famous composers, novelists, and scientists how they might improve their work; Mao imagined himself a great "theorist" as well as poet. Their loneliness and bitter alienation as young men were filled with hours of furious autodidact learning, gleaned in magpie fashion from whatever lay at hand in the extremist fashions of the day, that helped them spin the fantasies of the totalitarian new order they would impose on all others, finally recognized by all for their hidden genius. The interminable dinner-table monologues in which the Leader bangs on for hours with his insuperable insights into every aspect of human existence from ancient history to art, diet, and medical science is a hallmark of many of them, including Hitler, Stalin, and Castro.

Many of these men begin their rise to tyrannical power unusually early for success in conventional politics, generally a middle-aged vocation. Hitler was a major public figure in Germany by his thirties; Lenin became Bolshevik leader at thirty-three. Robespierre dominated the Jacobins at the same age. Their youthfulness often supplies a veneer of open-mindedness, vibrancy, forward-looking optimism and empathy for nonconformists masking their long-term aim for total control. Their thirst for absolute power absorbs and deflects drives for ordinary luxuries and amusements – the "Spartan" public image of Robespierre, Stalin, Hitler, Mao, Castro, Bin Laden, and others (whether authentic or not) appeared to confirm their selflessness and dedication to a just cause. Such men begin as revolutionaries and end as absolute despots. They appear in the guise of youthful idealists who invite other spirited and idealistic young people to join them in a revolution that will sweep away the old world of injustice, oppression, poverty, and class distinctions and create a new, fresh world in which all are free to flourish in a community that is simultaneously totally unified and allows every individual complete fulfillment. While Marat and Robespierre prepared their death machine for the slaughter of hundreds of thousands, the young poet Wordsworth truly felt that to be alive in Paris at this time was bliss, "but to be young was very heaven."

This vision of a brighter future in which the young, following their young leaders, will rise to their place in the sun is common to all modern revolutionary movements from the Jacobins through the Bolsheviks, Nazis, Maoists, Khmer Rouge, and today's Jihadists. Sometimes the leaders even pose as anarchists bent on smashing all authority for all time (both the Bolsheviks and Nazis early on had many anarchist adherents, and university students were one of the first major social classes to go over wholesale to Hitler). They attract hardened criminals and sadists who sense that "revolutionary justice" will provide a camouflage for their own psychoses, but also dewy-eyed idealists like the young Wordsworth (he came to know better) who genuinely want to help the downtrodden and believe that the Leader shares their hopes.

Those who hang onto the revolutionary movement are gradually drawn into the spiraling violence, the mass executions, the slaughter of racial and class enemies, on the way to total power, convincing themselves that the Leader does these things unwillingly, as regrettably necessary but temporary measures until full power is achieved and can be wielded justly or that he doesn't know about the excesses committed in his name. This was a common delusion about Stalin and Hitler among their dedicated followers. Then they wake up and find that the self-proclaimed revolutionary they believed was taking us all to a brighter world is in fact a tyrant bent on retaining total power forever. Stalin called them "useful idiots," including his admirers in Europe and America.

THE BEAUTIFICATION OF VIOLENCE

In understanding how revolutionary leaders amass their followings through the vision of a brighter future, we cannot underestimate the aesthetic appeal of youthful radicalism and political violence. It is mirrored in the literature, music, art, and film of the nineteenth and twentieth centuries, and, in turn, has inspired real-life revolutionary actors. That cultural context plays an important role in this book.

Think, for example, of the young nihilist Bazarov in Turgenev's *Fathers and Sons* or of Flaubert's Senecal in *Sentimental Education* (a would-be Jacobin in the Revolution of 1848 who ends up working for Napoleon III's secret police). Dostoyevsky's *Crime and Punishment* explores a young ex-student's cold-blooded murder of a crooked pawnbroker based on his conviction that he is a "great man" who will use her filthy lucre to perform good deeds, presaging later Bolshevik savagery in the name of social justice. Herman Hesse's *Demian* portrays a charismatic German student looking forward to World War I as the violent catharsis that will bring about the birth of a "new world." Solzhenitsyn's

Lenin In Zurich offers a fictionalized Lenin whose inhuman cold-bloodedness seems utterly convincing as an explanation of what he would later become. Strelnikov, the Trotsky stand-in in *Doctor Zhivago*, displaces his failure as a lover into an ascetic will to destroy counter-revolutionaries, ravaging Russia with his firing squads from his personal armored train.

Philosophy and music also contributed to romanticizing political violence. In addition to Marx's views on the therapeutic benefits of revolutionary violence, Nietzsche's Superman – his call for "a master race, the future masters of the earth" – certainly played a role (misinterpreted or otherwise) not only for the Nazis, but also for a Russian sect called the "God-builders," identified as an important precursor of the Bolsheviks. Existentialist philosopher Martin Heidegger extolled "the inner truth and greatness of National Socialism." Hitler saw in Wagner's *Rienzi* the beginning of his life mission – the opera is about a "tribune" of the People who leads their struggle against an oppressive aristocracy – while, in arranging for the Berlin Philharmonic to give Wagner's *Götterdämmerung* as its last performance as Berlin lay in flaming ruins in 1945, Albert Speer performed a final artistic service for his Führer. "Tomorrow Belongs To Me," sung by a beautiful Hitler Youth in the 1972 film *Cabaret*, captures precisely the appeal of National Socialism to the younger generation, a call for earth-shaking violence couched in bucolic Romantic imagery, and has been embraced by neo-Nazi groups today who think it actually comes from the Nazi era.

The trend continues into our own times. Charles Manson, who, in many ways, fits the pattern of an abused, brutalized and enraged youth who weaves his desire for murderous revenge against the upper orders who rejected his musical genius into an ideology of apocalyptic race warfare that might, in a setting other than the United States with its historical aversion for revolutionary extremism, have fueled an actual political movement, took the Beatles' *Helter-Skelter* as his oracle. The final scene of the 1999 film *Fight Club* in which Tyler Durden calmly blows up the New York skyline now seems eerily prescient about 9/11, and makes one wonder if it provided Al Qaeda and its young cadres with a source of inspiration. Reversing this possible imitation of art by life, German composer Karlheinz Stockhausen pronounced the destruction of the Twin Towers as "the greatest work of art imaginable for the whole cosmos." The beautification of violence is a rich and troubling trove of insights for our excavation of the tyrannical personality.

THE CHALLENGE OF TYRANNY IN TODAY'S WORLD

These dangerous young men, terrorists who are tyrants in waiting, will escape undetected – until it is too late – if we see the world as having already been transformed in such a way that, owing to the opportunity for individual freedom and self-interest, there should be no grounds for their anger. The problem with this assumption is that none of the millenarian tyrants I discuss in this book experienced an injustice in youth or childhood that, however real, remotely justified the vengeance they took through mass murder, terrorism, and genocide. In most cases, whatever injustice stung them as youths, they did not grow up in impoverished circumstances or lack the opportunity to rise in life through conventional careers. Robespierre was educated as a lawyer. Lenin's father belonged to the hereditary service nobility of the Tsarist regime and his family was prominent in Simbirsk. Mao's father was a wealthy land-owner. Pol Pot attended the Sorbonne. Bin Laden's family was worth millions. Most of them came from backgrounds that were middle class or higher.

Consequently, the sad truth is that, even if the blessings of liberal democracy were to spread around the globe (a dubious proposition at best), there is no guarantee that such violent and wrathful men will fade away. Indeed, their very contempt for what they perceive as the corrupt and spineless material-ism of the West might only intensify as liberal democracy spreads throughout the non-Western world, evoking Nietzsche's prediction that a new breed of "master" would emerge for the coming twentieth-century's struggle for the Earth precisely through their revulsion for the unbearable prevalence of bour-geois Last Man, "the herd man of democratic morality," a conceit embraced by many Bolshevik and Nazi revolutionaries. The revolutionary's zeal for punitive justice is, quite simply, an independent variable in political behavior that will never go away. It doesn't matter if the vast majority of people in the non-Western world would be content with a chance for prosperity and security in their personal lives. That won't necessarily deter the club of the righteously angry from their destructive mission, any more than it did in France, Russia, or Germany, all comparatively advanced countries, as we'll see in Part Three, at the time their revolutions broke out.

If we entertain this disturbing perspective, the world around us will not change. It remains what it was before. But we will see it differently, without the distorting lens of the modern social sciences and their inability to grasp tyranny as a permanent alternative, and we'll understand the need to keep a keen lookout for those wolves prowling the perimeters of liberal-democratic civilization in the nearby darkness. It's the same world, but our understanding of it and the contemporary threats posed by tyranny to democratic freedom will change considerably. That will involve teaching our young that real and aspiring tyrants still exist, just as they always have, and that it is important to learn what motivates them. The first step in confronting this danger, therefore, is to speak frankly about what it is and not cling to the comforting delusion that the spread of Western-style materialism will be sufficient to counteract it.

We also have to remember that, at bottom, our own liberal democratic civil-ization has *never* been premised solely on material well-being, greed, and com-fort. That is a caricature imposed on it by its opponents on the extreme Left and Right. Liberal democracy was not born primarily from the materialism of Hobbes, but from Spinoza's and Locke's more edifying accounts of liberty as the flourishing of the individual's full educational, civic, and spiritual potential, and it never lost sight of its classical heritage. Liberal democracy has its own account of a noble soul, one that does not try to hide from the possibly dangerous passions of righteous anger and zeal that are innate to spirited young men but can help young men understand themselves and become the vigorous defenders of the common good rather than its enemies. I hope this book will contribute to that educational effort. Consider it the equivalent of those old Mercator maps where, at the edge of known civilization, travelers were warned that *Hic Sunt Dragones* – Here there be dragons. I'm hoping to chart the map of tyranny past and present.

The career of tyranny is a complex and colorful tapestry in which human ambition, the forces of historical change, and revolutionary new thinking, both secular and religious, overlap and intertwine. Since tyranny has existed for as long as there has been recorded history, a complete history of it would run to thousands of pages, even if our focus were mainly the West. Because my purpose here is to provide a road map tracing the main varieties of tyranny from earliest times to the present – a Rick Steves' guide, to use another comparison, to despotism – within a single readable volume, a kind of portable one-semester course, I've had to be highly selective.

Part One is about tyranny in the ancient world. Part Two traces the emergence of the modern state against the backdrop of the Middle Ages. Part Three is about revolutionary violence and terror since the French Revolution. In each of the three parts, I've tried to show how tyranny has emerged and developed in conjunction with changes in moral philosophy, culture, and even art, poetry, and architecture, sometimes mirroring those influences, sometimes shaping them. That means that, in addition to focusing on some fundamental writers – Homer, Sophocles, Thucydides, Plato, Aristotle, Cicero, St. Augustine, St. Thomas, Machiavelli, Hobbes, Rousseau, Burke, Marx, and Nietzsche – I've also focused on individual tyrannical figures as standouts who are especially representative of one or more of the three categories, in part because they are still quite familiar to today's readers. They include Homer's Achilles, Alcibiades, Alexander the Great, Julius and Augustus Caesar among the ancients and, among the moderns, Henry VIII, who, I argue, blazes a path followed by other modern state-building despots including Peter the Great and Frederick the Great. When it comes to millenarian revolution, I open with the Jacobin Terror, including a psychological profile of Robespierre, and argue that all the hallmarks of totalitarian utopianism first emerge there. Using those hallmarks as a guide, I then offer successive diagnoses of revolutionary movements and their leaders – Lenin, Stalin and the Bolshevik Revolution, Hitler and Nazism, Maoism, the Khmer Rouge, down to today's Jihadist revolutionaries including former Iranian president Ahmadinejad – accompanied by a discussion of the shifting patterns of revolutionary ideology from Marx to Fanon and Ali Shariati.

In one sense, this is an old-fashioned book. I'm not talking about every kind of tyranny human beings encounter in life – the tyranny of parents over their children and *vice versa*, the physical or psychological oppression hidden in marriages; the tyranny of vindictive high school principles over cocky kids, of self-important bosses over sullen employees, of petty bureaucrats over helpless supplicants, of pompous professors (I'm told they exist) over cowed students. I'm talking about tyrannical *governments*. But that's the whole point – they're not old-fashioned. They're still around, and in some ways more dangerous than ever (think of ISIS capturing nuclear weapons). While I'll be arguing in this book that the danger of tyranny will always be with us, that doesn't mean I'm pessimistic about the prospects for freedom and self-government in the world, today and in the future, in the West and beyond the West. Far from it! As we'll see, the story of tyranny from earliest times to the present is also the story of its eventual defeat – from the Greeks' victory over the Great King of Persia at Marathon and Salamis to the struggle against ISIS as I write these words.

Free societies are often sluggish at first in responding to tyrannical aggression. Precisely because they are free, they bridle at concentrating so much power in the hands of their elected leaders. Themistocles and Churchill, among many other democratic war-leaders, found themselves pariahs after the danger had been vanquished. The Greek city-states were only slowly brought to see the need for united action against the Great King. When Britain finally did declare war on the Third Reich, eight months of "phony war" were to pass before it could actually put boots on the ground, while America's decisive entry was only sparked by Pearl Harbor. Republics are slow to rouse, but their wrath, once unleashed, is irresistible, because it is the wrath of an entire people, not a solitary despot, and it's based on hope, not fear.

All of our accumulated experience and knowledge about tyranny – ancient and modern, garden variety, reformist, and millenarian – is needed if we are to address the ways in which tyranny threatens democracy in the world today. While understandings of the character and motivation of tyranny have varied greatly over time, a fund of common sense and rich insight remains at our disposal not only from philosophers and artists, but also from historians and great statesmen – George Washington, Winston Churchill, Charles de Gaulle – who have reflected on their own motives for honor seeking and its permissible limits.

As the world was being inspired by the struggle for freedom unfolding across the Muslim lands during the Arab Spring, Freedom House reported that the forces of tyranny have been on the rise and the forces of democracy in retreat. We seem to be living in an era in which expectations for freedom and the proliferation of tyranny are intensifying simultaneously. The contest in today's world between tyranny and freedom reminds us that democratic self-government was first experienced in ancient Greece, along with an awareness of the threat posed by tyranny to self-governing communities under the rule of law. Plato's denunciation of the tyrant in the *Republic* has remained a standard throughout the ages. But as we have observed, an even more disturbing paradox, acknowledged by Plato and Aristotle themselves – one that is central to this book – is the extent to which intense political ambition can sometimes serve the common good.

According to Thucydides, the Athenian democracy expelled Alcibiades from command of the expedition to conquer Sicily because they felt he threatened to become their tyrant. And yet, Thucydides claims, Alcibiades might have won that war, whereas putting Nicias, leader of the peace party, in charge of the expedition guaranteed its failure, which brought about the decline of Athens. The study of history, political theory, and statecraft has always been greatly concerned with the question of how much political ambition is permissible. Can a love of honor that might otherwise derail into tyranny be converted to the robust and energetic service of the common good? History proves that while people sometimes loath tyrants, at other times they support and admire them as charismatic leaders who can get good things done even if it means violating tradition and precedent. Julius Caesar, for example, was adored by those who thought he was saving and revitalizing Rome from the purblind selfish and reactionary Senatorial class, and loathed by those who saw him as a tyrant and demagogue bent on destroying the republic forever. Napoleon was perceived in the same conflicted way throughout Europe – for some, a democratic liberator, for others an invading conqueror. Closer to home, both Abraham Lincoln and Franklin Roosevelt were regarded as national saviors by some, as tyrants by others.

This returns us to one of our central themes, one with which this Introduction began – exploring the paradox of how excessive and even tyrannical political ambition might conceivably be converted to serving democracy and the common good. This debate is more relevant than ever, as the pursuit of freedom in our own world sometimes requires us to make some rather difficult and uncomfortable choices between greater and lesser evils. The replacement of a dictator by a self-professed democratic movement does not necessarily mean something better will come about. Instead, a new kind of tyranny even worse than what preceded it might be the long-term outcome. We should ponder how the French, Russian, and Iranian revolutions all began as liberal reformist movements that were hijacked by collectivist extremists bent on genocide and war when we forecast a future for Egypt or Syria, or when we are tempted to throw over an imperfectly democratic authoritarian dictatorship when a totalitarian tyranny might be waiting in the wings to replace it. Again, might it be necessary to choose between relatively better and relatively worse nondemocratic kinds of authority? Does the removal of tyranny itself guarantee that people will naturally become democrats or might they want revenge against their former oppressors, thereby becoming oppressors themselves? These are not pleasant questions, but they are inescapable ones. The heritage of classical Greece is the indispensable starting point for thinking them through, and the place to begin is with the rage of Achilles.

Part One

The Rage of Achilles: From Homeric Heroes to Lord and God of the World

Achilles was in many ways the original Greek ideal of youth and manhood, a beautiful man with a divine aura, born of a sea goddess and a mortal king. Real conquerors and rulers including Alcibiades, Alexander the Great, Julius Caesar, and Napoleon took inspiration from him. And yet his primary passion was rage. The rage of Achilles is what sets Homer's great epic, the *Iliad*, into motion, a rage born of competition with his overlord, the older Agamemnon, which eventually left thousands of Greeks and Trojans dead in steaming heaps on the blood-soaked field before the great city.

The feud between the younger man and his elder is over who should rightfully be given the captive Trojan woman Briseis as a trophy of war. Achilles believes she is his by right because he has been by far the bravest warrior on the Greek side. But Agamemnon claims her for his own because he is not merely a king, but the King of Kings, the commander of the entire Greek force including Achilles. The mixture of erotic jealousy over the possession of the unfortunate woman and their resentment for each other over their status and prestige – Achilles thinks Agamemnon is a coward and a lightweight gaining glory through what are really his own achievements, while Agamemnon finds Achilles insufferably arrogant and insubordinate – boils over in their accusations of each other. You can fairly hear the words spitting through clenched teeth of these two kings clashing:

Then looking darkly at him Achilles of the swift feet spoke:

"O wrapped in shamelessness, with your mind forever on profit, how shall any one of the Achaians readily obey you either to go on a journey or to fight men strongly in battle? I for my part did not come here ... to fight against the Trojans, since to me they have done nothing ... For your sake, o great shamelessness, we followed, to do you a favor, you with the dog's eyes, to win your honor ... Always the greater part of the painful fighting is my work, but when the time comes to distribute the booty, yours is the far greater reward."

Then answered him in turn the lord of men Agamemnon:

"Run away by all means if your heart drives you. I will not entreat you to stay here for my sake ... To me you are the most hateful of all the kings whom the gods love. Forever quarreling is dear to your heart, and wars and battles ... Go home then with your ships, be king over the Myrmidons. I care nothing about you."

Who was right? It's easy to see in their feud an early version of a very old story – how a talented and ambitious young man is held back and kept down by an older man with position and power he is determined to hang onto all for himself, even though he is less able, and even if it harms everyone's collective interests. Think of Henry Ford II's jealousy of the young Lee Iacocca, who had done so much to revive the fortunes of Ford's own car company, which he had inherited. At their parting, when Iacocca wanted to know why he was being let go, Ford reportedly said, "Sometimes you just don't like somebody." Agamemnon knows that Achilles is indispensable to the war effort against Troy and should not be alienated, but he doesn't care about that in comparison with his own wounded pride. In Homer's poem, Agamemnon ruled the kingdom of Mycenae, and when the nineteenth-century archaeologist Friedrich Schliemann excavated the citadel there, he discovered a mask of pure gold that has ever since been known as "Agamemnon's mask." The link is doubtful, and scholars are divided over whether Agamemnon was even a historical figure at all. But the face is thin, angular, and sly, a tight little smile framed by the neatly trimmed spade beard of the complete villain, reminding one of evildoers and brutes from the Sheriff of Nottingham to the Klingons. It is hard not to picture Homer's portrait of the King of Kings in exactly this way. The citadel of Mycenae itself looms like a dark bird of prey over the surrounding rich farmland, and wandering around the palace remains, hemmed in by steep black peaks on all sides, one feels an electric charge of woe and tragedy, as if Agamemnon really could have been murdered here by his wife and her lover. This is a man who, after all, had cold-bloodedly made a human sacrifice of his own daughter in order to coax the gods into giving him a fair wind for the Greek fleet on its voyage to Troy.

But it's not so one-sided. After all, Achilles *is* insubordinate. The Greek chieftains agreed to Agamemnon being their commander-in-chief by common consent. Because of his personal anger at Agamemnon, Achilles not only withdraws from combat, but deliberately tries to sabotage the whole war effort. In other words, he commits treason against his own side. He does this by enlisting his mother, the goddess Thetis, to plead with the king of all the gods, the great Zeus – who, together with his fellow Olympians, is observing the war from their perch on Mount Olympus as if from the balcony of a movie theatre – to intervene in the war by enabling the Trojans to inflict a defeat on the Greek side in battle, proving that the Greeks can't win without their greatest warrior Achilles and demonstrating Agamemnon's foolishness for alienating him. Thetis had sided with Zeus in his own earlier war against his father, Kronos, whom he had overthrown (and castrated) to establish the rule of the Olympians over that of the earlier race of giants. The struggle for mastery among the gods parallels the one going on among men. Thetis is, therefore, calling in a favor, and Zeus reluctantly agrees. He is reluctant because he knows that when his wife, the formidable "cow-eyed" Hera, discovers that Zeus has sided with the Trojans against the Greeks, her chosen favorites, her fury will be implacable. (One rather pictures her brandishing a rolling pin). Zeus takes the heat, reminding Hera that he is the senior partner in their dynastic match, and that he had once had her hung by her heels weighted down by iron when she got out of line before. But a price will be paid by Achilles for forcing the direction of the war in this way – Achilles' best friend Patroclus will die fighting in his place.

Although Achilles bridles at the tyranny of his elder, Agamemnon, he is quite capable of being tyrannical himself. (And he's a king in his own right). After smugly watching the Greeks driven back all the way to their ships by the Trojans – Zeus' delivery on his promise to his mother – from the sidelines, Achilles comes back into the thick of the fighting out of his rage on learning that his beloved Patroclus has been killed in combat by the Trojans' greatest warrior, Hector, son of the Trojan king Priam. Achilles' rage is perhaps fueled by his own guilt upon learning that Patroclus had entered battle dressed in Achilles' armor, trying to compensate for the absence of the greatest Greek warrior by making it seem to the other Greeks as if he were present. Achilles had withdrawn from combat in a huff because of his feud with Agamemnon, and he now returns to fight solely to avenge a personal loss by killing Hector. There was a rule of chivalry that called for the body of a fallen opponent to be treated with respect and returned for burial, especially someone of princely rank like Hector. Not only did Achilles not return Hector's body, but in his bottomless fury over his friend Patroclus' death, he dragged Hector's body by its feet from the rear of his chariot around Patroclus' funeral bier for nine days. At this point, Zeus issues a stern warning to Thetis: Tell your son this has gone far enough. *We* get to do this kind of thing to humans because we're gods. Your son, who is mortal, does not. At length, the aged Priam comes under a flag of truce to Achilles' tent to beg for the return of his son's mangled corpse, falling to his knees and wrapping his arms in supplication, weeping, around Achilles' legs. Remembering with pity his own aged father back home, Achilles finally relents, and there is a lull in the war as both Greeks and Trojans solemnly hold funeral games for the noble fallen on both sides. It is a rare instance on Achilles' part of a capacity to feel sympathy for another human being against a backdrop of almost unrelieved narcissism and self-absorption.

Still and all, Achilles possesses a real magnificence, both in Homer's account and in other tales. It is not so difficult to see why the Greeks admired him and saw him as a model for young men. He was courageous in battle. He was proud. The flip side of his selfishness was that he was capable of real affection and loyalty toward those he loved. Personal life meant more to him than public life. Above all, it's hard not to side with him a little in his refusal to knuckle under to Agamemnon – whose claims were based on the preeminence of his kingdom and his right to avenge the abduction of his brother's wife, but who was a mediocre warrior – just as it's hard not to sympathize a little with any young man who bucks authority in order to push his way forward. There's something magical about him. Homer often likens him to a flash of sunlight, and when he heads out for his battle with Hector, his horse speaks to warn him he will die. Achilles knows he is doomed to a short life but is determined that his brief time on earth will be a blaze of glory. Homer's portrait of him is not uncritical, for Achilles is a complex, disturbed, and disturbing man. He alternates between spasms of blind fury and blue funks of despair over the meaninglessness of existence. His rage is projected upon the entire cosmos, which he tends to hold responsible for his own troubles. If the gods aren't on his side, he will even do battle with them, as when he draws his sword on the river god Skamander. He was the embodiment of what the Greeks called *hubris* – excessive pride verging on madness, a desire to shine and dominate that practically invites the gods to respond by crushing him, putting mere mortals back in their place. All in all, Achilles continued to inspire and haunt the imagination of the ancient Greeks, even as Greek civilization underwent deep changes.

HOMERIC KINGS AND HEROES

At this point, we have to add the realm of history to the realm of myth. Troy was real. Before I visited the site, people kept telling me, "don't expect too much." They knew I had been to extensive and magnificent ruins like those of Ephesus and Pergamon, where not much had to be left to the imagination to envision what they looked like in ancient times, and they didn't want me to get my hopes up that I was actually going to see Homer's Troy, with its enormous walls, temples, palaces, and citadel. But the site was nevertheless quite overwhelming for how evocative it was. True, all that's there are the multiple levels, mostly mere foundations, of the numerous cities (as many as nine) that have been built there, on top of each other, since the early Bronze Age, like a honeycomb of man-made caves where one epoch melds into the next. Yet, there are the clearly visible remains of a gate and rampart. Schliemann, whose excavation had been an act of faith based on his belief in the accuracy of Homer when many dismissed the epic as pure fiction, convinced himself that this had indeed been the main gate of the Troy of the Trojan War, through which the famous Trojan Horse might have been taken. The arch of the gate, one could fantasize, was gone because, as we know from Homer, the Trojans deliberately dismantled it because otherwise the marvelous wooden horse would have been too big to pass through.

Just as extraordinary for me, when you stood on the mound of the rampart, you could look straight out onto the plane that descended gently to the shore, imagining you were a Trojan looking down toward the Greek encampment and their ships. This is where the battles in Homer's tale took place, the plumed and gleaming columns of the Greeks moving toward the city as the equally splendid Trojan ranks issued from the gate to meet them head on – even though, I was told, the shoreline was located in a somewhat different place in the twelfth century BC, the date the war is assumed by some to have taken place. Traces have been found of a burned citadel, possibly the one the Greeks, according to Homer, torched when they successfully snuck into the city hidden inside the Trojan horse and opened the gates to their army waiting outside. Traces have been found nearby of fields that may have been cultivated by the Greeks during what Homer says was their ten-year siege. Supply lines back to the Peloponnesian mainland were poor, and the army would have had to grow its own crops. All in all, it is a deeply moving place, not the least because of its location in the Dardanelles and the nearby World War I battle site of Gallipoli, reminding one of just how often this patch of the world, linking the Mediterranean with the Black Sea, linking West with East, has been fought over.

But if there really was a Troy, and wars went on there, how can we be sure it's the war Homer recounts in the *Iliad*? Did Agamemnon, Achilles, Hector, Ajax, and the other heroes really exist? Was the war caused by the abduction of the world's most beautiful woman, Helen, from the palace of her rather hapless husband Menelaus, King of Sparta, by the visiting Trojan playboy Prince Paris?

The story of the Trojan War has come down to us through different layers, like the excavation of Troy itself. It is familiar to us as the Trojan War because the Romans called it Troy, and the British loved all things Roman. The city in the poem was actually called Ilion – I'm using Troy because everyone recognizes it. Similarly, the war was not really between "the Greeks" and "the Trojans." Homer calls Agamemnon and his allies Achaeans. We call the winning side the Greeks because Homer wrote the epic for an entirely different people than the ones the war is about. They called themselves Hellenes, but the Romans – hence the Brits, hence us – called them Greeks, so I do too.

Scholars are divided between those who believe that Homer's account was entirely fictional, those who believe it was very close to actual events, and all shades in between. Homer may have composed his tales in the ninth century BC, some four hundred years after the war took place. After the Minoan-Mycenean civilization that the war was set in mysteriously died and vanished, familiar to us through the stunning frescoes at Knossos, a dark age of several centuries set in, during which time warrior invaders from the north called Dorians swept down into the old Bronze Age kingdoms and established themselves. We know literally nothing from contemporary sources about Homer other than his supposed name. He was often simply referred to as "the poet." But it is clear that, in composing the *Iliad*, he was drawing upon legends from the Mycenean era to serve as a kind of national epic for an emerging new Greek culture, signaling the end of the dark age. So over time, the Greeks, led by Homer, projected themselves back onto this earlier golden age, becoming the army that invaded and defeated Troy.

(Interestingly, the composition of the Hebrew Bible started at around the same time, and about events that were roughly as far back in time as the Trojan War, and that epic narrative also served as a kind of national myth for the Jewish kingdom of that age and ever after).

Some scholars believe that, starting in Homer's time, the still primitive Greeks, coming across the imposing ruins and burial mounds of the Mycenean era, something they could not have built themselves, believed they were the palaces and tombs of heroes from a vanished Golden Age whose tales may originally have come from the Black Sea region. They chose the mound of some unknown Mycenean chieftain and proclaimed it to be that of Achilles or Agamemnon, venerating it as a shrine, making sacrifices, and perhaps reciting or chanting tales of the hero's great exploits (the distant beginning of ancient Greek tragedy). These scholars don't dispute that there was a war of some kind around 1244 BC between Ilion and mainland Mycenaeans, but it was probably a rather primitive affair. Others, though, believe that the heroes of Homer's poems were real people – maybe not the same in every way, but close – from Bronze Age Mycenean culture, and that they really did fight the Trojan War in heroic splendor, in bronze armor with plumed helmets. According to Barry Strauss, the strongest evidence comes from Hittite records, which contain the names of Bronze Age figures from the thirteenth century BC that are intriguingly similar to those of Agamemnon, Achilles, and others. At the time of the war, there was a huge Hittite empire based in what is now inland Turkey, with a magnificent capital called Hattusha, near today's Ankara. There is good evidence that Troy was an ally of the Hittite empire. The Hittites were not interested in directly ruling the coastal regions on the Aegean Sea. But they did not want the Mycenaeans of Peloponnesian Greece to gain a foothold there. The Greeks of that era – let's follow customary usage and call them that – were akin to the Vikings, sending frequent raiding parties along the Ionian coast. We can imagine that the real-life Agamemnon was one of these bold and avaricious warlords with a trim little fleet. Troy's job as the Hittites' ally was to prevent them from putting down roots on what is today the west coast of Turkey. Troy's location, which sat astride the shipping lanes through today's Dardanelles, made it an ideal buffer state, as well as making the city extraordinarily wealthy from the fees it charged for ships to shelter in their harbor while waiting for favorable winds. This is what we might call a *Realpolitik* explanation of the Trojan War: It was a proxy war on behalf of a great empire by one of its allies against an outside threat. However, it is entirely possible that the flash point for the particular war that Homer writes about was something akin to Paris' abduction of Helen. In the Bronze Age, wars were often justified as vengeance or punishment for some such personal outrage, often involving sexual passion, wounded honor, or a violation of the laws of hospitality. So the abduction of Helen might well have been a convenient pretext for a war that both sides saw coming for what we would now call geopolitical reasons. And that war may very well have been fought by men with names like Achilles and

Hector, who would seek glory from combat whatever the underlying economic incentives to victory might be.

As we saw, Achilles thinks that King Agamemnon has behaved toward him like a tyrant. Starting with the Greeks, monarchy was always closely connected to the danger of tyranny for the simple reason that a monarch with absolute power over his subjects is capable of oppressing them. For the ancient Greeks, some protection against this kind of oppression came from the fact that a proper king, what they called a *basileus*, was a king by hereditary descent, and, therefore, had a motive to respect established tradition, including the laws and customs of his realm. Since he received his throne as the property of his father, he was unlikely to violate the property of others or the right of other fathers to pass their property to their own children. Kingship also had a kind of divine aura – kings often claimed to be descended from a god, and sometimes they functioned as high priests. It was hoped that this would make kings observe the habits of piety themselves, including treating others justly, being moderate, avoiding arrogance or excessive pleasures, and venerating the ancestors. In ancient Rome, for example, whose history began unfolding in the ninth century BC, roughly around the time that Homer composed his lays, although largely unknown as yet to the Greeks, the king was also the *pontifex maximus*, the high priest. When the Romans got rid of their kings and established a republic, they kept the office of high priest, usually exercised by someone from the aristocracy, and the state provided him with an official residence that continued to be called the *Regia*, the king's house, in an echo of the former fusing of high priest with monarch. Its ruins have recently been excavated in the Roman Forum.

In the kind of kingship that Homer writes about in his poems, the king had two important functions. He was the chief of a band of warriors of similarly noble birth, and in peacetime, he ruled his subjects as if they belonged to a single enormous private household in which he was the father (hopefully a good father who ruled benevolently rather than a bad one who was violent and exploitive). The need for a king to be able to lead his fellow aristocrats in war demanded that he prove his worth, his fitness to rule, including through bravery in combat. And it also imposed a certain restraint on his capacity for arbitrary treatment, because he had to answer to his fellow warriors; in some ways, they were his equals, and should he fall short of the mark as a fighter, or treat them with contempt, one of them might fight him for his throne. At this time, there were not as yet standing armies that fought in massed columns, like the famous Greek phalanx or the Roman legion. A Bronze Age king entered the fray of battle surrounded by his fellow aristocratic warriors, more akin to the knights of the Middle Ages.

For the ancient Greeks, monarchy was also closely connected to the importance of the family and the family household. Their word for this was *oikos*, and the art of managing the household properly they called *oikonomia*, from which we get our words for economics and the economy. The family, in other words, was the realm of property, and also of marriage and child rearing. The king was, in effect, the chief householder of the realm, and his respect for property and family life acted as a symbol and a safeguard for the other householders. Of course, we are talking about a very small proportion of the population – the nobles who fought alongside the king in war were also the heads of their own households and lands during peacetime. Everyone else was a slave, serf, or tenant farmer. In both the *Iliad* and the *Odyssey*, and especially the *Odyssey*, we get glimpses of this peacetime life. The king's fellow warriors would gather at his palace – the word in ancient Greek was *megaron*, essentially meaning "the big place." It had little if anything in the way of government offices, as we would expect in a modern presidential palace. It was simply a very large private residence. The king was expected to provide the other warriors with regular lavish feasts at which they would gorge themselves with food and drink and recount their own exploits as well as tell stories about past heroes and about the gods, including, for instance, the very active sex life of Zeus, with his many liaisons with human women, and the wrath this provoked in his wife Hera. By feeding his nobles from his own table, the king acted as a kind of father toward them, and they in turn would exercise this role on a smaller scale with their own families and retainers.

Homer vividly depicts one of these gatherings in the *Odyssey* when Odysseus's son Telemachus sets out to find his father, absent for twenty years beginning with the Trojan War, and bring him home to his kingdom of Ithaca. Telemachus stops during his travels at the court of Menelaus, where he is warmly welcomed. With wry humor, Homer depicts how Helen, who ran away with Paris and thereby set in motion a ten-year war that cost a huge number of lives, has apparently returned to her husband absolutely unscathed and free of taint, confidently ruling the roost as much as ever, with her cuckolded husband looking on benignly. (I somehow picture Zsa Zsa Gabor gushing "Dah-link!" when young Telemachus arrives). There is an air of comfort and gracious living, including an after-dinner appearance by a traveling bard who sings songs about the great exploits of the Trojan War in which they were all key participants, a bit as if Homer had traveled back in time and made a cameo appearance in his own poem. The atmosphere is one of peace restored and harmony reestablished – king and queen are reunited, living happily in their household surrounded by their fellow nobles, and everyone is relaxing after the long years of sacrifice and struggle on the shores of Ilium. The royal household perfectly integrates the realms of family life and warrior honor under its broad roof.

Very different is the atmosphere in the royal palace of Ithaca from which Telemachus has journeyed. Because the king, Odysseus, is missing, everything is in disarray. The nobles, convinced Odysseus is dead, are behaving totally out of line. Instead of being invited by the king to feast, as would have happened if their ruler had been there, they simply invade the palace and consume its food and drink at will, loudly carousing and constantly pressing Odysseus's queen, Penelope, to choose one of them to marry. Although their pushiness was outrageous and bordered on being downright threatening, there was some justification for it. If, as seemed very likely after twenty years, Odysseus were indeed dead, it was urgent that the monarchy be restored as soon as possible. The best way to do this was for one of the other men of noble birth in the warrior aristocracy to take the dead king's widow as his own queen. This would preserve continuity and keep the throne among the bluest of blood. In other words, the badly behaving nobles were looking to establish a new leader who would restore order and keep them in line. In order to remain secure in the rule of their own households, they needed that man at the top heading the superhousehold that made up the entire kingdom of Ithaca. But because Penelope is fiercely loyal to her husband and totally convinced that he is still alive, she stubbornly resists their advances and refuses to join in their drunken partying. Her best hope is that Telemachus – whose own ascent to the throne would be imperiled should Penelope remarry and produce a new heir – will find his father and bring him back to restore royal order.

Odysseus, the hero of the *Odyssey*, provides a very interesting contrast with Achilles, the central character in the *Iliad*. Achilles is a man of action. War is his only element. Homer tells us almost nothing about Achilles' family life or about his son Neoptolemus because it isn't important for our understanding of him. He is brash and direct, never hiding his views, and willing at all times to use force to get his way. Odysseus, by contrast, is a man capable of foresight and subtle planning. He is a warrior, to be sure, but willing to achieve his aims through persuasion, strategy, and deception. Homer calls him the man "of many turns" and says that he possessed more than any of the other Greeks the quality of prudence or practical wisdom (he is repeatedly described as "wise in counsel"). While he does not play a large role in the *Iliad*, in the *Odyssey*, we learn that it was he who devised the strategy of the Trojan Horse, counting upon the curiosity of the Trojans to bring this wooden wonder into the city, bringing about the defeat of Troy through trickery more surely than all of Achilles' battlefield bravery had been able to. Just as Odysseus has a better understanding of human psychology than Achilles and is willing to achieve victory through being smarter rather than always heading for the battlefield, Odysseus is also more involved in his family life and the realm of love than is the single-mindedly violent Achilles. Whereas Achilles is always alone in his warrior's splendor, Odysseus has many interesting flings on his travels, including with a sorceress, and temporarily marries into another royal family, while remaining deeply in love with his wife and eager to return to his son, with whom he has a tear-drenched reunion. Unlike Achilles, he is a man of both war and peace. But that does not mean that Odysseus was a softy or a peace lover. When he returns home, with the help of his traveling companion, Athena, the goddess of wisdom, he is disguised as an old man so that he can observe the outrageous behavior of the nobles before revealing himself and reclaiming his throne. It is almost as if he wants to make himself as angry at them as possible. When he does announce himself, he proceeds to systematically slaughter over a hundred of the nobles in the great hall, until the floors are awash in blood. When necessary, he is capable of Achillean rage, one hallmark of a king.

When we put all the ingredients of Homer's depiction of kingship together, we see vividly before us a band of brothers in war, led by their chieftain, riding out with him on horseback into battle, then feasting merrily in a great hall with a roaring hearth, seated at tables groaning with food and drink, the king and his family at the head table, the hall pulsing with music and loud with jokes and tales. As dawn approaches, many of the men simply collapse onto the floor to sleep, while the king, his family, and his bodyguards withdraw from the great hall into his sleeping chamber. It is quintessentially Bronze Age, yet it also describes in broad strokes the way of life of the Visigoths and other Germanic tribes during the Roman Empire (before they became an occupying power in the imperial heartland itself), the Norman nobility of William the Conqueror, the Viking longhouses excavated in Newfoundland, and the raucous court of Henry VIII. We often think of history as progressing in a single direction, with one era simply obliterating the traces of the previous one. In this view, the Bronze Age is "over." But it's probably more accurate to think of history in layers. New layers go over the old ones, but the old ones continue on their own time line. As we are about to see, ancient Greece did change profoundly within a couple of centuries of Homer composing his epics, and in ways that did make the Bronze Age culture he had re-created a thing of the distant past (although it continued to inspire). In other ways, though, that Bronze Age culture of knightly combat simply continued on and developed elsewhere, among Germanic tribal kings and feudal courts. It will make its re-appearance in our story in due course. Before we follow the career of tyranny in the classical era of ancient Greece, however, we have to go down a rather different but equally important trail.

KINGS OF THE WORLD: UNIVERSAL MONARCHY

Visitors to the ruins of Mycenae in Greece and those of the Hittite imperial capital of Hattusha in present-day Turkey are often intrigued by the fact that the entrances to both have massive "lion gates" with twin lions carved in relief, symbolic guardians of the city. The resemblance, however, ends there. The seat of the Mycenaean kings – including Agamemnon, I choose to believe – was a compact little cluster of buildings linked by a single road, including some beehive and shaft tombs for prominent people and surrounded by a low-lying wall for defense, nestled for protection between two mountain peaks. It's barely visible until you get to the Lion's Gate, looking from a distance like a mere ridge of rock (and it wouldn't have been much different in ancient times). It may have laid low for an extra measure of security from attack, rather like the farmers in medieval Sicily who built their huts in clusters behind the ridge of a hill for self-defense. You can walk the entire length of the compound, including the megaron, in under an hour. By contrast, the ruins of Hattusha are absolutely staggering in their monumental size and complexity, covering nine square miles. The enormous foundation platforms still convey how gigantic these structures must have been. There were huge palaces, temples, markets, offices for an administrative bureaucracy, and numerous spacious houses protected by massive walls with guard towers and sally ports. Far from hugging the ground, Hattusha must have risen up towering in proud and unconquerable magnificence, visible for miles around. Whereas Agamemnon's fortress was that of a small local kingdom of farmers, Hattusha was the capital of an empire embracing much of present-day Turkey, Syria, and Iran, with many major cities and ports and hundreds of thousands of subjects. (Troy, so impressive to the Greeks in the *Iliad* with its walls and citadel, was, in all likelihood, as we have seen, merely one of the Hittites' client-states.) It is also the very symbol of the orderliness and might that the Hittites wielded, a might that offered security for their multitudes of subjects in exchange for absolute obedience. The city was, in effect, the symbol of an orderly world created by tyrannical power.

Hattusha was itself one of a sequence of imperial centers in the east attempting to impose order on the world through force stretching back to the very dawn of human history, including the ancient cities of Nineveh, Sumer, and Babylon, home of the famous hanging gardens of Nebudchadnezzar and an enormous ziggurat – the distinctive terraced stepped pyramid style of Mesopotamia – that may have inspired the Tower of Babel told about in the Bible. People still find what remains of these incredibly ancient places breathtaking when they visit them in London and Berlin. One side benefit of being an empire is that you get to house the remains of previous empires. The British Museum in London and the Pergamon museum in Berlin contain between them one of the greatest collections of archaeological loot in history, acquired by conquest, payment, a gun held to the head, or payment combined with a gun held to the head. London has some beautiful glazed brick reliefs of animals from Babylon (and the wonderful man-headed winged bull from the palace of an Assyrian king, Ashurnasipal II), but Berlin wins hands down in the Babylonian department by housing the restored remains of the enormous Ishtar Gate, still dazzling in blue, studded with graceful golden lions and bulls strolling across its vast surface. The Gate bears the following inscription:

Nebudchadnezzar, King of Babylon, the faithful prince appointed by the will of Marduk, beloved of Nabu, of prudent counsel, who has learned to embrace wisdom, who fathomed their divine being and reveres their majesty, the untiring governor, who always takes to heart the care of the cult of Esagila and Ezida and is constantly concerned with the well-being of Babylon and Borsippa, the wise, the humble ... the firstborn son of Nabopolasser, the King of Babylon.

Nebudchadnezzar makes it good and clear who is responsible for the magnificent city you are about to enter:

Both gate entrances ... following the filling of the street from Babylon have become increasingly lower. Therefore I pulled down these gates and laid their foundations at the water-table with asphalt and bricks and had them made of bricks with blue stone on which wonderful bulls and dragons were depicted. I covered their roofs by laying majestic cedars length-wise over them. I hung doors of cedar adorned with bronze at all the gate openings. I placed wild bulls and Ishtar ferocious dragons in the gateways and thus adorned with luxurious splendor so that people might gaze on them in wonder. I let the temple, the highest festival house of Marduk the Lord of the Gods, a place of joy and celebration … be built firm like a mountain in the precinct of Babylon …

Look at the list of qualities and skills Nebudchadnezzar is claiming for himself and it's clear how far we are from those free-wheeling raiders the Bronze Age Greeks chronicled by Homer knew as kings. Nebudchadnezzar says he is prudent and has "embraced wisdom." He is the most loyal servant of the gods. He is tireless in his concern for the well-being of the city and spends every hour of the day devoted to good government. He claims – one can hear Achilles and Agamemnon roaring with laughter at this, one of their few areas of agreement – to be *humble*. For good measure, throw in that he is an architect, urban planner, and chose the city's adornments himself. Again, it's hard to imagine Agamemnon deciding on tile colors.

These eastern monarchs wanted to be nothing less than kings of the entire world. And they pursued this ambition not only for the sake of their own wealth and pleasure – although they certainly achieved that too – but to impose order on chaos, refined civilization on barbarism, and to bring security to their subjects so that they would be free to work and prosper in peace. Their ranks include the pharaohs of Egypt (perhaps the most ancient kingdom of them all), the Babylonian, Assyrian, and Median empires, culminating in one of the most impressive figures in all of history, Cyrus the Great, Great King of the Persian Empire, whose successors placed ancient Greece in its gravest peril.

The kings depicted in Homer's poems might more accurately be described as chieftains or warlords when compared with what it meant to be a king in these vast eastern empires. Agamemnon, as depicted by Homer, is out for himself, cynical, capable of cruelty and calculation. Never once is he depicted as expressing concern about the well-being of his people, especially the common people. All that would have mattered for him would have been his own clan and the need to keep the other aristocratic clans satisfied and in line. He doesn't claim to be wise – prudence can be left to a counselor like Odysseus – and he certainly isn't humble. But he can be approached. He can even be challenged by his fellow noblemen. He is first among equals, but the other clan chiefs have a say in what goes on. Sophocles' tragedy *Oedipus Tyrannus* gives an interesting insight into the power structure in Bronze Age monarchies, although it was written much later, during the Age of Pericles in the fifth century BC. In public, Oedipus appears to be the unchallenged master of the city of Thebes. Indoors, however, we learn that he has to share his power with Cleon, a member of the clan aristocracy, in part because he is a "new man" who did not arrive at his position by hereditary descent but through his own extraordinary prowess in defeating the Sphinx that was laying waste to the countryside after the throne fell vacant upon King Laius' murder. That is why he is a "tyrant" rather than a king. We'll come back to this important distinction later.

As rendered by Homer, the gods worshipped by the Greeks, the immortal Olympians headed by Zeus, reflect the same qualities as their mortal worshippers. They fight, squabble, cheat on their partners, and can barely be kept in line by their overlord. In one of the funniest scenes in the *Iliad*, they actually come down from Olympus one day and fight alongside their chosen humans, whether Greek or Trojan, and it verges on slapstick as Athena punches Aphrodite in the breasts. The independence of the gods in their colorful variety mirrors the Greeks' dogged refusal to be yoked under any kind of universal multinational authority. For them, the meaning of life centered on the *polis* or "city-state," a small, neighborly community where, if everyone didn't know everyone else, they came close. As a famous classical scholar, Sir Ernest Barker, once observed, living in one of these small, cohesive societies was almost like being the member of a church congregation. Each city had its own gods, its own legends, its own heroes. The Athenians believed that their city began when Athena defeated the sea god Poseidon in a battle on the site where the Acropolis still sits today. Many Greek cities believed that they had been there from time immemorial, literally bred from that soil. They were not necessarily self-governing. Popular government was not generally a Bronze Age concept, and does not appear for a while longer in our story. But they were fiercely independent. By the time of the fateful encounter between these Greeks and the vast multinational empire founded by Cyrus the Great, there were some three thousand of these tiny statelets spread throughout what is today Greece and the coast of Turkey, then known as Ionia.

It would go too far to say that the mission of bringing civilization, order, and the art of good government to the world, or at least to their own peoples, had *no* presence in ancient Greek history, or among its Mycenaean and Minoan predecessors. The Minoan palace at Knossos with its beautiful, Klimt-like frescoes, excavated by Sir Arthur Evans, shared some of the qualities of Hittite and Babylonian structures as a kind of mirror of the cosmos. Built somewhat like a ziggurat, at the top, the famous bull-wrestling games took place in view of the mountain where Zeus had supposedly been born. The movements of the wrestlers leaping over the bulls may have been meant to mirror the movements of the stars. Its huge, twisting, multichambered interior gave rise to the legend of the Labyrinth, where the struggle of the Athenian hero Theseus against the Minotaur, a monstrous half-man and half-bull, may have echoed the young city-state's struggle to throw off the weight of Minoan hegemony.

The ancient Greeks also developed the legend of the so-called Battle Against the Giants, the *gigantomachia*, depicted on temple reliefs in numerous and far-flung Greek city-states, the most magnificent remaining example of which is from Pergamon, housed (you guessed it) at the Pergamon Museum in Berlin. A fierce and bloody war in which the Olympian gods finally defeat an earlier race of monstrous gods called titans, it, too, can be interpreted as the struggle against barbarism, ugliness, and brute physical strength by the forces of beauty, order, and justice, or even the struggle within man between his own lower animal side of unconstrained passion, lust, and aggression and his higher side of nobility, art and the intellect. In short, a tyranny on behalf of civilization (the Olympians and their overlord Zeus) vanquishes a tyranny based on barbarism, ignorance, and savagery.

Another impressive example of the Greeks' early association of their own way of life with a higher, civilizing mission for mankind is the temple of Apollo at Delphi. According to murky myths, a fierce barbarian warrior god is said to have come down to the site from the distant north, where he fought and slew a dragon guarding a spring sacred to the Earth Mother, Gaia. He then somehow magically absorbed the feminine qualities of Gaia, who is morphed into the "Pythia," the Python Lady (called this because of her guardian dragon), first of a succession of priestesses who ever afterward interpreted the meaning of steam which was supposed to issue from a crack in the earth inside Apollo's sanctuary, revealing the god's oracles. Apollo also absorbed the wisdom associated with the vanquished snake, who ever afterward appears coiled at his feet, the once fierce dragon now shrunken and tame. Hence Apollo was always referred to at Delphi as "Pythian Apollo," the Apollo of the Python. More than that, by absorbing these feminine, instinctual, and snaky qualities, the original barbaric war god from the north is transformed into the sublimely beautiful Apollo seen in the statues of Praxiteles and other great sculptors from the classical era. Because he combines masculine strength with feminine instinct and a connection to the wisdom of nature through the snake, Apollo is very youthful and sometimes almost androgynous in appearance, with full round hips and large breasts. The exertion of brute, tyrannical might over the fertile forces of nature leads to a blend of qualities in which courage is supplemented with knowledge – Pythian Apollo is the special patron of the fine arts and the art of good government. The site of the temple embodies this very tension between civilization and barbarism, and can be readily felt by anyone who makes the journey there today. After climbing for a very long time through steep, dark, looming cliffs, you suddenly emerge into a stunning skyscape at the top of the world, the ruins of the temple gleaming at precisely the point where earth meets sky, the sanctuary of Apollo holding the forces of darkness at bay on behalf of the sunlight. Its significance as a symbol of the Greek civilizing mission is especially demonstrated by the fact that, during the classical era of the fifth century BC, Delphi functioned almost as a kind of United Nations headquarters for many city-states. Negotiations over war or trade were frequently conducted there, and there was an international precinct clustered around the main temple where numerous city-states built their own shrines to the god and left precious tributes. Apollo, then, was the closest the Greeks came to a kind of "international" god. Still, that's as far as it went. No attempt was ever made to turn these mechanisms for negotiation into some kind of actual central state, as opposed to mere temporary alliances or trade treaties. On the eve of the war with the Great King of Persia, the Greeks remained disunited and happy to be that way. For the complete model of the world-state and its drive to impose order and peace everywhere, you had to look to those very old empires of the east going back to the pharaohs.

If the Bronze Age kings were approachable and lived in what were basically rather large houses, the eastern monarchs of Egypt, Babylon, Assyria, and Persia lived in palace-cities that were quite staggering in size. They contained not only unbelievably lavish living quarters with gigantic gardens and fountains, but large quarters for secretaries, retainers, and other bureaucrats. The gardens of Cyrus the Great's palace, which he tended personally, were so large and gorgeous that they give us our word for "paradise" (the Greek word for these gardens was *paradeisos,* which came in the Bible to mean the Garden of Eden or heaven). Something of the superhuman and imposing qualities of these palace-cities can still be felt at Karnak in Egypt, with its forest of columns and processional alley of sphinxes straight out of a Cecil B. DeMille screen epic. Although not a lot remains of Cyrus the Great's palace at Persepolis, one can still sense its humongous extent. Eventually, as we'll see, this model of Eastern universal monarchy moved West, and the remains of the Flavian Palace on the Palatine Hill in Rome, the forum and palace of the Byzantine emperors in Constantinople, as well as Muslim royal palaces like Topkapi and the Alhambra also allow us to re-capture the atmosphere of these absolute kings.

Whereas the Homeric chieftains were fairly approachable, living among their equals without a great deal of ceremony, from the pharaohs on, the eastern rulers were surrounded by the most elaborate ceremonial and ritual conceivable, ensconced at the center of their sprawling palace complexes, constantly attended by serried ranks of officials and retainers, each rank's status marked by how close they could approach the royal personage. Usually even the highest-ranking nobles had to prostrate themselves on the ground in the Presence – all men, high or low, were his slaves. The kings themselves were bred to hold themselves stiff and erect like human statues, the living embodiment of their own monumental sculptures spread far and wide across the realm. The closest we could come to this atmosphere today might be a Mass at St. Peter's, which was itself a kind of throne room for God and his deputy on earth. Whereas in Homer, even among the kings, you can smell the leather, the horses, and hear the clank of their swords, the atmosphere of the god-king's palace was hushed, full of luxurious hangings, the aroma of incense, the tinkling of bells.

As we've already seen with the case of Nebudchadnezzar, these eastern kings were closely associated with the gods, in some way embodying the divine in their own mortal lives. It's especially pronounced in the Egyptian pharaohs, whose passage from death to immortal life was in some way still not clearly understood the central organizing principle of Egyptian civilization, culminating in the still-breathtaking pyramids and Valley of the Kings. It seems as if the pharaohs' transmission to the heavens and eternal life was somehow collectively shared in by Egyptians as a whole, or at least it pointed out the path for them as well. Egypt at its height, like its successor empires in the east, maintained complex road systems, a postal service, and beautiful cities with baths, schools, markets, theaters, and libraries. It is said that when Octavian Caesar first glimpsed the Egyptian capital of Alexandria, he was so overwhelmed that he vowed then and there to put Rome on the same level (later boasting "I found it a city of brick, and left it a city of marble"). There were law codes, health facilities, military outposts, courts, and of course numerous holy sites, all maintained by the pharaonic superstate.

One of the most striking differences between the great eastern monarchies and the ancient Greeks was military. While the loosely-organized bands of knights riding into battle with their chieftains from Homer's epics gave way to the organized columns of the Spartan phalanx, Greek armies remained small and, for the most part, made up of citizens who, when not needed for actual fighting, would be back home plowing their fields. Unique in the world with which the Greeks were familiar, and especially so in the case of Persia, the eastern empires, by contrast, maintained enormous standing armies of hundreds of thousands of men, including wave after wave of infantry, cavalry, and armored chariots (to say nothing of their vast fleets of warships).

Whether the god-king personally led his armies varied from one time and place to another. While there were great military men among the pharaohs like Ramses II, some scholars think that illustrations of what look like Egyptian victories were often mainly symbolic – that is, the pharaoh in his war chariot leading his troops in a bas-relief is not so much triumphing over an actual foe as over the forces of chaos and disorder, often personified as serpents and other vicious animals. The founder of the Persian Empire, Cyrus the Great, was unquestionably one of the greatest generals in history, whose battle plans are still studied at West Point and other military academies. He was also a great builder who welcomed his new subjects, if they were willing to submit to his rule, to prosper economically, and to enter his own army and bureaucracy and rise based on their merit. Another hallmark of these empires, and especially that of Cyrus, was their cosmopolitanism. In contrast with the Greeks, whose city-states were tribal in the extreme and generally not friendly to outsiders – it was said that anyone showing up at the Spartan border would immediately be politely but firmly turned away – Cyrus welcomed those he had conquered as his subjects with the same privileges as his native Persians.

Another sign of Cyrus' greatness and foresight as a statesman is that he inaugurated a policy of religious tolerance. All the states and peoples spanned by his empire were not only permitted but actively encouraged to worship the gods of their choice. Most famously, this led to his allowing the Jews held captive in Babylon to return to Jerusalem and build the Second Temple, an act of generosity that is generously recognized in the Hebrew Bible, where Cyrus is described as God's anointed, "Cyrus, whom He has taken by his right hand to subdue nations before him and strip the loins of kings." Cyrus apparently believed religious tolerance would not only preserve peace within his far-scattered realms – dozens of peoples totaling a population of tens of millions throughout Asia Minor, Babylon, and Egypt – but would contribute to the moral fiber and character of the empire's peoples. It was a policy followed later with great success by Alexander the Great and especially the Romans.

Another striking difference between the Greek city-states and the eastern monarchies is that the eastern monarchs, while tolerant toward many forms of worship, tended themselves to be monotheistic (though perhaps less the case with the pharaohs) in the sense of favoring one god ahead of the others, or at least a good deal more so than their Greek contemporaries. The Babylonian kings identified themselves with their supreme god, Marduk, while Cyrus devoted himself to a version of Zoroastrianism, always accompanied by its priests or "Magi" and dedicating many lavish temples to the cult. Zoroastrianism was not only monotheistic but was also in a way messianic. Zoroastrians believed the world was divided between a realm of light – and, therefore, of goodness, virtue, and justice – and a realm of darkness – and, therefore, of evil, vice, and injustice. Followers of Zoroaster were called upon throughout their lives on earth to struggle on behalf of the light against the darkness, thereby progressively making the world a better place and bringing about a better future. While Cyrus tolerated all forms of worship, it is not accidental that, in striving to create a universal empire based on peace, justice, and prosperity, he should embrace a universal god and present himself as that god's chief earthly ally in making a better world. This messianic dimension of supreme political authority will return time and again throughout our tracing of tyranny's career – sometimes with terrifying consequences. In Cyrus' case, the political consequences of monotheism were generally benign. As we've already seen, the pluralism of the pagan Olympian gods made such a universal divine authority, mirroring a universal political authority, next to impossible for the ancient Greeks to embrace. In the late Roman Empire, it culminates in the triumph of Christ as the *Pantacrator*, the universal divine monarch, over the discredited multiple gods of the pagans, whose deputy on earth was the universal Emperor.

Not all eastern kingdoms embraced the model of the god-king. Most famously, the Hebrew people of the Bible wanted to have a king "like other nations," especially to lead them in war. But they also feared displeasing God, who was indeed angry that they were not content to be ruled directly by Him and His law, although he gave into their wish by telling the Prophet Samuel to choose Saul as king. The choice of a king by the prophet placed a kind of buffer between that king and any illusion he might have that he was absolutely supreme, or even divine himself. The rich and vivid chronicles of the Kings of Israel – in some way reminiscent of Homer's tales – unfolds a whole little minihistory of monarchy and the danger that it may degenerate into tyranny. The election of a king represents the Israelites' recognition that, although their people alone worship the one true God (meaning not merely the first among the gods, but the *only* God), they face the trials of any "normal" state, especially the need for military self-defense under a single commander in chief.

The first king, Saul, begins well, but, like many monarchs throughout history, eventually becomes more arrogant, demanding, intolerant of interference, and suspicious of those who might be plotting against his throne. David, by proving himself the greatest warrior and befriending the king's son and heir Jonathan, eventually usurps the throne, with a mixture of bravery, merit, and Machiavellian skullduggery. David is himself versed in music and the arts, but his son Solomon carries the Israelite kingdom to new and unmatched heights of might, glory, luxury, and culture. In many ways, Solomon is rather like his neighboring eastern monarchs. One pictures him in a purple robe, relaxing in his palace surrounded by fountains, singers, and musicians, enjoying many sexual dalliances, composing poetry, but also riding out to war with his large and imposing fleet of chariots. He also builds the magnificent first Temple, widely regarded as one of the marvels of the world. For all that, though, Solomon never crosses the line into *becoming* a god-king. Ever since the exodus from bondage in Egypt, the Israelites had always bewared of their leaders becoming "pharaoh" – that is, becoming megalomaniacal despots with no respect for justice, mercy, and submission to God.

And this brings us to a moral quandary that will come up again and again as we trace the career of tyranny. Whatever their achievements for the peoples they ruled, these eastern monarchs *were* tyrants. They had the absolute power of life and death over their subjects, and were unconstrained by an aristocracy of near-equals (as were Greek kings), let alone the rule of law (that was something they may have enforced for the benefit of their subjects, but it never applied to themselves). While some were benign despots like Cyrus, others, even some of the effective generals and administrators, were notoriously depraved and cruel. The Assyrian king Ashurnasirpal boasted in his royal inscriptions about the thousands he had beheaded, impaled, or skinned alive, draping their skins over the city walls, and the hundreds of captive boys and girls he burned alive. The anthropologist Geoffrey Clarfield expressed his misgivings about a recent joint exhibition at the British Museum and Toronto's Royal Ontario Museum that, in celebrating the state-building achievements of these eastern rulers, never identifies them as tyrants and their rule as tyrannical. It is hard not to share those misgivings. But it's also hard to deny the achievements. The question about whether tyranny can achieve good things will come up repeatedly as we go forward.

TYRANNY OR REPUBLIC? THE EMERGENCE OF THE WEST

The clash between the fierce independence of the tiny Greek city-states and the universal empire created by Cyrus the Great could have been predicted. Not content with checking the power of the Greeks in Ionia through a proxy (Troy) as had the Hittites, Cyrus conquered the entire region and appointed tyrants to rule its independent-minded cities, pitting the Greeks against quislings drawn from among their own number. From the outset, then, the conflict between

Greece and Persia was a conflict between the spirit of political independence and a sometimes benevolent but always overwhelming despotism. Chafing under this tyrannical yoke imposed by Persia and its local collaborators, all of Ionia rose in rebellion in 493 BC and, with the support of Athens in the Peloponnesian mainland of Greece, captured and torched the Persian regional capital of Sardis. Faced with this act of rebellion from these troublesome pip-squeaks, the Persian Empire decided that all of Greece, the mainland included, must be brought decisively under its control and taught once and for all who was master. The first Persian invasion, led by King Darius, was defeated at the Battle of Marathon. In 480 BC, his son Xerxes led one of the largest armies ever assembled over a bridge created by yoking hundreds of ships together across the narrow isthmus (the Hellespont, today's Dardanelles) separating Ionia from Europe (near Troy, always the crossroads between East and West). At Thermopylae, famously, three hundred Spartans, the cream of their small but superbly trained army made up of the warrior aristocrats of the ruling class, miraculously held off a Persian force of tens of thousands for seven days by wedging themselves into a small canyon opening onto the plain, enduring wave after wave of the Persian ranks in their chain mail, cavalry, and chariots, fighting to the last man. Breaking through, Xerxes then captured and torched Athens. It looked as if the fractious and tiny Greek city-states didn't stand a chance against the Persian juggernaut, a confrontation between the passion for independence and the drive for centralized control and subjugation that has been repeated many times in the history of the West down to the Allies' refusal to knuckle under to Nazi aggression in WWII. Just when it looked like all was lost, the combined Greek fleet inflicted a shattering defeat on the Persians at the Battle of Salamis, and the following year, the Greeks decisively defeated the Persians on land at the Battle of Plataea, effectively ending the invasion. Talk about the mouse that roared!

The century or so bookended by the Persian invasion and the trial and execution of the Athenian philosopher Socrates in 399 BC is one of the most extraordinary periods in all of human history, the height of what we now call the Classical Age. Ironically, it opened with the defeat of a tyranny by free cities and ended with an act of tyranny by the city that claimed to be the most free of them all, Athens, against a man in their own midst who defended the life of the mind and freedom of thought. It was an era of tumultuous social and political change, and of prodigious achievements in art, drama, and the writing of history. This was when the splendor of Greek architecture flowered in the Athenian Acropolis, still dominating the skyline of Athens today, in the sculpture of Phidias, the histories of Herodotus and Thucydides, the tragedies of Aeschylus and Sophocles, and the philosophy of Socrates' follower Plato. It was also an era in which the Greeks, reflecting on what a near thing their avoidance of conquest by the Persian empire had been, began to set forth the basic categories of government – the different varieties of tyranny, how tyr-annical rule differed from free self-government, and whether the best form of free self-government was a democracy of the common people, an aristocracy based on the bluebloods, or an oligarchy made up of the rich (who sometimes claimed to be the blue bloods as well). They'd had ample opportunity to observe all these forms of government in action during the life-and-death struggle with Persia and to reflect on their merits and drawbacks. In the course of these reflections, the Greeks also thought about the Homeric understanding of manly honor, centering on Achilles, that had influenced them for so long, and whether it was entirely adequate for the new era after what they had gone through in the Persian Wars. The vocabulary of government they came up with shapes our understanding of just and unjust authority to this very day, when we talk about Ukraine's desire for democracy as opposed to the tyranny of Putin, the longing of Syrians for independence from the iron grip of the tyrant Assad, the struggle of black South Africans to throw off the yoke of the ugly racist dictatorship of apartheid, or the excessive wealth of the global oligarchs making up the "top 1 percent". Until very recently, "Oriental despotism" was a byword for the monolithic imperialism with which the Greeks were threatened by Persia, and which has re-appeared to menace the West in various forms including the Ottoman Empire, Stalin's Russia, and Western rulers who themselves aimed to exercise such total power including Napoleon and Hitler. As we'll see, though, the clash between East and West is also the ongoing story of how they and their principles of government penetrated and influenced each other.

The classical age of Greece also saw the rise of writers who did not compose myths, as had Homer, but who claimed to write about historical fact, often from their own observation, and this is where we must pick up our story. Herodotus and Thucydides invoke the importance of evidence and reasoned judgment in contrast with Homer's magical tales of gods and heroes from the distant past. Herodotus in his travels amassed a great deal of information about Persia and the even older empires of Egypt and Assyria. He also chronicled the division in Athenian leadership during the Persian Wars, including the suspicion that their great wartime leader Themistocles might have been on the take from the Great King Darius. Thucydides is especially assertive about the superiority of history to myth, dismissing the Trojan War as having been in reality a rather primitive tussle between rustic tribesmen with little in the way of organized military power or technique, dressed up by Homer in the language of gods and heroes. The gods play no role at all in Thucydides' kind of history. In order to understand how history really works and what human nature is really like, he says, we have to look at the Peloponnesian War that broke out in 431 BC between Athens and its former main ally against the Persian invasion, Sparta. This was the first war in human history, according to Thucydides (who lived through it), where the material scale of the conflict – the size and wealth of the cities, their fleets, armies, and economic reach – created a canvas on which the leading personality types could emerge. Those types – tyrants, demagogues, warriors, the virtuous, the vicious, aristocrats, and humble people – were all further intertwined with and shaped by the kind of government they lived under or desired, such as tyranny, monarchy, democracy, oligarchy, and aristocracy. As he famously claimed, all future political and military conflicts will give rise to similar human types, since human nature will always be the same. There will always be leaders like Pericles, Nicias, Alcibiades, and the other outstanding figures of the Peloponnesian War, not identical to them, but akin to them in broad outline. In order to understand why these former allies turned on each other after achieving such a great victory together, Thucydides tells us, we have to go back in time to before the Persian Wars themselves and then examine the motivations of the Athenians and Spartans in making common cause against the invader and why they afterward fell out.

As Greek civilization emerged from the Dark Age, inspired by Homer's tales of a vanished Golden Age to which the Greeks themselves might now aspire, the city-states sprinkled throughout the Peloponnesian mainland and Ionia began to develop economic and military strength, building walls and harbors, and each had its own fortified keep, the acropolis. Often, as Thucydides recounts, these efforts were headed by tyrants, which is why, from early on, to describe a ruler as a tyrant was not necessarily a criticism, or at least not entirely so. Yes, early on as well, some tyrants were notorious for their cruelty, gargantuan pleasures, and suspicion of potential competitors for absolute power. Dionysius I of Syracuse was said to have installed an echo chamber near his throne room, the "ear," which made voices reverberate and allowed him to listen in on possibly treasonous conversations while hidden from view, or, more sinisterly, that it amplified for his pleasure the screams of prisoners being tortured. (It's still there, and might have been nothing but a passageway.) But often they were successful as state builders, military commanders, and urban planners, more effective at governing than the local blue bloods or a king who possessed his throne by birthright. As we've already observed, Sophocles' tale of Oedipus provides a sketch of such a man in the garb of a very old myth. Tyrants were "new men" who gained absolute power, unconstrained by the rule of law, and not of hereditary descent like a true king. But the really successful ones could sometimes make their tyranny hereditary, like the Peisistratids in Athens or the eavesdropping Dionysius I. For all that, they never entirely threw off the taint of illegitimacy, of an ambition that violated the traditional order of things. Because they came to power by disrupting hereditary descent, they committed a kind of impiety, since legitimate monarchs were regarded as sanctioned by the gods themselves (and most ordinary Greeks, whatever Thucydides with his emphasis on factual evidence and disdain for poetic fancies might have thought, continued to believe in the old gods). In a certain sense, these early Greek tyrants might be compared to the Shogun in Japan – a strongman whose talents were needed for war and effective government because the Emperor, a sacred figure descended from the gods, had to be enshrined and protected from the peril or grubby taint of actual battle or political infighting. All in all, then, from early on in the ancient Greek world, the tyrant's reception was *mixed*.

Some were good at governing, others weren't. Some were downright oppressive, and unfortunately the ones good at governing in the sense of making their cities more secure and prosperous might have those nasty qualities as well, pouncing on anyone suspected as a potential rival, capable of large-scale greed and acts of rapine or cruelty toward their subjects, reformer and garden-variety kleptocrat rolled into one. Sophocles' Oedipus, who saved Thebes from devastation by solving the riddle of the Sphinx – like Homer's Odysseus, relying more on brains than brawn – was also capable, like Homer's Achilles, of splenetic rage toward anyone who opposed him or even questioned his judgment.

This ambiguous take on tyranny – in some ways appreciating the need for a "strong man" to take the reins of government when the legitimate authorities were incompetent, but uneasy about the sometimes vulgar origins of such men, their willingness to trample on tradition, and their ruthlessness – is conveyed in our ancient sources by the recurring dual accounts of the origins of great rulers. Oedipus thinks of himself as a new man, an orphan from another country, not knowing that he is in reality the son and heir of the legitimate king of Thebes, Laius, whom he unwittingly murders when Laius' retainers treat him scornfully, with the horrible consequence that he then unwittingly marries his own mother after being offered the throne, setting his doom in motion. Laius, it turns out, had Oedipus exposed at birth after the oracle at Delphi had prophesied that Oedipus would one day kill him (which, in fact, he did). According to Herodotus, Cyrus was the grandson of the legitimate King of Media, Astyages, who ordered his death as a baby due to (wait for it!) an oracle who foretold he would grow up and seize the throne from Astyages' son and heir – like Oedipus, the baby was saved by a compassionate herdsman. Cyrus was the offspring of a marriage between his mother, a Median princess, and a Persian chieftain whose people chaffed under the domination of the Medes. When Cyrus grows up, he then leads a rebellion of the Persians against their Median suzerain, the beginning of his conquests, even though he is actually of royal Median blood himself.

Perhaps the best example of this ambiguous judgment about the origins of power is in the dual accounts of the origins of Rome, which, we must remind ourselves – even though mostly absent from our Greek sources for what was going on in the fourth and fifth centuries BC – was developing on its own by the Tiber in a lot of ways like a typical Greek-style city-state. (The Greeks will become unpleasantly aware of them soon enough.) According to one account, the future of Rome was established by the Trojan hero Aeneas, who, on escaping the burning ruins of Troy, journeyed westward and rejected the advances of Dido, Queen of Carthage, before settling in the land of the Latins, Rome's future location, and marrying its King's daughter. In this way, the poet Virgil sets up the coming great conflict between Carthage and Rome as predestined Dido commits suicide on a funeral pyre, shrieking with fury, when Aeneas takes ship and deserts her. In the other account, however, Rome is founded by a band of brigands headed by the brothers Romulus and Remus, who establish a campsite on what later became the Palatine Hill and took in whatever thieves and scoundrels wanted to join their raiding band. They were so rough they couldn't even find wives except by abducting them from the nearby Sabines. Like other famous squabbling brothers including Cain and Abel, only one of them could be top dog, and Remus early on was jealous of his brother's coming out on top, while Romulus did not trust his brother to be a loyal junior partner. When Romulus established the sacred trench surrounding the new city – this was a common practice among Greek city-states, basically marking out a sacred enclosure within which the gods would be venerated, and free of pollution such as the burial of the dead – Remus, in a fit of jealousy, jumped on top of the mound before it had been properly dedicated, an act of impiety that Romulus promptly punished by killing him with his spear, thereby solving his problem.

How can these two totally differing accounts both be true – that the destiny of Rome was foreseen and pursued by the great and noble Trojan hero Aeneas, who becomes the prince of Latium, or that Rome was founded by a mangy gang of cutthroats and rapists whose leader rubbed out his brother like a Mafiosi? In Virgil's *Aeneid,* the two accounts are connected by the slenderest possible of tendrils, whereby two brothers (another quarrelsome duo) descended from Aeneas, Amulius and Numitor, fought each other for power, ending in Numitor's defeat and the exile of his daughter, Rhea Sylvia who, although a Vestal Virgin, gave birth to twins fathered by Mars; those twins were Romulus and Remus. When Amulius killed Rhea Sylvia and exposed the twin babies to die, they were rescued and suckled by a she-wolf until a shepherd adopted them. Since Aeneas had joined the royal family of Latium centuries earlier, that meant Romulus and Remus were, however narrowly and with however pale a shade of blue blood, also royal, although for good measure they were also half-divine on their mother's side. At the same time, their possibly true origins as feral children and brigands is symbolized by the famous tale of the she-wolf, from whose milk they presumably absorbed a wolf's cunning and ferocity, and also emphasizing what outsiders they were. Common to all these accounts of the origins of great rulers is the desire to have one's cake and eat it too about whether they were legitimate kings or tyrants. Typically, they rise to power through tyrannical ruthlessness, violence, and ambition, but then – surprise, surprise – they turn out to have been royal heirs all along! It's as if the ancients liked to flirt with the notion of tyrants rising from nothing entirely through their own daring and talent, but then hastened to restore traditional legitimacy by grafting them back onto a hereditary royal bloodline.

Let's get back to the Greeks. On the island of Sicily, near Syracuse, you can visit the remains of a tiny perfect city-state called Akrai that sums up Greek civilization on the eve of the Peloponnesian War. There is a small theater built into the side of a hill where tragedies were performed and where Dionysos could be worshipped in the caves running along the outside. Right next to the theater, there's a small enclosure of benches made of stone steps. This was the *bouleuterion*, the council chamber, of their little community, where the city's leaders would gather to debate and make needed decisions. The ancient Greeks invented self-government.

By the outbreak of the Peloponnesian War, which went on for twenty-seven years, two basic forms of self-government had developed, represented by Sparta and Athens. The words *Sparta* and *Spartans* come from the name the Romans gave them, taken from their chief village Sparta, although they actually called their country as a whole Lacedaemonia and themselves Lacedaemonians. We'll use the more familiar Roman names. (I know, it's a bit like Magill who called herself Lil and so on in *Rocky Raccoon*, with all these English versions of Roman versions of Greek names). Sparta was a military aristocracy whose men trained all their lives for war. It invented the famous phalanx, a massed infantry formation that usually defeated all before it, a precursor of the Roman legion. Although an aristocracy, they lived frugally, without luxury, and were entirely dedicated to the common good without thought, or so it was claimed, of individual advancement (didn't always work, of course). I tell my students they were a bit like the Klingons, though truth be told the Klingons and their architecture have a bit of Genghis Khan about them. Their capacity for endurance and self-sacrifice became legendary throughout Greek and Roman antiquity, captured in many tales, true or not, such as a boy allowing himself to be mauled by a fox under his cloak rather than cry out, and the mothers who shouted as their sons left for battle: "Come back with your shield – or on it!" (No Mother's Day card for them).

Wealth was agricultural – there was little trade or commerce. The Spartans did not welcome outsiders, and resisted innovation. Thucydides tells us their way of life and form of government had remained unchanged since their founder Lycurgus had established them some four hundred years previously. Unlike Athens, they had no great cities or grand architecture. Thucydides predicted that future centuries would not be able to gauge Sparta's power accurately based on the meager remains of her habitations, and he was right. There's not much there today but some foundations, whereas the Acropolis in Athens still takes your breath away in its mammoth glory. The plush palace of the earlier Mycenaean kings of Sparta described in the *Odyssey* was long gone. The Spartan men, while they had families, spent much of their time together in a brotherhood based on combat, and may have lived in communal block-houses with a common mess. The Spartans are sometimes thought to have been descendants of the main rump of Dorian invaders said to have come down from the north as Mycenean-Minoan culture was disintegrating, imposing military discipline and order on a more sybaritic and free-wheeling way of life just as the stern war-god Apollo (as he was then, pre-snakiness) came down from the north to suppress the mother goddess and her serpent. The Doric columns in their temples were stout and unadorned, like rows of hoplites, as compared to the fruity, frothy Corinthian order with its carved grapes and animals. In many ways they had absorbed the heroic code of manly fortitude praised by Homer, but without any of the nihilistic and insubordinate individualism of Achilles. Among the Homeric heroes, they were perhaps more like Hector, a Hector collectivized – brave in a solid, unflashy way, loyal to country and ancestors, deeply pious. Personally, I have always sensed a cultural connection between the Trojans, Spartans, and Romans, as opposed to the flamboyant Athenians.

The Spartans trained for warfare constantly, but were in fact an isolationist power that fought only when there was no alternative. That was because they ruled over a population of slaves ("helots") who vastly outnumbered their masters, and whom they treated with extreme brutality. The helots were Sparta's Achilles' heel. Their warrior aristocrat masters were constantly on guard against a desire for freedom spreading among their slaves. Foreign wars meant destabilization, a chance for rebellion when the army was away fighting. Wars also led to an ambition for glory and loot, and hence a dangerous kind of individualism in what was supposed to be a collective. The Spartans had observed to their dismay during the Persian Wars that their commanders, when stationed abroad, often turned into violent and greedy mini-tyrants, like Kurtz in *Heart of Darkness*. Staying at home was a protection against corruption. Wars also meant the spread of dangerous new ideas from the outside world, like democracy. Fighting the Persian invaders had been an absolute necessity if the Spartans were to avoid being enslaved themselves. But once the common struggle was over, all the Spartans wanted to do was go home and resume normal life. Aside from a buffer zone of allied states with which they had surrounded the Peloponnesian homeland, Sparta had no imperial ambitions. There was no public debate in Sparta. There were two kings whose main role was as military commanders – their powers were hemmed in by an elected council, the Ephors, and a Council of Elders whose decisions were final. Spartans as a whole, rather like the heroes in Westerns played by John Wayne and Clint Eastwood, didn't like talking much and distrusted fancy talk in others. *Laconic* (from their country's actual name, Lacedaemonia) became a description of people who didn't waste words.

The career of Athens as a consequence of the Persian invasion could hardly have been more different. As a maritime power, Athens had always been open to contact with other countries through trade. With foreign trade came new ideas and innovations. Athens was home to a large immigrant population of merchants and traders, and they were very welcome. Sometimes they even served in the military. Because they lived by trade and commerce and not so much through agriculture, Athenians always had a taste for luxury and bling (such as fancy brooches and hair clasps from Ionia, says Thucydides). While different segments of the population favored democracy and oligarchy, and having tried one-man rule – the tyrant Peisistratos defended the common people against the aristocracy, while Solon, their original law-giver, had been granted extraordinary individual authority – by the time of the Persian invasion, they were a full-fledged democracy, history's first. Whereas Sparta was ruled by a council that deliberated behind closed doors, the entire free adult male population of

Athens, some forty thousand citizens, gathered in the central square, the agora, where issues would be debated by anyone who cared to speak and resolved by a majority vote. Because the ability to speak persuasively in public was such a prized asset in democratic politics, professional teachers of the art of rhetoric from Ionia and elsewhere frequently trawled for business in Athens, looking for the sons of the rich as clients, figures like Gorgias and Protagoras who show up in the dialogues of Plato.

One reason Athens became a democracy was that, under Themistocles, it had begun to maintain a huge fleet, and needed large numbers of men for crews and shipyards. Since they were expected to outfit and man the ships, they also expected a say in government. Before that, like many Greek city-states, the military had been made up of knights from the landed gentry who could afford the horses and armor. That way of life was gone now. Athens and Sparta made a perfect combination for fighting off the Persians – the best navy combined with the best army. The other city-states lined up behind their joint leadership. But after the war, whereas the Spartans wanted to go home and have things return to normal, the Athenians enjoyed the heady sense of power as well as the wave of prosperity that victory over the Persians had brought. Claiming that the fleet had to be maintained in case the Persians came back, they craftily told the allies that instead of going to the bother of sending their own ships, they should give the Athenians a cash equivalent and Athens would build the ships themselves. In this way, Athens became both wealthier and more powerful, gradually turning what had been an alliance into a kind of hegemony. It was this wealth and power that enabled the adornment of the city with the Acropolis and a more comfortable way of life for all Athenians.

The Athenian leader Themistocles, over the objections of the Spartans, built the Long Walls from the center of the city all the way on either side to the harbor of Piraeus and brought most of the population inside. In effect, this made Athens relatively immune to an invasion by land, while retaining the upper hand by sea, the early equivalent of an ABM system. The Spartans understood this, but, inward looking and sluggish as always about goings-on elsewhere, they were too late with their protests. Over time, the so-called allies were more and more resentful of Athenian arrogance and power over them. As Themistocles' successor Pericles warned his fellow citizens, they were perceived as a "tyrant city," and could not afford to relinquish their grip on their hegemony because those whom they had oppressed would exact revenge. Many believed that, having led the effort along with Sparta to repulse the Persian Empire, Athens was now attempting to establish its own version of that empire over all the other Peloponnesian states.

Sparta, roused at last from its isolationist slumber by cities like Corinth that resented Athens' domineering ways, was finally convinced that, if they waited any longer, Athens would be unstoppable and a threat to Sparta's own way of life. That began a long and terrible three-decade struggle in which the other Peloponnesian city-states lined up on one side or the other. It was not only a war based on conflicting interests but also on conflicting understandings of just government. The other democracies tended to rally behind Athens, while the other oligarchies – small self-governing groups of the rich and wellborn – lined up behind aristocratic Sparta. That struggle between the leading democracy and the leading aristocracy, not surprisingly, began to infiltrate the domestic politics of all the combatants. In other words, the oligarchies backing Sparta found themselves being challenged, even toppled, by democratic movements in their own cities that were loyal to Athens and were egged on by her, while the same thing happened in reverse in the democracies – the oligarchs, backed by Sparta, would try to install the rich as rulers. The carnage unleashed across the whole of the Peloponessus by this civil war was terrible indeed. As Greeks slaughtered Greeks, stole each other's property, violated each other's families, law and order broke down and anarchy reigned. "War," Thucydides wrote on describing this civil strife, the human equivalent of an infectious disease like the Plague that had wracked Athens in 430 BC, "is a terrible teacher."

As the war unfolded, the conflict between these clashing principles of government was nowhere more extreme than in Athens itself. As we've seen, its own great wartime leader Pericles frankly stated in the Assembly that Athens was a "tyrant city" ruling over other cities. But within itself, it was a self-governing democracy. If its commanders were victorious in extending Athenian power over their external enemies led by Sparta, what prevented those victorious men from returning home with their forces to establish themselves as tyrants in Athens? The Athenian people were increasingly preoccupied with this danger.

As long as Pericles lived, the problem was held at bay. Pericles advocated a measured imperialism. It was too dangerous to let the empire go, and Sparta had to be defeated. But new entanglements and wars of acquisition should be avoided unless they clearly squared with the city's resources. Let's be clear – Pericles was no peacenik. He never entertained the idea that Athens should cut back, much less give up, her dependence on the luxuries and riches that came with imperial power. No bicycles, only gas-guzzlers. In his great funeral oration for the fallen in a battle early in the war, he praised the beauty and culture of the city, and boasted that Athens was a "school" for all Greece. While enjoying the peacetime benefits of pleasure and the arts, tolerant of innovation and new ideas – unlike the grimly provincial Spartans with their huts and porridge – Athenians could at a moment's notice turn around and become unconquerable warriors. They had the best of both worlds. Pericles held out Athens as a shining vision, a civilizational beacon, for friend and foe alike. In the early phases of the war, before things went south, the Athenians seemed to truly believe that, unlike other imperial aggressors, they were bringing a better way of life to all. It was the first version in history of what we might call a liberal empire (but not the last).

According to Thucydides, although Pericles was, in effect, a monarch without the title – so great was his sway with the Assembly – he was content with the degree of power and honor that came from serving the common good by steering the ship of state through this middle passage of prudent imperialism. With his successors, this middle ground was abandoned for the extremes of excessive imperial expansion and a desire to shed the burden of being a "tyrant city" altogether. In Thucydides' view, neither side necessarily acted on behalf of the common good. The war party was led by Alcibiades, the brilliant, beautiful, bold and charismatic nephew of Pericles, a member of the wealthy and aristocratic Alcmaeonid clan. Given to extravagance in his personal life, including a passion for racehorses and all manner of luxurious living, Alcibiades had a vested interest in expanding Athens' empire and bringing in ever greater loot. The peace party was led by an older man, the general Nicias, known for his moderate and pious character. He wanted a quiet life. When the Athenians successfully grabbed Sparta's Achilles heel by conducting a naval assault on an island off their coast, thereby making the Spartans more nervous than ever about a helot uprising sparked by the arrival of a liberating democratic army, Nicias used the opportunity to move Athens toward a concluding peace treaty with the foe.

But then Alcibiades began whipping up support for invading the island of Sicily, full of rich cities led by Syracuse, ripe for the picking. Nicias opposed this as madness when Sparta had not yet been properly knocked out of the war, attempting to continue Pericles' policy of no new imperial projects without the means to back them up. Alcibiades, by contrast, planned to move right on to the conquest of Carthage after polishing off Sicily – he believed there was "no limit" on the empire's future expansion. Was he a megalomaniac? Or was he something new – an Achilles who aspired to be Cyrus the Great, reflecting the impact of the Persian superpower on the Greek city-state as a model of authority? The assembly, enflamed by Alcibiades' promise of untold riches, backed the invasion of Sicily. Seriously misinformed about just how strong the Sicilian cities, especially Syracuse, actually were, the Athenians were defeated in a bloody rout. Five thousand of them died miserably of starvation and exposure, held prisoner in a canyon-sized quarry pit, which you can see outside of the ruins of Syracuse to this day. But the key reason for the expedition's failure, according to Thucydides, was that, having begun by sending out Alcibiades as leader of the expedition, the Athenians recalled him and sent out Nicias in his place. In other words, they replaced the man most in favor of the expedition, and in Thucydides' view most capable of winning victory, and replaced him with the man most opposed to it (who did not have a great track record as a general to boot). Why? Because the Athenians had begun to fear that Alcibiades would use his success as conqueror of Sicily to return and set himself up as tyrant at home. Their fear was sparked by the widespread belief that, on the eve of his departure, Alcibiades and his posse of rich aristocratic bullyboys had gotten plastered and mutilated some statues of Hermes, a god dear to the common people – seemingly an insult to the democracy. They also began to think about an unpleasant experience Athens had suffered some years previously during the tyranny of the Peisistratids.

Peisistratus had been a "new man" who took power by force, but ruled effectively and made Athens richer. He led their wars, adorned the city while balancing the budget, promoted commerce, and enforced the law, displaying (according to Thucydides) "wisdom and virtue." He was the classic reforming tyrant. But Peisistratus' successor, his son Hippias, became more despotic. Hippias' brother Hipparchus was enamored of a beautiful youth, Harmodius. But Harmodius was the beloved of an older man, Aristogeiton – who, when he learned of Hipparchus' unwanted advances toward Harmodius, was enraged and vowed to kill Hipparchus and overthrow his brother, the tyrant, as well. The personal quickly boiled over into the political. Just as with Achilles' feud with Agamemnon over the possession of Briseis, sexual passion and possessiveness mixed together with a perceived insult to one's honor in a combustible brew, a private vendetta that had serious consequences for political affairs. Hipparchus reacted to Aristogeitons's rejection of his advances by publicly humiliating his sister, pronouncing her unfit to participate in a public festival, perhaps hinting at her lack of virginity. Harmodius was angrier now than ever on his beloved's behalf. Knives hidden in their cloaks, the two lovers resolved to kill Hippias at the Panathaneiac procession, punishing the tyrant for his brother's outrages, but they lost their nerve and fled. Coming upon Hipparchus by accident, they killed him on the spot. After this, Hippias became fearful of plotters and began executing many Athenians. Finally the Spartans deposed him in alliance with the powerful Alcmaeonid clan, and a democracy was established.

The story confirms that although tyrants can sometimes rule well, their power can also tempt them and their cronies to treat whole cities as if they were their personal property, including their people, which can extend to public humiliation and sexual exploitation. It was because Hipparchus was the tyrant's brother that he could press his unwanted advances on Aristogeiton and shame his sister in public. The Athenians were resolved never to let anyone have this kind of power over them again. The arrogant and licentious Alcibiades, a distinctly Achillean kind of personality who, along with his rich prep-school pals, wore his hair long in the Spartan fashion to imply that he preferred the Spartans' aristocratic code to the sovereignty of the masses (the *hoi polloi*) was target number one. The catastrophic defeat of the cream of the Athenian army and navy in Sicily, which may well have been guaranteed by the recall of Alcibiades, led to the city's decline and the eventual loss of the war with Sparta. The contradiction between democracy at home and empire abroad eventually ground Athens up.

The conflict between the imperial expansionism of Alcibiades and the longing for peace of Nicias mirrored a division within Athenian society that deepened as the war unfolded. On the one hand, the professional teachers of rhetoric, who came to be known as the Sophists, taught that it was human nature to pursue power and wealth, to "get the better" of others, and that anyone who can get away with being a tyrant will want to do so. Short of that, you can pull the wool over your fellow citizens' eyes by practicing the art of deceitful rhetoric in order to get ahead in democratic politics. An especially brazen version of the Sophists' teaching was put by Thucydides into the mouths of a group of Athenian generals, members of Alcibiades' war party, who state that "Of the gods we believe, and of men we know, that by a necessary law of nature they rule wherever they can." This is often taken to be the original classic statement of *Realpolitik*, that might makes right. It implies, if not outright atheism, a belief that the gods couldn't care less about whether we behave justly or unjustly; on the contrary, they believe that might makes right themselves, and act on it. Tyranny and imperial conquest are the way of the world. You can either try to get it for it yourself, or knuckle under when an unusually generous conqueror like Athens offers you the chance to submit and live in peace.

On the other hand, especially as the war went badly, there were Athenians who began to feel guilty about provoking the Spartans to war in the first place through their pursuit of hegemony. They believed that the terrible plague that devastated the city (and killed Pericles) was the gods' punishment for their hubris. Bringing the population inside the Long Walls had also disrupted the traditional worship of the ancestors, in which the family hearth was used both to cook food and to provide burnt offerings in sacrifice to the ancestors, who were buried directly beneath the hearth on the family homestead in the countryside. These Athenians began to feel that Athens' rise to power had led to a breakdown of old-fashioned morality, that the pursuit of self-interest and power had corroded the old virtues of loyalty to family, country, and the gods, and the respect of the young for the old. The contrast was summed up in Aristophanes' play the *Clouds* in the debate between the Just Speech and the Unjust Speech. The Just Speech laments the passing of the old morality, the Homeric code of manliness that reached its finest flowering at the Battle of Marathon in the struggle to repulse the Persians. In contrast with the Just Speech, who is a bit of an old fogey, the Unjust Speech is brazen and shameless in his defense of imperialism, power, unbridled pleasure, and the need for the young to seize their place in the sun away from their decrepit elders. Alcibiades is parodied in the play as a lisping, arrogant, long-haired fop with expensive tastes including horses (the character's name, Pheidippides, runs together "son of thrift," expressing his self-made father's hope that he will be a good businessman, and "concerning horses," reflecting his aristocratic mother's approval of his extravagance), and he sides, of course, with the Unjust Speech.

The division in Athenian society that the comic poet Aristophanes presents as humorous is presented as tragedy by Sophocles, who served as a general and whose lifespan corresponded with the rise and fall of the Athenian empire. He makes use of the ancient legend of Oedipus – known at least since Homer's time – in order to examine the moral dilemmas of Athenian statesmanship in the present. Like Shakespeare's history plays, Sophocles' plays rise to the level of the universal and enduring in their teaching, while at the same time they are closely engaged in the world around

him. In Sophocles' depiction, Oedipus believes in the power of reason, allied
with his supreme ambition, to make him the master of Thebes. He came to
power by defeating the Sphinx, and when the land is once again laid waste
by plague, he offers to save the day by uncovering and punishing the murderer of Laius, who, as he eventually learns to his horror, is, in fact, himself.
The blind wise man of Thebes, Teresias, urges Oedipus not to probe further
into Laius' murder. For Teresias, sometimes it's best not to know; it's best to
be blind to the truth. Men should lay low and avoid excessive ambition lest
the gods strike you down for presuming too high a place. Oedipus violently
castigates Teresias for refusing to reveal what he knows. He invokes Apollo,
god of the art of government, as his special patron. When his insistence on
investigating Laius' murder leads to the revelation that he killed his father
and slept with his mother Jocasta, driving Jocasta to hang herself, Oedipus
blinds himself with the pins of her disheveled tunic, cursing Apollo for aban-
doning him. His self-inflicted blindness at the play's end matches the wisdom of the blind Teresias, who was right: Sometimes it's best not to know.
Oedipus' reliance on reason, coupled with his ambitious pride, leads to his
nemesis. Throughout the play, the chorus, representing the Theban citizenry,
are torn between their desire for a statesman whose ambition will serve the
state and their revulsion for tyrants. The problem is, they're not sure which
is which, and neither is Oedipus, who learns the full truth about himself only
at the end. The play teaches us that, unfortunately, some of the same qualities of excessive ambition, ruthlessness and intolerance for disagreement
marking a tyrant may be needed by successful statesmen as they defend and
protect their cities.

Scholars have long speculated that Oedipus might be a stand-in for Pericles
himself. The play was first presented in 430 BC, around the time of Pericles'
death from the plague, and Oedipus begins his tragic downward spiral by confronting the danger presented by a plague to Thebes. If the parallel is a valid
one, Sophocles seems to be endorsing the view that the rise of Athens, reaching
its zenith in the rule of Pericles, later sometimes even called the Periclean Age,
was guilty of a hubristic ambition that eventually would have to be brought
low. It was also a warning to the average Athenian: Curb your desires and your
love of wielding tyrannical power over other cities. Interestingly, the worldview
of Teresias – lie low, avoid excessive ambition, trust in the virtue of your fellow citizens rather than in your own presumed brilliance and originality – is
presented by Thucydides, through the speech of the Spartan King Archidamus
to the Council of Ephors opposing war with Athens, as very much the Spartan
code as well. We sense that, as their fortunes decline, many Athenians start to
wonder whether the more modest and old-fashioned Spartans might have had
the right approach to life all along.

Even so, Sophocles' depiction of contemporary Athenian life through the
filter of myth shows how much things have changed since Homer's code of
Bronze Age heroism, reflecting the crisis of values and the felt lack of a moral

compass in Athens as it rose to empire. In Homer's poems, the gods are very close to men, moving among them, becoming their friends and lovers, and very like them in their passions and needs. In Sophocles' tragedies, by contrast, the gods seem very distant, their interest in human affairs uncertain, their will bleak and inscrutable. When they do strike, it comes out of the blue, a tidal wave of sheer necessity, crushing Oedipus, who thought Apollo was his patron, for aiming too high. Have the gods gone away? Have they left man's world empty?

Even in Homer, though, as well as in other respected poetic works like those of Pindar, the gods seem disturbingly inconsistent or ambivalent about the meaning of human virtue. People reflecting on these venerated sources began to question their worth, in light of the moral decline that many felt had been sparked by Athens' rise to empire and the civil strife it provoked among the Greek city-states in the Peloponnesian War. Do the gods, as the poets sometimes present them, consistently punish vice and reward virtue? Or, as the poets present them at other times, can they be swayed by a wicked man's lavish sacrifices to overlook his crimes in rising to tyranny? Do they care about what we do at all? If virtue is supposed to be the best way of life, its own reward, why do so many of the poets stress how difficult it is, how harsh and painful a climb? Could the best way of life for a man make him unhappy? If you avoid gaining wealth and power at the expense of others in order to be pious and moderate, aren't you really just being played for a sucker? The poets, many began to feel, provided no clear answers.

The thoughtful young men who surround him in Plato's dialogues, looking for guidance, ask these questions of Socrates. They lead us back to the rage of Achilles with which we began Part One, and a wholesale reassessment and critique of Homer's code of manliness as summed up by the hero of the *Iliad*. Although much had happened in the history of ancient Greece since Homer composed his lays, for many, his works remained authoritative, with the shining hero Achilles at their core – as the Victorian poet Matthew Arnold put it, Homer's poems were nothing less than the Bible of the Greeks. As we saw in our look at the *Iliad*, although Achilles does not actually rule as a tyrant – he is one king in a league of kings headed by Agamemnon – his unbridled selfishness, passion, and craving for honor make him very capable of tyrannical behavior. Everything is personal, everything is about him. Whether he fights or refuses to fight alongside his allies, it's over a personal vendetta or passion.

For Socrates, Achilles is the supreme example of "the love of one's own" – one's own status, pleasures, property, at the expense of any concern with the common good. And he is, therefore, the very quintessence of a tyrannically inclined personality. Because he is so totally wrapped up in himself, he personifies the external world that places obstacles in the way of his desires as his personal foe, raging against the cosmos and even threatening the gods with battle. Socrates belittles his rage by presenting it as akin to that of a sulky teenager who has been sent to his room and kicks his chair in anger, becoming even more furious when he stubs his toe, and so must punish the chair with a stronger kick, or maybe, like Keith Moon, trash the whole room. As Socrates dismissively puts it in the *Republic*, Achilles' constant bewailing of his fate reminds one of a little boy who has hurt his finger and goes around crying for someone to kiss it better. Achilles is, therefore, everything that a young man should not be, and the proper education of young men can be summed up as the need to be the opposite of Achilles in every case.

According to Socrates, young men need to be educated from an early age to moderate and restrain their passions and to cooperate with others. Excessive rage must be redirected toward the vigorous and spirited service of the common good in cooperation with your fellow citizens. Excessive hedonistic pleasures are to be avoided. There's nothing wrong with ambition in itself. In this respect, Socrates and the other ancient thinkers do not share a later tendency common to Christians like St. Augustine and early modern thinkers like Hobbes to think that the longing for political honor should somehow be expelled from the soul (views we'll explore in Part Two). No, it all depends on where the ambition is *directed*. Honor seeking should be deflected away from a tyrannical outlet and channeled toward seeking honor from your fellow citizens for serving the city and upholding justice.

Whether entirely fair to Homer or not (as we saw earlier, Homer is not entirely uncritical of Achilles), Socrates' new ways of education offered a powerful alternative to the moral ambiguities of the traditional poets. Book 9 of the *Republic* offers a critique of tyranny and the tyrannical life that has, in many ways, remained the template down to the present, with variations by Sallust, Erasmus, and many others. The disordered soul of the tyrant flows directly from the licentiousness of democracy itself. He begins as a populist demagogue who takes the lead in indulging the worst excesses of democratic hedonism and stirs up the resentment of the mob against their betters. On becoming tyrant, as Socrates puts it, his bloated erotic passion acts as a demagogue within his own character, focusing all his energies on the selfish pursuit of pleasure and glory. Because he rules through fear and force, he can never trust those around him, and is constantly on guard for conspiracies, gloomy, suspicious, and prone to spasms of cruelty. The only effective cure for this tyrannical longing is to curb those unruly passions, and that can only be done if the mind rules the passions and redirects their energies toward justice and civic virtue. Philosophy itself must show the way. If the world is chaotic, our passions and our behavior will be too. If the world is reasonable, there's a chance our passions can be enlisted in the service of reason as well. Because Achilles believes the world is chaotic, he careens between mad daring and a blue funk. What's needed is *steadiness*.

To be sure, Plato's depiction of tyranny is not always so unqualifiedly scathing. In Book 4 of the *Laws*, he entertains the possibility that a tyrant could play a constructive role in founding a just society – the Tyrant as Reformer from our three categories. But this won't be possible unless the ambitious young tyrant is guided by a wise counselor. A hallmark of the classical approach to the danger of tyrannical ambition is this search for the wise advisor. Plato's exploration of this partnership in the *Laws* is taken up by Cicero, who presents an idealized portrait of Scipio Africanus the Younger as having received instruction in a dream from the spirit of his dead father on a journey through the heavens to serve his country as a brave and patriotic Roman, but to place a concern with eternity and one's immortal soul even higher than a concern with martial and civic virtue and honor. The pedigree continues down to Erasmus' *Education of a Christian Prince*, with its advocacy of a blend of Christian humility and faith with an education in classical statecraft and the exploits of ancient heroes like Cyrus the Great as depicted by Socrates' companion Xenophon. For Erasmus, a love of properly directed honor is a perfectly acceptable motive for a Christian prince to cultivate his sense of duty. A desire for immortal fame of the kind extolled by the ancients in virtuous statesmen is a rung on the ladder to the higher concern with the immortality of the soul promised by Christian revelation.

As we'll explore further, these partnerships between wisdom and political power didn't always work out in real life. Socrates' mentoring role with Alcibiades didn't seem to succeed in restraining the younger man's excessive ambition. Plato later picked a dud when he thought the young tyrant Dionysius II of Syracuse could be turned into a philosopher-king. In the *Laws*, after flirting with the idea of a young tyrant guided by a wise mentor to found a just city, he abandons it as too risky – you might wake up to find the young man you trusted to serve justice was a monster, and even if he did found a just regime, could he be persuaded to give up absolute power over it? The Romans believed one of their early dictators, Cincinnatus, voluntarily returned to his plow after his term with absolute power was up. But how often does that happen? As for Cicero, in attempting to try on the role of wise older advisor with the twenty-year-old Octavian Caesar, he came a complete cropper.

We began our discussion of the tumultuous panoply of the fifth century BC with the clash between the fierce independence of the Greek city-states and the universal empire created by Cyrus the Great, heir to the god-kings of the east who wanted to impose order on chaos throughout the world, to bring the benefits of peace, prosperity, and good government to all. The new code of civic virtue set forth by Plato, reforming Homer in order to downplay his emphasis on Achilles' kind of overweening ambition and emphasizing instead the collective service of citizens to the common good, in many ways re-affirmed the superior way of life of republics to that of empires. Plato's *Republic*, whose citizen-soldiers renounce private gain and live communally in a barracks, has been compared to an idealized version of Sparta.

But not everyone drew the same conclusions from the crisis in moral values that saw out the century. An interesting fork in the road was reached that will have a deep impact on the continuing career of tyranny. Although the Greeks had come perilously close to being overwhelmed by the Persian Empire, many of them were fascinated by it, admired it, and even saw in it a solution to the Greeks' own woes – the lamentable fractiousness and fragmentation of their thousands of tiny statelets, their comparative military and economic weakness, their inability to unite, their frequent internal political upheavals. Their temporary alliance against Persia had created a new spirit of unity that many wanted to see made permanent.

In writing his own life of Cyrus the Great, Xenophon, who was both a philosophic companion of Socrates and a general with combat experience, not least in aiding a younger Cyrus to reclaim the throne of Persia, set forth what we can describe as a utopian monarchy to counter the utopian republic of Plato. Ostensibly about a great leader from the past, it openly invites the Greeks to consider whether they might not want to create a multinational empire of their own. We have already seen that, from early on, through their art and poetry, through their great architecture, the Greek city-states believed they, too, had a civilizational mission from which all Greeks, and even peoples beyond Greece, might benefit. The temple at Delphi, the many depictions of the Gigantomachia, represented a Greek version of the eastern god-kings' campaign to conquer disorder and establish the rule of reason, law, and art. Indeed, their very use of the term *barbarian* suggested a sense of superiority to those outside the Greek world, although literally it originally simply meant people who went around saying bar-bar-bar (that's how eastern languages sounded to them). Before now, the dogged independence of the city-states prevented the creation of a universal state that would mirror this civilizational mission. That would all be changed by Alexander the Great; in a way he was the answer to Xenophon's prayer. Through the empire he established, the model of a universal monarchy from the east found a new home in the west.

We've already suggested that Alcibiades, in many ways evocative of Achilles' narcissistic splendor and excess, was feeling his way toward conquering an empire of limitless extent when the Athenian democracy brought him down – that, in his aspirations, he may have been a combination of Achilles and Cyrus the Great. Alcibiades' imperial ambitions were held back by the small city-state and the constraints of democracy, but with Alexander the Great, in the following century, the bounds are burst and the death knell sounded for the polis as a small, truly independent community. A mosaic of Alexander's smashing victory over the Great King of Persia, Darius, after which the entire Persian empire fell into his hands intact, shows Alexander leading a charge directly toward the Great King himself, normally ensconced among his retainers and protected from direct exposure to combat. Alexander, young, lean, and tousled, careens forward at the head of his comrades from the left-hand side, while on the right, Darius and his bodyguard, suddenly realizing that this madman is hurtling straight toward them, rear back in terror. Achillean daring transforms the beautiful young Macedonian into the new Great King.

Alexander combined the prowess in generalship of Cyrus the Great with the personal heroism in combat of his avowed model, Achilles. In carving out his empire all the way to Egypt, restrained from invading India only by the exhaustion of his men, Alexander saw himself as blazing a Homeric trail of glory fit for future myth. He even had his own Patroclus, his bosom buddy Hephaestion. He was more than a little prone to drunken rages and brawls before flaming out at the age of thirty-three. The project of creating a rational universal monarchy brought to fruition by the first Cyrus is now reinvigorated by the still vibrant code of manly honor and the pursuit of immortal individual glory inherited from Homer. The mosaic of Alexander charging for Darius in a melee of panicked horses and fleeing men recalls the earlier depictions of the pharaohs waging war on the forces of disorder, only now, the civilizational mission has been transferred from the east to the west.

Alexander, son of the Macedonian King Philip, having grown up in a kingdom that was considered somewhat beyond the pale of being properly Greek, heavily identified with the culture of Greece and drunk it in. Aristotle had been his tutor, and while conquering Asia, Alexander wrote to him claiming that "I had rather excel others in the knowledge of what is excellent, than in the extent of my power and dominion" – the very model of the young tyrant who acknowledges his need for a wise counselor, though it plainly didn't get in the way of his gaining "power and dominion." Like other famous political outsiders – think of Napoleon – as a Macedonian, he aimed to be the hero of the Greek civilization he wanted into. He saved the Greeks by conquering them and finally making them united. Aristotle, like Xenophon, had already envisioned a perfect monarch exercising superlative judgment who would establish his authority over "many cities and peoples." In aiming to do just that, Alexander added a distinctively Greek tincture to the older agenda of the eastern universal god-kings in improving life for their subjects. The numerous cities he founded were, in effect, replicas of the Greek *polis* air-lifted to Mesopotamia, Assyria, and Egypt, each one complete with an agora, a local council, gymnasium, temples, theater, and schools. In this way, unlike his eastern predecessors, Alexander spread with his conquests something of that republican preference for local self-government. At the same time, he wisely followed Cyrus the Great's policy of religious tolerance that would in turn be taken up by the Romans. It was taken for granted that the Greek way of life was not true simply for Greeks, but for human nature everywhere, which meant that Alexander could do his conquered subjects no greater service than to enable them to become Greeks. The result was something of a patchwork that we now refer to as "Hellenistic monarchy." After Alexander's death, his empire was divided among his main generals, and the kingdoms they set up – the Seleucids in Assyria and the Ptolemies in Egypt – became unique hothouse blends of Greek and Asian influences, with the elaborate ceremonial of the traditional god-king mixed up with a passion for Greek literature, art, and sport, and men who had originally won their kingdoms through demonstrating their military and administrative merit under Alexander establishing traditional hereditary monarchies to be passed down to their descendants after intermarriage with the former royal lines. It's well summed up in the stunning Ptolemaic temples that can still be visited along the Nile, where Greek and Egyptian styles seamlessly intertwine, columns alternating with sphinxes, and where the Ptolemaic pharaohs made an annual visit to the "birth house" of Horus to be reborn with the god in order to make sure their Greek blood was now sufficiently Egyptian.

THE GREATEST REPUBLIC

If the ancient Greeks were concerned about tyranny, one might say that Republican Rome was obsessed by it. In their great national epic composed by their historians such as Livy and Polybius (actually a Greek) and their own Homer, the poet Virgil, Rome's entire existence was dedicated to preventing the arbitrary authority of one man over the common good. The Greeks, as we have seen, distinguished between legitimate monarchs and tyrants who had usurped power, and had allowed that even the latter could sometimes do good things for their countries. For the Romans, these distinctions were brutally collapsed into one simple, hated, and all-encompassing term – *Rex*. While we translate it as "king," for the Romans, it was indistinguishable from what the Greeks had meant by tyranny at its worst. *Regnum* – kingship – was the most detested form of authority, reducing free citizens to the status of slaves. It made no difference whether kings did good things or bad, their power over citizens was intolerable. For the Greeks, it made a difference that Sophocles had called Oedipus a tyrant rather than a king (*basileus*). For the Romans, it made no difference at all, which is why they translated it as *Oedipus Rex*, Oedipus the King – in other words, the tyrant.

For the Romans, this lesson was learned, one might say seared into their historical or at least their mythological memory, by the tyrannical excesses of their last king, Tarquinius, surnamed the Proud or Haughty (*Superbus*) whose overthrow established the Republic. The tale is so drenched in bloodshed, usurpation, patricide, cruelty, rape, outrage, revenge and bravery as to rival the most lurid Greek tales of sex, murder, and power like the curse on the House of Atreus.

Tarquin (no need to use his full name Lucius Tarquinius Superbus) had married his sister-in-law Tullia after she left her first husband, whom she despised as a wimp. She and her lover Tarquin murdered Tarquin's first wife, the gentle Tullia (yes, same name). Encouraged by his virago of a new wife, Tarquin seized the throne by armed force, flinging the legitimate King Servius – his new wife's father – from the steps of the Senate House into the street. Tarquin's henchmen then slew Servius, with the encouragement of his own daughter, who drove the wheels of a chariot over her father's corpse for good measure. (Aren't these people sweethearts?). The new King Tarquin refused to bury the dead Servius (thereby denying him passage to join the ancestors, a serious crime as we know from Sophocles' *Antigone*). Next came a reign of terror in which Tarquin executed without trial anyone he suspected of disloyalty. Interestingly, it's conceded that, like our reforming tyrants among the Greeks such as Peisistratos, Tarquin did some good things for Rome. He won a number of wars, used the spoils to beautify the city with temples, including the great national shrine the Temple of Jupiter on the Capitoline Hill, improved a theater, and built a sewer system, the *cloaca maxima*, that can be glimpsed to this day in the Forum. Historians have speculated that the Romans never entirely wanted to concede just how much these Etruscan kings had done for them. In fact, they adopted a lot of their religious rituals and symbols of rank including the elegantly turned curule chair used by magistrates.

The flash point for Tarquin's overthrow came over sexual passion and outrage, broadly akin to the stories of Harmodius and Aristogeiton, Achilles' feud with Agamemnon, and Agamemnon's murder by his wife and her lover. The king's son, Sextus Tarquinius, was enflamed by the beauty and virtue of Lucretia, his cousin's wife. Lucretia was the model of Roman womanhood, devoted to her household chores while the other noble ladies lunched. Sextus pressed Lucretia to give herself to him, threatening to kill her and claim it was because he caught her having sex with a slave, the worst imaginable crime. To spare her husband's family this shame, she submitted to rape by Sextus, then killed herself in revulsion for what had happened. Appalled by this abuse of power by Tarquin's son, a band of young nobles led by Lucius Junius Brutus swore an oath to drive the Tarquin family from Rome. It worked, but Tarquin continued plotting to subvert some of the leading citizens into restoring him, including Brutus' own sons, whom Brutus unflinchingly condemned to death when the plot was uncovered. In a last ditch bid to come back, Tarquin convinced the king of Clusium to march on Rome, where the Romans' defense of the city saved the day, thanks to Horatius' legendary defense of the bridge over the Tiber. The Tarquins were done, and the Republic was founded, lasting for a thousand years, the longest single-running system of government in human history. (How it kept on thinking of itself as a republic after becoming an empire is a fascinating aspect of the story).

The story of Tarquin's overthrow telescopes a number of key themes that dominate the history of the Roman Republic – the hatred of tyranny, the passion for civic liberty, loyalty to family, the duty to use force in the service of justice, bravery in combat, and a loyalty to the common good so uncompromising that it led a father to have his own sons executed. Like the Spartans, the Romans claimed that citizens must always place the common good above one's own. Bravery in war such as that of Horatius at the bridge was the mark of a true man. Other virtues like knowing how to govern were important, but meant little absent battlefield courage – so much so that the Roman word for virtue, *virtus*, was originally almost indistinguishable from manliness demonstrated in combat. As we have observed, Cicero, inspired by Greek philosophy, tried much later on to set a higher standard in which martial and civic virtue were subordinate to the life of the mind. But many of Cicero's associates in the ruling class snickered at his obvious distaste for battlefield combat (he was "timorous in arms," as Plutarch put it), including an embarrassing scene where he appeared ready to faint at the sight of a column of burly legionaries in the Forum. Until the closing days of the Republic, its greatest dynasts including Marius, Sulla, Pompey, and Julius Caesar took the field at the head of their troops, in Caesar's case hand-to-hand combat right in the line. Above all, every citizen had a duty to oppose, by assassination if necessary, anyone coveting the title or power of a king. Even Romulus himself, in one version of his death, might have been set upon by the senators, who bridled at his increasing arrogance and hacked him to death. Certainly Marcus Brutus, whose family claimed descent from the founder of the Republic, Marcus Junius Brutus, felt a special obligation to take similar action against Julius Caesar when it appeared he coveted the kingship.

When we talk about the Roman understanding of the common good – the term for republic, *Res Publica*, meant, roughly, "the public matter" – we must always bear in mind that for many upper-class Romans, this did not include the mob, the plebs, whom their betters sometimes sneeringly labeled "the sewer of the city." Educated Romans regarded the Athenian experiment in democracy as a disaster, not least because the Greeks' own leading minds, including Plato, had taken such a withering view of it. Like Sparta before it, the Roman Republic was a self-governing aristocracy who called themselves the "patricians" because they claimed descent from the fathers, from the original great families going back to the time of Romulus.

Between the patricians and the plebes, there was a middle class of equestrians. In the earliest, semilegendary period of the republic – paralleling archaic Greece – these men were knights, men with enough money to keep a couple of horses, armor, and a squire. When cavalry later gave way to the famous Roman legion of massed columns of infantry, the knights, while retaining their ancient title, became the business and commerce class of Rome, and hence very influential in their own right. Senators were not supposed to engage directly in business because it was thought vulgar, even though many of them were extremely rich, so equestrians would function as their agents, stewards, and bankers. The three classes functioned together in the path of honor, the *cursus honorum*. It was complicated and changed a great deal over time, but essentially, membership in the Senate, along with high military commands, was in principle confined to the patricians. The equestrians could aspire to certain offices short of the Senate, while the main role of the plebs was to vote for their betters in elections that were rigged to favor the wealthy. But there were numerous exceptions. In the course of the republic's history, equestrians and even plebs had become senators and consuls.

The main thing to bear in mind as we follow the career of tyranny is that, following the overthrow of the Tarquins, the Romans gradually developed a complex series of constitutional checks and balances aimed at preventing any man from achieving kingly power again, or any faction from grabbing the lion's share of influence. The aristocracy was determined to avoid the extremes of tyranny on the one hand and mob rule on the other. The American Founders had it in mind as one of their own models for the division of powers in the American constitution. The war-making authority of the kings was transferred to two consuls elected annually, the chief magistrates of the Republic and the greatest honor to which any man could aspire. Originally, they led Rome's armies into battle. Later on, these commands were usually assigned on the basis of military competence to "pro-consuls," men who fought wars "in the place of the consuls." The consuls exercised the mysterious quality the Romans called *imperium*. Originally it meant the power over life and death without trial that military commanders must exercise in war, not only over the enemy but over unruly or cowardly troops. It came to mean more generally (as one scholar put it) "the power vested by the state in a person to do what he considers in the best interest of the state." Always vigilant lest this power be turned against Romans themselves by an aspiring tyrant returning home at the head of his army, the consulship was limited to a year, and when, later on, imperium was exercised by the most competent commanders, its terms were strictly set by the Senate – a certain period of time in a certain place for a certain task, after which, when completed, the precious imperium must be returned. Pompey the Great, for example, was granted imperium for the explicit task of ridding Rome's sea-lanes of pirates. Crassus received it to defeat Spartacus' slave revolt. On occasion, the troops would spontaneously proclaim a victorious field commander as "imperator," the guy with the imperium, from where we later get our term "emperor." Above all, it was maintained, a commander must never enter the city of Rome with his forces; that would be tantamount to the establishment of tyranny – the use of the military against fellow citizens.

Yet, inevitably, in times of crisis caused by the threat of foreign invasion or internal insurrection, exceptions had to be granted, changes had to be made. The office of Dictator was established so that a magistrate appointed by the Senate could exercise imperium for a longer period than the consuls, and within Rome itself – in effect, martial law. Power sharing by the Senate was also unavoidable. The plebs, feeling oppressed by their aristocratic betters, once threatened to withdraw as a body to the nearby Sacred Mount and establish a new city of their own. The patricians, realizing they couldn't function without servants and soldiers, coaxed them back by giving them their own representatives, the Tribunes, who could veto measures of the Senate and whose bodies could not be violated by the laying on of force. Sometimes the tribunes really were men of the people. Other times, aristocrats scheming for greater influence would run for this office too. Over several centuries, this Rubik's Cube of interlocking, overlapping and somewhat contradictory institutions and social forces, clashing and checking, brought the Republic, which had become a great empire stretching from modern-day

France to Syria, to its final blood-soaked forty years of civil war culminating in the assassination of Julius Caesar.

Early Rome's history is shrouded in a mixture of legend and fact, but it is clear from early on that the Romans sought military victory over their surrounding neighbors in Italy, perhaps initially to give Rome a buffer zone from attack, but eventually for power and plunder. Just as Romulus' door was always open to newcomers who wanted to join his Palatine Gang, when the Romans conquered a neighboring city, they tried to convert the populace into allies and sometimes made them Roman citizens. In this way, Rome's original armies were swollen with newcomers, who then turned outward and added new conquests to an ever-expanding perimeter.

The shroud of legend gives way to definite historical reality when Rome acquired its first truly foreign possession, Sicily, which invited the wrath of Carthage. That began a century-long battle to the death between the great maritime commercial empire and the upstart Romans. As we mentioned earlier, when Virgil came to write his Homeric-scale epic of the founding of Rome by Aeneas, he wove into the tale a hatred between Rome and Carthage going all the way back to Aeneas' rejection of Dido – their life and death struggle was destined! The Punic Wars began with the great Carthaginian general Hannibal's near defeat of Rome in its own Italian heartland and ended with the decisive victory of Scipio Africanus the Younger. Carthage was leveled and her soil sewn with salt to suggest no one would ever live there again (actually, it rebounded pretty quickly under Roman control).

Rome woke up the next morning to find itself the greatest power in the Mediterranean. Barely known to the Greeks in her first several centuries of growth as a *polis* much like their own, the Romans now crashed relentlessly into the historical window of the ancient Greek world, picking off Macedonia, the Seleucid monarchy left by Alexander, and finally Greece itself. These victories brought tremendous wealth to Rome, but they also introduced the tensions that would eventually bring the republic down. The plebs who fought in the legions wanted farmland in recompense for their sacrifices. The senators, whose greed for landed estates was insatiable, didn't want to give it to them. Roman politics became divided between the "optimates" (the "best men," as they called themselves) and a new faction, the "populares" or champions of the people, sometimes led by patricians themselves. When their champions, the Gracchi, used their authority as Tribunes to begin redistributing some senatorial landholdings, the aristocrats hit back using armed mobs. Under the dictatorship of Sulla ("pot-marked"), who broke the sacred taboo by occupying Rome with his army, as many as nine thousand populares were executed. But the populares regained the upper hand when the illustrious general Marius, a commoner, became dictator himself. He also marched on Rome. Among his protégés was the young Julius Caesar.

The contradiction that blew the Republic apart was the fact that it was basically a Greek city-state attempting to rule a world-wide empire. Surveying

Roman ruins from Britain to Jordan, you will find that the greatest boast to be made by the local Roman governor, or later a visiting emperor, was that he had been made a consul of Rome so and so number of times. It's a little as if the mayor of Cleveland just happened to be supreme commander of a force of two hundred thousand troops in Iraq, all the while stoutly maintaining that he was only the mayor of Cleveland, and could conceive of no higher honor than being the mayor of Cleveland. Because of the republic's ingrained fear of tyrants, it refused to modify or change its basic structure – a town council dominated by local notables who had the final say about everything. In the meantime, it sent out a string of successful conquerors – Scipio, Pompey, Caesar to mention a few – who emerged from their victories swollen with plunder and controlling vast new fiefdoms of territory whose inhabitants regarded them as their new kings, even as gods. Pompey, in particular, benefited from conquering the east, the heartland of the old Assyrian and Hellenistic domains. Not only was Pompey acclaimed locally as a god, but he acquired sizable "off the book" armies from his new client kingdoms as well as tons of loot.

Yet in all cases, these men were expected to simply return at the end of their fixed term as commanders and resume their status as equal citizens. Although the Senate often honored them, it could not always hide its collective resentment of their achievements, their fear that one of these grand dynasts might court the mob or proclaim himself openly as King of Rome. Scipio, for example, was criticized in the Senate for indulging his troops with lax discipline so as to win them over to advance his ambitions back home. Cicero managed to blunt Crassus' claims to victory over Spartacus by inviting the more powerful Pompey home to claim credit for it himself, using one dynast to check another. Frequently, too, as soon as these great men resigned their commands, they would be hit with a flurry of lawsuits, from which they had enjoyed legal immunity while in office, by fellow aristocrats jealous of them and determined to prove they had used their power corruptly.

The flash point was reached when Julius Caesar, having conquered huge territories for Rome in Gaul, adding thousands of slaves and tons of booty to Rome's coffers, had to come home because his appointment was up. Normally, to prevent someone from getting above himself, the Senate insisted that he give up his current command and return to Rome as a private citizen, before becoming eligible for another appointment. Caesar, fearing that on returning to Rome lawsuits would descend on him like jackals (he had been pretty high-handed, after all, including making war on and plundering people in Gaul who in fact were already Roman citizens, and raising off the book legions), asked the Senate to let him proceed immediately to his expected consulship. They refused. He refused to resign his command. When he crossed the Rubicon, it was at the head of an army to which he was no longer entitled – an invasion force for war on the Republic. Pompey and much of the Senate – they had enlisted Caesar's rival dynast to crush him – fled south and eventually to Illyria, where Caesar routed him at the battle of Pharsalis. Following the remnants of Pompey's forces to Egypt, Caesar was horrified when he was presented with Pompey's severed head by a minion of Queen Cleopatra; she thought it would please him. The republican firebrand Cato (descendant of the scourge of Carthage who ended every speech in the Senate with the words: "Carthage must be destroyed") refused to accept Caesar's authority and killed himself, but the young Brutus (descendant of the man who expelled the Tarquins) was reconciled.

Caesar was triumphant, and during his dictatorship he proved to be the classic reforming tyrant. He sponsored huge public works. He reorganized the legal system, had much personal debt forgiven, and provided at last for a fair distribution of land among his veterans. Unlike Sulla, he did not carry out mass reprisals against his enemies. He much prized the virtue of clemency, and was willing to accept as a friend any man who had once opposed him but now was willing to relent. Learned and urbane, and an excellent prose stylist, even Cicero found him charming company, albeit the death of republican liberty.

It's been suggested that the spread of Greek literature – especially Homer – to Republican Rome had led young men to forsake the austere collective virtue of the old code and to long to imitate the world-conquering heroism and godlike magnanimity of Achilles and Alexander. The world was their oyster. Caesar's adventures in Egypt appear to savor of this longing. In the midst of his torrid affair with Cleopatra, the last descendant of the Ptolemies and a captivating and supremely well-educated woman, he brought Egypt under Roman suzerainty while touring the wonders of the Nile on Cleopatra's royal barge. Finally, he brought her to Rome, erected a statue of her in the Forum, and ensconced her in a villa while maintaining the open sham of a marriage with his wife, the virtuous Calpurnia. A rumor spread that he intended to recognize his son by Cleopatra as his legal heir. These events were a flash point. Long suspected of aiming to proclaim himself openly as king, the Roman aristocracy was appalled that he now apparently intended to rule over them beside a foreign queen, and install the strumpet's bastard as heir to the new throne. Things came to a head when Caesar was stabbed brutally to death in the Senate, the result of a plot led by Brutus, another of those small-town aristocratic mob hits against an overreaching *capo* going back to Romulus.

Another spasm of civil war followed when the eighteen-year-old Octavian Caesar, named earlier by his grand-uncle Julius as his heir, clashed both with the assassins and with Mark Antony, Caesar's right-hand man who disdained this young upstart's pretensions and expected to lead the Caesarean party himself. Cicero, ever angling to preserve the old Senatorial order by playing off one dynast against another, tried to pit Octavian (he referred to him behind his back disdainfully as "the boy") against the seasoned commander Antony, whom Cicero thought of as the much greater threat. Octavian stabbed Cicero in the back by forming a pact with Antony, leading to a reign of terror in which Cicero lost his life. Predictably short-lived, the pact ended when Antony went out to Egypt to try to fill Caesar's shoes with Cleopatra. Their combined forces were decisively defeated at the Battle of Actium. Antony and Cleopatra committed suicide, and the young Octavian Caesar found himself undisputed master of the Roman world, bringing forty years of civil war to an end. What he did next changed everything.

THE UNIVERSAL LANDLORD: FROM REPUBLIC TO EMPIRE

Octavian, or as he later became known, Augustus Caesar, resolved the conflict between the self-governing republic Rome had started out as and the universal empire it had become by establishing a permanent world state disguised as a republic, ruled by a Hellenistic universal monarch disguised as merely the "first citizen" of that republic. He was walking in the footsteps of Cyrus and Alexander and bringing their project of a universal state to completion. It's impossible to know whether he planned this all along, or found his way by stages, just as it is impossible to know whether Caesar was also planning to establish a hereditary monarchy. When his uncle was assassinated, Octavian was compelled to protect his *dignitas* as a Roman aristocrat by returning to the dangerous city to claim his inheritance – the same argument Caesar had made when he crossed the Rubicon. An aristocrat cannot allow himself to be publicly slighted or denied his rights. But if that's all it started as, it became much more.

Augustus' rise to power was marked by political mass murder of a kind Julius Caesar had avoided, returning to the proscriptions of Sulla. Several hundred senators and upward of two thousand knights were killed. Sometimes they were opponents. Often they were cynically murdered so that their estates could be confiscated. His temporary partner, Antony, claimed Cicero for his list of victims, whose tongue was cut out after he was run through, and nailed to the doors of the Senate House for some insulting speeches he had given about Antony. Cold and calculating to an extraordinary degree, devoid of frivolity, good-looking but distant and reserved, Augustus was a young god of death, climbing over heaps of corpses to his legendary stature in later life. ("I like treachery," he once remarked, "but I cannot say anything good about about traitors."). Starting out as what his greatest biographer Ronald Syme described as a "young generalissimo and putschist," he ended as an avuncular old man given to wisecracks and who loved plain bread and cheese. He was widely respected and loved, the guarantor of peace after decades of strife. He was possibly the most Machiavellian politician who has ever existed, although Machiavelli, as a patriot of the Florentine Republic and admirer of early Rome, detested his memory for destroying the liberty of the Roman Republic for good.

How Augustus managed to reign as an absolute monarch garbed in the outward appearance of merely the first magistrate of the Republic came about through an absolutely ingenious rejigging and combining of existing Roman offices and institutions, such that his powers as monarch seemed nothing more than a consolidation of venerated past practice – hence his propagandistic claim that he had "restored" the Republic, not overthrown it forever. There were three constitutional pillars to his supreme authority. First, he was permanent commander-in-chief of all Roman military forces. The authority of the emperors was first and foremost based on military might. He claimed the term *imperator*, which had once been accorded spontaneously to victorious commanders by their forces in the field, for his own exclusive and permanent use, turning an informal accolade into a formal position. Eventually this title, the origin of our word *emperor,* became the chief designation for the autocrat of the Roman world.

Secondly, Augustus had the Senate endow him with the powers of the tribunes for life, while letting the original office dwindle into a merely honorary position. This gave him the aura of the champion of the common people, the heir of his grand-uncle Julius, Marius, and the populares. The empire was indeed liked from the get go by the common people, as opposed to the aristocracy who understood the reality behind the outward appearance – Augustus was now their absolute master. For the people, it meant peace, safety, and the freedom to prosper in private life. Plato might have said that the Caesars' identification of themselves with the common people confirmed his diagnosis of the tyrant as a demagogue who panders to the mob at the expense of the best men. The tribunician power also made the person of the emperor inviolable, indeed sacrosanct, buttressed by his taking on the title Augustus, a word evocative of the most ancient Roman piety, which could be translated as "the venerated one."

Augustus also assumed for life the office of Pontifex Maximus or High Priest, once exercised by the kings, which further endowed him with an aura of sanctity as well as placing in his gift many rich sinecures of priesthoods with which to reward his supporters (getting a Roman priesthood was rather like a fellowship at Oxford – nice digs and lots of great dinners). Finally, he possessed the right to speak first in the Senate in any deliberation, which meant that if he didn't wish to speak, no matter could go forward. (For good measure, as holder of the former tribunes' power, he also had an absolute veto over any Senate measure). This combination of powers gave Augustus and his successors absolute control over every aspect of life. Augustus himself was most often referred to as *princeps,* the leading man.

Augustus and his close advisors Agrippa (his military right-hand man and chief architectural planner) and Maecenas (bagman, shake-down artist, propagandist, and all-around political fixer) left nothing to chance. Every aspect of Roman life including art, literature, architecture, and religion must conform to and glorify the new Augustan principate. Rome was festooned with beautiful new temples and markets. It takes nothing away from the genius of Virgil to say that he was, in effect, Augustus' spin doctor, perhaps rewarded financially by Maecenas. His masterpiece, the *Aeneid*, recasts the entire history of the Roman Republic as preparing the way for Augustus, heir to Aeneas and Romulus, and harbinger of a mission to bring peace to the entire world. In this way, one might say that Augustus invented the Roman Republic retroactively as a narrative that progresses from the earliest origins of a clutch of huts on the Tiber to its magnificent fulfillment in him. More than that: By linking Augustus to Aeneas, and thereby to Troy, in a sense Virgil presents Augustus as the fulfillment and zenith of the entire age of Greek and Roman antiquity. In this return to the ancestral origins, the feline, fractious, and overly subtle qualities of the Greeks – this is how the Romans often thought of them, much as they admired their culture – are bypassed in favor of pious, solid, manly Troy.

In the fourth *Eclogue,* in a passage later identified with the birth of Christ, Virgil describes a "divine child" sent into this world to bring peace. Although dates are uncertain, the poem may have been composed around the same time that the Senate, now under the thumb of Octavian and Antony, declared Julius Caesar posthumously a god – which made Octavian, as he now repeatedly claimed, "the son of a god." In the *Aeneid,* his grand-uncle Julius Caesar's usurpation of authority, and especially his own much bloodier proscriptions on his violent path to victory, are carefully air-brushed so that the greatest achievements of the Republic prior to the civil wars segue directly and smoothly into its highest product, himself. Virgil also claims that Augustus embodies the highest moral and civic virtues praised by the Stoic school of philosophy, which, originating in Greece as a legacy of Socrates, became a favorite among well-educated Roman aristocrats because it offered a philosophical justification for the strength of character, courage, and magnanimity that they identified with their own gentlemanly code of honor. It's not surprising that Augustus wrapped himself in the mantel of Stoic self-discipline, moderation, piety, and service of the common good, since he most definitely didn't want any of his fellow aristocrats trying on what he had once done! The revolution was over.

Beginning with Augustus, the emperors made a great show of patronizing the achievements of ancient Greek art, literature, and philosophy and their Roman followers. They made the Roman empire into a kind of museum culture for what we now call "Greco-Roman antiquity," electing themselves as the stewards of a high culture from a politically defunct region. Greek culture was in the best of taste. The poor bastards (Romans thought) didn't know much about governing or the art of war, but oh were they on the mark when it came to poetry, philosophy, and sculpture. One of the best collections of Greek bronzes survives intact in the archaeological museum in Naples because Julius Caesar's wealthy father-in-law had reserved one of his villas near Pompeii for no other purpose than to house his collection. The emperor Trajan's villa near Tivoli, once believed to be a summer villa for him, is now thought to have been something more akin to the Bellagio Center on Lake Como, providing quarters for visiting scholars from throughout the empire to do their work with beautiful grounds to stroll through, lined with statues of the greatest Greek and Roman authors.

Stoicism became the philosophical school that received the patronage of the emperors, who wanted to be seen as representing its high standard of moral

conduct – Epicureanism was less favored because it encouraged personal pleasure over civic duty. Cicero, who had given his life to oppose what became
the Augustan principate, was rehabilitated as a part of Augustus' "restored"
republic. It was touchingly related that he told his daughter Julia to read Cicero
because he was "the best of the Romans," perhaps indicating a gentle regret
over unfortunate events in the past now best left unmentioned.

The public cult of Augustus is best summed up in the remarkable Prima Porta
Equestrian Statue, at once a masterpiece of classical sculpture and propaganda.
Dressed in the uniform of the order of knights, a beautified Augustus stretches
out his hand in a gesture of benevolent authority often associated with Apollo.
As I mentioned earlier, the equestrians were in actuality the business class, and
often formed the senatorial elite in Italy's provincial towns even though they
were barred from becoming senators in Rome. They represented the values of
hard work and small-town decency as against what many felt was the corrupt
pleasure seeking and political maneuvering of the patricians in the capital during the late Republic, including their notoriously licentious and scheming wives
(think of Polly Walker's portrayal of Octavian's mother Atia in the television
series *Rome*). By wearing the uniform of the Equestrian order in the statue, it
has been argued, Augustus was identifying himself with their solid, bourgeois,
and countrified code, part of his claim to have restored old-fashioned republican morals.

At the same time, he was also claiming a special relationship with Apollo, his
patron among the gods. His house on the Palatine hill had a temple to Apollo
directly connected to it. It also sat right next to the primitive settlement of huts
supposedly established by Romulus, thus endowing Augustus with the aura
of the city's founder. His house was comfortably large but by no means pala-
tial, reinforcing his image as merely the first among equals. As his biographer
Adrian Goldsworthy puts it, "Augustus lived in a fitting style for a leading
senator." Yet it was all something of a sham, an Abe Lincoln Log Cabin. For,
carefully hidden from public view, Augustus enjoyed enormous villas and gardens in Capri and on the islands of Pandataria, Pontia, and Planasia. (For the
emperors, the Bay of Naples was to the Palatine as Malibu is to Beverley Hills).
His relatively modest complex on the Palatine, linking him both to Romulus
and Apollo, was a stage set.

Augustus' connection to Apollo had another significance. Just as Apollo
subdued the forces of barbarism when he slew the dragon at Delphi, Augustus
depicted his victory over Antony and Cleopatra at Actium as holding off the
forces of barbarism represented by the lusty and flamboyant couple, the victory
of stern old-fashioned Roman virtue over the sybaritic luxury and Egyptian
despotism that had corrupted Antony. As Virgil depicted the battle of Actium,
"on one side Augustus Caesar stands on the lofty stern ... with the gods of the
households and the state," on the other, the "barbaric" East, with Antony and
Cleopatra leading "monstrous gods of every form." In effect, Augustus was the

first Orientalist. The monarch's role as the defender of civilization against barbarism that had begun in the east under the pharaohs now moves west. And there may have been a real threat to Roman political culture from the east. It's possible that Julius Caesar, in hooking up with Cleopatra, did plan to install himself as a Hellenistic-style supreme monarch with an eastern queen – possibly the only solution to the strife of the civil wars. In heading east to take Caesar's place with Cleopatra, Antony may have had a similar idea. Augustus' first act in entering the temple where Antony and Cleopatra had killed themselves was to order his men to smash their faces from carvings that depicted them as new versions of Osiris and Isis – as if he were worried that they might become the center of a new religious cult surpassing the Olympian gods of Greece and Rome.

Once firmly in control, Augustus was the very model of the reforming tyrant. He was immensely popular among the common people in the provinces because he had brought them peace – relieved of the dangers of civil war, they could go about their business and try to prosper. Aided by his chief paladin Agrippa, he added enormously to the beauty of Rome and to its public facilities. Like Alexander the Great earlier, beginning under Augustus, Rome built cookie-cutter cities, miniature Romes, all over the empire, from Britain to Syria, from the Danube to North Africa, each with its own forum, senate house, theater, schools, and baths. The imperial government, represented by the local proconsul, relied heavily on the local land-owning elites and their town councils – one of the empire's secrets of longevity was that the class of rich men everywhere benefited from its protection of their privileges. Augustus also imitated Cyrus's and Alexander's policy of religious tolerance. Rome regarded piety as a source of good morals, and, therefore, of loyal citizens and subjects. It didn't care which gods you worshipped as long as you worshipped some. As a part of his first-among-equals pose, Augustus never allowed the sanctity in which his person was wrapped to cross the line into an outright claim to divinity. But it was permissible to pay divine honors to his soul – his "genius" or "guardian spirit" – and he was, of course, the adopted son of the deified Julius Caesar. Soon enough, though, Augustus was worshipped openly as a god in Asia Minor, which had long been accustomed to monarchs claiming divinity.

As for Augustus' personality, Churchill's phrase about Russia comes to mind – a riddle wrapped in a mystery inside an enigma. In *Antony and Cleopatra,* Shakespeare has Thidias refer to him as "the universal landlord," implying that his triumph has brought an end to the old Roman republican code of martial honor in favor of middle-class money making. He has been derided for avoiding leading his forces into combat, unlike his famous granduncle who fought in the line alongside the legionaries. But he was not necessarily a physical coward; returning to Rome after Caesar's assassination when his enemies ruled the city took guts, and he had served with his grand-uncle on campaigns in Spain. He tried to raise Roman society's moral tone after the debauchery of the late republic and mostly practiced what he preached (his wife Livia was said to bring him girls on the side rather than have him cheat on her). Over time, the extraordinarily cold-blooded and self-controlled young man gave way to a rather rumpled, cheerful old man given to quaint sayings ("Never look round when you're running away!" "Quicker than boiled asparagus!"). Yet he never lost the capacity to strike like a cobra when his power was threatened.

Late in his reign, a murky conspiracy centering around his daughter Julia momentarily shook the dynasty. Augustus had tried to convert the Senate into a service aristocracy, hoping that by appointing the patricians as his magistrates, generals, and governors, and continuing to appoint annual consuls, they would be bought off by these honors and opportunities for advancement. Some were, but not all – some young patricians doubtless dreamed of bringing back the real republic, where their class would control everything once again. Julia seems to have had liaisons with several young bearers of famous old names – Gracchus, Claudius, Scipio and, in particular, the son of Mark Antony. (It's possible that Augustus still craved the social acceptance of these blue bloods himself, after killing off so many of their fathers). Together they may have aimed at forming a regency if Augustus were incapacitated by illness so as to protect Julia's sons by Agrippa from the schemes of Livia and her son by a previous marriage, Tiberius. The plot against Augustus was exposed and crushed. Rather than let the public know that some of the patricians, supposedly his loyal partners in the "restored" republic, were so dissatisfied that they were contemplating replacing him, Augustus allowed his daughter to take the heat. All the public knew was that her broken-hearted father had reluctantly banished her for life for her corrupt morals. Having already been married off three times for purely political reasons, Julia may well have hated her father's guts, even though he had taken great pains over seeing that she received the same education in the classics as a boy.

On his way to Naples just before he died, the passengers and crew of a ship who sighted him broke into spontaneous cheers, declaring they owed him their lives, freedom, and prosperity. He was definitely loved. But the price he paid for his success, it seems, was that he was trapped for his entire life in a largely artificial role and could never break character. It's summed up in the story that his last words were to joke about passing the hat and asking for tips if the audience had been satisfied with his performance, which is how Roman stage plays commonly ended.

Augustus' wife Livia, of course, has gone down in history as the virago who poisoned Augustus' heirs one by one to pave the way to the throne for her gloomy son Tiberius. Over time, if Tacitus and Suetonius are to be believed, the Julio-Claudian emperors, heirs to Livia's and Augustus' bloodlines, turned the Palatine Hill into a hotbed of orgies, gluttony, plotting, perversion, and murder. Each new emperor added his own palace until the entire hill was covered with a honeycomb of interlocking luxurious dwellings, the scene of debased excesses worthy of the worst of the Greek tyrannies, recalling the House of

Atreus, Harmodius and Aristogeiton and cruel eastern royals like Salome and Herod. The lethal blend of sexual betrayal, revenge, ambition and parricide was a reversion to the outrages of Tarquin the Proud that had led to the founding of the Republic. Tiberius supposedly had naked children swimming around him in the blue grotto at Capri licking his private parts (his "minnows"). Caligula made his favorite horse a senator and forced aristocratic ladies to become prostitutes. Claudius' wife Messalina cuckolded him with the entire imperial bodyguard. Nero staged a public marriage ceremony in the Forum in which he played the woman. Afterward, the crowd could hear his screams of delight from behind the curtains as his new husband deflowered him there and then. Nero also had a pleasure craft ingeniously designed to break in half and drown his mother while she was cruising in the Bay of Naples (if the Romans had movies, it would have been *Throw Momma from the Trireme*). Are the stories true? It's hard to say. Tacitus, who may have had access to imperial state records, wrote his annals during the reign of the Emperor Trajan, who had an interest in blackening the Julio-Claudians so as to firm up the legitimacy of his own dynasty. On the other hand, even slander must contain a kernel of truth in order to be believable. We wouldn't believe a story about Richard Nixon having had a secret torrid love affair for years with Lillian Hellman. But we might believe a story that he drank too heavily and sometimes soliloquized in front of George Washington's portrait.

Beyond question is the steady growth of the emperor's position from the charade of being merely "first citizen" into open, bare-fisted despotism. Whereas the army was not allowed to enter Rome under the Republic because the threat of military force was considered an affront to a free citizenry, the emperors were always accompanied by an armed bodyguard, like the tyrants of old Greece and the middle east, including (for the Julio-Claudians) a group of giant Germans for whom the emperor was their tribal war-chief. This bodyguard swelled into a force of five thousand, the Praetorian Guard, permanently stationed near the city to enforce the emperor's autocratic power (when they weren't bribed into overthrowing him in favor of a new master). Gradually, even patricians lost the protection of the law against the emperor's decision, sometimes whimsical, to have them killed. According to Cassius Dio, when Tiberius turned on his cruel and ambitious Praetorian Prefect Sejanus and ordered his children executed, the soldiers first had to rape his daughter Junilla, because there was no precedent for the capital punishment of a virgin. Later, even this kind of ugly pretense of legality was dropped. As I mentioned in the Introduction, when a distinguished architect criticized the blueprint for a temple drawn up by Hadrian, the new emperor ordered him executed. Disrespect for the "greatness" (*majestas*) of the Emperor became a capital offense, and to be denounced for it was often tantamount to being found guilty. Augustus' original pretense of not claiming to be divine also slowly dissolved under his successors – the emperor Domitian was openly addressed as "Lord and God of the World." A telling sign of this transformation is that, whereas the Julio-Claudian palaces on the Palatine were still essentially private dwellings of very great size, when the Flavians built their palace nearby, it was basically the headquarters of a Roman military governor expanded to gargantuan scale. Rome was, in effect, merely another occupied territory for the emperors.

Yet the empire's claims to protect its people and to promote the values of Greco-Roman civilization were not hollow. After a series of civil wars over the succession sparked by the assassination of Nero, the hereditary principle was discarded, and for ninety years, each emperor chose his successor based on who was the best man. This period of the Good Emperors was described by the historian Edward Gibbon in *The Decline and Fall of the Roman Empire* as "the happiest period of mankind." Though capable of cruel acts and tolerating no dissent (Hadrian, who expelled the Jews from Jerusalem and began building a temple to Jupiter on the site of the Temple earlier destroyed by Titus, was among them), in general these emperors maintained the peace through the might of Roman arms, built roads and aqueducts, and lavished public improvements on the empire's cities. Imperial rule at its best was expressed in the marvelous Forum of Trajan, whose vast remains still inspire awe in Rome today. At its center was the magnificent column chronicling Trajan's many military victories – the empire reached its greatest extent under him. Surrounding it was a spacious curved structure with markets on the lower floors. Towering above them, and reaching even higher than the victory column, was a splendid library. That summed up the entire creed of the emperors at their best, bringing to fruition the legacy of Greek culture going back to Homer, Plato, Thucydides, and Sophocles, and its Roman inheritors including Cicero. Martial virtue is higher than the life of peacetime commerce that it protects. But higher even than martial virtue is the life of the mind.

Sadly, this dream was broken when Marcus Aurelius, whether out of a father's misguided affection or the lack of an alternative when the deputy he was grooming unexpectedly died, broke the principle of elective emperors and allowed his son Commodus to succeed him – a man as worthless, vicious, and corrupt as the worst of the Julio-Claudians. That instigated the collapse of the Augustan principate and the beginning of a century of violent mayhem, until the empire was finally rescued by descendants of those it had once conquered and regarded as barbarians. As we'll see in Part Two, it was not the same Rome.

Let's sum up the stops we've made in following the career of tyranny so far. Our theme in Part One has been the saga of how the ancient Greek ideal of manhood captured by Homer's depiction of Achilles developed over the centuries into the unprecedented power and magnificence of the Roman Empire. How that beautiful, valorous, and unruly youth turned into the cold and orderly splendor of the Roman emperors, first immortalized in the Porta Prima statue of Augustus, is, as we have seen, an enthralling tale, full of unpredictable twists and turns.

The world of Achilles and the Trojan War was lost to the Greeks of Homer's time in the shrouds of heroic myth surrounding the exploits of a now vanished superior people. By recovering it in his poems, Homer enabled the Greeks to venerate this past as their own, an inspiring precedent for their own slow emergence from a Dark Age of strife. It had been a world of warrior chieftains leading their men directly into battle, a pattern of authority that, as we'll discuss in Part Two, lived on in Europe for centuries to come. After Homer, however, the Greeks themselves began to move away from the heritage of the Bronze Age warlord to develop their own unique civic culture – one that was centered on the public life of free city-states. Nevertheless, their admiration for Achilles remained intense.

These city-states – be they democracies or oligarchies – would not permit any citizen in their own midst the kind of swaggering personal authority that had been exercised by Homeric kings like Agamemnon and Achilles. As we saw, even when the office of king survived in city-states like Sparta, it was severely hemmed in. By the same token, prominent men and families like the Alcmaeonids in Athens might exercise an influence far beyond their official status as mere citizens. Moreover, as Thucydides tells it, in the centuries between the Trojan War and the Persian and Peloponnesian Wars, tyrants emerged in a number of city-states who used their executive power to promote their cities' security from attack and protect agriculture and commerce. Still, the Greeks always felt a tension between the occasional need for a tyrant's vigorous and hopefully temporary authority and their overwhelming love of liberty.

Although the Greek polis did not in general allow its citizens to exercise the kingly power of an Achilles, the ideal of Achilles as the flower of young Greek manhood remained deeply influential, a part of the education of every Greek nobleman. While tyrants of the kind described by Thucydides could be tolerated when they were sober and business-like about defending the city's interests, letting everyone get a piece of the pie as they lined their own pockets, the ever-shining image of Achilles offered a more dangerous and subversive alternative – an ambition for supreme glory, wealth, pleasure, and immortal fame through victorious conquest, a great adventure in which bold young men could throw off the shackles of their tired elders and set the world ablaze in comradely might.

At the crossroads between the ideal of Achilles, the Greek love of liberty, and the threat of the Great King is where a fascinating combination of historical forces took place. As the city-states united to repel the Persian invasion, the manly and valiant ideal of Achilles and the other Homeric heroes, many felt, had its finest flowering in Greek victories like Marathon. But something else happened. Having almost been overwhelmed by the vast power of Persia and the godlike power of its supreme leader, the Greeks began to absorb in fascination its diametrically opposed pattern of authority. Some wondered openly whether the Greeks with their numerous tiny fractious city-states might learn something from the vast, multinational, powerful, and centralized Persian Empire.

That fusion of a personal ambition for glory inspired by Achilles with the new vision of a world empire inspired by the Great King of Persia first emerged in Alcibiades, who believed that "no limit could be set" on the extent of Athens' power. It came to full fruition in Alexander the Great – consciously modeling himself on Achilles, he led his army of adventurous young men personally into battle. He brought the whole Persian Empire crashing down, but then proceeded to make its universal monarchical authority his own. In this way, what began as the rage and lust for glory of the tribal warlord Achilles, a legendary past claimed by the Greeks at the dawn of their history, ends up fueling the construction of a new universal empire originally created by the Persians and other eastern god-kings, but now infused with Greek culture – a structure that, as we saw, was in turn brought to an even higher peak of perfection by the Roman Empire beginning with Augustus, which also saw itself as the steward and exporter of Greek culture and of the Roman culture steeped in it to the barbarians.

In sculpture, Augustus is endowed with a divine beauty and splendor representative both of Achilles' heroism and of his special divine protector, the ever-young Apollo, guardian of the art of government and of music, wearing a military uniform so that the manly virtue of Romans in battle, itself a part of the heritage they claimed from Troy, would always stand forth as the basis for the emperors' claim to authority. And yet, as we saw from looking at the career of that greatest of political sphinxes, Augustus, this image of Achilles-like youthful courage and sublime beauty was the outward camouflage for what was in fact a universal despotism, pharaoh in a toga. But as we'll see in Part Two, all that changed in the centuries to come, as men began to look for a happiness beyond the Roman world of honor and military glory altogether. Political authority, including tyranny, would never be the same.

Part Two

City of God or City of Man? The Tyrant as Modern State Builder

In 410 AD, Rome, the Eternal City was sacked by Alaric the Visigoth and his forces. They didn't do tremendous damage. Alaric had been a Roman ally and general. He felt the imperial government had welched on their deal – occupying the city was meant to apply bargaining pressure. Rome at this point was not even the capital of the western empire – it had moved to Ravenna. Yet so famous was her name and history that the entire Roman world was traumatized. The city had not been invaded for eight hundred years. As Saint Jerome wrote, "if Rome can perish, who can be safe?"

The psychological impact was akin to the German occupation of Paris in 1870 or the attack on New York on September the 11th – a devastating blow from without that was felt by many to be the earned comeuppance for years of moral drift and corruption. Many believed that the newly dominant religion of Christianity was responsible for sapping the manly fiber of old Roman virtue. Christianity, they claimed, was pacifistic, whereas Rome's glory was based on her strength of arms. Christians had divided loyalties, and placed their otherworldly salvation above their loyalty to the state. Far from honoring Rome's unmatched success in war, Christians actively disapproved of it. The Christian emperor Constantius II ordered the removal from the Senate of the famous Altar of Victory, containing a magnificent gold statue of the goddess Victory holding a palm branch (peace for the defeated) and offering a laurel wreath (glory to the victors). Captured during the Romans' wars of subjugation against Greece, Augustus had it placed on the Altar of Victory in the Senate to commemorate his defeat of Antony and Cleopatra at Actium. Its removal by Constantius could not have been a more stinging repudiation of the first Emperor and Rome's entire tradition of military honor. Now, pagans believed, we are paying the price for turning our back on the martial virtues that made us great.

St. Augustine wrote his classic *The City of God* to refute the charge that Christianity had weakened Roman virtue and so invited the barbarian invasion of the legendary and hitherto invulnerable capital. Christians, he argued, have high moral standards, higher than those of the pagans (worshipping gods who are sex fiends), and these virtues of moderation, chastity, and decency make them good citizens. If anything, the empire has lasted longer than it would have otherwise because of them. He had a point, of course – then as now, Christians are perfectly capable of good citizenship and patriotism. Moreover, their belief in God has often acted as a spur of conscience to oppose tyranny and injustice, even at the risk of their lives. On the other hand, though, it's hard not to detect in Augustine's writing a withering evaluation of worldly glory and martial prowess. They are mere tinsel in comparison to the eternal salvation that awaits those who accept Christ.

The ancient moral thinkers from Plato to Cicero were careful to distinguish between permissible and impermissible forms of honor seeking. Being honored for serving the common good, whether in war or as a statesman, was entirely admirable. Satisfying a drive for honor by becoming a tyrant, on the other hand, was to be condemned. St. Augustine, by contrast, tends to dismiss *all* love of worldly honor as selfishly motivated, not virtuous at all, but an impulse for crude "dominion," and a sign of sinful vanity for believing man can accomplish anything worthwhile or admirable without completely submitting himself to the will of God. Whether you're the depraved Nero or a Stoic like Marcus Aurelius, it's the same delusion. Stoicism may be a classier-looking broad than Epicureanism, as St. Augustine puts it in *The City of God*, but at bottom she's just another streetwalker.

Moreover, while Greco-Roman civilization in its entirety, stretching all the way back to the Bronze Age heroes depicted by Homer, continuing throughout the history of Rome's rise from a village on the Tiber to a Mediterranean empire and, finally, world monarchy, had been thoroughly and relentlessly aristocratic. It was premised on the unquestioned assumption that some men were born to rule over others – the "beautiful and good ones" as the Greek aristocracies called themselves, the "best ones" as Rome's elite called itself. The Alexandrian empire, like the Roman empire that followed it, extended civic culture universally regardless of national origin. Alexander thought that "Greekness" could be exported everywhere, just as the Roman Emperors eventually made every free man within their vast domains a *civis Romanus*. But it was an aristocratic kind of universality – the upper orders were everywhere protected and their privileges and status guaranteed.

Christianity, by contrast, was at its core a thoroughly egalitarian religion. All men were equal in the sight of God, equally vulnerable to sin, equally capable of salvation. Although this did not necessarily lead to any direct assault on the established hierarchy of Roman wealth and rank – swelled by the more recent ecclesiastical hierarchy of bishops with their palaces and cathedrals – it did lead to a change in society's moral tone, a disapproval, for instance, of the gratuitous violence of the gladiatorial games, the encouragement of slave-owners to free their slaves and buy no others, and in the long run this change in moral tone would contribute to a struggle in the here and now to make men equal on earth as well as in heaven. The contrast is perhaps best summed up in the classical emphasis on pride as the highest human virtue, the crown of martial, moral and civic excellence as opposed to the Christian emphasis on humility. For Aristotle, while pride in one's earned achievements was the highest virtue in civic life (and not to be confused with mere vain boasting about honors not truly deserved), humility was actually a *vice* because only a man with a "small soul" (a Greek word rendered marvelously in Middle English as "pusillanimous") would avoid claiming an honor to which his virtue or rank entitled him. For Augustine, by contrast, *all* pride, deserved or not, was reducible to vanity because it was based on the folly that man can achieve anything good on his own without God.

The ancients had also thought carefully about the good and bad varieties of government – monarchy was better than tyranny, a republic was better than mob rule. Although these distinctions were usually honored in the breach under the emperors, who were at best absolute despots and at worst monsters of tyrannical excess, the classical moral outlook did at least keep alive in mens' minds the difference between just and unjust authority. On occasion, the emperors themselves could be brought to aspire to practice these virtues despite their absolute power. It was said that whenever the emperor Vespasian failed to perform a good deed before going to bed, he would exclaim, "I have lost a day!" Marcus Aurelius, this most peaceable of men who spent much of his reign on campaign with his legions in order to fend off barbarian invasions along the Danube Valley, truly believed that those Rome conquered would benefit from peace and a higher form of civilization. In his own life, he felt that being emperor was a burdensome duty to which fate had consigned him. His greatest personal pleasure came from studying philosophy. But he still had to "man his post," as the Stoic saying went, to preserve the Roman Empire as a sphere of light – of peace, culture, and civilization – holding the surrounding barbarian realm of savagery, bestiality, and darkness at bay, for the benefit of all his subjects.

St. Augustine tends to dismiss these gradations between good and bad government here on earth, including the distinction between a tyrant and a good monarch, as crashingly unimportant compared with our inescapable mortality and our overriding need to prepare for eternal salvation and avoid eternal damnation. He writes: "Is it reasonable and wise to glory in the extent and greatness of the Empire when you can in no way prove that there is any real happiness in men perpetually living amid the horrors of war, perpetually wading in blood? ... In the absence of justice, what is sovereignty but organized brigandage?" As for Rome's civilizing mission, he openly compares the city's origins to a gang of thieves whose only motive for collective loyalty was to increase every gangster's share of the loot. He grudgingly concedes that this brand of honor among thieves has brought Rome unprecedented worldly power, but will set its value no higher than that. When he compares the way of life of a prominent Roman citizen ("haunted by fear, heavy with cares, feverish with greed, never secure") and a humble, obscure man of God ("loved by his own, enjoying the sweetness of peace in his relations with kindred, chaste in morals"), there's no question that the man of God's way of life is to be preferred in every way. As for the empire, for Augustine, its *only* legitimate role is to preserve law and order and, as the earthly outpost of the City of God amidst the City of Man, protect the One True Church – if need be, by using its absolute power to persecute heretics.

The charge that Christianity undermined the moral fiber of the Roman empire and thereby sped its decline by dividing men's loyalties between what Augustine saw as a merely fleshly, sinful, and temporary sojourn here on earth and the infinitely greater happiness of the afterlife that awaits us has been echoed down through the centuries by writers on politics and morals including Machiavelli, Rousseau, and the historian Edward Gibbon, who traced to that religion the central cause of the empire's fall. In recent years, it's become fashionable to debunk this critique and stress how gradual the decline was, and how for many decades under the predominance of Christianity, the empire continued to field great armies and repel invasion. I still lean to Gibbon's view, but I'll leave it to readers to decide as we go on to talk about the late Empire and the beginning of the Middle Ages.

The Roman Empire underwent a huge transformation after Marcus Aurelius' cataclysmic decision (willing or forced on him due to the untimely death of his junior colleague Verus) to allow his son Commodus to inherit the throne, ending the golden age of the Good Emperors, each of whom had chosen his successor based on merit rather than direct descent. Rivals quickly murdered Commodus, and the following year saw five men claim the title of Emperor. Septimius Severus, a native of North Africa who had risen through military service, achieved stability. Brutal but effective, he placed securing the legions' loyalty above all else, which at least established some basic order. ("Enrich the soldiers and scorn the world!" was his motto). After the last Severan emperor, Alexander Severus, was murdered by his own troops, fifty years of usurpation and civil war raged during which there were twenty-six claimants to the throne, mostly generals (sometimes called "barracks emperors"). Finally, under a line of exceptionally vigorous and domineering emperors from Illyria (today's western Balkans) such as Diocletian and Constantine the Great, the empire revived, discipline was restored over the legions, and civil war ceased.

But it was a different culture. Emperors now often rose through the ranks of the military, without a shred of aristocratic lineage. In effect, the empire was saved by the now partly Romanized descendants of the peoples it had originally conquered, especially in the Balkans. Diocletian was born in a military colony established some two centuries earlier by Julius Caesar and embellished by Augustus into one of his numerous instant mini-Romes complete with forum and baths. The genius of the Augustan principate in establishing these colonies, often populated by retired soldiers who intermarried with the locals, in effect incubators for future generations of loyal legionaries from once hostile lands, now came to the rescue, saving the empire from the spent force of its original Italian nobility. But these new emperors from the once conquered territories dropped all pretense of being the "first citizens" of a republic – they rarely even visited Rome. (It's a little as if the United States was ruled from Vietnam by presidents who never visited Washington). They ruled openly as soldier-kings, military autocrats. The connection with high Greco-Roman civilization that the Augustan principate maintained as its inheritors and stewards, a steward-ship continued by the Good Emperors, was shattered. When Constantine had a triumphal arch erected in Rome, they simply hacked off pieces of older sculpture from the reign of Marcus Aurelius and stuck it onto his. They couldn't reproduce the old masterpieces.

The emperor Diocletian tried to freeze all occupations throughout the empire as hereditary in order to guarantee tax revenues. If you were a farmer, your son would have to be a farmer too. In principle, it was the beginning of feudalism. The centralization of all power in the hands of the emperors had led to a huge growth in the bureaucracy. That increased when Diocletian dealt with the vast size of the empire by dividing it up between Western and Eastern emperors. Each "Augustus" was also to groom a junior partner and successor, a "Caesar," so as to prevent civil war every time the throne fell vacant, in effect creating four separate imperial courts, each with its own enormous staff. A general shift to the more populous and prosperous East was symbolized by Constantine's creation of his new capital, Constantinople, not far from our old friend Troy, which soon eclipsed Rome. The imperial ceremonial became correspondingly more elaborate, hearkening back to the eastern god-kings, the Pharaohs, Nebuchadnezzar, and Cyrus the Great. A contemporary described Constantius II as having the ideal ceremonial presence in his chariot of state: "As if his neck were in a vice, he kept the gaze of his eyes straight ahead, and turned his face neither to the right nor left, nor ... did he nod when the wheel jolted." It was a melding of west and east. The best way to bring this home is to compare the Equestrian statue of Augustus we discussed in Part One, a perfect fusion of Greek beauty with Roman strength of purpose, with the 300 AD statue of Diocletian's college of four coemperors embracing. Dressed in heavy cloaks and with large swords at their side, they already look like medieval kings, but they also recall the eastern monarchies of Babylon and Persia. With their square trunks, stubby legs, and stout frames, each face indistinguishable from the others, blocky and stiff in their ritualistic pose, this sculpture group represents, according to art historian Ernst Kitzinger, "an almost complete rejection of the classical tradition." In another sign of an "easternization" that also points ahead to the medieval world, the Romans began to rely less on infantry and more on heavily armed cavalry units, and they replaced the short skirt, leather cuirass, and dagger sword of the Republic and Augustan principate with

long trousers, large swords and chain mail – a reversion to eastern-style warfare, which at the same time starts to look like the Middle Ages. As historian
Greg Woolf writes, by the late third and fourth centuries, "the military landscape came to look more and more medieval, a world of knights and castles
amidst a landscape of peasant villages."

After the dynamic interventions of Diocletian (he thought he was the human
embodiment of Jupiter), Constantine was the other major architect of the late
Roman Empire by making Christianity the preferred religion of the state.
Christianity's champion was a ruthless, brutal despot knee-deep in blood –
he strangled his own son with his bare hands for suspected plotting. Here
is Gibbon's description of him as a young man: "In his whole conduct, the
active spirit of youth was tempered by habitual prudence; and while his mind
was engrossed with ambition, he appeared cold and insensible to the allure-
ments of pleasure." After dabbling with Mithraism, the favorite religion of the
soldiers, he chose Christianity to patronize – to what extent out of genuine
conviction or because of its popularity remains a matter for debate. Possibly
he believed that the notion of a single God above complemented the rule of a
single Emperor on earth. It was a largely urban and eastern religion (Christians
referred to nonbelievers as *pagani*, country dwellers, implying they were rural
hicks, since it was indeed in the more agrarian west that belief in the old gods
lasted the longest) and, contrary to myth, had rarely been severely persecuted.
According to recent scholarship about the Colosseum, however many times
it's been done in the movies, there's scant proof Christians were ever "fed to
the lions." (Constantine's predecessor Diocletian was an exception – suspect-
ing their pacifistic and other-worldly values threatened Rome's authority, he
cracked down hard, but it was too late; Christian influence was too widespread
and entrenched.) From early on, the new religion aspired to exercise a universal authority over believers akin to the empire's political authority. The pattern
for the cathedral was the Roman basilica, a combination of law-court and
throne room, with the bishop taking the place of the emperor or proconsul on
his throne. Imperial patronage brought the Church's hierarchy lavish incomes
and perks. The emperors often employed the bishops as the equivalent of their
governors and representatives in the provinces.

Finally becoming, under the emperor Theodosius, the *only* state-sanctioned
religion, Christians used their alliance with the absolute power of the emperors to gleefully lay waste to pagan temples, art, and libraries (not unlike the
Taliban in our own time dynamiting priceless Buddhist statues), and persecuted with equal ferocity – including torture and execution – Christian sects
deemed heretical. It could cost you your life to give the wrong answer when
asked if the Holy Spirit proceeded "from the Father" or "from the Father and
Son." The Academy of Plato and Lyceum of Aristotle, patronized for centuries by the pagan emperors, were shut down by Justinian early in the sixth
century. The City of God's representatives on earth were more than happy

to employ the murderous tools of the imperial City of Man once they had it on their side.

Paganism's pluralism and tolerance of many beliefs was replaced by a single, all-encompassing theocratic creed claiming to be the only true guide for every aspect of life, backed by the authority of an absolute ruler. Even the emperors, including Constantine and Theodosius, dabbled in abstruse theological disputes about, for example, the character of the Trinity, and were willing to back up their chosen doctrines with lethal force against the other viewpoints. Tyranny started to become ideological, a religious predecessor of later secular ideologies like Communism claiming to possess "the unity of theory and practice" enforced by an all-powerful state. This was a watershed change in the career of tyranny in the West, with reverberations throughout the centuries to come down to the present day. Not all Christians, of course, were happy with these newfound trappings of worldly power. Some retreated into monastic communities or a hermit's cave in order to preserve the spiritual purity of the faith and its original renunciation of worldly wealth and power – a tension within the faith that would undulate through the centuries to come and reach a head in the Reformation.

Finally, the Roman Empire split irrevocably into two halves as the west fell under wave after wave of invaders from beyond the Danube. When the Goth warlord Odoacer deposed the last western emperor (eerily named Romulus Augustulus, "Romulus the Little Augustus," combining the name of Rome's founder with an oddly contemptuous version of that of the first emperor), only the Eastern Empire of Byzantium remained. As we saw in Part One, starting with Augustus, the eastern principle of universal monarchy traveled west, becoming a Hellenistic monarchy based in Rome outwardly clad as a republican first magistrate. Now, the remainder of what still claimed to be the *Imperium Romanum* merges back into the east altogether. "Byzantine" becomes a byword for palace intrigue, betrayal, plots, and a swollen bureaucracy and court ceremonial making extensive use of eunuchs, as had the Pharaohs and the Persian kings of old. The ruler still called himself "the Emperor of the Romans," maintaining a slender tendril of historical loyalty to that rough and ready village of brigands founded on the Tiber a thousand years before. But the steamy, inbred atmosphere of the palace in Constantinople, swirling with intrigue over sex and power (the Emperor Justinian's wife Theodora was rumored to be a former prostitute), puts one in mind of the Forbidden City in Beijing and the palace-cities of Babylon, Persepolis, and Alexandria. When Constantinople at last fell in 1453 to the Ottoman Turks, the new Muslim rulers, rather as had happened when the Mongols invaded China beginning in the thirteenth century, absorbed much of the elaborate ceremonial of their Byzantine predecessors, witnessed by the remains of the magnificent Topkapi palace in Istanbul today, a blend of an imperial Roman palace with the interconnecting pavilions evocative of China and Japan, perhaps a memory of their nomadic origins and tents.

THE FALL OF THE WEST

The mystique of Roman military invincibility under the Emperors was essential to holding together such a vast empire with a standing army of no more than around three hundred and fifty thousand front-line forces, the famous legions. There was no way that Roman rule could literally be maintained by military force – there just weren't enough troops to go around. Even a major province like Syria had no more than a few legions under the legate's command. Some had none at all. As procurator (chief magistrate and tax collector) for Judea, Pontius Pilate commanded a second-tier force of locally recruited auxiliaries, a cross in American terms between a police department and the National Guard.

Ever since Augustus, Rome's policy had been to create client-states or neutral buffer states on its borders so as to avoid the need for war. But when war could not be avoided, Rome's victory had to be absolutely crushing, in order to convince everyone that, at the end of the day, rebellion would always fail. Hence, the extreme brutality of Rome's suppression of the two Jewish rebellions, including the grueling siege of Masada, which, although strategically insignificant, was necessary to demonstrate that not even a single fortress could resist Roman power. The second rebellion ended with the Emperor Hadrian building a temple to Jupiter on the site of the Jewish Temple that had been destroyed by Titus in the first Jewish war, and expelling the Jews from Jerusalem. Two strikes and you're out. When Rome's military might in the West finally collapsed under relentless waves of invaders – Visigoths followed by Huns – so did the mystique of the empire's invincibility and, therefore, the psychological grip of its central control.

When the central authority of the western empire dissolved, many of the major nations of Europe we are familiar with today were coming into view in rough outline, their identities established earlier by Roman conquest and conversion into provinces. These included Spain, Gaul (the future France, more or less), Britain, the Balkans, and Italy, although they were divided into internal fiefdoms and statelets that would take many centuries to absorb into the modern nation-state. Germany, beyond the Rhine and Danube, had never been conquered, the Romans having wisely conceded in the time of Augustus that the Germans were too ferocious and independent to ever be contained within the empire. The greatness and authority of the vanished empire continued to haunt the imagination of its former subjects, an epoch of glory, peace, prosperity, and civilization now lost, but one that would never be forgotten. Roman military titles from the late Empire like *Dux* and *Comitus* become the titles of medieval authority, "duke" and "count," a sign of Rome's continuing prestige and the wish to somehow latch onto the legitimacy of the vanished Caesars (origin of the German *Kaiser* and Russian *Tsar*).

At the same time, the development of feudal monarchy – the king and his knights supported by peasant farmers – was in a way a return to a very old pattern of authority reaching all the way back to the chieftains described by

Homer, a pattern that had been overlain by the growth of the universal empires of Alexander and Rome but had never entirely gone away. The "barbarian" tribes, as the Romans regarded them, that swept into the western empire and finally overwhelmed it might have been Bronze Age chieftains, warlords who ride into battle at the head of their own clan of fellow fighters, and who had to prove their personal courage in combat or risk being challenged and overthrown by a stronger competitor. The invaders the Romans called Goths were succeeded by peoples variously known as Vikings or Norsemen who continued to invade the fragmentary states that the collapse of imperial authority had left behind, merging with the conquered Gauls (themselves already intermixed with earlier Germanic invaders), for instance, to become Norman and with the Celtic natives of England who knew them as Saxon.

On the Orkney Islands that they conquered, the Viking chieftains were buried in shaft tombs built by an earlier Neolithic people, broadly reminiscent of the tombs left behind by Mycenaean kings. As fans of the TV show *Vikings* will know, when these frightening bearded giants with their broadswords and axes, in chain-mail, furs, and war paint, descended like Homeric warriors on the old monastery on Lindisfarne, chanting epic verse about their gods and heroes as they slashed away, they looted it and slaughtered the terrified monks. Initially, the Vikings reacted to Christianity as had the pagans of the old Roman Empire – they despised it as cowardly and unmanly. In the long run, however, even these ferocious warriors could not resist its promise of eternal salvation, especially as they interacted with their newly conquered Christian subjects. One of their Earls on Orkney built the magnificent St. Magnus Cathedral to mark his conversion, with the model of a cute little Viking longboat placed on the altar. Some precautions were taken as the barbarians were gradually won over to the new faith. When St. Saba converted the Goths, his translation of the Bible into their language did not include the Book of Kings – the saint felt they didn't need stirring up by the exploits of the Judaean kings when they were already so aggressive.

Meanwhile, astonishingly, the Eastern Empire rolled on for another thousand years, its capital of Constantinople being virtually impregnable with its vast system of fortifications. One of its greatest emperors, Justinian I, for a time actually succeeded in reconquering former territories of the vanished Western empire in North Africa and Italy. Along with his shrewd and glamorous wife Theodora, rumored to have begun life in a brothel, a kind of Constantinopolitan Eva Peron, the vigorous Justinian bequeathed to posterity his famous Code of all previous Roman law. At its lowest ebb, on the other hand, foreign invaders reduced Byzantium to little more than the capital city and its outskirts. In the Byzantine empire, intensifying a trend already underway when Christian emperors like Constantine laid down the law about theological issues such as the Nicene Creed, the emperors were the head both of the Church and of the Roman state – the source of all authority both spiritual and temporal, including the appointment of the Patriarch of Constantinople and the rest of the ecclesiastical hierarchy. Scholars later called this fusion of temporal and divine authority "Caesaropapism" – emperor and pope in one. Although often resisted by priests and ordinary worshippers, the Byzantine emperor's headship of the church as well as the state was especially strong from the sixth to eighth centuries. Indeed, when Justinian I established Byzantium's temporary foothold in Italy, he appointed the next three popes of the Occidental church as well. Caesaropapism was adopted and strengthened by Tsarist Russia, beginning with Ivan the Terrible in 1547, until under Peter the Great (more on him in due course), the Patriarchate was abolished and the Church became a department of his government. That's why today, strictly speaking, the Russian Orthodox Church lacks a supreme head since the last Tsar was executed in 1918.

The Roman Empire going back to Augustus had always more or less recognized people's right to their own property – its protection of rich men everywhere was a great source of the empire's legitimacy. Still, because it was a Hellenistic monarchy outwardly camouflaged as a "republic," as time went on, the emperors reverted increasingly to the older eastern pattern of the god-kings of Egypt, Mesopotamia, and Persia, where, in practice, the monarch owned *everything*. The Julio-Claudians frequently had Roman nobles executed for treason, or drove them to suicide, so as to grab their property. During unstable periods like that of the "barracks emperors," usurpers would confiscate property wholesale to pay off the legions who backed their seizure of the throne. This pattern of imperial control of property rights intensified under the Russian tsars, heirs to Orthodox Christianity and Byzantium's caesaropapist model of authority. Whereas in Europe, feudal lords came to enjoy large landed estates in their own right, including large bodies of armed retainers, even though they recognized (at least in principle) the king's authority over them, the tsars were careful never to allow the nobility to amass large fiefdoms of this kind that might threaten their absolute power.

On the whole, the Byzantine Empire continued to maintain a high Roman level of civilization with great cities, baths, roads, schools, and libraries, while Europe, after the collapse of the Western Empire in the fifth century, entered what is commonly known as the Dark Ages. How dark? It has become fashionable in recent years to challenge this notion. Life in the early centuries of the Middle Ages, some scholars say, wasn't as bleak, backward, and stupid as in *Monty Python and the Holy Grail,* with peasants up to their necks in mud and manure struggling to move carts with square wheels. Debating this isn't central to our purpose of following the career of tyranny, but to me, one set of figures stands out. The greatest of the Roman Empire's libraries, in Alexandria, is recorded as having four hundred and ninety thousand rolls of papyrus. The private library of the third-century poet Serenus Sammonicus contained sixty-two thousand rolls. By the seventh century, after the fall of the Western Empire, the Bishop of Seville's library of 475 works was regarded as very large. The monastic library used by the Venerable Bede totaled 200 texts. The two thousand-book collection of the monastery in Fulda in eighth century

Germany was considered a true marvel. In other words, since the collapse of the Western Empire, hundreds of thousands of books had been lost, thrown away, allowed to rot, or willfully destroyed by Christian enemies of all things pagan. That seems pretty dark to me. Fortunately both Byzantium and the Islamic world preserved a lot of those books for later recovery.

Of main interest for us in tracing the career of tyranny is to stress how different was the pattern of authority in the former Western Empire in contrast with Byzantium. The collapse of imperial authority in the West created a vacuum to be filled by the authority of the Popes, who had steadily progressed from being merely the bishops of Rome to claiming supreme headship of the universal church. In the fifth century, they took the title of Pontifex Maximus, originally the high priesthood of the Roman kings of old (a role also exercised by the ancient eastern monares), then assumed by Augustus and the emperors, now vacated by the collapse of the imperial line. While the popes were mainly concerned with establishing unified spiritual guidance for Christians, they also vied with the new secular rulers of feudal Europe for total control of affairs. This tug of war went on for centuries, one side gaining the upper hand, then the other.

Meanwhile, in spite of Christianity's elevation of the City of God over the City of Man, the allure of the departed Roman Empire continued to inspire events and enabled men to dream of a better future, one that would be like the Roman past. Beginning in 768, the Frankish King Charlemagne carved out a large domain incorporating most of Western Europe with its capital at Aachen. This was the first successful large-scale political entity created since the western Roman Empire's demise, and in 800 AD, Charlemagne confidently assumed the titles of Augustus and Emperor of the Romans, claiming to revive the glorious legacy of the Caesars and laying the basis for the Holy Roman Empire, a shifting clutch of states and principalities ruled by successive dynasties of Hohenstauffens and Hapsburgs. It was dissolved by the victorious Napoleon in 1806, but returned to life in a somewhat different, more eastward-looking configuration, and shorn of its claim to holiness, as the Austro-Hungarian Empire. The Prussian kings' later assumption of the title of Emperor (*Kaiser*) starting with Wilhelm I, as well as Queen Victoria's being hailed as the Empress of India, shows the enduring allure of this old Roman title *Imperator*.

Beginning with that cheeky contrarian Voltaire during the Enlightenment in France, it used to be joked about the Holy Roman Empire that it was neither holy, nor Roman, nor really an empire. It was an uneasy blend of secular and divine authority that could never achieve the Caesaropapist fusion of the two spheres because of the spiritual supremacy of the Popes. No Holy Roman Emperor ever achieved the complete authority over church and state exercised, at least in principle, by the Byzantine Emperor or the Russian Tsar. By the same token, neither did any Pope. Back and forth the struggle went, symbolized by what came to be called the "investiture crisis" – in other words, does the Pope, as the font of both religious and political authority, crown the Emperor, or does the Emperor, as God's deputy on earth, crown himself? Charlemagne claimed that he would never have attended Mass at St Peter's in Rome had he known that the Pope intended to sneak up and crown him on the spot, ahead of the scheduled coronation. By contrast, the Holy Roman Emperor Otto I voluntarily allowed himself to be crowned by the Archbishop of Mainz, signifying his subordination to the ecclesiastical hierarchy. In yet another variation, William the Conqueror, having flown the papal banner during his invasion of Britain, ducked the Pope's invitation to Rome to pay homage to the Holy See for his new kingdom. Still later, ostensibly mutinous forces of the Holy Roman Emperor Charles V invaded Rome, sacked the city including the Vatican, and imprisoned the Pope (Charles' degree of complicity is still debated). This conflict between temporal and spiritual authority also bounced into the individual kingdoms of the Middle Ages, as in the famous clash between Thomas a'Becket and Henry II that ended in the Archbishop's martyrdom at the hands of Henry's knights.

As we'll see, the different way in which authority developed in the West and the East had a profound impact on the continuing career of tyranny and its contest with free government. The Caesaropapist model of Byzantium endowed the emperor with absolute personal authority over affairs both spiritual and temporal, with state and religious appointments to be distributed at his pleasure. The Russian tsars inherited this model. There was no separation between church and state. The state, being also divinely mandated, was all-powerful. In the west, by contrast, from early on, a rough division of spheres between the secular and the sacred was established, owing to the inability of either the pope or the emperor to establish Caesaropapist supremacy over the other.

Moreover, whereas in the Caesaropapist model all patronage flowed from the Emperor, the West continued to recognize that, other things being equal, people, and especially the great lords, should be able to enjoy their lands and fortunes without fear of their arbitrary seizure. England, in particular, cherished a vision of itself as having always defended the right of property and due process of law against the encroachments of the crown, first said to have been agreed upon in Magna Carta when the nobility clipped Bad King John's wings. Whether that amounted to a full-blown recognition of the right to private property and other liberties is debatable, but when that right was legally established in England through the Glorious Revolution in 1688, the conservative philosopher and statesman Edmund Burke among others regarded it not so much a break with the past as the continuation of venerable English tradition. (More about this in Part Three.)

Some argue that you can map the prospects for democracy in Europe according to this East-West divide. If you draw a line down the map of Europe, they say, between Europe proper and where it starts to join the east, you'll find that on the left-hand side of that line, democracy gradually took root because Occidental Christianity had already recognized the autonomy of the secular sphere of politics, the economy, and society, and its independence from complete control by the Church. By contrast, on the right-hand side of the line, where Orthodox Christianity regarded the state as all-powerful over both temporal and religious affairs, not surprisingly, democracy has had a harder time taking root. My instinct is that there is something to this view. In Ukraine, presently resisting being gobbled up by Russia, the prodemocratic western half of the country that longs for full integration into Western Europe is also largely Occidental Christian, whereas the pro-Russian half in the east, who want to join their Slavic brethren, is largely Orthodox. Some say that the monolithic control exercised by Stalin and the Soviet Communist dictatorship was in effect a continuation of tsarist absolutism dressed up in Marxist ideology, hearkening back to the original Byzantine pattern for all power to be concentrated in the hands of one man. In this view, Caesaropapism was reborn as what Communist doctrine called "the unity of theory and practice," meaning that the Party, in turn meaning its Leader, possesses the absolute truth. I'll be arguing later in Part Three that Communist tyranny was far, far worse than anything to be found under the tsars, or indeed under any traditional form of despotism. But the parallel, while limited, is valid.

FEUDAL MONARCHY AND THE GREAT CHAIN OF BEING

Medieval kings were considered to be God's representatives on earth. In what historian Arthur Lovejoy called The Great Chain of Being, society was designed by God to be an orderly hierarchy in which the common people submitted to the authority of the lords, the lords submitted to the authority of the king, and the king submitted on everyone else's behalf to the authority of God (and, the popes tried to insist, to the Church headed by them). The identification of the king as God's deputy, at least as regards temporal affairs, had a tendency to muffle the traditional debate about tyrants versus true kings that we examined in Part One. Royal authority was hereditary. Anyone exercising royal power was assumed to have God's sanction – he was anointed, as Kings Saul and David had been by the prophet Samuel. How else, after all, could he be on the throne? Since all human freedom of action was ultimately in the control of Providence, the political status quo presumably had His blessing.

It was certainly recognized that kings were capable of tyrannical acts. By our own standards, they were very capable of selfish and wanton cruelty – Edward I's expulsion of the Jews from England; Philip IV of France's suppression and execution by burning at the stake of the Knights Templar after seizing their wealth; the annihilation, jointly undertaken by the papacy and the kings of France, of the heretical sect of Cathars in southern France. Even these excesses, however, were applauded by most of their subjects as righteous Christian acts. There were few instances of popular rebellion before the fourteenth century, when a growing gap between wealthy and poor sparked a number of peasant uprisings that were invariably crushed. Not until the religious wars of the Reformation, brought about by a deep division over the meaning of Christianity, was the feudal order shaken to its foundations by new levels of religious strife and persecution, with each side hoping the king would bring to bear his powers of execution, torture, banishment, and imprisonment to destroy the heretics on the other side. Before that explosion of sectarian violence, medieval monarchy rolls on rather placidly, sometimes stained with the gluttony, avarice, and adultery that has always been the garden-variety tyrant's stock-in-trade, sometimes graced with beautiful music and art, as at the legendarily gracious court of the Dukes of Burgundy, an atmosphere captured in the famous Lady and the Unicorn tapestries. Sometimes, as in Greek and Roman tyrannies, both kinds of activity went on at once. Some kings, though, were extremely pious, including Edmund the Confessor, so named because of his saintly life.

The greatest theologian of the Middle Ages, St. Thomas Aquinas, departed somewhat from his predecessor St. Augustine's general disinterest in distinguishing between better and worse forms of earthly government. In doing so, he drew upon what remained of classical learning in the West, especially Aristotle. But, tellingly, whereas for Aristotle the best form of government was an aristocracy of virtuous gentlemen, for Aquinas it was a kind and just monarch who followed God's law in all his affairs – a single omnipotent king to deputize on earth for a single omnipotent God. The lack of legal restraints on royal power was all to the good if the king was pious and benevolent, because he could act more efficiently than if constrained by the law. The next-best form of government was an aristocracy of God-fearing men ruling collectively for the benefit of all – but it wasn't as efficient because more people's views had to be consulted. Democracy, if its citizens were just and God fearing, could be a good form of government, but least efficient of all because everyone's view had to be consulted.

As for unjust government, Thomas thinks democracy is the least bad variety because, even if the people are vicious and selfish, democracies move too slowly to get much done, and no one, even among a corrupt populace, would want to have a tyrant ruling over them. A corrupt aristocracy is worse than a corrupt democracy because it can act more quickly. Worst of all is tyranny, because it allows a wicked man to act selfishly with the absolute unchecked power of what in a good government would be a monarch.

Sensible as these distinctions are, they bore little resemblance to the actual medieval world. Kings, princes, and dukes ruled most countries; their power was close to absolute. Nothing resembling republican self-government would emerge until the rise of wealthy trading states in the late Middle Ages, such as Florence, Genoa, Venice, and the Hanseatic League – whereas Europe's monarchies were predominantly connected to the landed aristocracy, republican self-government early on took root where the merchant classes became prominent. As for a purely democratic form of government in which every citizen participated equally, it had existed nowhere in the West since Athens in the fifth century BC, and been thoroughly discredited, starting with Plato, in the eyes of all educated men. Nothing close to it would come into existence again until

1776, when America's founders would have to labor mightily with their pens and speeches to convince the better elements of society both in America and Europe that they were not going to return to the dreaded mob rule and demagoguery of ancient Athens.

Strictly speaking, Thomas allowed for the overthrow of a tyrant. But he hedged this in so carefully that, in practice, it could probably never happen according to his rules. Even in the most extreme instances of tyranny, he insisted, subjects must never rise in armed rebellion. They should simply withhold their obedience and wait for another great lord to overthrow the evil king. The common people do not have any direct responsibility in the feudal chain of command for improving government– this larger responsibility for the common good belongs exclusively to the nobility. For the common people to overthrow a tyrant in a popular uprising will very likely lead, in Thomas's view, to chaos and injustice worse than that of the tyrant himself. Better in most cases to bear with an oppressive ruler and hope things get better: "If there be not an excess of tyranny it is more expedient to tolerate for a while the milder tyranny than, by acting against the tyrant, to be involved in many perils which are more grievous than the tyranny itself."

Despite the greater leeway in his thinking for distinguishing between better and worse kinds of government than in that of Augustine, at the end of the day, Thomas is at one with his predecessor in believing that no form of political life can even remotely approach the beatitude that will be experienced for all eternity by those who are saved. While the ancient Greeks and Romans really believed that illustrious political action – martial prowess, great statesmanship, civic virtue – could bring human beings authentic happiness and fulfillment in the here and now, for the Christian theologians it paled in comparison with the prospect of salvation and the danger of hell. Unlike Augustine, Thomas's conceded that citizen virtue had its place in the Great Chain of Being as the first rung on an ascent that enabled us to aspire to goodness and, therefore, prepare for our future in heaven. But it was no more than the first rung. The main role of government was to maintain order so that people could devote themselves to their duty to God, and, of course, to defend God's Church and its ecclesiastical hierarchy.

Thomas's model of the good king with a kind heart ruling justly on behalf of God was idealized in song and verse and became a deep part of the texture of European tradition. I remember as the child of English parents being enchanted by the Christmas carol *Good King Wenceslas* as sung by the Canterbury Cathedral choir, with its portrait of a saintly king who is concerned enough about the suffering of a poor peasant whom he spots desperately gathering wood for his fire on a bitterly cold night to send out someone to bring him Christmas dinner and firewood. It seemed quintessentially English in a deeply primeval way – I didn't realize that Wenceslas was actually a Duke of Bavaria, but that only points to how widespread this idealization of Christian monarchy was. Not that this act of charity was the first step in creating the welfare state, of course. Medieval kings are praised for individual, spontaneous acts of charity and good will toward their subjects, all the more moving and miraculous for being so rare, nothing on which any subject could rely, let alone insist. The limited character of royal charity was preserved in the Maundy Thursday ceremony, continuing as late as the Tudors, in which the monarch, in an imitation of Christ, would wash the feet of a selected group of poor people from the London streets. Feet cleaned, each soul would be given a new cloak, a few coins, and sent back into the miserable stinking poverty of the city, their lives basically unchanged. What counted in these moments was the graciousness and mercy of the monarch.

The Victorian historian and clergyman John Richard Green wrote the following description of King Harold the Great, long a sentimental favorite among English monarchs because of his tragic defeat at Hastings by the ruthless Normans, the last "true" English King (never mind that he was himself descended from Saxons who had previously come across the Channel as conquerors). He was the very model of a medieval monarch, indeed, according to Green, a paragon of all human perfection:

Alfred was the noblest as he was the most complete embodiment of all that is great, all that is lovable, in the English temperament. He combined as no other man has ever combined its practical energy, its patient and enduring force, its profound sense of duty, the reserve and self-control that steady in it a wide outlook and a restless daring, its temperance and fairness, its frank geniality, its sensitiveness to actions, its poetic tenderness, its deep and passionate religion. Religion, indeed, was the groundwork of Alfred's character. His temper was instinct with piety. Everywhere throughout his writings that remain to us the name of God, the thought of God, stir him to outbursts of ecstatic adoration. . . "So long as I have lived," said the King as life closed about him, "I have striven to live worthily."

In Shakespeare's *Richard the Second,* written around 1595 about events that took place in the fourteenth century, at the very cusp of the medieval era as it is about to give way to the Renaissance and Reformation, John of Gaunt gives expression to an even more romanticized account of medieval monarchy at its most ancient and honorable, a world of seamless unity between monarch and subject, between royal authority, ancient descent, and their rootedness in the age-old soil of England, that is all about to fall apart owing to the evil actions of Richard: "This seat of Mars/This other Eden, demi-paradise, this fortress built by Nature for herself ... This nurse, this teeming womb of royal kings."

Through Shakespeare's history plays, we can sense Elizabethan England looking back on what once had been, on the Great Chain of Being – with a degree of nostalgia, but also with a sense of the inevitable momentum of the future. For, once again, everything in the career of tyranny was about to change.

GOD'S SHADOW ON EARTH: THE OTTOMAN CALIPHATE

In order to set the stage for this new act in the drama, we have to consider the impact on medieval Europe of the rise of Islam, last in the historical sequence of the three great monotheistic religions, and especially the impact of the Ottoman Empire. If the rise of Christianity in the old Roman Empire had fundamentally changed its culture and created the transition to the feudal middle ages, the second great challenge to Europe after the fall of the Western empire was the rise of the Ottomans.

The spread of Islam, which began in the seventh century, had already been accompanied by waves of conquests that absorbed the former Roman provinces of the Middle East, northern Africa, parts of Sicily, and the southern part of Spain into its fold. Like the civilizing imperialism of Rome and Alexander the Great before them, the Muslim conquerors built beautiful mosques, public buildings, libraries, and schools wherever they went. At a time when very little of the precious literary and philosophical heritage of Greco-Roman antiquity survived in Europe, large libraries and universities for studying the Greek and Roman classics – which had been preserved after the fall of the Byzantine Empire and translated into Arabic – sprung up in Baghdad, Toledo, and Palermo. The intellectual currents filtering into Western Europe from the Islamic philosopher Averroes' revival of Aristotelianism influenced Thomas Aquinas.

But while Western Christendom managed to hold the initial Muslim advances at bay in their footholds in Africa, Spain, and Sicily, the Ottomans created something unique, a new world empire that would threaten Europe's very existence and preoccupy it for a hundred years. For, whereas the Arabic Saracen conquerors had focused on taking possessions in the Mediterranean basin, the Ottomans were determined that their new empire would also extend into the very heartland of Europe itself.

The Ottomans, named for the founder of their dynasty, Osman, ruler of a Ghazi emirate, captured great Constantinople in 1453 after years of chipping away at Byzantium's ever-shrinking regional power, racked by civil war and partition after the Fourth Crusade. Beginning with the conqueror of Constantinople, Mehmed II, the Ottoman dynasty remained in power through lineal succession until the last sultan was exiled in 1922, a record rivaled in Europe only by the Hapsburgs, and never matched elsewhere in the Islamic world. At its height under Suleiman the Magnificent, the Ottoman Empire became one of the most powerful states in history, in many ways the Roman Empire's first real successor. It was a multinational empire totaling some twelve million people by the mid-sixteenth century, controlling much of Southeast Europe, Western Asia, the Caucasus and North Africa. The Ottoman army during the Middle Ages was perhaps the most advanced in the world, one of the first to employ muskets and cannons. Its fleet dominated the Mediterranean. Having gobbled up the former Roman province of Illyria, the Ottomans under

Suleiman took most of Hungary and laid siege to Vienna twice, reaching the very gates of the city before being checked. But Suleiman's ambitions went much further: Styling himself "Caesar of the lands of Rome," he dreamt of reuniting by conquest Rome, the capital of the former Western Empire, with the former Constantinople, now Ottoman Istanbul, east and west joined together again under the Caliphate. Some said he wanted to be the new Alexander the Great.

Any visitor to Istanbul today will immediately grasp that it is one of the world's great cities and civilizational centers. The vista of its gleaming domes studding the sparkling waters of the Bosporus is almost beyond description, as if the beauties of Rome, Venice, and Cairo were rolled into one. Its very name Istanbul, from an ancient Greek phrase, simply means "the city," as if there were no other. Spread out over hills originally chosen as a site by the Emperor Constantine for his New Rome in part because they evoked the seven hills of the original Rome, walking around the old city requires mountain-goat stamina. My favorite spot is the remains of the old Roman Hippodrome. Its shaded quiet provides a welcome relief from the ceaseless bustle and throngs of the huge city. You can sit on the cool stone foundations and contemplate the historical layers of this very ancient place, which tie together every epoch we have considered so far in following the career of tyranny and the struggle against it. There's an Egyptian Obelisk from the reign of Pharaoh Tutmosis III, brought to Constantinople by the Emperor Theodosius I. A column depicting intertwined serpents, celebrating the final Greek victory over the Persians at the Battle of Plataea in 479 BC, arrived courtesy of Constantine, who looted it from Delphi. On one side of the square is the magnificent palace of the Grand Viziers, second in command to the Sultans. On the other side, where the palace of the Byzantine Emperors once stood, rises the airy dome of the Blue Mosque.

What kind of impact did it have on the Ottoman conquerors of this city to gaze upon the almost superhuman architecture of the Byzantines? Whatever it was, they set about to create a new synthesis of their own way of life with that of the now-defunct Byzantine realm. They took over the caesaropapist model of supreme monarchical authority developed by the Byzantine emperors and injected it with their own culture and the values of their Muslim faith. Just as the Byzantine emperor had been the apex of both earthly and divine authority, so too would be the Ottoman sultan (meaning "lord of kings"), who claimed the highest position in Islam, the caliphate. As caliph, he was the "sword of the prophet" and "the shadow of God" on earth. Like the Roman emperors, he was the supreme head of the armed forces. The state was divided into a military administration and a civil administration, with the empire's provinces governed on behalf of the Sultan by pashas (not unlike the role of the proconsuls under the Augustan principate). The sultan was advised by a council of tribal elders, later including top military men and administrators, the Divan. On religious matters, although the sultan might consult a council of mullahs, he ultimately decided on all clerical appointments and doctrinal issues. All these spheres of government intersected in his person and his absolute power. Beginning in the fourteenth century, the Sultan was assisted by the Grand Viziers, an office originally created by the earlier Abbassid caliphate. Sometimes likened to a prime minister, but also akin to the role of powerful Praetorian Prefects like Sejanus under the emperor Tiberius, the Grand Vizier sometimes exercised an almost unlimited authority on the Sultan's behalf, and was romanticized as the evil villain of fairy tales. But no one – at least during the medieval period – ever forgot who the true master was. While adopting some features of the Byzantine model, we should bear in mind that the Ottoman caliphate was in another way returning behind the legacy of Rome to the much more ancient god-kings of the east, from the pharaohs to Cyrus the Great, and their universal empires.

From the time they first conquered Constantinople and dissolved the Byzantine Empire, the Ottomans practiced religious tolerance toward Christians and Jews. On one level, they were continuing a policy of tolerance begun by Cyrus the Great and continued by Alexander the Great and the Caesars, one which, as we have seen, contributed greatly to the peace and prosperity of those earlier universal empires. But the Ottomans added variations that came strictly from their own Islamic convictions. For, like the Jews and Christians, they, too, were strict monotheists. While those earlier empires were able to practice tolerance toward all sects in part because their rulers and nearly all their subjects were polytheists (even if they were partial to one god among others), the Ottomans believed in the One True God, the God of Abraham, and rejected all others as false.

Mehmed II allowed the Orthodox Church and its lands to continue unmolested as long as Christians accepted Ottoman authority. Most Orthodox Christians actually preferred to take their chances with their new Muslim rulers than with the Venetians and Serbs who had previously gained control of Byzantine affairs – they knew full well that Occidental Christians regarded them as heretics and might well burn them at the stake. Since until the late-fifteenth century Christians were still in the majority in the Ottoman domains, the arrangement must have worked fairly well. But Ottoman tolerance for Christians and Jews had its limits. In the Muslim tradition, as "peoples of the Book," they deserved some respect as Islam's Abrahamic predecessors. But they weren't equals, because their earlier revelations had now been surpassed and completed by that of the Prophet Mohammed, the final and true teaching. Under the Ottomans, Christians and Jews had the right to worship, but could not bear arms or even ride horses, or build a house higher than that of a Muslim. They were subjected to a special tax. On the plus side, Jews and Christians were given their own court system with their own coreligionists appointed by the caliphate as judges. The patriarch of the Orthodox Church had considerable autonomy, and Christian clergy were paid by the Ottoman state. From early on, the sultans welcomed Jews as emigrants from Europe, where they suffered terrible persecution at the hands of Christian monarchs and the Inquisition. All in all, though it was hardly the model of complete tolerance that it (along with the period of Muslim rule in Granada) has recently sometimes been romanticized as, Jews and Orthodox Christians probably fared much better under the Ottomans than they would have in most of Europe. In 1656, the Greek patriarch of Antioch, mourning the atrocities committed by Polish Catholics against Orthodox Christians, proclaimed: "God perpetuate the empire of the Turks for ever and ever! They take their taxes and enter no account of religion, be their subjects Christians or Nazerenes."

For the Ottomans, religious tolerance went hand in hand with encouraging a flourishing economy. Jews were welcomed in part because, denied ownership of land in Europe, they were frequently merchants and traders. The Ottoman state turned major cities including Istanbul, Bursa, and Adrianople into what we might now call "economic zones" in which non-Muslim shopkeepers, tradesmen, and artisans were left free to prosper. The empire developed roadways and trade routes throughout its vast domains, and encouraged the cultivation of new land. By performing these basic economic functions, the Ottomans were an early example of what we might now call a "mercantilist" or "statist" approach to economic development, in which the state partners with the private sector in order to generate prosperity for both. The system of cantonments it created with large non-Muslim populations of merchants and traders anticipates the Chinese practice during the nineteenth century of granting foreign powers rights of commercial development in certain coastal enclaves. As in the Chinese case, in the Ottoman case as well it was probably also meant to keep these valuable foreigners sealed off from too much contact with the Muslim population, lest they corrupt the pious humble folk with their love of money. (Islamic theology, like its Thomistic counterpart in medieval Europe, was conflicted over the issue of commerce. Must the acquisition of money and the pleasures its possession enables us to gratify not get in the way of a devotion to God?). All in all, the Ottoman economic model was in a category of its own for its era. Certainly the old Roman Empire had never taken much of an interest in using the power of the state to develop the economy.

In doing so, however, the Ottomans were hearkening back to a very ancient model that has undergone a remarkable revival in our world today. For, as we saw in Part One, the idea that the monarch possesses his country as if it were his personal property, his household, is one that goes back to the ancient Greeks – an overlap of political authority with economic domination that ancient thinkers like Aristotle warned could easily lapse into a tyrannical form of government. Xenophon, less republican in his leanings (and an admirer of the Persian Empire who assisted Cyrus the Younger in his bid for the throne with a Greek expeditionary force), encouraged tyrants in his political treatises such as the *Hiero* to promote trade and commerce so that their subjects would be loyal out of self-interest and both ruler and ruled would prosper alike. Beginning as far back as Cyrus the Great, the Persian Empire had put into practice the control and encouragement of the economy by a central state. But in none of these models for the state's development of the economy, it must be stressed, was the freedom of people to prosper and flourish through agriculture or commercial enterprise ever meant to be extended to political liberty. You were free to prosper in private so long as you never questioned the ultimate authority of the Great King or the Sultan.

It has been noted that the Ottoman caliphate's encouragement of zones or spheres of economic autonomy in order to garner greater revenues for itself, while never relaxing its ultimate grip on total authority, has for a long time remained the preferred model in the Middle East, as in, for instance, Saudi Arabia's insistence that foreign oil companies will only ever be granted the right to extract Saudi oil for a generous cut of the profits, never actual ownership of the oil fields. And in today's world, of course, nondemocratic regimes like Russia and, above all, China, have revived the idea of a state-directed or mercantilist economy. Not to mention the "sovereign wealth funds," enormous concentrations of capital owned by governments (usually nondemocratic) rather than business corporations that play a major role in global financial markets today. This divide in the road between the state as the master of the economy (what Aristotle, we recall, termed *oikonomia*, the art of household management that was in its essence also despotic) and the view that the right of the individual to prosper economically must be part and parcel of his right to be a free citizen with a say in government becomes a major barrier between east and west as we follow the career of tyranny into the modern age.

Like their Byzantine predecessors, the sultans ensconced themselves in ever-greater luxury and ever more elaborate ceremonial. Surrounded by concentric circles of courtiers, few ordinary human beings ever laid eyes on them. Like their predecessors among the universal monarchs of the east including Cyrus the Great, the most impressive of the sultans, best exemplified by Suleiman the Magnificent, led their armies in person during times of war and cultivated gracious peacetime lives in their gorgeous gardens and palaces. Suleiman – named for his counterpart among the kings of Judea, the paragon of a ruler brave in war, just in peace, and magnanimous toward his subjects – codified the laws and spent lavishly on building schools, hospitals, and libraries. A talented poet himself, he was a generous patron of the arts, and his court hosted religious thinkers and philosophers. The ancient Greek and Roman classics survived alongside Muslim theology. The meandering pavilions, gardens, and fountains of Topkapi palace, much of it still visible in Istanbul, were less a personal dwelling than a kind of microcosm of an orderly and beautiful world, like the earlier capitals of Babylon and Persepolis.

It is possible that the greatest church of Constantinople, Hagia Sophia with its enormous dome, inspired the sultans to build the equally imposing Blue Mosque and Suleiman Mosque on a similar pattern. But at this point, it becomes hard to disentangle whether west was influencing east or east influencing west. Sinan, architect of the Suleiman Mosque, may have influenced Michelangelo's dome at St. Peter's and Palladio's churches, but the influence might have run in the other direction – Palladio's patron was also the Venetian envoy to Istanbul. In building enormous domed structures like the Pantheon and Hadrian's tomb, Romans of the Augustan principate may have already been influenced by eastern structures, the earlier Roman domes in turn influencing Hagia Sophia, which in turn influenced the mosques. Like their Christian counterparts, the basilicas and great medieval cathedrals of Europe, the Ottoman mosque, reaching its height in the architecture of Sinan, was definitely an architectural symbol for an orderly cosmos presided over by God and his deputy on earth. Outside, the large dome and surrounding smaller ones represented the circular movements of the heavens, Plato's music of the spheres. Inside, the vast dome represented the orb of the world reaching up toward God. The large light fixtures were slung very close to the floor, not only to provide illumination, but to show symbolically how much greater God's majesty, soaring up to the distant roof, was than even the light-giving heavenly bodies He had created like the sun and the stars.

Before we get too carried away by the accomplishments of the Sultanate, we should add that, within the sprawling labyrinth of Topkapi, there was an endless atmosphere of sexual and political intrigue, not unlike the atmosphere on the Palatine Hill under the Julio-Claudians. Like the Roman emperors before them, the sultans at their best were reforming tyrants, often with a sybaritic dash of the garden-variety tyrant in their private pleasures, and capable of spasms of cruelty, too – reminding us once again of the uncomfortable truth that the psychological traits of good rulers and tyrants often have a lot in common. Sometimes they were nothing more than garden-variety tyrants, in the same league as Caligula and Nero. Nor was their court free of dissension and ambition. Although the Ottoman dynasty was never overthrown, on eleven occasions, sultans deemed unfit, whether because of jealousy or because they really were disasters at ruling, were deposed and replaced by a brother, son, or nephew – in which case, the deposed sultan's remaining heirs would be mercilessly strangled. (Mehmed III did in no fewer than nineteen of his brothers and half-brothers). The famous harem created a steamy swirl of carnal delight and vying for influence among the Sultan's wives, who bribed officials and sometimes affected the succession. As in any system where one man has absolute power unconstrained by law, excesses were committed rivaling those of the worst Greek and Roman tyrants. One sultan, Murad IV, used to amuse himself by standing on the palace walls and picking off innocent bystanders below with his musket. Sometimes he would run through the streets killing anyone he encountered with his sword. Who could stop him? Like the Caesars, at bottom, the sultans were tyrants – sometimes reforming tyrants, but tyrants all the same.

A major hallmark of the Ottomans was that they strove to create a multinational meritocracy in which men of ability could rise in the imperial service regardless of their origin, including peoples the Ottomans had conquered. The Persian, Alexandrian, and Roman empires had also been open to people rising through their merit (black Africans reportedly held seats in the Roman Senate by the Antonine age), but the Ottomans devised institutions specifically aimed at creating this meritocratic elite. A series of palace schools culled the most promising young men and groomed them for future service as administrators of the state, including deliberately searching for promising children among the poor. It is striking that the Ottoman sultanate was especially bent on drawing its service class from among the conquered peoples of the Balkans. Three thousand boys were recruited annually from Christian families there. The sultans looked toward Europe for their future, not toward the tribal communities and clan chieftains of Anatolia from which they had sprung long ago as nomads. I don't think the sultans did this because they thought Europeans were superior – far from it – but because they wanted to create an elite of administrators loyal only to themselves. Among their Turcic kinsmen, the sultans as "lords of kings" never entirely escaped the role of tribal head chieftain, constrained to listen to the lesser chiefs somewhat as Bronze Age kings like Agamemnon had been. By contrast, their authority over these European recruits was absolute, a necessary bridge to their emergence as full-blown universal monarchs in the league of Cyrus, Alexander, and Augustus.

Their most extraordinary innovation in pursuing this aim was the creation in 1383 of a full-time standing army, the Janissaries, drawn exclusively from among promising Balkan Christian boys. Chosen between the ages of six and fourteen by government talent scouts and taken from their parents, they received a superb education in warfare, administration, and liberal learning. Doubtless they and their parents were often forced to part unwillingly, so when we stress that the sultans promoted meritocracy, we should also bear in mind the potential cruelty of the method, itself an act of tyranny, albeit reforming tyranny. Conversion to Islam was mandatory, of course, for the Janissaries. Trained as engineers, artisans, riflemen, and clerics, they became the elite of the Ottoman army and state. Their effectiveness as an army was legendary. Slaves of the sultans, they checked the influence of older Turkish tribal and ethnic loyalties, in keeping with Ottoman policy from the outset once Byzantium was taken. At first, like the warrior class in Plato's utopian blueprint, the *Republic*, they were unmarried, celibate, and owned no property of their own. They could not pass their status on to a family heir. Each generation was chosen anew on the basis of merit. But in the course of time, like most elites, the Janissaries did not want their privileges to end with each generation. By the late sixteenth century, the purity of the meritocracy fell apart and declined into a caste when the Janissaries starting having families and their status became hereditary, passed down to their relations whether they deserved it or not. The barracks were abandoned for private homes. They became more interested in becoming tradesmen, making money, acquiring property, and enriching their families than in selfless service to the Sultanate. Corruption had set in – or was it simply human nature?

PRINCES AND PEOPLES: THE REBIRTH OF THE WEST

The defeat in 1571 of the Ottoman fleet at the Battle of Lepanto by a coalition including Spain and Venice, followed in 1683 by the final victory over
the Ottoman army at the gates of Vienna by the forces of Poland and the
Holy Roman Empire, gave Europe a new sense of security, strength, and
glory, bolstering the Renaissance or "rebirth" underway since the fourteenth
century, reflected in the magnificent neoclassical architecture of Bramante,
Michelangelo, and Palladio, and flourishing studies of the classics of Greek and
Roman antiquity, partly owing to their transmission from the Muslim east. No
longer overwhelmed by the splendor of Ottoman court culture and learning,
Europe began to reforge its connection with its Greek and Roman past.

The Renaissance also opened a whole new epoch in the career of the reforming tyrant. Whether they were perceived as tyrants or statesmen depended on
whose interests were furthered or harmed. But a series of dynamic and extraordinary leaders including Henry VIII, Elizabeth I, Louis XIV, Peter the Great,
and Frederick the Great carved out a huge new scope for the extension of
centralized state power to create the instruments of national sovereignty, security, commerce, even culture and religion. For the first time, we encounter the
absolute monarch as the builder of the modern state.

Aided by the rise of modern science with its emphasis on discovering and
developing practical benefits for mankind at large, in contrast with the ancient
view of science as the contemplative study of the cosmos, these state-building
despots also developed modern weaponry, fleets for both war and commerce,
and fostered the beginning of modern industry. With the Tudors at the fore-
front, Europe began its penetration of the New World and the fabulous vista it
offered for future colonization, wealth, and trade. Reforming despots including
Catherine the Great and Frederick the Great could even claim to have brought
a new spirit of human equality and tolerance, the lessons of the Age of Reason
and the Enlightenment, to their backward peoples, or at least to their elites –
true democracy remained as much as ever a feared and loathsome prospect.
But ordinary people's lives could certainly be improved by the expansion of
the state into schooling, promoting trade and commerce, and care for the sick
and impoverished.

The beginning of the modern age faces us as never before with the profound and uncomfortable paradox that absolute monarchical power can sometimes achieve great things for everyone, or as Machiavelli put it, "security and
well-being" for "princes and peoples." It also raised in sharp relief a related
paradox – that the aggressive, ambitious, and willful qualities of tyrants can
shade into those of great statesmen to the point where it's difficult to tell them
apart. The shaky multinationalism of medieval Europe – the claims to universal predominance of both the Holy Roman Empire and the Church, neither
of which could ever really enforce this authority – gave way to the rise of
robust, powerful, independent nations including Britain, France, Spain and,

later, Germany and Italy, each one with a predominant language, ethnicity and sense of its own unique history.

The rise of modern state building was born of two great revolutionary movements in the sixteenth century, the Renaissance and the Reformation. These secular and religious dimensions of the modern age would continue to clash, repel, and intertwine for centuries to come. The "rebirth" hailed by the Renaissance was primarily the rebirth of ancient learning and of the Greek and early Roman ideals of republican liberty and self-government, now embraced anew by Florence and other small city-states with pedigrees going back to antiquity. The church had already transformed itself from being the enemy of pagan culture to becoming its steadfast promoter, commissioning scholars to translate the priceless library of Greek and Roman classics in Toledo that fell into European hands with the expulsion of the Moors from Spain. While the church believed these recovered classics would add to the greater glory of God's creation – Plato and Aristotle could now be approved of as "virtuous pagans" who would have accepted Christ had they been born later on – inevitably they produced a sense of liberation from old-fashioned religious absolutism, what we now call Renaissance humanism.

Most humanists were by no means antireligious; many were devout. But they did believe that the sphere of secular learning and civic life should be allowed much greater freedom from religious supervision than previously, and that differing interpretations of religion should be tolerated. In his portrait of a Christian prince, for example, Erasmus argued that a well-reared monarch should combine faith in Christian revelation with a deep immersion in the Greek and Roman classics, adding to his piety the heroic virtues extolled by Xenophon in his *Education of Cyrus*. Erasmus trod a fine line between conventional Christian beliefs and an assertion of free-thinking independence. His writings were investigated several times for heresy by the Spanish Inquisition, but no conclusion was reached.

If the humanists' relationship with the Church was not always an easy one, a wholesale assault on it came from within its own ranks, led by the theologian Martin Luther. (He reproached Erasmus for being a lily-livered compromiser). Luther wanted a "reformed" church. He wanted to purify the papal church of its involvement in political power brokering and its financial corruption. To Luther's followers, St. Peter's in Rome seemed almost like the throne room of an earthly monarch rather than a spiritual leader, while papal excesses – flagrant family cronyism, popes with illegitimate children whom they then pushed forward as cardinals or princes, the selling of blessings for bribes, sybaritic luxury and debauchery – recalled the excesses of the Caesars. Luther saw himself as returning to the pure spirituality of St. Augustine, with its almost agonizing chasm between the City of God and an earthly realm mired hopelessly in sin. Not surprisingly, Luther detested Thomism, which he believed glorified the church's worldly power and its claims to doctrinal as well as political supremacy (the model of a Christian monarchy under papal supervision) – he called it "the theology of glory," and, therefore, of sin. Luther's call for reform reexploded a buried tension within Christianity that went back to its origins – the conflict between those who eagerly embraced Roman patronage and state power and maintained that salvation could only come through the priestly hierarchy and those who wanted a more pure way of life, devoid of worldly ambition, and the freedom as individuals to find their own way to God without priestly intervention.

The Reformation's attempt to disentangle Christian faith from worldly power opened the way to greater autonomy for the secular state. Disentangling the church from politics might purify the faith – Luther's main concern – but it inevitably liberated politics from religious oversight as well. Early on, regional princes such as the Landgrave of Hesse and the Elector of Saxony supported Luther. The Schmalkaldic League of Lutheran princes was established both to defend the cause of the Reformed Church and to break away from allegiance to the Holy Roman Emperor. Not surprisingly, the Holy Roman Emperor Charles V viewed Luther both as a heretic and a subversive who encouraged what were supposed to be his vassal princes to assert their own autonomy. The Emperor's claim to possess caesaropapist authority over both temporal and religious affairs had always, as we've observed, been a shaky one. The combination of religious dissent and political autonomy asserted by the Lutheran princes weakened it further.

The Reformation's stress on the freedom of each believer to commune directly with God and follow his own conscience, as opposed to the liturgy of the church and the priesthood, harmonized with the Renaissance's emphasis on individual freedom of thought and creativity and a renewed emphasis on civic virtue and republican liberty in Italy's ancient city-states like Florence. Florentine publicists for republican liberty like Guicciardini made common cause with the Lutheran call for a reformed church. The modern age emerges from this fusion of religious and secular individualism. For the first time since ancient Greece and early Rome, the denunciation of tyranny – the tyranny of the church over the conscience of the individual believer and the tyranny of despotic authority, whether papal or monarchical, over republican liberty – a denunciation paid lip service under the Roman Empire and pretty much squelched in the Middle Ages, found its full-throated voice again, so that, as the Renaissance humanist Petrarch wrote, "the old Roman valor is not dead, Nor in the Italians' breasts extinguished." From the very beginning, though, there was a conflict between how best to bring about more liberty for the individual. Through a return to ancient republicanism? Or through an all-powerful secular ruler who would throw off the shackles of papal control and religious superstition and build a powerful, prosperous, and well-run state for the benefit of all his subjects? The reforming tyrant makes a big comeback.

Preparing the way for the tyrant as modern state builder was sixteenth century Florentine political thinker Niccolo Machiavelli, whose name is still a byword for deceit, manipulation, political murder, and the notion that great things can be accomplished through skullduggery. Here is the essence of his new view of statecraft, from chapter 15 of *The Prince*:

Many have imagined republics that have never been seen or known to exist in reality. For there is such a distance between how one really lives and how one ought to live that he who overlooks what is really done for what ought to be done achieves his own ruin rather than his preservation. For a man who tries to be good in all regards must come to ruin among so many who are not good.

In these few lines, Machiavelli overturns the entire tradition of previous moral and religious philosophy going back to Plato. According to him, whatever differences might exist between pagan philosophy and Christian revelation, both put forward an impossibly high standard for human beings to live up to – the "imagined" republics included both the utopia of Plato's *Republic* and St. Augustine's otherworldly City (literally, republic) of God. Francis Bacon, a pioneer of modern physics and one of Machiavelli's greatest admirers, summarized the argument with a clear reference to the lines I just quoted from *The Prince*: "We are much beholden to Machiavelli and others that write what men do, and not what they ought to do … As for the philosophers, their discourses are as the stars, which give little light because they are so high."

Instead of trying to encourage men to live as they *ought*, according to Machiavelli, we should accept them as they *are*. Whereas the ancients, joined by Christianity, had called upon men to rise above selfish passions and greed and devote themselves to a higher morality, Machiavelli is all in favor of everyone pursuing his material self-interest. The only way for states to achieve lasting stability and prosperity is to cooperate with what the vast majority of human beings really want – survival, prosperity, and comfort. We remember that St. Augustine saw in the City of God our hope for eternal salvation, while in the fleshly and sinful City of Man, all human achievement, whatever its pretensions to virtue, came down to material wealth and dominion over others. Machiavelli in effect simply lops off the City of God, tosses it aside as sheerly "imaginary," and says: The City of Man, the world of wealth and power, is all there is. Go for it!

A republican by inclination, Machiavelli hoped his native Florence could govern itself freely. (After the expulsion of the Medicis who had ruled there for sixty years, Machiavelli served as diplomat and organizer of the militia for the Republic of Florence before the Medicis returned to power, fired him, and had him tortured). But what matters at bottom for any society is "security and well-being," and if that takes one-man rule, it's better than civil war or being ripe for foreign conquest. Whereas the ancient thinkers and medieval theologians always made a distinction between tyranny as an unjust form of rule by a man mired in vice and monarchy as the rule of a virtuous man for the benefit of the common good, however rare they knew such kings to be in practice, Machiavelli abandons the distinction altogether as useless, part of the "imagined" standards of the tradition. He calls them all "princes," whether it be a Nero or a Marcus Aurelius, a Romulus or a Moses. He won't make a moral judgment about their legitimacy as long as they are effective.

Besides, he argues, republics from time to time need tyrannical personalities who restore order, discipline, and the rule of law, purging the citizens of an excessive love of peace and comfort and restoring the vigor of their virtue. Sometimes, in other words, a tyrant wearing the toga of a citizen might be needed to counteract other would-be tyrants who would overthrow the republic altogether by pandering to the licentiousness of the mob. That's why the Romans created the office of Dictator, in effect a legal (though temporary) tyranny. In the annals of republican Rome, Machiavelli preferred the harsh code of Manlius, who ordered the execution of his own son for showing off in battle, to the softness of Scipio, whom hardliners in the Senate accused of pampering his troops. Righteous anger is better than kindness in the statesmen of republics. The harshness of Manlius preserved the equality of Romans before the law, whereas Scipio verged on becoming a tyrannical demagogue by subverting the army through soft treatment into his personal faction.

The history of the Roman republic was always Machiavelli's favorite model. He regarded it as the greatest state that had ever existed, a model for imitation today. As I mentioned in the Introduction, in the opening to his book *Discourses on Livy*, he compared himself to a kind of Columbus of political thought who had taken a path "no one has trodden before," more dangerous than the exploration of the New World. Eerily, he seems to foresee that the newly discovered world to the west will provide the home for the New Rome that he hopes his readers will build after he uncovers for them the lessons of the original Rome's climb from a republic to an empire unsurpassed in history. An empty canvas of limitless extent awaited across the ocean to the west in which old Europe's errors could be left behind and a fresh start made (empty, of course, only if you overlooked the peoples who already lived there).

The history of the Roman republic showed that, in order for a republic to grow in power through conquest and achieve long-term prosperity, it had to postpone its material gratifications so as to keep military and civic virtue keen and energetic: Have your cake, but don't eat it yet. Machiavelli also admired the Roman constitution with its checks and balances among the clashing ambitions and selfish interests of the Senate and People, which we discussed in Part One. Rather than preaching that everyone should be good, like the ancient philosophers, the Roman republic recognized that everyone is inevitably out for themselves. Harnessing this aggressive energy outward in foreign conquest, while blocking it internally through the division of powers so that no one class or faction could get the upper hand, was the secret of Rome's incredible expansionary dynamism and success.

As we'll see, transmitted through his English followers like Harrington and the French philosopher Montesquieu, the theory of checks and balances will have a profound impact on the American founding. As Madison wrote in a

Machiavellian-sounding moment, the purpose of the new American constitution was "to let ambition counter-act ambition," a fruitful struggle in which everyone's fortunes would improve. Did Machiavelli see any contradiction between encouraging republican civic-spiritedness and self-sacrifice in the present so as to bring about a rise to imperial power and prosperity that would eventually undermine republican virtue by engulfing it in luxury, ease, and a craving for the peace to enjoy them? He certainly knew that the Roman republic had eventually been undone by its very success, a battle among dynasts that could only end when the final victor, Octavian, imposed a tyranny that could never be shaken off. He understood as well that, once the emperors offered the Roman people the chance to give up their stern martial code and enjoy the fruits of empire in peace, as long as they were willing to trade political liberty for an absolute ruler, they went for it in droves. That was why Machiavelli so detested Augustus and Julius Caesar – courageous and skilled as they were, they were the death-knell of liberty. But to Machiavelli, such cycles of rise and decline were an inevitable part of history and human nature. The New Rome he foresaw might well eventually undermine itself in this same way. But what a glorious ride it would be to the top!

Machiavelli was considerably more critical of Christianity than the other Renaissance humanists. He revived the old pagan charge that Christianity made men pacifistic and weak, dividing their loyalties and making them neglect affairs in this world in anticipation of eternal salvation in the next. Citizens were less and less willing to fight and die in the defense of their homeland. The compassion that was so highly prized in the Christian moral code led, in the real world, to disastrous politics. Flinching at the use of force to suppress civil discord out of compassion was ultimately more cruel to your subjects in the long run if it plunged society into anarchy and strife.

According to Machiavelli, leaders should always be ready to use violence now in order to prevent worse violence later; always ready to wage a preventive war today in order to stave off a far worse war later on when the odds may not be in your favor. If another country threatens you, don't wait to be attacked – take it out now. History is full of examples that confirm this hardheaded if cynical advice. Had the Western allies hit back hard against Hitler when he illegally occupied the Rhineland, their two hundred divisions would have overwhelmed his mere ten; his own generals would probably have overthrown him in order to avoid a full-scale invasion of Germany. Because the allies flinched at the use of force, Hitler had time to build up the Wehrmacht. He was convinced his enemies did not have the stomach to fight, which emboldened him to further acts of aggression, and his overwhelming prestige and apparent military genius soon made his overthrow impossible. By failing to use a small amount of force in the first place, the allies guaranteed a war that went on for years and cost tens of millions of lives and unparalleled destruction.

When thinking about how Machiavelli's maxims would apply to real events, it's important to bear in mind that he was not an advocate of large-scale, mindless, and excessive political violence. Precisely by allowing ambitions to check and clash as energies for self-advancement, rather than repressing them to simmer and boil underground, he maintains, there was very little actual violence or killing in the early history of Rome. Machiavelli was as much opposed to tyrants like Nero or Caligula who were cruel for the pleasure of cruelty as the traditional teachings had been, but for a completely different reason. The ancients opposed excessive violence because it was the sign of a flawed soul. Machiavelli opposed excessive violence because it got in the way of one's ultimate success. He believed that a short burst of efficiently targeted force in the present – against a potential foe abroad or a disturber of the peace at home – would remove the need for widespread carnage down the road when things got out of hand. It's the political equivalent of what we now call a "surgical strike" by the military. According to Machiavelli, the new prince will not merely achieve power and glory as had ancient conquerors like Alexander and Caesar, although that would be a great place to start in comparison with the feckless Christian rulers of today, but will be a kind of *scientist* of power, rebuilding society methodically for the sake of maximizing everyone's security and well-being. The Romans, who are always Machiavelli's heroes in contrast with the weak and irresolute states of his own era, are likened by him to surgeons or horticulturalists of power.

We recall from Part One that the ancients emphasized the educational shaping of a good character – *paideia* – as the best way of forestalling potentially tyrannical ambition and rechanneling it into the service of the common good. The mad ambition of an Achilles must be rechanneled into the honor a citizen receives from serving his fellow citizens. Machiavelli rejects this educational approach to citizenship. He simply doesn't believe it works. No truly ambitious person will ever forsake the chance to be absolute master in order to participate in the rather pale second-best honor bestowed by one's equals. Anyone with the brains and guts to think he can get away with becoming top dog will go for broke. Even citizens will always try to avoid their duty to the common good if they can focus on their own personal wealth and status.

What's required is not moral education but a disciplined *method* for the application of force to achieve power, and that means that princes must employ force and violence with a cool head. Referring to an old fable, Machiavelli remarks that a prince must know how to combine the ferocity of a lion with the cunning of a fox. But in a pinch, the cunning of the fox is preferable to the anger of the lion, because anger is a passion that we can get carried away with, until our rage, hatred, indignation, or joy at the prospect of revenge blinds us to what actually needs to be done to remove a foe or an obstacle to our supremacy. Princes don't need a philosophic mentor to moderate their ambitions, as Plato and the ancients had taught. They need to exercise this rational control over themselves, not to moderate their ambition, but, on the contrary, to fulfill it beyond their wildest dreams. Princes, in other words, do need to be wise. But they don't need the wisdom of the philosophers or the church to guide them, which will only lead to failure. They need to be wise in the ways of success. They don't need to read Plato's *Republic*, but they do need to know about Machiavelli's Romans.

The ancients had taught that we should live within the order of nature and rein in our impulses. Machiavelli now offers the heady prospect that man can master nature, control his own destiny, "conquer Fortuna" through bold and cool-headed action. Sometimes he suggests that human rulers could achieve a godlike scope for their power. In *The Prince*, he says that the most outstanding princes of the past – Romulus, Cyrus the Great, Moses – were literally able to "impose onto matter whatever form they pleased" through their strength of will. Any reader of that time would recognize that Machiavelli was transferring God's capacity to impose form on matter – a standard formula in Christian theology – to a secular human ruler. We've seen that past rulers from the pharoahs to Cyrus the Great to the Roman Emperors and the Ottoman Sultan had likened themselves to gods, claimed they had the favor of the gods, said they were gods in human form, or claimed to be God's deputy on earth. But no one before Machiavelli had suggested a ruler could actually and quite literally *be* God, recreating the world of man.

Machiavelli's summons to conquer Fortuna is acknowledged by Francis Bacon as the larger inspiration for his own new natural science, whose purpose is to master nature through scientific investigation (he compares it to torture) so as to unlock her powers "for the relief of man's estate." In this way, Machiavelli's new method of ruling is linked to modern natural science's project for mastering nature to create expanding economic opportunity and wealth for the common man, the early origins of the industrial age and global technology. To Machiavelli's expansion of tyrannical political power is added something even more novel – man's power to tyrannize over nature and the world itself. No wonder many of Machiavelli's readers then and later regarded him as Satanic – "Old Nick" (from Niccolo) became a name for the Devil himself.

BY GOD AND MY RIGHT: THOSE FASCINATING TUDORS

One of Europe's first Machiavellian monarchs was Henry VIII. The fascination with Henry VIII today seems endless. If you accept that Henry was a tyrant – more on that debate shortly – then he perfectly illustrates what I said about tyrants at the beginning of this book. They are outsized, larger-than-life personalities who fascinate as well as repel. His rowdy charm, coupled with his serpentine ruthlessness, were beautifully portrayed by the actor Robert Shaw in the film of *A Man for All Seasons*, when he alternates with Paul Scofield's scholarly Thomas More between manly slaps on the back laced with raucous laughter and glowering threats over any lack of cooperation More might be contemplating about Henry becoming head of the church in England.

More recently, the actor Jonathan Rhys Meyers provided a nuanced and complex portrait of Henry through all the stages of his life in the TV series *The Tudors*. Beginning as a rough and ready, laddish, and athletic young prince, head shaved almost like a soccer thug, he progresses from the brutal amusements of jousting and hunting to seize ever-greater control over the affairs of the kingdom through his great ministers and confidants Cardinal Wolsey, More, and Thomas Cromwell. New grabs for power alternate with endless bed hopping (some of it in search of a woman to bear him an heir, much just for fun) and ever-mounting gluttony. Especially convincing in Rhys Meyers' depiction is Henry's quicksilver mood swings. One moment he hugs Cromwell with tears in his eyes on learning of the birth of his minister's son – moments later he turns on him in blazing fury and blames him for his every frustration, heavily hinting that Cromwell will pay with his life if things don't work out.

Henry's serial dalliances with other women, openly cuckolding their frightened and cravenly ambitious husbands, begin as charming games of chivalry and courtship, all sighs, love letters, and pinning his lady's sash to the reins of his jousting horse, and become increasingly more desperate as his body and jaded appetites fail, while increasingly intertwined with court politics of the most literally deadly kind, including sending two of his own six wives to the block. Novelist Hillary Mantel, in her masterful layering of the enigmatic Thomas Cromwell in her novels *Wolf Hall* and *Bring Up the Bodies*, has added her own Henry – in his early years essentially a big, cheerful, ruddy-cheeked, and red-haired boy who is already discovering his power to lash out and destroy. Tall, handsome, and well-formed as a young monarch, like a prince from a fairy tale, Henry ended as the monster of gluttony in the famous Holbein painting, where it seems as if the very wealth of England is wrapped in blankets of silk around his gigantic carcass, a veritable dirigible of jewels and velvet, perhaps a boast that all his subjects have grown fat and rich along with him.

Put it all together – a craving for honor in war (abandoned after the capture of Boulogne in an alliance with the Holy Roman Empire against France was left hanging by the Emperor's deserting Henry and making peace with Francis I of France); sexual acrobat without equal; titanic appetites; endless hunting, jousting, male carousing, seduction, adultery; the wild mood swings careening between spasms of jealousy, joy, vanity, fear, and libido – and you've got the tyrant to beat all tyrants. Yet like all the Tudors, Henry was in many ways a true Renaissance prince, exceptionally learned and cultured, possibly the best-educated of English monarchs. His court glittered with musical entertainments and elaborate masques. He knew Greek and Latin and studied theology. He played the flute, trombone, and trumpet and may have composed "Greensleeves." Above all, *everything* was personal. Everything was about *him*. Eventually he forced Parliament to pass a law proclaiming that his will, written or spoken, had the force of absolute law. The royal motto favored by the Tudors, "By God and my Right," displays in Henry's case a kind of fist-clenched narcissism akin to a child whose angry blows at being denied a candy would, if endowed with adult strength, kill the nearest person.

In short, Henry combined all the ingredients of a tyrannical personality we have seen in this book going back to Achilles. The explosions of erotic excess and violence that swept around him in dark clouds recall the worst of garden-variety tyrants like Caligula. But his large-scale efforts to transform England into a major economic and military player recall the best of reforming tyrants like Julius Caesar (who shared his libidinous side as well). He is a compelling example of the paradox we have seen before – how the psychological qualities of aggression and ruthlessness that characterize the tyrant can also characterize the great statesman. For make no mistake – a real case can be made for Henry's greatness. When Henry ascended the throne at the age of eighteen, he inherited a full treasury that he quickly depleted through high living and ill-considered military adventures, along with fractious and rebellious nobles, and he was confronted by France's reduction of England's once extensive continental possessions to almost nothing. Although he never regained England's Angevin empire, by the end of his reign, his amassment of absolute despotic power laid the basis for England's transformation into a great, powerful, and prosperous modern nation. Henry's foreign policy tried to steer a neutral path between Europe's two great rivals, France and the Holy Roman Empire. He made alliances first with King Francis, then with the Emperor Charles – neither endured. Realizing that England with its small population could never compete as a continental land power, he began focusing on building the navy, expanding the five warships he inherited from his father to upward of 150 ships, making England a major sea power. By the end of his reign, England had a foothold in the New World (salt cod from Newfoundland was already a delicacy in England's great houses). His record at expanding the state's power was extended by his daughter Elizabeth, in many ways Henry in a skirt. When Henry came to the throne, the age of chivalry was, while mostly a memory, still in the air. By the time he died, England was a mightier and more formidable country, but also a harsher, colder, and more cynical one. Something had been broken, but something had been born – a modern state.

There's a story that when Thomas Cromwell, who closely followed Italian literature, read Machiavelli's *The Prince*, he resolved on applying its maxims in the service of his royal master Henry. We'll never know whether this story is true, just as we'll never know whether Stalin kept a copy of *The Prince* on his nightstand. But it's by no means impossible, and I incline to believe it. Cromwell was a voracious reader and an intellectually curious man. Vagabond, soldier (he served in the French army in Italy), merchant (in Florence and Antwerp), lawyer, banker, bon vivant, devout Protestant, master schemer, he embodied the conflicting values of this rambunctious age of intertwining religious and secular upheaval. Why might he not have read *The Prince*? Machiavelli had advised princes to crush the authority of the church over their affairs. He advised them to enlist the support of the common people at the expense of the nobles. Whereas the nobles were too arrogant to ever accept a prince's supreme authority over them, the common people would be grateful for being left in peace with their possessions and allowed to get along and prosper. To this end, the prince should actively promote trade and commerce. Henry VIII did every one of these things. Whether he or Cromwell knew about Machiavelli or not, Henry was the ultimate Machiavellian ruler.

I asked earlier whether he should be regarded as a tyrant. He was certainly not a usurper, having received the throne from his father Henry VII (who was). But his expansion of royal authority burst the bounds of feudal restraint and became close to omnipotent. His first mentor, Cardinal Wolsey, was eminently capable of skullduggery and deceit. But he could not secure an annulment of Henry's marriage to Catherine of Aragon (she had produced no male heir) so that Henry could marry Anne Boleyn and, as he expected, sire a son, and the Boleyn clique whispered that the Cardinal was deliberately dragging his heels. He was charged with treason and died en route to trial. After Henry's next advisor, Thomas More, could not reconcile his loyalty to the Universal Church with Henry's efforts to become its supreme head in England, he too had to go. He was held for interrogation in the Tower by Cromwell, waiting hungrily in the wings to fill his place. We can believe that Henry's tears and loud lamentations at having to send to the block a learned man who had shaped his youthful mind as a father figure were real – but they didn't prevent the axe from falling.

In Thomas Cromwell, Henry finally met his perfect partner, a man whose fervent Protestantism, which included Luther's original insistence that the church must absolutely divest itself of its corrupting entanglements with the secular state, combined with his complete lack of scruples, enabled him to help Henry build his absolute power while advancing the cause of the Reformed religion. Henry amassed unprecedented power by seizing the lands and wealth of the church in England. Assisting him at every turn, touring churches and abbeys so as to inventory their wealth and then supervise their systematic plunder, Cromwell purified the faith (as he saw it) of its worldly possessions while forcing the Church of Rome and its hierarchy in England to yield and accept the Reformed Church.

Like every school child, I was told that Henry VIII wanted to divorce his wife, Catherine of Aragon, who had not given him a son, so he could marry Anne Boleyn, who he was certain would produce the required heir. When the pope refused to grant him the divorce, Henry took over the church in England and forced it out of them. While he was at it, he stole the Church's wealth for his own. Although this is all true as far as it goes, it's an overly simplistic explanation. It's no more true that Henry made himself head of the Church of England simply because he wanted to remarry, produce an heir, and steal church treasure than it is that Constantine made Christianity his preferred religion simply because he wanted to make his dynasty more popular. In both cases, issues of religious principle were involved, a sea change in religious belief.

Certainly Henry chaffed at marriage to his wife, seven years his elder and a censorious prude surrounded by black-clad rosary-clutching duennas. He was infatuated with the pert and vivacious Anne Boleyn, who it was said had learned at the racier French court how to, so to speak, hold a man's interest for a very long time through a special technique. Anne, who followed her sister Mary into Henry's bed, was the daughter of the relentless political climber the Earl of Wiltshire and niece of the crusty old warhorse the Duke of Norfolk, possessor of a title so old that the Norfolks looked down on the Tudors as upstarts. (His son the Earl of Surrey eventually lost his head for displaying a royal coat of arms). He and his brother-in-law Wiltshire whored out Wiltshire's daughters without blinking an eye in order to advance their clan. A part of Henry's fury at being denied the divorce was the hypocrisy involved. The pope had granted them before on similar grounds, most recently in 1498 when Louis XII of France got his marriage annulled by Pope Alexander VI so that he could marry Anne of Brittany. Pope Eugene had annulled Eleanor of Aquitaine's marriage to Prince Louis of France when it produced no male heir. Henry's divorce was blocked because his outraged wife Catherine of Aragon enlisted the help of her nephew, the Emperor Charles V, who held the pope virtual prisoner and, indignant over his aunt's shabby treatment, would not hear of Henry being accommodated.

When Henry VIII took matters into his own hands by establishing his supremacy over the Church of England in matters both temporal and spiritual, he was reviving the Caesaropapist model for the unification of imperial and religious authority that had disappeared in Europe when the Roman Empire split into two halves, migrating east, as we saw earlier, with the Byzantine emperors and later north to the Tsars. The trail had been blazed by the emperor Constantine, who never hesitated to dictate doctrinal matters to his bishops. Moreover, just as Constantine's legalization of Christianity was a recognition of its already widespread popularity and prominence – it hadn't come out of nowhere – when Henry broke with Rome, the Reformation already had a very large base of support in England. Henry didn't invent it from above. The Lollards, followers of John Wycliffe's denunciation of papal corruption starting back in the 1380s, together with the more recent influence of Erasmus' Christian humanism, planted the seeds for English Protestantism. Many of Henry's most prominent advisors were a part of the movement, including Anne Boleyn and her father. Avid as they were for the riches and influence that would come from Anne being Queen, they also saw her as a way of advancing the cause of the Reformed Church. It was typical of the era that people could sincerely hold these motivations at the same time. The same went for Henry's seizure of the church's lands and wealth. New men like Cromwell, along with a host of noblemen loyal to Henry's supremacy over the church and to the cause of Reform, made out like bandits from their share of the plunder, while rejoicing in it as a victory for the new religious movement of purification.

A case can be made that the confiscated lands, properties, and treasure of the church, a fantastic amount of wealth in today's money, helped enrich the English economy by a quantum leap and created a whole new social class who owed its wealth to the Tudors as they helped themselves to the seemingly bottomless cornucopia of dispossessed abbeys, farms, and houses. Often, the newly enriched lords made a former church into the great hall of their new manor, building wings of other rooms around it. Fans of the TV series *Downton Abbey* will remember how its original church structure rises above the later additions, a very common design in the great houses of the period.

Another important fall-out from Henry's confiscation of the church's property is that it brought to a sudden halt the role the church had assumed for centuries of providing regular charity for the poor in their monasteries and churches, including food and shelter. Suddenly the Tudor state had to assume responsibility for these services, the beginning of the modern state's creation of social welfare services, a secular replacement for Christian charity. To be sure, it wasn't very much at first, as the poor themselves complained. Sometimes the Tudor state's way of dealing with poverty was brutal, as in a law that ordered all beggars to be whipped through the streets and expelled from town. But it was the beginning of the idea that government is responsible for the care of its poorer subjects.

Henry's struggle to exert his supremacy over the church inevitably went hand in hand with his struggle to exert his supremacy over the nobility. When he took the throne as a young man, his authority was limited by a handful of great feudal magnates like Norfolk. This is how it had always been in England. On their vast estates with their private armies, they ruled as kings in their own domain. Their acknowledgment of the king's suzerainty over them in the feudal pecking order was grudging and often openly contemptuous. By breaking the power of the church, Henry also amassed the power to break the old feudal nobility. After a number of plots and attempts to overthrow him were crushed, by the end of Henry's reign, these former magnates had been reduced to creatures of his court, hanging around the palace feeding on gossip and hoping for a piece of the King's generosity through titles, sinecures, and offices.

Beginning with Henry VII, the Tudors had infuriated the old nobility by elevating men of humble origins to high positions as advisors, men who, therefore, owed everything to the king. Wolsey and Cromwell under Henry VIII both fit this mold. The movement for the Reformed Church, although it had adherents among the nobility, was predominantly middle class, from the merchant and trading classes of the large towns and seaports, particularly in Kent, Essex, and East Anglia, whose port of Boston had close connections with the Protestant Hanseatic League. The rise of this commercial middle class illustrates perfectly how the religious freedom of conscience first promoted by Luther dovetailed smoothly with the liberation of material self-interest first encouraged by Machiavelli, along with a keen interest in public affairs of a kind absolutely forbidden to the common people in the Middle Ages, but which the civic humanism of the Renaissance was making widespread. The two new forces of individualism – religious and secular – made common cause.

Luther had urged that the laity be encouraged to read and think about the scriptures in their own language, and to find their own path of conscience to God independent of the priesthood. Predictably, this freedom of thought in religious matters led to a new free-thinking attitude about secular and political affairs as well. It's not surprising that, a century later, John Milton would be both the poet of a Protestant masterpiece, *Paradise Lost*, and an advocate for the spread of learning and debate through the printing-press and the abolition of all censorship. The high intellectual tone of the Reformation, its encouragement of independent thought and new learning, suited Henry's own temperament to a degree, which was remarkably open-minded in any matter not threatening his own self-interest. Cromwell himself, who entertained a lively circle of humanists and scholars under his patronage at his urban palace in Austin Friars, reflected this tone as well. Henry actively promoted education, through the creation of grammar schools – meant to cull the meritorious from among the lower orders and give them the benefit of a liberal education in the classics – and endowing King's College, Cambridge. It is said that for the first time during Henry's reign, the sons of the nobility began attending the universities – hitherto the domain of pale-faced clerics. No longer content with riding, hunting, and fighting, they wanted high learning and cultural polish as well – to become "gentle men."

For all these reasons, Henry's reign brought the Reform-minded middle class to a newfound prominence, and it disturbed many at first. The famous Peasants' Rebellion of 1536, which Henry's reliable warhorse the Duke of Norfolk crushed with blood-thirsty thoroughness, was actually a rebellion of old-fashioned peasants who rejected both Henry's new church and closure of the monasteries – ending their ministrations to the poor – and objected to his elevation of commoners over them like Cromwell. They actually *wanted* aristocrats to be their masters, and resented having to doff their hats to the likes of themselves! It was probably Europe's last revolution in favor of privilege.

When we say that Henry followed the Machiavellian prescription for crushing the church, we should bear in mind that he was personally ambivalent about the Reform movement. His own view seems to have been that, with the one difference that he was now head of the church in England, rather than the pope, and owner of all its property, its liturgy, hierarchy, and doctrines would remain the same. There was as yet no sense for most people that this was to be a completely *separate* church. The church to be reformed was still the One True Church. But certain fundamental conflicts in the movement for reform were emerging. Cromwell and his Lutheran followers believed that the laity should be able to read the scriptures in their own language, to study and think about Christ's teachings on their own, independent of the priesthood. They also disputed the doctrine of transubstantiation that equated the wine and bread of the Eucharist with the actual blood and flesh of Christ – the wine and bread, they maintained, were merely symbolic of Christ's divinity. For traditional believers, that threatened the status of the sacraments as man's sole certain path to salvation, and threatened as well to put self-appointed lay preachers on the level of the priesthood. Cromwell made sure the churches were run by priests who followed the Reformed path. But while some of the outwardly compliant clergy secretly harbored continuing loyalty to Rome, others among them wanted to go even further than Cromwell – abolish the priesthood and mass altogether and have congregations elect their own spiritual leaders. Maybe it was even time for men to be equal on earth as they were in heaven, instead of under the thumb of lords. This was all too much for the king. Cromwell eventually fell because Henry did not trust him to contain these more radical trends, which he abhorred as much as the most devout Catholic. (Henry also blamed Cromwell for inveigling Henry into marriage with Anne of Cleaves, wife number four. "She is nothing so fair as has been reported," he groused on meeting her, and complained of her body odor and sagging breasts. Henry could not perform with her for England, although his own vast size by this point didn't help matters).

Anyone who visits England today will frequently come across what are misleadingly described as the "ruins" of religious buildings, such as the remains of the huge Abbey next to Canterbury Cathedral. These structures did not fall apart due to their age or natural causes. Rather, they were dismantled brick by brick by Henry's agents after being sacked. Often it was done out of sheer avarice. But just as often it was fueled by religious zealotry. Just as the early Christians had gleefully laid waste to pagan temples and destroyed their art, just as the religious fanatics of the Taliban would destroy Buddhist art centuries later, some who espoused the cause of the Reformed Church felt called upon to destroy the art of England's great churches. In Ely Cathedral, one of Europe's most magnificent churches, zealots deliberately smashed the delicate reliefs lining the walls of the Mary Chapel. It was an ugly time. (Interestingly enough, Ely was later the family hometown of Oliver Cromwell, future Protestant Generalissimo and Lord Protector, who for a time had a job as its tithes collector and could have seen the cathedral's spires from his modest house).

Henry's establishment of his supremacy over the church was often violent in the extreme, both in terms of human lives and the destruction of property. The Tudor motto "By God and My Right" now inspired methods that anticipated Stalin. We often use the term "medieval torture" to describe the agonies inflicted by the Rack and other instruments of torment in the dungeons of the Tower. In truth, it had rarely been used in the Middle Ages. It only becomes commonplace under Henry VIII and successors, and is, therefore, more a glimpse of things to come in the dungeons of the People's Commissariat for Internal Affairs (NKVD) and the Schutzstaffel (SS) than it is a throwback to a barbaric past. A particularly sinister figure, Richard Topcliffe, who subjected Catholics to the rack under Elizabeth I, had a torture chamber in his own house, raped one of his prisoners repeatedly until she agreed to testify against a Jesuit, and was accused of torturing his assistant's father to death when the son denounced him so as to inherit his estates and share them with Topcliffe. He was an early example of state-employed psychopaths like Lavrenti Beria and Klaus Barbie. As Allan Massie put it, Topcliffe was "as sadistic as any officer of the Gestapo or the Soviet NKVD." The rule of law rapidly eroded, so that people could be snatched off the streets and subjected to these torments under suspicion of political disloyalty or religious dissent – they were often treated as identical.

Henry's reign was violent, but it was only one part of a vast conflagration unfolding across Europe among the conflicting forces of the Church of Rome, the Reformation, and secular authority, and it would go on for 120 years. Countries like Austria became largely Protestant then largely Catholic again through force of arms. During its Protestant interval, the great palace-monastery of Melk in Austria replaced its marble toilet seats with modest Puritan wooden ones. When Catholicism returned, so did the marble. Some twenty years after Henry's VIII's death, Catherine de Medici trod cautiously in his footsteps of defying Rome by granting limited tolerance to the Protestant Huguenot minority in France. It triggered massacre and war until Henry IV of France reaffirmed and extended the Protestants' rights in the Edict of Nantes. He tried to promote tolerance of religious differences, hoping his subjects would come to see themselves as French, regardless of religion, rather than (as the vast majority did) as Catholic. But the revocation of the Edict in 1685 by Louis XIV drove thousands of Protestants out of France and heightened tensions with the Protestant countries next door.

Both sides in the religious struggle committed horrible atrocities in this long-lasting conflict. Thomas More, widely regarded as a gentle scholar and heroic martyr to conscience largely because of Robert Bolt's play *A Man for All Seasons*, was in truth a fanatic who, as Henry VIII's Chancellor, had men burned alive for the crime of possessing an English translation of the Bible. His professions of humanism did not sit well with his complete intolerance for even the slightest departure from traditions that held that the laity were not fit to read the scriptures or reflect on the meaning of the faith. His profession of friendship for the great humanist Erasmus – who was hounded by the Inquisition for encouraging a degree of independence in religious speculation and who maintained that heretics should not be executed but persuaded of their error – is puzzling too. Perhaps, like many people, even very gifted ones, More was not fully aware of the contradictions in his own principles. More's willingness to die rather than renounce the Church of Rome was no doubt sincere, but he only brought on himself what he had very readily done to others who also acted out of conscience.

It's a sign of how interested we remain in the Tudors that More's character and motivations remain a matter of intense debate even today. Some were incensed at Hillary Mantel's depiction in her novels of More as gleefully torturing heretics in a private dungeon in his own house. Mantel's response was that she wanted to correct the overly idealized portrait of More in the Bolt play as a pure martyr to conscience. The allegations of torture are at best unproven, possibly Protestant propaganda. But no one appears to dispute that, in the words of historian Richard Fox, "the number of heretics burned at the stake under More's chancellorship is generally agreed to have been six, with three cases in which More was himself directly involved." To me, that is enough for serious slippage of his halo. But the deeper issue, I think, is the extent to which people no longer accept without reservation the Whig theory of history that I mentioned in the Introduction. For an earlier generation of scholars like G. R. Elton, the despotic power amassed by Henry VIII through Cromwell's ruthless methods was a necessary interlude for laying the foundations of a modern, prosperous, eventually tolerant and self-governing England. What bothers people about this today (and it bothers people about Mantel's version of events) is that it implies that Cromwell's own frequent use of execution and torture in serving Henry was somehow okay because such measures were necessary for progress, whereas More was fighting a rearguard action to preserve the outmoded past. People are not so certain any more that they accept the historical necessity of Henry's revolution from above, because they're not certain about the whole notion of the progress of history in general. Some ask, might not Catholic humanism have evolved toward an accommodation with modern secular liberty on its own, bypassing the intense conflicts sparked by the Reformation and the ambitions of state-building despots like Henry? We can't answer that question, because we are still living in its shadow.

Henry's successor, Mary, employed mass execution and torture to restore the Catholic Church; her successor, Elizabeth I, used the same measures to restore the Church of England. When "Bloody Mary," as Protestants called her, briefly and disastrously married the king of Spain, her subjects were loud in protest that the horrors of the Inquisition might come to their shores. The Tudors' will was carried out by a series of dreaded viziers starting with Thomas Cromwell and continuing under Elizabeth with the widely detested William Cecil, another Protestant fanatic of humble origins who feathered his family's nest with sinecures and titles like there was no tomorrow, parodied in a way instantly recognizable to Elizabethan audiences as the social-climbing sneak and windbag Polonius in Shakespeare's *Hamlet*.

The terrible moral turmoil of the Tudor age as, like Europe as a whole, it careened in fratricidal bloodshed between Protestant and Catholic predominance inextricably intertwined with struggles for political supremacy is accurately reflected in Elizabethan drama. Hamlet's self-annihilating doubt about what to do in a world empty of purpose points to Lutheranism's rejection of Thomism's celebration of the natural goodness of the Great Chain of Being at whose apex presided the Roman Church with its orderly, splendid, and all-encompassing hierarchy, dispensing authoritative guidance on every aspect of how to live and what to believe. Individualism had its liberating side. But it also made men feel solitary and anchorless in a world drained of enchantment. Tellingly, Shakespeare's Hamlet had studied at Wittenburg, where Luther launched the Reformation. (Never mind that the legend of Hamlet dated back to at least the thirteenth century – Elizabethans knew of the connection between Wittenburg and the Reformed Church.) In *Richard the Second*, projecting back onto the late Middle Ages what had happened to England under the Tudors, Shakespeare draws a sharp contrast between the flawed medieval monarch Richard – given to spouting Augustinian poetry about man's sinful fragility as his royal power slips away – and the cold, laconic, calculating new Machiavellian prince, Henry Bolingbroke, who slides beneath events like a barracuda moving inevitably toward his goal of taking the throne. Like the Tudors, he too, as depicted by Shakespeare, follows the Machiavellian formula by befriending the common people and crushing the nobility. He cuts them down like the Gardener in Act III, who proclaims, "all must be even in our commonwealth."

Summing it all up, Christopher Marlowe has Machiavelli himself appear on stage at the beginning of *The Jew of Malta*, where he famously proclaims: "The only sin I know of is the sin of ignorance." There were still enough traditionalists in the audience to find this a horrifying remark, innocuous as it sounds to us now. For all three of the Abrahamic faiths, the presumption that man can achieve knowledge on his own, unaided by God, is the greatest possible sin, the height of ruinous pride. So far from being the only sin, ignorance, if accompanied by faith in and complete submission to God, is vastly to be preferred to a merely human and, therefore, fallen knowledge of worldly matters. Marlowe's depiction of Machiavelli accurately reflects the man himself and the rise of the modern age he helped to launch. The Florentine is celebrating man's capacity to understand the world entirely on his own and, therefore, master it for the maximization of secular power and wealth. The only true sin, in other words, is a lack of willpower to forge your own destiny, to take God's place as the master of the universe.

We began our look at the modern state-building tyrant by discussing Machiavelli's encouragement of "princes and peoples" to achieve "security and well-being" through the creation of powerful, patriotic, and prosperous states free from papal interference and Christian pacifism. In both alternatives – the authority of princes and of peoples – Machiavelli envisioned the secular state increasing its power at the expense of all other local, class or religious authorities. In the feudal order of the Middle Ages, authority had on one level been divided – king versus church, pope versus emperor, each in their separate if sometimes clashing spheres. On another level, however, authority had been shared. The nobility, while nominally the vassals of the king, had a great deal of autonomous power, including extensive lands, agricultural produce, and their own military forces (which the king himself had to call upon in times of war), while the church, notwithstanding Good King Wenceslas and Maundy Sunday, took care of ministering to the needy as well as of education. To complicate matters further, noblemen could be prelates, and archbishops could rule principalities. The hallmark of the modern state, by contrast, is that it concentrates all these instruments of sovereignty – military, economic, educational, social welfare – under a single centralized government divested of ecclesiastical oversight. The dilemma going back to Machiavelli and the Renaissance was whether that was *best* done by an all-powerful monarch or by a self-governing republic. Machiavelli's preference was republicanism, which he hoped his beloved Florence would rekindle, but he realistically understood the attractions of stable and effective one-man rule. Henry VIII was, for good or ill, one of the first examples of how a reforming tyrant could begin to achieve modernization from above.

The truly remarkable thing about England's evolution is how it *combined* these two paths: A reforming tyrant paved the way for the emergence of the English people as free and self-governing. Unlike, say, the dictatorship of Julius Caesar, which led inevitably to the permanent despotism of the emperors, the Tudors' centralization of power in the Crown led, after a century of civil war, to the establishment of constitutional and parliamentary government in the Glorious Revolution of 1688. How did this happen?

First of all, the English Channel protected England from the truly vast scale of destruction unleashed in central Europe by the wars over religion and state building among the Holy Roman Empire, France, and Spain. The German Peasants' war of 1524 cost hundred thousand lives. During the Thirty Years' War in the next century, the population of the German and Czech lands was reduced by a third. In England, there was civil strife to be sure, under both Henry and Elizabeth and in the later civil wars sparked by the Stuarts, but nothing like the devastation in Europe. This was a huge incentive to peaceful economic growth, along with England's growing sea power and increasing ties with the prosperous Protestant Low Countries, beehives of business and trading and a haven for religious tolerance.

Feared while alive, Henry was increasingly appreciated in retrospect for how he had built the kingdom through his titanic strength of will into a powerful and flourishing state, though debate still rages about whether he was an egocentric monster, a far-seeing statesman, or a combination of both. The reign of Elizabeth I began in peril and ended in triumph. Succeeding to the throne after a militant Protestant (Henry's son the short-lived Edward VI) and a militant Catholic (Mary I, the vengeful daughter of Henry's cast-aside wife Catherine of Aragon), she steered a dangerous but ultimately successful middle course. The Church of England was once again Protestant, but it retained Catholic symbols such as the crucifix and priestly vestments. The more radical puritans were out of favor, while heresy laws were repealed. Church attendance was compulsory, but the penalties for absence were mild. The perceived threat of a Catholic crusade against England undermined Elizabeth's inclination to leave her own Catholic subjects in peace; many were persecuted as agents of treason sponsored from abroad. But she stated that she had no wish to pry into her subjects' inner religious beliefs so long as they were loyal to her realm, and this pragmatic approach took increasing hold in English politics and society.

Meanwhile, Elizabeth encouraged the exploration of the New World for the joint benefit of the Crown and its merchant partners. The Province of Virginia, named for her, the "Virgin Queen," by Sir Walter Raleigh, was the first colony in what eventually became the British Empire and the beginning of what is now known as mercantilism – a partnership between the state and the private sector to carve out large swaths of territory or resources for their mutual profit, a model for economic development alive and well today in Russia and China (anticipated, as we saw earlier, by the Ottoman Sultanate). Her successor, James I, chartered a joint stock company known as the Virginia Company, first of a number of such ventures including the Hudson's Bay Company. Already under Elizabeth, middle-class economic enterprise, encouraged and supported by the Crown, was going further in England than just about anywhere else in Europe. She also turned a blind eye to swashbuckling pirates including her paramour Sir Francis Drake, who looted the fat treasure galleons of Spain in the New World to fill her treasury after taking his own cut.

In the life and death struggle against the Spanish Armada – a razor's edge victory that anticipated Dunkirk and the Battle of Britain – Elizabeth came into her own, along with a new sense of English national pride. King Philip II of Spain, one of Europe's most powerful monarchs, had been bent on annihilating this heretical English pipsqueak Elizabeth in the name of the One True Church. For Elizabethan England, Spain with its Inquisition was a bogeyman that in today's terms combined Mordor, Darth Vader and Voldemort. Emerging from the final defeat of the Armada and therefore of Catholic Spain's overwhelming dark power, Elizabeth was transformed into Gloriana, her fairy-tale gowns, white make-up and enormous pearl-splayed headdresses making her an earthly, secular equivalent of the Virgin Mary. (Was she really a virgin? Or rather, like Doris Day, did she *become* one? The jury of historians is still out.) With her Tudor red hair, love of learning (she supposedly knew nine languages) and gusto for music, saucy humor, dancing, and flirtation, she was her father's true heir, especially for willpower, resolute character, and singularity of purpose. She once upbraided her council for failing to provide clear advice by telling them that if *she* were cast out of her kingdom the next morning wearing nothing but her petticoats, *she* would be prospering by sundown, whereas everything *they* were they owed to her. She could truly claim, as she rode on horseback unguarded and in full armor among her awe-struck troops as the invasion force of the Armada descended that, although a mere woman, she had "the heart of a king." In English national myth, the Armada's defeat was akin to the Greeks' defeat of Persia and Wellington's later defeat of Napoleon, a doughty little people who stand up to a monolithic tyrannical aggressor with his hordes bent on robbing their liberty.

When the mighty Tudor dynasty ended with the childless Elizabeth and the Scottish House of Stuart came to the throne, all the vying forces that the

Tudors had managed to contain through their indomitable personalities as they built a unified English state came roaring into their own. The conflict at the heart of Machiavelli's dual endorsement of "princes" and "peoples" – monarchy and republic as alternative paths to a nation's success – now exploded in ten years of civil war, the overthrow of the monarchy followed by the establishment of a republic ruled by Parliament alone, and then the one-man rule of the Lord Protector, Oliver Cromwell. The opposing sides combined both the conflict between the Reformation and the old faith and the growing demand to curtail the power of kings in favor of some form of popular authority and self-government. This tension was at the very heart of the Renaissance itself, for Machiavelli the advocate of absolute despotism in *The Prince* was also the Machiavelli who called for a revival of ancient republican liberty in the *Discourses*.

While the philosopher and historian Thomas Hobbes carried on Machiavelli's endorsement of absolute monarchy in the *Leviathan*, justifying the Stuarts' bid for supremacy over Parliament as the only alternative to civil strife and anarchy, English republicans including James Harrington (in his utopian work *Oceana)* envisioned a future English republic modeled on Machiavelli's Rome, but adapted to specifically English characteristics – a sea-faring, commercial republic "bent on increase." In other words, Harrington envisioned material prosperity, with a balance of powers among commons, nobility, and a "Lord Archon," a supreme citizen-magistrate somewhat like the Roman dictators of old, not a hereditary monarch. The contrast between Harrington's and Hobbes' visions of England was roughly akin to that between Sir Francis Drake and *A Clockwork Orange*. Whereas Harrington's Britannia would rule the waves with its daring corsairs, Hobbes wanted all forms of rebellious and unruly behavior to be crushed.

Although Hobbes' main aim was to defend the Stuarts' claim to absolute monarchy and thereby avoid the horrors of civil war (he hearkened back to Thucydides' descriptions of it in *The Peloponnesian War* as well as the actual strife of the English Civil War going on around him), Hobbes' claim that the "Sovereign" should have the limitless authority to crush all resistance through terror if necessary and even to dictate people's religious beliefs looked ahead to the totalitarian regimes of Robespierre, Stalin, and Hitler, as we'll explore in Part Three. As for Harrington, his vision of a prosperous self-governing republic became known as a part of the "Atlanticist Republican" tradition, originating with Machiavelli, that came to fruition, it can be argued, in the future United States of America. We recall that Machiavelli himself was looking to the New World discovered by Columbus as a blank slate upon which the history of the New Rome would be written. In England, as early as Thomas More's *Utopia*, another imaginary island realm, Renaissance England was looking to the New World for a future of greater prosperity and power; Shakespeare's *The Tempest*, where a philosopher uses the secrets of nature to regain political power, was (many believe) set in Bermuda. Meanwhile, Francis Bacon in his utopian fantasy *The House of Solomon*, another magic island, foresaw a future in which modern science would create technical marvels (including telephones, airplanes, and submarines) that would end poverty, hard labor, and disease.

The new individualism introduced by the Reformation in matters of religious conscience bolstered the Renaissance's emphasis on individual self-interest and political liberty, each reinforcing the other. As R. H. Tawney observed in his classic *Religion and the Rise of Capitalism*, the repression of the desires called for by Protestantism to purify Christians of their worldly attachments struck a surprising partnership with the repression of the desires required to work hard and be thrifty and diligent so as to get ahead in business – it became known as "the Protestant work ethic," or what Tawney called "worldly asceticism." These forces coalesced in the antiroyalist side in the English Civil War, known as the Roundheads – made up of fierce Protestant zealots (they cropped their hair to show they were not vain about their appearance) who wanted an end to all traces of popery, including the remaining Catholic overtones of the Church of England, along with proponents of secular republican liberty and commercial enterprise, frequently the same people and overwhelmingly middle class. Facing them on the opposing side were the Cavaliers – defenders of the absolute authority of the Crown by divine right, leaning toward Catholicism or at least a very Roman or "high" version of the Anglican liturgy (bells and smells), overwhelmingly aristocratic, with the long tresses, plumed hats, and rich clothing of a Renaissance fop, hunters and horsemen, dissolute and chivalrous.

In some ways, the Stuarts were ideal Renaissance monarchs. Their impeccable sense of style is captured in Van Dyke's portraits. They were patrons of the arts and scientific discovery (the Royal Society, partly inspired by Bacon's *House of Solomon*, was founded by Charles II). James I, by commissioning an authoritative English translation of the Bible, made possible a literary masterpiece that also, by James' conscious intention, straddled the strictness of the Puritan approach with a richness of expression that suited the more "Roman" Anglican liturgy, hoping the new Bible would help bring these extremes together. But the Stuarts also tried to exercise the absolute power established by Henry VIII in order to levy taxes without parliament's consent, and Parliament was not having it from these Scotsmen – besides which, one of them (Charles I) was suspiciously popish in his religious leanings, while James II, by going public with his secret conversion to Catholicism, was forced to abdicate.

The more radical antiroyalist forces like the Levelers were even advocating an early version of communism, in which men's possessions would be equal and all class distinctions eradicated. But most Roundheads, who included some lords, gentry, and many well-off merchants and tradesmen, didn't want to go this far. The defeat and execution by beheading of Charles I sent a shock wave throughout Europe. Never before had a crowned king, still thought by many to be God's anointed and deputy on earth, been bound and executed in public like a criminal, when it once would have meant the death penalty merely to lay hands on him. The Stuarts were followed by a republic whose squabbling led to its forcible dissolution and the six-year Protectorate of Oliver Cromwell, the Lord Protector whom Harrington had idealized as the Lord Archon of his utopian island republic Oceana.

Cromwell was a man who embodied the contradictions of the age. A member of the minor gentry and, before the Civil War, an undistinguished MP and tax collector, it would be hard to know whether to describe him as a Puritan Machiavellian or a Machiavellian Puritan. He advocated with equal force an end to arbitrary royal power on behalf of republican liberty and a strict Puritan version of the Protestant faith, with no mass, no incense, no trappings, and the Presbyterian practice of a church government elected by the congregation in place of an ordained priesthood. He preached complete individual freedom of worship, although in practice he loathed Catholics (his campaign in Ireland was extremely brutal). The Protectorate sponsored a nationwide campaign of "Godly reformation" to encourage hard work by abolishing inns, theaters, and sports. Cromwell might be described as a Puritan republican dictator, somewhat, as suggested earlier, like the Roman dictators of old, except a prim, straitlaced, and choleric Lutheran to boot. Although a complete amateur at war, he proved a brilliant general and created the New Model Army out of peasants and tradesmen that unexpectedly defeated the plumed professional cavalrymen of the Stuarts. When Cromwell died of a urinary infection in 1658, many believed that his own dictatorial power had come to rival that of the toppled Stuarts, including some of the trappings of a monarch.

Two years later, tired of this experiment in republican and Godly dictatorship, Parliament brought back the Stuarts who, although they promised to be good and not attempt to rule without Parliament's consent, were soon up to their old tricks. James II tipped the scales by openly proclaiming his fealty to the Church of Rome. He was driven into exile, and Parliament invited Prince William of Orange from friendly, business-minded, Protestant Holland to assume the throne, a marriage to James' daughter (with whom he was to reign jointly) grafting him onto the legitimate bloodline. He solemnly undertook to consult Parliament on all money matters, while Parliament decreed that as head of the Church of England, he and all his successors must be Protestant.

In this way, the religious, economic, and social forces once suppressed by the iron hand of the Tudors, and which burst their bonds during the Civil War, were now reconciled in what was called the Glorious Revolution of 1688, one of three great revolutions of the modern world, followed by the American Revolution of 1776 and the French Revolution of 1789, about which more in Part Three. With an elected House of Commons that was the source of all legislative and budgetary authority and a monarch who, although still rather powerful (especially in military affairs), could not rule arbitrarily but was himself subject to the rule of law, and who over time began to consult as his first minister whoever commanded a majority of votes in the Commons, the Westminster model of government – "the Crown in Parliament" – assumed its basic outline. Now the monarch truly was a monarch – a constitutional monarch – rather than a tyrant, even a reforming tyrant or a tyrant who came to the throne by legitimate descent like Henry VIII. It was an ingenious combination of the venerable aura of hereditary royalty with limited powers that amounted increasingly over time to those of a largely symbolic figurehead. To be sure, the new arrangements created by the Glorious Revolution did not quite add up to a republic, but it was a balance of powers among commons, lords, and crown not unlike what Machiavelli had praised about ancient Rome.

As we've seen, Thomas Hobbes had provided a theoretical justification for the absolute monarchy to which the Stuarts aspired. Ironically, the Stuarts did not like Hobbes' defense of their despotism, because he based it on utilitarian arguments about what was best for society and its material interests, whereas they truly believed in the divine right of kings as God's sole arbiters on earth of both religious and secular affairs originating with Henry VIII's importation of Caesaropapism to England. After the Stuarts were swept from the throne once and for all, the script for the Glorious Revolution was written by the Cambridge philosopher John Locke. Religious tolerance (but not yet for Catholics); the inalienable natural right to acquire private property, which no government could infringe upon without proving itself tyrannical; the prohibition against Parliament raising taxes without the consent of the property-owners whose interests they were elected to represent; a general endorsement of freedom of thought; more humane methods of child rearing; independence of women from the absolute authority of their husbands; and the importance of a liberal education in the classics – this was to be the new England at its best in Locke's vision.

Locke struggled unsuccessfully to find a way of distinguishing between the private religious beliefs of Catholics, which should be tolerated, and their supposed political loyalty to a hostile foreign power, the papacy. Gradually, toleration was extended to Catholics, and by 1829 they possessed close to equal civil rights. Was this the outcome of the secular reasoning about the rights of man that began in the Renaissance and Enlightenment, or did Protestantism itself contribute to religious tolerance in the long run? It's an open question. We've seen how closely connected the Reformation was in England to the Parliamentary cause. The Glorious Revolution both limited the powers of the Crown and insisted that no one but a Protestant monarch could be the "defender of the faith," serving both the Renaissance aim of free self-government and the sectarian aims of the Reformation. Throughout the English Civil War and the religious wars in Europe, both Catholics and Protestants committed atrocities against each other. During Cromwell's Protectorate, many Protestants wanted a theocracy every bit as overbearing as anything that had existed under the papacy. But while Protestantism initially may have been no more open to tolerance than its Catholic foe, it might be fair to say that the *inner logic* of the Reformation compelled it over time to practice just such tolerance of other denominations and creeds. For the entire Lutheran claim to the right to break away from Rome was based in the first place on the central conviction that every individual ought to be able to commune with God in his own way. If this was every man's right – extending, fairly quickly, to freedom of thought not just about religion but about everything – then it must eventually reach the conclusion that Catholics and people of other faiths possessed these same rights. It was long in coming, but as a matter of principle, it seems to me that it had to come.

Although tyranny did not disappear from British life (you could have asked the Scottish and English tenant farmers driven out during the "enclosure" of common lands by greedy nobles, or the Irish whose lands were seized for being Catholic), it was never again a danger on English soil in the sense of taking the form of the entire government (as opposed to periodic reprehensible actions), as it had been, in the view of many, under the Tudors, Stuarts, and Cromwell. During the eighteenth century, the Church of England became a national institution of religious reconciliation as Elizabeth had originally hoped it would. From Low Anglican to High Anglican, it contained all but the most independent-minded of Puritans who could abide no form of ordained clergy (many of them went to the New World) and those who, aside from not accepting that "the Bishop of Rome" was head of their church, in all liturgical and theological matters, including the Eucharist, were almost identical to Roman Catholics, including reciting the Nicene Creed, and all shades in between. It was a powerful source of social cohesion until only just recently.

Earlier, we mentioned the theory that there is an overlap between the prospects for liberal democracy and its resistance to tyranny and the geographical spheres of the Occidental Church and the Orthodox Church. Before the Reformation, there was already relatively greater leeway for secular political authority independent of the church than there was in the Caesaropapist east, and the prospects for free government, if the theory is valid, were, therefore, greater in Europe with its Occidental rite than in the Orthodox east. When the new sphere of the Reformation is added to Occidental Christianity, it is striking that those countries where Protestantism early on became the main religious preference – England, its colonies in the New World, the Low Countries, Lutheran northern Germany – are also the modern countries where secular democracy and a market economy have taken deepest root, while countries that remained predominantly in the Latin Church – France, Italy and Spain – have had a rockier path toward democratic self-government and an economy based on market forces. Spain is a telling case in point. At the time of the Spanish Armada, Spain was a world superpower. Yet because a strong middle-class work ethic did not take root there due to a traditional religious distrust of commercial enterprise and the contempt of the aristocracy for the life of a tradesman, the vast plunder the Spanish monarchy acquired in the New World was squandered on magnificent palaces and cathedrals, not invested in the economy to create lasting wealth. Spain declined into a creaking, parochial backwater. As for France, it eventually became a liberal democracy, but only (as we'll see in Part Three) after a revolution much more violent than those of England and America, and only after successive waves of imperial rule and further revolutionary outbreaks among its never fully reconciled democratic, royalist, and ecclesiastical factions.

Now of course one only has to state this theory to see how many holes there might be in it. If democracy's roots were deeper in Protestant Germany than in the Latin south, how to explain National Socialism, one of the worst tyrannies in history? (I will try to answer this in Part Three). Still, while it may not be a flawless match, on the whole, the possibility that liberal democracy is a better fit with countries with a heritage of Protestant individualism remains an intriguing one to which we will return.

THE TYRANT AS STATE BUILDER LIVES ON:
BENEVOLENT DESPOTISM

As our discussion of the reforming tyrant as modern state builder comes to a close, we have to bear in mind that much of Europe took a very different route after the Glorious Revolution. The trail blazed by Henry VIII – modernization from above through royal autocracy – goes on for another century in much of Europe, and comes to be known as Enlightened or Benevolent Despotism. The outstanding examples are Louis XIV (1638–1715), Peter the Great (1672–1725), Frederick the Great (1712–1786) and Catherine the Great (1729–1796). History's bestowal of the title "great" on a string of them was not necessarily because they were *morally* great (far from it) but because their ambition, belligerence, and Machiavellian lack of scruples were necessary to wrench their own pre-modern societies out of the feudal past and force them by a breached passage into the future. Like Henry, they came to their thrones through hereditary descent and so weren't reforming tyrants in the strict sense of charismatic usurpers – "new men," like Oedipus or Julius Caesar. But also like Henry, they were revolutionaries who used their powers to set aside traditional and legal restraints in order to build more powerful societies, hallmarks of the classic reforming tyrant. They combined reform at home with aggressive imperialism abroad. After all, you couldn't carry out big reforms until you had acquired a big country to transform. While different in many ways, they shared the domineering strength of will to shape human nature and external circumstances that Machiavelli regarded as the unique stamp of "the most outstandingly virtuous princes" – the capacity, as he put it, to "master Fortuna" and "introduce form into matter" so as to create "new modes and orders." When crossed, they were also capable of the titanic rage that marks the tyrannical personality throughout history all the way back to Achilles.

On a scale that exceeded even the Tudors, Louis XIV followed Machiavelli's script for modernization by crushing the nobility, raising the common people, and controlling religion. His reign of seventy-two years, a length unmatched in European history, laid the basis for a centralized, powerful, and prosperous

France. For much of this time, France was Europe's leading power and fought three major wars. Like Caesar with Mark Antony and Octavian with Agrippa, Louis knew how to delegate authority to able men (including his ministers Mazarin and Colbert and his general Turenne) and wasn't jealous of their achievements so long as they served him unswervingly. This is often a hallmark of the most successful reforming tyrants, unlike ordinary tyrants such as Caligula who take anyone else's merit as a personal insult, destroying them even if it means weakening their own regime. In this, Louis was more consistent than Henry VIII, who sometimes (as in the case of Thomas Cromwell) succumbed to resentment of his advisors' eminence (or, later, Stalin, who would execute generals and scientists who outclassed him). Louis encouraged the rise of talent and also lavishly patronized artists (Le Brun), writers (Moliere, La Fontaine) and composers (Lully, Couperin) as adornments of his reign, leading to his famous nickname, "the Sun King," the source of all enlightenment, beauty, and grace.

An early revolt by the aristocracy against the Bourbon monarchy's centralization of authority, which threatened their feudal autonomy and privileges, was put down by Cardinal Mazarin, who played a role comparable to that of Thomas Cromwell for Henry. The peace of Westphalia, which added Alsace and Strasbourg to France, was followed by a final aristocratic revolt, the Fronde. Just as with the Tudors, the old aristocracy resented being replaced by royal bureaucrats elevated from among the commoners. Louis preferred them because they were loyal only to him. (As Machiavelli had advised, the common people will love the prince for whatever benefits he gives them, even just being left in peace to work and prosper, whereas the nobles will always resent having to acknowledge his pre-eminence). After defeating the Fronde, Louis played to the French people's desire for an end to civil strife in order to extend his control. His minister Colbert bolstered French commerce and trade through mercantilist policies as had the Tudors and Stuarts and, like the Ottomans, Colbert invited craftsman from all over Europe to work in France. Like the Tudors as well, Louis acquired colonies, not only in America but in Africa and Asia, sponsoring explorers like La Salle (who established Louisiana along the Mississippi). The military was professionalized, with senior ranks no longer automatically reserved for noblemen, whose private feudal armies were outlawed as they had been in England.

The Code Louis was the first system of laws for all of France, a mark of reforming despots going all the way back to Hammurabi, Julius Caesar, and Justinian. Like a number of the Caesars, Louis was an avid urban planner who adorned Paris and created the boulevards. His intended masterpiece was the palace of Versailles. With what has always struck me as its cold, almost inhuman grandeur, long reflecting pools stretching to the horizon, vast statue-studded, geometrically carved groves imposed on an enormous artificially flattened landscape, and its hundreds of gilded, art-plastered rooms each more resplendent than the last, it was meant to overawe and dazzle. Like the ancient god-king palaces of the east that we discussed in Part One, including more recent versions such as Topkapi and the Alhambra, Versailles was a microcosm of a world made orderly through royal control, with Louis literally at its center. Like the Sultans and the late Roman emperors, he was unapproachable by all but the highest ranks. These great nobles, dukes, marquises, and counts, formerly akin to monarchs on their own estates, now waited on Louis as participants in an elaborate court ceremonial recalling the Ottomans and Byzantines, living permanently at Versailles and anxiously vying for the incomparable privilege of handing the Sun King his napkin, fork, or toilet paper. Owners of enormous chateaux back home, they lived in tiny warrens at Versailles rather than forsake their place near Louis the Great.

The court at Versailles promoted the pursuit of wit, elegance, amorous intrigue, and foppishness like the Stuarts to the power of ten (beautifully captured in the 1996 French film *Ridicule*). Louis himself danced in ballets staged at court some eighty times, recalling the performing aspirations of Nero, though fortunately not resembling him in other respects. By contrast, it is hard to picture William of Orange dancing in a ballet in Protestant England. The palace of the Louvre, established by Louis as a national gallery, acquired some of the exiled Stuarts' extraordinary art collection of Renaissance masters from the grim-wig Puritans at fire-sale prices. (Too many breasts swirling licentiously in the clouds).

Louis consolidated his absolute power over the Catholic Church in France, imitating the caesaropapist model of the Byzantine emperors first revived in the West by Henry VIII. He controlled all appointments of bishops and all doctrinal matters. No appeal over his head to the pope was allowed, and the clergy were forbidden to excommunicate any official who carried out the King's orders. With his revocation of the Edict of Nantes, Louis also outlawed Protestantism. For him, the lack of complete religious conformity in France suggested a lack of complete royal control over the entire country, which was intolerable. In other words, he had the same motive as the Tudors – control of religion by the state – with merely a different outcome. He was less guided by piety in this policy than by modern theorists of absolute monarchy like Hobbes, who argued that the Sovereign can and must dictate his subjects' religious beliefs. Unlike England, which had a strong Protestant presence by Henry's time, France had remained overwhelmingly Catholic. It therefore suited Louis' grab for complete control to patronize Catholicism exclusively, just as it had suited Henry's grab for complete control to suppress it. As a practical matter, Louis' domination of the Church in France was every bit as complete as Henry's domination of it in England. The pope, needless to say, protested this exclusion of Rome's authority within France, to no avail. We need not doubt the reports that, on a personal level, Louis was devout and pious – that was not incompatible with a Machiavellian drive to subordinate religion to the crown. Henry had also continued to love the old Roman mass once the pope had been jettisoned.

In the shifting chessboard of wars of dynastic succession that convulsed Europe throughout his reign, Louis first faced an alliance led by the Holy Roman Empire including Spain. William of Orange, now William III of England, brought his new Protestant kingdom into this anti-French coalition over Louis' support of the exiled Catholic Stuarts. No sooner was this conflict settled than a dispute erupted over the succession to the Spanish throne, which passed from the childless Charles II of Spain to Louis' kinsman the Duke of Anjou, now to be Philip V of Spain. The prospect of this dual Gallican-Iberian monarchy added to France's growing reputation for arrogance and aggression and provoked a new alliance against Louis. Threatened with an invasion of France by the brilliant English commander Marlborough and the equally brilliant Eugene of Savoy, Louis made peace by agreeing that the Spanish crown should pass instead to the Archduke Charles, brother of the Holy Roman Emperor. But when the Archduke succeeded his brother, becoming both Holy Roman Emperor and King of Spain, England and the Dutch Republic were suddenly more worried about this vast new superpower than they were about France, and they turned from foes of France into allies.

As a result of his dexterous machinations in war and diplomacy, by the end of Louis' reign, France's expanded borders were largely preserved, and remained unchanged until the French Revolution. The French court had meanwhile become admired throughout Europe for its exquisite manners, culture, and style, and French became the dominant language of Europe's upper crust. Like all great despots, the Sun King was loathed by some and idolized by others. Saint-Simon claimed that "there was nothing he liked so much as flattery." But Napoleon, who generally hated the Bourbons, described him as "the only King of France worthy of the name." For Lord Acton, he was "by far the ablest man who was born in modern times on the steps of a throne," a happy combination of royal birth with a fierce in-born natural ability. While vain, Louis was not cruel, and was credited with a generally mild and gracious character. Married twice and relatively amicably, he took a long series of mistresses and sired many illegitimate children, blending the reforming tyrant with the garden-variety hedonist, as had Caesar, Henry, and so many others. Recalling the Roman imperial cult beginning with Augustus, there was a systematic cult of personality surrounding Louis, including the standardized depiction of him in hundreds of portraits and sculptures throughout France, often blending his features with those of major Roman emperors, the god Apollo or Alexander the Great. There is no proof he ever said "*L'etat, c'est moi,*" but he did say, "It is legal because I wish it," along with the observation, straight out of Machiavelli's *The Prince,* "there is little that can withstand a man who can conquer himself."

In our gallery of tyrants, reforming or otherwise, Peter the Great must be one of the more bizarre personalities. Towering at six feet eight inches over most of his fellow Russians, but with a head too small for his giant's frame, afflicted with a nervous tic of the mouth, he was both a pinhead and a weirdo. He had a crippling phobia about insects. The mere sight of a cockroach sent him into convulsions, and wherever he traveled in Russia, new houses had to be built for him that were cockroach free.

At times, he seemed like a large, guileless boy and tech nerd. During his grand tours of Europe, he studied the latest advances in shipbuilding (Amsterdam), architecture and urban planning (Manchester), agronomy, dentistry (believe it!), how to catch and mount butterflies, and the use of a firehose. He met with locksmiths, shipwrights, and seamen to learn their skills, sometimes (unthinkable for most monarchs) doing manual labor himself. He would naively write reports of these experiences as "Farmer Peter" and so forth, apparently actually believing he was traveling incognito, despite an enormous entourage of courtiers. In England, he met William III. In Amsterdam he was exposed to European art, while the neoclassical beauty of Leipzig, Dresden, and Vienna fired his dreams of his own new capital. Yet for all his love of technical learning and willingness to be instructed by what he regarded as superior European culture, he was immensely ambitious, calculating, forceful, and capable of great brutality, having his own son pitilessly tortured in order to extract a confession when he was suspected of plotting his father's overthrow. His son later died from the injuries he received during this savage treatment.

It doesn't go too far to say that Peter literally willed Russia into existence as a great modern nation. He followed the same general script as the Tudors and Bourbons for state-building at home and imperial (including naval) expansion abroad. In keeping with Machiavelli's original Renaissance vision of princely supremacy, he, too, crushed the power of the nobility, promoted meritocracy and commerce, and centralized the state's power. Through a combination of wars that expanded Russian power abroad and a cultural revolution at home to eradicate the medieval past, Peter left Russia a major power bent on scientific and technological progress like Europe.

Whereas, beginning with the Tudors, formerly feudal European monarchies imported the caesaropapist model from the east in order to modernize their countries from the top down in keeping with the values of the Renaissance and Reformation, Peter did the opposite. Having inherited an already absolute eastern autocracy, that of tsardom, Peter imported the western project of modernization from Europe in order to impose it from the top down, revitalizing an ancient eastern people with new European ideas. Unlike Henry VIII and Louis XIV, who had to modernize ancient European nations, Peter first had to *create* a European country from above in order to modernize it. Whereas they had to win their way to autocratic power by degrees, Peter was born a Caesaropapist autocrat. Like the Byzantine emperors and Ottoman Sultans, he owned everything and everyone. Although he relied heavily on technical advisors from Europe to carry out the reorganization of the Russian army along modern lines, as well as on certain top generals like James Bruce, he appeared not to have a major *eminence grise* on the order of Thomas Cromwell, who at his height was almost Henry's partner in power. Peter did everything important by his own direct command. Ordering his own son to be tortured to death was a sign of absolute mastery that even European despots like Henry or Louis had quailed at asserting over those of noble blood. Their nobles, to say nothing of their heirs, were exempt from such horrors – in England, even convicted traitors, if noble, were merely beheaded rather than subjected to the agony of being hanged, drawn, and quartered as were commoners. But Peter owned every Russian body and soul as literally as the master class of ancient Rome had owned its slaves. Serf or lord, the Tsar could order them clubbed to death on the spot on any pretext.

In effect, Peter colonized his own country from above in order to make it accept what he saw as the superiority of European culture, science, and technical advancements – but never, of course, self-government of the English sort. The contrast between how he found Russia and how he left it is symbolized by the contrast between Moscow and St. Petersburg. Moscow, with its colorful onion domes, hearkened back to the connection between Russia and Byzantium, including the Orthodox rite, dating back to the conversion of Vladimir the Great, Prince of Novgorod, in 987. Petersburg, by contrast, was a magnificent Baroque capital inspired by Rome and Paris, as if airlifted and set down fully built near the Arctic Circle by a titanic act of despotic will (thousands perished building it). Its construction was the most spectacular effort at using architecture to encode imperial values since the Roman Empire.

When Peter came to the throne, Russia's nobility, the boyars, traced their culture to Byzantium and their distant Mongolian origins – they wore long caftans, soft turban-like hats, and full beards. By the time Peter was through with them, this traditional Muscovite look had been forcibly transformed literally overnight into the frock coats, tight breeches, and powdered wigs of Versailles. Peter personally supervised the shearing of the boyars' beards. The cultural tug of war between Peter's Europhile vision for Russia, summed up by Petersburg, and its older eastern or Eurasian roots summed up by Moscow, has been a driving force in Russian history down to the present day – Turgenev versus Dostoeievsky, Sakharov versus Solzhenitsyn, Gorbachev versus Putin, the Enlightenment versus Slavophile tribal nationalism. As we'll see in Part Three, this cultural struggle decisively shaped Russia's engagement with its final European colonization from above, Marxism-Leninism.

Although officially an autocrat when he ascended the throne at the age of ten, in practice, of course, it took time for Peter to seize the reins of the untrammeled power to which he was entitled. Like the Byzantine and Ottoman courts, the gloomy recesses of the Kremlin swirled with intrigue. The Streltsy, Russia's feudal military aristocracy, aided Peter in his struggle to win his powers from a sister and mother who ruled as regents when he was young. But later, as they realized the threat that absolute monarchy posed to their traditional status (the same threat posed by the Tudors and Louis XIV to the feudal nobility), the Streltsy plotted against him. Rushing home from one of his European tours to crush their rebellion, he had over 1200 of the rebels tortured and executed. After that, the Russian nobles took peacefully to their frock coats. All such rebellions during his reign were crushed with similar thoroughness and violence.

Like Louis, Peter reorganized the army along professional lines, robbing the Strelsty of their hereditary right to be commanders, further alienating them in the same way as had the Tudors and Bourbons with their own noble orders. He rapidly constructed a modern navy and dreamt of Russia becoming a great maritime power. His foreign policy, like that of his successors including Catherine the Great, was driven by the search for sea ports in the north and south, pitting him in a long dual struggle with Sweden and the Ottoman empire. The capture of the Ottoman Black Sea port Azov in 1696 marked a first victory for his new navy. He visited Europe the following year to try and drum up an anti-Ottoman alliance. He didn't succeed – France and Austria did not want a new confrontation with the Ottomans while preoccupied with the war over the Spanish Succession that we discussed earlier in connection with Louis.

Peter declared war on Sweden in a bid to gain control of the Baltic Sea, enlisting the help of the Poles and Lithuanians. After ups and downs including a naval defeat at Narva in 1700, Russia decisively defeated the Swedish army at the battle of Poltava nine years later. Overreaching, Peter turned immediately to renewed war with the Ottomans, which ended in disaster as he was forced to return his Black Sea ports and the Ottomans acquired a chunk of today's Latvia. But Peter made up for these setbacks by seizing great chunks of the former Swedish sphere of influence including Estonia and Finland. In both foreign and domestic affairs, Peter set the course for Russia's development. Catherine the Great continued Peter's dual efforts at Europeanization and imperial expansion. She conducted a long correspondence with Voltaire, the famous French intellectual, skeptic, political liberal, critic of aristocratic privilege, drawing room wit, and all-purpose man of letters, whom she regarded as her mentor, and brought German farmers to settle along the Volga river, regarding them as harder and more intelligent workers than Russians. She also destroyed the Ottoman fleet and partitioned Poland with Austria and Prussia.

The enormous multinational Russian Empire founded by Peter filled the uneasy vacuum where Occidental Christianity and the modern West met the unstable zone of Orthodox Christianity and a declining Ottoman East, buffered in central and eastern Europe by the fragmentary hodgepodge of the Austro-Hungarian Empire. After the Ottoman Empire fell in 1917, the ensuing tug of war between Russia and the Austro-Hungarians for control of the vacuum left in the Balkans helped ignite WWI and was finally brutally resolved by Stalin, who gobbled up nearly all of it after WWII. Vladimir Putin's annexation of the Crimea and menacing of Ukraine shows that, despite the subsequent collapse of the Soviet Empire in central Europe in 1989, domination of the region by a latter-day autocrat may be up for grabs again and is of a piece with Russian geopolitics since Peter and Catherine (which does not excuse its complete illegality).

In the later years of his reign, Peter continued to methodically concentrate power in his own hands. While away on his military campaigns, instead of following tradition and having the Duma, the old council of the boyars (whom he still mistrusted) govern in his place, he abolished it and created a "senate" of ten members completely loyal to himself. He also diluted the power of the patriarch of Moscow, traditional head of the Orthodox Church, by letting the office lapse and replacing it with a council of ten clergymen, also Petrine loyalists. New rules prevented men from becoming monks – Peter felt that too many Russians were wasting themselves as clerics instead of joining his new professional army. In 1721 he was officially proclaimed "Emperor of all Russia" – trumping the older title "Tsar," derived from "Caesar" – in a bid to place himself on the same level of precedence as the Holy Roman Emperor. He had rejected the alternative title of "Emperor of the East," with its overtones of a restored Byzantium and implicit fencing off of Russia from the European West. Like Henry VIII and Louis XIV, as a modernizing despot, Peter wanted to be known as the founder of a new nationality, not an old-fogey feudal or Christian dynast. One of the ironies of the tyrant as state builder is that the origin of modern national identity as something territorial and often ethnically homogeneous often begins with enlightened despotism, as opposed to the feudal polyglot of widely dispersed fiefdoms based on centuries-old royal blood ties and intermarriage that could, weirdly to us today, make the Netherlands belong to Spain or Sicily to a family of Norman knights.

A year later, codifying his efforts to replace the influence of the hereditary boyar nobility with a new service aristocracy based on merit, Peter created the Table of Ranks. Like the Tudors and Louis XIV, he was determined that status would no longer be determined solely by birth, but by talent demonstrated in service to the Emperor. This hierarchy of officialdom remained in effect until the Russian Revolution in 1917, led by a man whose father had been ennobled for his abilities as a Tsarist bureaucrat. Like Henry, who had encouraged English nobles to become "gentlemen" through attending university, and also like the Ottoman vision of the Janissaries, an elite of soldier-administrators, Peter decreed compulsory education, especially in mathematics and geometry, for the children of noblemen and of imperial officials. He did not live to see the completion of his palace near St. Petersburg, a sprawling complex of gardens, fountains, gilt, and loot that became known as the Russian Versailles.

Throughout Part Two, we have seen how the Renaissance, in partnership with the new spirit of independence spread by the Reformation, and summed up in Machiavelli's recipe for either republican liberty *or* the improvement of the common people's lot through rational despotism, sought inspiration in the greatness of Greco-Roman antiquity – its civic spiritedness, its philosophical, literary, and artistic treasures, and its heroism – to build a better, brighter world of the future.

Louis XVI and Peter the Great adorned their own new national kingdoms with the splendors of neoclassical architecture, art, and sculpture. Our final Great, Frederick, built the first of Berlin's magnificent museums, a collection of antiquities housed in a pavilion of stern Doric columns suggesting that Prussia was the inheritor of ancient Spartan manliness. Frederick also built a beautiful folly of pseudo-Roman "ruins" that can be viewed at the end of a long park from the terrace of his magnificent baroque palace with its Bernini-like circular colonnade, *Sans Souci*. It really does look like something you might glimpse from a distance down a shady lane in Rome or in the Campagna – just suggestive traces of the remains of an ancient amphitheater and the columns of a temple framed by poplars. Yet Frederick was so busy conquering countries for his new Prussian Empire – including Silesia and a large swath of Poland – that he was never able to go on the Grand Tour. He never saw those ruins himself, but had to rely on prints by Piranesi and others in order to envision them. The architectural folly at San Souci was an act of instant nostalgia, the "recollection" of something he had never laid eyes on. There is something touching about how much he loved the classical heritage whose remains were barred to him. But, of course, they were barred to him because he had made war on half of Europe! It's hard to be a tourist when you're always at the head of an army of invasion.

Like the other enlightened despots, Frederick combined a lust for imperial conquest with a profound admiration for the modern age's new ideals of tolerance, open-mindedness, intellectual ferment, and liberal education – as long as he was the unquestioned master. His palaces were crammed with treasures of ancient and Renaissance art. He hosted Voltaire near Sans Souci for three years, just for the handsomely reimbursed pleasure of his irreverent and sparkling conversation, starring in lavish dinners mounted by Frederick for any local or visiting intellectual luminaries he could find. (Eventually he and Voltaire fell out over Voltaire's dislike of militarism). Frederick's large library contained all the Greek and Roman classics, which he read in the original languages, much French literature and philosophy, but not a single volume in German. The French culture of the Enlightenment, with its emphasis on clarity, proportion, finesse, elegance, polished manners, and emotional detachment, was still considered the high-water mark. German Romanticism and the storm and stress of passionate emotion, both personal and political, that it opened up were only beginning to be born.

A gifted musician, Frederick composed a hundred flute sonatas. He built up the reputation of the Prussian Academy, making it a home for distinguished intellectuals including Immanuel Kant and Jean le Rond D'Alembert. With Voltaire's help, he wrote a tract called the *Anti-Machiavel*, a defense of high moral virtue as the best guide for government in contrast with the Florentine's unscrupulous recommendations for power seeking in *The Prince*, very popular as a guidebook for benevolent despotism in the eighteenth century. But as Voltaire drolly remarked about Frederick's essay, the first thing someone who truly understood Machiavelli would do would be to write a high-minded critique of him, disguising his own ruthless pursuit of power under the mantle of idealism. In other words, Voltaire saw through Frederick, although it's possible that Frederick really did believe he was acting out of a desire to do good for his people as a virtuous prince. As we've seen throughout this book, many reforming tyrants see themselves that way.

Frederick was miserable with his arranged marriage to Elizabeth of Brunswick – the two lived apart and Frederick may have been homosexual. He aspired to rule as a philosopher-king, taking Marcus Aurelius as his model. It's fair to say that he did combine the spirit of both Sparta and Athens to a high degree – he was both a warrior and a promoter of the Enlightenment. He was fearless in battle, leading his troops personally, and had six horses shot out from under him. He was also regarded as a military genius for his reorganization of the Prussian army and the studies he wrote on strategy and tactics. Like the other enlightened despots, he promoted internal trade (through high tariffs) and a civil service based on meritocracy rather than on noble birth. (Commoners now could become judges and senior administrators). Government grain stores protected the common people in times of famine. He promoted religious tolerance throughout his realm, but Protestantism, with its emphasis on self-control and hard work, became the favored faith.

The dark and aggressive side of Fredrick's benevolence was manifest in his detestation of the Poles, whom he regarded as backward and barbaric (he referred to them as "all these people with surnames ending with –ski" and as "vile apes") and he was determined to civilize them through conquest. The plunder of Poland was extensive, along with the dissolution of its nobility. On the other hand, by draining swamps to create new farmland, building new canals, introducing new crops, and founding a thousand new farming villages – he described these transformations, with a perhaps unconscious echo of Machiavelli, as "conquering" nature – he really did improve the economic prosperity of his conquered territories through a kind of "Germanization." When he ascended the throne, Prussia was a backwater – on his death, it was one of Europe's major powers. Frederick in these ways embodied many of the traits of the reforming tyrant we have seen throughout this book – capable of good works, enlightened, and magnanimous, but also ruthless in his ambition and his conviction that people must be forced to live better lives under his unquestioned authority.

Let's take a break from the historical account for a moment and make some comparisons between ancient and modern reforming tyrants, because there *are* some differences. Modern reforming tyrants share with their ancient predecessors that same potent mixture of qualities – limitless ambition, a passion for glory, military genius, generosity toward their subjects combined with lethal violence toward anyone getting in their way, a love of learning and beautiful art – that we saw in their most impressive ancient counterparts including Alexander the Great and Julius Caesar. The modern "benevolent despots" we've examined also shared with many of those ancient rulers an ambition to beautify their cities, codify the laws, and to surround themselves with an imposing court ceremonial.

We can put what's *different* into focus by looking at the Roman Empire, the culmination, as we saw in Part One, of the fusion between the Greek heroic ideal of manliness first celebrated by Homer and the universal rational despotism evolved by the god-kings of the east. Although Roman citizens possessed equal rights under the law, it never entered the mind of any Roman emperor to work for the equality of opportunity, let alone equality of condition, for the great mass of toiling mankind. That would not only have been beyond Rome's economic capacity, but would also have violated the very order of nature that the empire claimed to embody as its aristocratic creed of legitimacy. For all moral philosophy going back to Plato had emphatically maintained that superior and inferior human beings existed by nature; that people fated to toil for a living would never possess the leisure of the propertied classes to cultivate their virtues, and that to encourage them to rise in life could only come at the expense of the naturally superior and the great wealth they needed in order to live like gentlemen. Moreover, although Rome built roads and fleets to support commerce within its domains, its technology evolved very little throughout hundreds of years. The notion that scientific knowledge could serve any public purpose – military, economic, or social – was also unknown, since the purpose of natural philosophy was to contemplate the beautiful order of the cosmos, Plato's "music of the spheres," a contemplative activity also reserved for the educated rich.

As much as the glorious precedent of Rome inspired modern state-building despots, their project differed from the Roman Empire on just about every point. It was guided by the supreme value of the individual, rooted in the Renaissance and the Reformation, and also, in time, the notion that every individual, simply by virtue of being human, should have the opportunity to rise in life based on their merits. Even though modern state-building despots amassed as much power for themselves as they could, broached no opposition, and often brutally suppressed the voices of dissent and demands for the sharing of power, they believed themselves to be working on behalf of the *eventual* triumph of individual rights, self-advancement, and the economic betterment of all.

Moreover, a completely different relationship between state power and scientific and technological knowledge emerged through modern state building than anything to be found in the example of the Roman Empire. Ever since Bacon, modern science no longer saw itself as merely contemplating the beautiful order of nature but, instead, as extracting from nature the technical power to improve the health and longevity of the common man and relieve the masses of their crushing toil. Europe's benevolent despots increasingly encouraged the development of science and technology as ways of improving the lives of their subjects, as well as making technical improvements in manufacture and trade, thereby enhancing their own power. In the longer run, of course, the development of modern machine technology, rail, and electricity also enabled the modern state to centralize its authority – for good or for ill – in a way the Roman Empire never remotely approached.

Meanwhile, back in England as we head into the eighteenth century, life seems tranquil in comparison with these world-shaping titans of war and reform on the continent. No need for enlightened despotism after the Glorious Revolution. Now, in England, the King did not so much rule as reign, with the consent of Parliament and within the limits set by an independent judiciary, though he still had some leeway in military matters. Englishmen were free to work hard and prosper – as the French Enlightenment philosopher Montesquieu observed, a part of England's political genius was that aristocrats were willing to dirty their hands and make money, while successful businessmen were invited into the aristocracy. Ambition was increasingly transferred from war and dueling to economic competition. English life might now lack the peril, the grandeur, the bold ideas and the outsized personalities of the Tudor era, but everyone was humming along in ever-greater comfort. Some, like the arch reactionary Jonathan Swift, nostalgic for the medieval and ancient past, saw his contemporaries as mediocre little busybodies and money-grubbers, parodying the England of William and Mary in *Gulliver's Travels* as "Lilliput," a well-groomed, prim and proper little kingdom of midgets in comparison with the heroic giants of classical antiquity, his Sparta-like aristocratic republic of Brobdignag.

But that was not the mainstream view. If some still found John Locke too much of a leveling radical, with his insistence on the inalienable natural rights of all people, including the right of revolution, religious tolerance, freedom of speech, and the right of women to own property along with men, Edmund Burke came along and dressed up the rise of the Lockean bourgeoisie as a steady, progressive march forward out of the feudal past into the modern present – why, the Glorious Revolution wasn't a revolution all, but an *evolution*. (It had been all but bloodless). Today's earls and dukes might increasingly be shipping or mining magnates, but in Burke's mind they still formed a feudal hierarchy to which the common people owed their deference. (And Burke, an Irish outsider, longed to be accepted by them, bankrupting himself over an expensive country house where he aspired to be regarded as one of the gentry). After all, hadn't Britons as far back as Magna Carta insisted on their property rights (never mind that it really only involved the greatest nobles)?

As we first mentioned in the Introduction, this was the beginning of what came to be known as the Whig theory of history. Covering over the revolutionary violence and brutality of the Tudors and the civil wars, along with the vicious conflicts over religion, it saw history as progressing from earliest times steadily and by stages toward the present. Edward Gibbon, for instance, author of *The Decline and Fall of the Roman Empire*, believed that Enlightenment Europe was finally equaling – and even surpassing – the accomplishments of the Roman Empire in terms of peace, prosperity, and a better life for the common man. Gibbon was well aware of the dangers of tyranny, but tended to believe that the benevolent progress of history toward ever greater liberty, prosperity, and tolerance would make such barbarism less and less possible in the future: "We cannot determine to what height the human species may aspire in their future advance toward perfection; but it may safely be presumed that no people ... will relapse into their original barbarism ... The benefits of law and policy, of trade and manufactures, of arts and sciences, are more solid and permanent." If only he could have seen what would happen in the twentieth century!

In "the New England," as the American colonies were called, Americans were from the get-go pure Lockean individualists in a continent empty of the Burkean vestiges of aristocratic privilege. As Calvinists and Puritans who could not abide even the gentle claims of the Church of England to possess an ecclesiastical hierarchy, they also mixed a talent for agriculture and commerce with a staunch sense of individual liberty and freedom of conscience. Able as in nowhere else on earth to rise on their merits and hard work, Americans on the eve of the American Revolution were on average considerably better off than Englishmen. The complaint that sparked their own revolution – that the Parliament in Westminster taxed them without their consent, lacking as they did representatives there – was straight out of the ninth chapter of John Locke's *Second Treatise of Government*: No taxation without representation. A consistent Whig who believed in freedom and progress (not a Tory, as is sometimes imagined), Edmund Burke supported the American cousins against the imperial war party bent on crushing colonial rebellion gathered around George III, revealing his Lockean true colors under a celebration of Ye Olde England with its cap ever doffed to tradition and precedent. All the Americans wanted, he argued, was the extension of the Glorious Revolution to themselves.

Little did Englishmen or Americans know, regardless of who they sided with in 1776, that only a few years later, a new kind of revolution would make the "tyranny" of George III look like a comic opera martinet, ushering in an era of unprecedented tyrannical aggression, genocide, and totalitarianism, the millenarian brand of tyranny that is still racking the world today. There had always been tyrants as reformers. Now we will see something new – tyrants who lead movements of collective fanaticism whose method of reform is the systematic extermination of hundreds of thousands, then millions, of people. Moreover, whereas both ancients and early moderns like Machiavelli had understood tyranny to be primarily a form of one-man rule, now we will see entire populations animated by the passion for destroying other races or peoples in order to bring about heaven on earth. Their aim, beginning with the French Revolution, is not to replace one kind of authority with another but to end *all* authority on earth forever – "neither God nor master!"

Part Three

The Eagles Will Drop Dead from the Skies: Millenarian Tyranny from Robespierre to Al Qaeda

As the mass executions during the Jacobin Terror of the French Revolution spiraled toward their bloody peak between 1792 and 1794, at the same time, ever more elaborate "Festivals of Virtue" were being staged. These pageants were a curious attempt to create a secular political religion with ancient Greek and Roman overtones, the beginning of the operatic spectacles we associate with subsequent totalitarian movements and regimes from the Bolsheviks' May Day parades and the Nazis' Nuremberg Rallies to the massing of hundreds of thousands of human puppets in the North Korean stage-set "capital" of Pyongyang.

The French Revolution's festivals emphasized a purity and innocence that played in bizarre counterpoint to the daily scenes of unbelievable savagery and sadism unfolding alongside them, and featuring the same players. Alternating with these sentimental and bucolic idylls were intervals of organized horror that even today cannot be read about without amazement. Christopher Hibbert writes about the executions in Paris: "As the heaps of corpses mounted, carts drawn by horses ... were obtained to take them away to the Montrouge quarries. Women helped to load them, breaking off occasionally to dance the Carmagnole, then stood laughing on the slippery flesh ... some with ears pinned to their dresses." He quotes an eyewitness account: "The carts were full of men and women who had just been slaughtered and whose limbs were still flexible because they had not had time to grow cold, so that legs and arms and heads nodded and dangled on either side." Hibbert goes on: "Men were reported by reliable witnesses to have been seen drinking, eating and smoking amidst the carnage, using for tables and chairs the naked bodies of their victims whose clothes had been removed   ." A special public spectacle was designed for the Princesse de Lamballe, Queen Marie Antoinette's closest friend – she "had been stripped and raped; her breasts had been cut off; the rest of her body mutilated" and exposed to the public's jeering. "A man was later accused of having cut off her genitals which he impaled upon a pike and of having ripped out her heart which he ate 'after having roasted it on a cooking-stove.'"

Near-victims of the Terror (a very few of the accused got off) noted how rapidly the executioners could switch from being murderous to sentimental and back again, at one and the same time psychopathic killers and acolytes of the new religion of love, a psychological distortion later termed, in connection with Fascism, "sentimental brutality." They described "men who seemed quite prepared to murder them at one moment" who "were at the next hugging them enthusiastically ... One assassin, refusing an offer of recompense, wept with emotion as he restored a father to his children. 'The nation pays us for killing,' said another who also refused a reward, 'but not for saving lives.'"

The makers of the French Revolution had long fantasized about restoring the stern virtues of the Roman Republic. The leader of the Terror, Maximilien Robespierre, had drunk in this atmosphere of nostalgia for ancient Rome while still a student. One of the revolution's first radical leaders, Jean-Paul Marat ("the time has come," he had proclaimed, "to establish a temporary despotism of freedom to end the despotism of kings"), was given a hero's funeral with overtones of the civil religion sketched by Jean-Jacques Rousseau in *The Social Contract* including pseudo-Roman touches, enflaming Robespierre's own ambition to play a leading role. Hibbert writes: "(Marat's) coffin was followed by young girls in white dresses who strewed flowers upon it, by boys carrying branches of cyprus ... His ashes were later given a place of honor in the Pantheon ... Poems and hymns were composed in his honor ... No less than thirty-seven towns ... were named after him." We can already look ahead to the Soviet Union's portrayal of its own leading executioners as possessing the heroic, larger-than-life status required for the reconstruction of entire societies through genocide, renaming cities after Lenin, Stalin, Sverdlov (the murderer of Czar Nicholas II and his family), and Kirov, Leningrad party boss and killer of thousands of "bourgeois" during the civil war. (Grotesquely, the Imperial Ballet was renamed after this thug and drunkard and is today still widely known as the Kirov Ballet, rather as if there were a Goering Philharmonic or a Heydrich School of Fine Arts in today's Germany).

Another leading Jacobin, Joseph Fouche, a frail former school teacher who implemented the Terror in Lyon, became a prototype of the revolutionary mass murderer and secret police chief (a position he held under Napoleon), the political ancestor of Beria and Himmler. He took particular delight in laying waste to churches and using them to stage his own festivals of virtue. Many of the revolution's leaders followed what they saw as Rousseau's call for a new myth, a new civil religion, to replace both the superstitions of traditional Christianity and the arid rationalism of the Enlightenment. At the peak of his power, Robespierre mounted an especially extravagant spectacle. The deputies of the National Assembly were "surrounded by groups of little boys with garlands of violets on their heads, by young men with wreaths of myrtle, by older men wearing oak, ivy and olive leaves ... An orchestra began to play; the various groups began to sing; the young men drew swords and swore to their elders to defend the fatherland ... "

These sharply contrasting scenes – maidens in white carrying wheat sheaves alternating with mobs howling before a blood-soaked guillotine – illustrate the pathology of Jacobinism, and of all subsequent millenarian revolutions. The people must be broken down and crushed, all their traditions and customary attachments destroyed, in order to be reconstructed into a purer, more harmonious collective. Savagery and sadism run in counterpoint with outbursts of emotion and affection as the people's vices are purged by terror so as to allow their underlying natural goodness to emerge. The return to the "Year One," as the Jacobins proclaimed it, the pageantry of rural greenery and peasant simplicity, of Roman austerity, drove their belief that the people could be stripped of their selfish materialism and vice and forcibly restored to the vanished Golden Age of what Rousseau had called man's "natural condition."

Many of the specific features of later revolutionary genocide are already in evidence in the Jacobin Terror. As the scope of the terror intensifies, so does its sadism. As in the later millenarian revolutions of the Bolsheviks, Nazis, Mao, and the Khmer Rouge, hidden sadists who would ordinarily have to conceal their urges or confine them to private crime are invited to assume a leading role in politics, with accompanying honors and high status. Large-scale political violence is worshipped almost as a mystical religious force. (One deputy of the National Assembly exulted in what he called the "Red Mass" performed daily on "the great altar of the holy guillotine"). Fouche, finding the guillotine too slow for the number of "counterrevolutionary" deaths required, experimented with opening cannon fire into a crowd of detainees, killing three hundred at once, leaving "heaps of mutilated, screaming, half-dead victims who had to be finished off with sabers and musket fire by soldiers physically sickened at the task." Fouche exulted: "Terror, salutary terror, is now the order of the day ... We are causing much impure blood to flow, but it is our duty to do so, it is for humanity's sake." Just as the Bolsheviks would later maintain about class enemies such as the Kulaks, and the Nazis about the Jewish race, the Jacobins believed that violence against the Revolution's enemies was justified by the fact that this single mass bloodletting would usher in a new age of bliss for the rest of mankind for all time. The Jacobin Terror also established the hallmark of future millenarian revolutions that to be suspected of or denounced for disloyalty was almost always tantamount to proof of guilt.

As the Terror spread beyond Paris into the countryside, where further mass executions were organized in areas like the Vendee, which was still loyal to the Church and the *ancien regime*, it became increasingly apparent that most of the victims were not aristocrats at all, but ordinary peasants and workers. For in the end, millenarian revolutionaries are not concerned with serving the actual people around them, even the downtrodden whom they claim to champion. They worship the ideal of a purely virtuous collective for whose sake the endless vices and perfidy of the actual masses must be mercilessly uprooted. As

Lenin was later to put it, Britain's proletariat may have been vastly larger than that of Russia, but that was merely the "empirical" proletariat, so the fact that it did not support a socialist revolution was irrelevant. What mattered was not the support of actual workers, or even their presence in large numbers, but the genuinely revolutionary "proletarian consciousness" of those appointed by history (almost none of whom were actual laborers) to create the workers' new world of collectivized labor. It was to be, as Flaubert's *Sentimental Education* depicted the aims of the revolution of 1848, an "American Sparta" in which the workers would be chained to their lathes and ruled by lawyers, professors, and cafe intellectuals. The same reasoning permitted Lenin and Stalin to identify modestly well-off peasants – the Kulaks – as devious enemies of the revolution deserving nothing but liquidation because their possession of a cow or a few chickens stood in the way of a world untainted by the corruption of private property.

Clearly, in the Terror of 1793, we are already stepping into the world of the Gulag, Auschwitz, the Cultural Revolution, the Killing Fields, and ISIS. How did this madness occur in the heart of Enlightenment Europe?

THE NATURAL CONDITION OF MAN: ROUSSEAU'S MURDEROUS DREAM

If John Locke wrote the script for the Glorious Revolution and the American Revolution, the script for the French Revolution – certainly its culmination in the Jacobin Terror – was written by Jean-Jacques Rousseau, as was recognized at the time by Edmund Burke, later by Robespierre's best (to my mind) biographer Hilaire Belloc, and most recently in Simon Schama's great history of the French Revolution, *Citizens*. Rousseau, intentionally or not (a long debate), was the godfather of the French Revolution and all subsequent millenarian revolutions. The first two great modern revolutions, the Glorious Revolution and the American Revolution, were liberal revolutions for the rights of man and the liberty of the individual. They were revolutions sparked by the Age of Reason and the Enlightenment. Rousseau begins the great Romantic protest against the Enlightenment and calls for "the people's" collective return to a Golden Age of Arcadian bliss without property, class, or religion, and the submersion of the individual in the General Will.

By the time Rousseau started to become a well-known writer in the 1750s, Europe had undergone a remarkable transformation since a century or so earlier. The old feudal order was giving way to absolute monarchs who, as we saw in Part Two, promoted the spread of commerce and the advancement of knowledge for the benefit of the masses. Locke, "the founder of the Enlightenment" according to Peter Gay, who was deeply admired by the French *philosophes* including Voltaire (for whom he was "the man of the greatest wisdom ... What he has not seen clearly, I despair of ever seeing"), had argued that the social contract exists solely to enhance the self-interest and security of the individual. If the representatives we elect protect our interests, especially our property rights, that government is legitimate, and its role should end there. Governments should encourage the rise of peaceful private enterprise but otherwise leave people to live as they please, as long as they don't harm others. The state should not legislate public morality or any particular religious doctrine (as another of Locke's admirers Thomas Jefferson wrote, "it neither picks my pocket nor breaks my leg" if my neighbor says "there are twenty gods or no God"). This transformation took a long time to take hold and did so at an uneven rate. But by Rousseau's era, the height of the French Enlightenment, government had found its own power increased by promoting these measures, while the *philosophes* mounted attacks on all remnants of the old public morality – against censorship, against intolerance, against militarism. It was the systematic repudiation of the old classical-Christian civilization, the Great Chain of Being, a critique that had begun with the Renaissance and the Reformation but was now carried to a far more radical pitch. Forget about eternal salvation, holiness, and martial glory. Instead, as Voltaire wrote, "cultivate your garden" – make money, relax, enjoy yourself, put away your dueling pistols, live and let live.

Not surprisingly, therefore, Rousseau became an overnight celebrity in the French intellectual world when he won an essay contest by contending that the Enlightenment had *not* improved mankind. It caused a sensation. In the spirit of the *philosophes*, every other contestant wrote that, yes, of course it had. "No more sincere friendships," Rousseau lamented in describing the France he claimed the *philosophes* wanted, "no more real esteem; no more well-based confidence. Suspicions, offenses, fears, boldness, reserve, hate, betrayal will hide constantly under that uniform and false veil of politeness, under that much vaunted urbanity, which we owe to the enlightenment of our century."

Rousseau thought there were two authentic ways for human beings to live – Natural Man and The Citizen. In the distant dawn of history, he believed, before civilization crushed our natural impulses, every man lived entirely for himself, able to survive living off the nuts and berries. It was good simply to be alive – "the sweet sentiment of existence." No one thought of exploiting others; everyone was equal. There was no private property, no social hierarchy, no religion, no government. The Citizen, by contrast, was entirely *unnatural*. He had to totally submerge his individuality in stern, selfless service to the common good, as in the ancient virtuous republics of Sparta and early Rome. But while completely unnatural, the life of the Citizen was dignified. Modern, Enlightenment man was a bastardized cross between these two genuine extremes – like Natural Man, he was selfish, but unlike Natural Man, whose simple need for self-preservation could survive by living off nature, modern man could only survive by exploiting others in order to feed his bloated passions for wealth and status, which meant he could not be a good citizen either. This hated new breed Rousseau labeled "the bourgeois," taking a word that hitherto had simply meant a person from a town (like the German *Burger*) and turning it into the symbol of everything most corrupt, degraded, and spiritually empty about the modern age, taken up with enthusiasm by Marx and numerous radical firebrands.

"Property is theft," Rousseau had thundered in the *Discourse on the Origins of Inequality*. In the *Social Contract* (whose opening proclaims that "man is born free, and everywhere we find him in chains"), he argued that "man must be forced to be free" – everyone must be curtailed from acting on their bourgeois impulses to dominate and exploit others so as to be protected from such treatment *by* others. Set up to regulate these selfish impulses for our own collective good, a government embodying the General Will "can never make mistakes" – a formulation seen by later scholars such as J. L. Talmond as a predecessor of the "totalitarian democracy" of the Soviet Union and Third Reich and the principle that the Party (meaning its dictatorial leader) can never be wrong. It may well be, as Rousseau's defenders maintain, that the *Social Contract* was at bottom a moderate recipe for reform, doing no more than adding a dash of compassion for the disadvantaged to an otherwise standard Lockean defense of private property so as to allow room for social welfare measures, dressed up with a vague call for more civic spiritedness and a wacky pagan civil religion. In this view, and it's probably correct, Rousseau was (in today's language) more of a social democrat than a revolutionary. Unfortunately, the extravagance of Rousseau's rhetoric made it easy for less careful readers like Robespierre to overlook the moderate core and get carried away by the most inflammatory formulations. In carrying out the Terror, he considered himself "Jean-Jacques'" most loyal disciple.

Stripped of their nuances and qualifications, reduced to their most memorable purple prose, Rousseau's writings appeared to be calling for a collectivist society that would use force to make men virtuous. In the *Social Contract* he also wrote ominously about "the Legislator," the man who founds such a just society, as needing to be equipped with godlike powers to remake human nature: "He who dares the making of a people's institutions ought to feel himself capable, so to speak, of changing human nature, of transforming each individual ... into part of a greater whole from which he in a manner receives his life and being." This godlike mandate to submerge the individual in the collective goes far beyond Machiavelli's call for the "outstanding prince" to assert his will over nature, because even state-building despots like Henry VIII and Frederick the Great, in following Machiavelli's playbook, were ultimately laying the foundations for societies in which the individual would be free to pursue his economic self-interest and prosper, along with the other rights of man. Rousseau, by contrast, wanted men to be whole, which meant that government could not simply facilitate the individual's self-interest, but must, on the contrary, cure him of it.

Rousseau wanted to rekindle the spirit of the ancient republics like Sparta and Rome. But it was a very different vision of the ancient republics than the one that had been embraced by the Renaissance and Enlightenment.

While the Romans, as depicted by early modern thinkers like Machiavelli and Montesquieu, were coolly calculating rationalists bent on power and prosperity, Rousseau's nostalgic view makes them ardently heroic, totally collectivistic, and fiercely patriotic. Whereas Machiavelli envisioned a new Rome rising from Republic to Empire – a vision acted out in English and American commercial expansionism – Rousseau wants Rome always to remain a clutch of huts and campfires on the Tiber, austere and self-sufficient. His view of early Rome is shaped by his longing for our return to a vanished innocence. His belief that human beings were once happy in the primitive state of nature, but made miserable by material corruption, vanity, and competition for honors and riches, set a standard for political legitimacy that no actual government could ever satisfy, and so was a catalyst for endless revolutionary upheaval.

Rousseau sparks the call for a founder who will strip away by force man's acquired traits of bourgeois selfishness and return us all to a mythical state of collective purity and innocence, "the natural condition of man." In encouraging the individual to openly pursue his self-interest, Machiavelli and his English followers like Harrington and Hobbes were simply lifting a few conventional moral restraints near the surface of what human nature was really like anyway. Rousseau, by contrast, opens the door to the use of political authority to make us all completely selfless, something there is no proof that human societies, even the most primitive, have ever really been. (Even Iron Age tribes had private property, different sized houses, locks on their doors, and engaged in trade and commerce). He was holding up the baseless dream of collective innocence at the beginning of time as the guide for political action in the present.

Is it any wonder, then, that fanatics like Robespierre felt called upon to impose this recipe in practice in the most literal-minded and violent way, enflamed by the conviction that the imposition of the General Will by revolutionary terror and violence on a corrupt human nature would be for mankind's own good, forcing us to return to the "sweet sentiment of existence" that we all once enjoyed in the state of nature and can again, once we have been forcibly liberated from the burdensome psychological agonies of private property, the competition for wealth and status, and the delusions fostered by religion in making the tyranny of privilege appear to be sanctioned by God? As Simon Schama observed, the contradictions in Rousseau's philosophy are caught in Jacques-Louis David's painting, *The Oath of the Horatii*. On the right-hand side, a family huddles in tender affection. On the left-hand side, stern Roman warriors swear an oath to avenge them. The French Revolution exploded in the Jacobins' zeal for using what they saw as Roman strength and force to bring about a world of love for all the victims of privilege.

Rousseau's summons back to the Golden Age transformed the French Revolution from another liberal and modernizing revolution into something entirely new. The Jacobins, led by Robespierre, aimed to carry out Rousseau's vision quite literally by the first methodically planned extermination campaigns based on class, regional loyalty, and religious faith – the beginning of utopian genocide. The results are unprecedented scenes of the mass execution of hundreds of thousands of "counterrevolutionaries," class enemies like the Catholic peasantry in the Vendee. A new kind of leader, the technician of murder, the idealist of death, emerges.

ROBESPIERRE AND THE ALGEBRA OF MASS MURDER

When the French Revolution first broke out in 1789, it was led by men like Mirabeau, Talleyrand, and Lafayette who wanted to bring to their own country the benefits of the American Revolution and its predecessor, the Glorious Revolution. A constitutional monarchy, representative government, the rule of law, freedom of speech, worship, assembly, and the right to acquire property – in other words, they were Lockeans. Lafayette, of course, had famously fought on the American side during its war of independence, becoming a kind of surrogate son for George Washington. These men also shared the American founders' concern, voiced especially by Washington, that an honorable ambition to serve one's country must never be allowed to cross over into an ambition to tyrannize over it. One must always emulate Cato, not Caesar.

The path to the French Revolution was paved by the reformist monarchy of Louis XVI. This is difficult to grasp if, like me, you were raised on Dickensian images of the Revolution being sparked by the arrogance and greed of the Bourbons, running over starving street urchins in their carriages while swilling champagne as Marie Antoinette joked "if they don't have enough bread, let them eat cake!" In truth, Louis XVI was a reform-minded monarch who had supported the American Revolution and tried to govern France according to the principles of the Enlightenment. Through his ministers Turgot and Necker, the hated *taille* or tax on all peasant households was decreased, efforts were made to abolish serfdom, the aristocracy's monopoly over the grain trade was broken up, and middle class merchants encouraged to rise. This alienated much of the aristocracy, who regarded the King as a class traitor, such that they largely stood aside when he was toppled from his throne. Louis also summoned a parliament, but then hesitated over how much power he was actually willing to let it have. When they asserted it anyway, the revolution began. But the King refused to suppress it with armed force, and his power to do so soon melted away. Louis' partial reforms opened the floodgate to more radical forces waiting in the wings. Impatient with the moderate agenda of Mirabeau and Lafayette, the true firebrands like Marat, Danton, and Robespierre took over. They didn't want mere rights. They wanted total equality, the leveling and expropriation (even the abolition) of private property, and the end of monarchy.

Alexis de Tocqueville drew from these events a theory that later came to be called "the revolution of rising expectations." In other words, it wasn't because the monarchy resisted reform that revolution came about. It was precisely *because* it undertook reform, but in a fitful, half-hearted, and cautious way, that it aroused expectations it could not fulfill, and was swept away. This is a pattern we see repeated again and again in the great revolutions of the coming centuries: A reforming despot sponsors an agenda for gradual and limited reform in order to bring about constitutional government without yielding monarchical authority, only to be overwhelmed by the true radicals.

As Rousseau's self-proclaimed disciple, Robespierre believed that the French Revolution could return "the people" to the bliss of the original state of nature through the revolutionary destruction of both modern and premodern civilization, including the systematic extermination of classes and social forces thought to be terminally infected by the defects of bourgeois self-interest, religious faith, regional loyalty and royalist sentiments. What began as a revolution in the American mold, with a constitutional balance of powers derived from Montesquieu and guarantees of individual liberty – continued by the Jacobins' main opponents, the *Girondistes* – ends with the Jacobins attempting to bring heaven to earth through terror. The Jacobin Terror was the prototype for all future totalitarian movements. It aimed to increase the pace of modernization by centralizing the power of the state. But whereas the modern state builders we looked at in Part Two, including the Tudors, Peter the Great, and Frederick the Great, built such states in order to foster the modern emphasis on individual self-interest, the Jacobins sought to restore an Arcadian origin so distant and unsullied by greed, selfishness, hierarchy, and vanity that all intervening traditions of patriotism, religion, class, and caste must be obliterated. Its aim was to destroy *both* the premodern authorities of Throne and Altar *and* the early modern project for the rights of the individual.

As would happen again and again with the Russian, National Socialist, Maoist, and Iranian revolutions, many people – especially young people – welcomed the French Revolution with starry-eyed optimism, only later to be shattered by the revelations of immense brutality and cruelty. The young Wordsworth was living in Paris when the revolution broke out, and later recalled in *The Preludes* his exultation over "speculative schemes/that promised to abstract the hopes of Man/out of his feelings, to be fixed thenceforward/For ever in a purer element ...." The Revolution's wholesale attack on all "feelings" rooted in ancient tradition on behalf of the rationality of pure human equality, he writes, especially "Flattered the young, pleased with extremes/Nor least with that which makes our Reason's naked self/the object of its fervor." The only sincere way to live, in other words, was to be stripped "naked" of all customary ties, inherited loyalties, and habits of deference, reduced to a pure (meaning empty) self ready to be collectivized with other empty selves. It was, Wordsworth at that time had believed, a fresh start for all mankind, the wish "that man/should start out of his earthly, worm-like state, and spread abroad the wings of Liberty/Lord of himself, in undisturbed delight ... Dragging all precepts, judgements, maxims, creeds/Like culprits to the bar."

Across the Channel in England, Edmund Burke had viewed this attempt to "abstract" or rip man out of the context of all received tradition and apply pure reason to reconstruct society through revolutionary force very differently. His Whig comrades like Charles James Fox were puzzled by his fierce criticism of the French Revolution after his support of the American Revolution in 1776. But unlike them, Burke foresaw early on that the French Revolution was not merely a new installment of the Glorious and American Revolutions, but something unprecedented and sinister. Even before the full culmination of the Terror, whose harbinger was the public execution by guillotine of the vain and foolish but politically guiltless Queen, he predicted that "all the pleasing illusions which made power gentle and obedience liberal, which harmonized the different shades of life ... are to be dissolved by this new conquering empire of light and reason." He anticipates Wordsworth's description of the aim of the French Revolution as the relentless exposure of "our Reason's naked self" when he writes: "All the decent drapery of life is to be rudely torn off. On this scheme of things, a king is but a man, a queen is but a woman, a woman is but an animal, and an animal not of the highest order." The revolutionaries' zeal for imposing abstract blueprints for achieving equality overnight, Burke argued, had been nurtured for decades previously by the *philosophes*, whom he lumped together (perhaps unfairly) with the man he regarded as their leading villain, Rousseau. In Burke's view, it led to a secular fanaticism intolerant of all opposing, especially traditional views based on rank, faith, and merit, a taste for vicious diatribe, and a drive to purge the people of their vices. Equally happy to have their blueprint imposed by a mob or a tyrant, "these Atheistical fathers have a bigotry of their own; and they have learned to talk against monks with the spirit of a monk ... By hating vices too much, they have come to love men too little." The pure equality of Rousseau's state of nature was completely "devoid of habit, tradition, custom, and variety. Hence, when it becomes the model for the state, differences must be sheared off, like canceling equations in algebra." Rousseau and the *philosophes*' utopian schemes of reform, however idealistically motivated, made revolutionary violence and mass murder inevitable: "At the end of all their vistas stands a gallows."

Robespierre was born to carry to its zenith of violence this revolution on behalf of the *philosophes*' abstract utopia as Burke diagnosed it. His most insightful biographer, Hillaire Belloc, establishes the centrality of Rousseau to Robespierre and the entire Jacobin project: "The general philosophy and trend of the (eighteenth) century," he writes, "was gathered up, woven, stamped by the genius of Rousseau ... To ignore it is to miss the very spirit of the revolution." He continues: "In his sincerity, his backward yearning for a past Eden, his inhuman sensitiveness at the contact of the world, (Rousseau) had all the character of the men that impel the origins of religions and he was found ... to be the agent of a mission ... " Rousseau, Belloc argues, was to eighteenth-century France what the King James Bible had been to England: "Men who profess astonishment at the spell he threw over the nation are like foreigners who misread half our own history because they cannot weigh the power the (King James Version) of the Bible has exercised over the English race." In a passage that shows why Rousseau's political theory demanded a kind of geometrician of political violence who would, as Burke had put it, "shear off" inequality like cancelling equations in algebra, Belloc writes, "In the shortest of his pamphlets, the *Contrat Social*, he fixed in little adamantine clauses the political creed which men demanded ... What is common to all men is utterly beyond the accidents by which they differ, as in mathematical science" and those "accidents" (of birth, faith, status, talent) must, therefore, be planed off.

Robespierre was the man to carry out the planing off, the algebra of mass murder, with the guillotine as his slide rule. Belloc writes: "(Robespierre) could not but accept all this ... as a mathematical truth, nor could he help revering its exponent as the seer and guide of a necessary change. He took the first postulates of the *Contrat Social* for granted, knowing well that everyone around him did the same. He deduced from them, and still deduced with a fatal accuracy of process, with a fatal ignorance of things, and with no appreciation of the increasing chances of error." When his attempts to impose pure reason on reality met with reality's resistance, and especially the resistance of human nature to giving up its achievements and loyalties, that could only be due to the vices of his opponents: "The resistance which such absurdities met he thought to be a willful rejection of strict logic, due to the corruption of private motives or to the casuistry of wicked men. In such a path, wholly of the mind and divorced from reality, his being was absorbed." Whereas the makers of the Glorious and American Revolutions strove never to confuse an honorable ambition to serve the cause of free self-government with a desire to tyrannize, the very character of the Jacobin project to bring heaven to earth overnight not only tolerated tyranny, but required its worst extremes. Belloc concludes about Robespierre: "He has been called a puritan; he was partly an inquisitor. His idea that he was the servant and agent of pure right made him" in both respects "a tyrant, just where tyranny is most monstrous." Or as Robespierre himself summed up his mission on behalf of pure right: "We must smother the internal and external enemies of the Republic, or perish with them ... Terror is nothing but prompt, severe, inflexible justice; it is therefore an emanation of virtue."

THE HALLMARKS OF MILLENARIAN TYRANNY

I've argued in this book that, of the three major types of tyranny, millenarian tyranny is unique to the modern era – that it doesn't appear until the French Revolution and reaches a zenith in the Jacobin Terror of 1793, the pattern for all the millenarian tyrannies to come. How does millenarian tyranny differ from the other two types? Let's look at it in broad strokes before turning to the Jacobins' successors – the Bolsheviks, Nazis, and other totalitarian movements of the twentieth and twenty-first centuries down to the International Jihad.

Millenarian tyranny is driven by a utopian aim in which society is to be completely transformed from being unjust, materialistic, and selfish in the present to being spiritually pure, selfless, and communal in the future. This transformation is a night-and-day difference – almost nothing can be salvaged from the corrupt present in order to bring this spiritually cleansed new world about. That's why it's frequently likened to a secular version of religious Messianism and Apocalypticism, like the Biblical coming of the Last Judgment before (or, depending on the theology, after) the 1000-year Kingdom of God (hence the term "millenarian," echoed in the Nazis' "thousand-year Reich") or the coming of the Messiah. Millenarian revolution is an earthly version of this complete transformation of nature and human nature – no longer an object of faith to be devoutly hoped for whenever at long last God in his mysterious ways decides to grant it, but a quite literal struggle to recarve the world we live in right now with frightening and monstrous consequences.

All millenarian revolutionary movements have a common set of genocidal aims. They all envision the return of "the people" to the simplicity of its origins, to what the Jacobins called "the Year One," to be achieved by a grimly repressive collectivist utopia of pure duty, submission, and self-sacrifice, in which individual freedom is obliterated by being stripped of all sources of "alienation" from the collective, including property, freedom of thought, religious faith, and the satisfactions of family and private life. Beginning with the Jacobins, this return to the origins is sparked by an intense loathing for the modern age of the Enlightenment and its alleged vulgarity, selfishness, and materialism. Paradoxically, returning to a past so distant requires a leap into the future that will destroy all intervening, ordinary, and received traditions, including those of patriotism and religious custom. As nineteenth-century composer Richard Wagner put it about the anarchist Mikhail Bakhunin: "The annihilation of all civilization was the objective on which he had set his heart ... It was necessary, he said, to picture the whole European world ... transformed into a pile of rubble."

The second aim that all these revolutionary movements share is the identification of class or race enemies standing in the way of the coming nirvana, an enemy that sums up in itself all the modern world's worst qualities. This enemy becomes the embodiment of all human evil, whose destruction will cleanse the planet. For the Jacobins, it was the bourgeoisie and the aristocrats. For Stalin, it was the "kulaks," the so-called rich peasants, while for Hitler it was the Jews. Annihilating this enemy is necessary to bring about a better world, and the violence necessitated by doing so also provides an emotional catharsis for the revolutionaries. Needless to say, the demonology identifying these classes or peoples as the source of all evil in the world is a complete delusion required to sanction genocide and endow its violence with a supposedly absolute moral justification.

Reforming tyrannies or universal monarchies in the past certainly aimed at large-scale social and political transformations, as we saw in Part One with Cyrus the Great, Alexander the Great, and Julius Caesar. But these transformations were always confined to imposing an already familiar and long-standing historical and cultural pattern on other peoples not yet fortunate enough to share in it – for instance, the Romans' spread of Greco-Roman culture throughout their domains. The authority structures of world empires like Rome were developments and extensions of the original cultural patterns in the conqueror's homeland – for instance, each Romanized town had its own Senate. Moreover, these transformations were a more fully developed version of the aristocratic culture that was already widespread in the ancient world. Landowners and chieftains among the conquered peoples need only conform to the culture of the new master, donning togas and learning Latin in order to retain their privileged status as wealthy Spaniards and Syrians now Romanized.

By contrast, millenarian tyranny is profoundly egalitarian in its aims. It is not democratic – that would imply self-government by the people and individual rights – but an absolute, overnight equality of condition to be imposed by revolutionary force through the leveling of all wealth, talent, and status, maintained by a totalitarian state. That is why the modern states built by figures like Henry VIII, Louis XIV, and the "enlightened despots" of Europe – states which, however brutal their methods may have been, tried to promote over time economic prosperity and some degree of individual freedom and religious tolerance for their peoples – according to the Jacobins had to be destroyed every bit as much as the class-bound feudal hierarchy which had preceded them. In the eyes of millenarian tyranny, both the modern state and the old feudal order are hopelessly tainted. If anything, the modern state is worse, because it robs people of even that flawed illusion of social harmony they had possessed as vassals of feudalism and replaces it with open, naked, crass individual selfishness and an obsession with economic success. The new order must be without rank or hierarchy, whether political, economic, cultural, or religious, meaning, again, that everything traditional has to be destroyed. Appeals to egalitarian populism were characteristic, for example, of Hitler. He repeatedly stressed that, in the Third Reich, hereditary rank, education, status, and wealth would count for nothing. He really meant the "Socialist" part in National Socialism. If the Führer's power was limitless today, that was only so that he could bring about the "National Socialist World-Blessing" of tomorrow.

A consistent paradox of millenarian tyranny is that the slate has to be wiped clean of all traditional authorities and customs in the future in order to recapture an alleged Golden Age of the most distant past, the "return to the Year One" (the Jacobins), "the community of destiny" (Nazism), "the Year Zero" (the Khmer Rouge) or the original community of Islam. Revolutionary action reshapes the present in order to bring about a future guided by a past *behind* the past, *behind* all received tradition. For, however deeply rooted and long established a people's past traditions might appear to be – the centuries-long histories of France, Germany, and Russia with their complex layerings – they, too, are tainted by corruption and vice from the ground up and so must be entirely jettisoned, along with more recent Enlightenment influences, in order to transport us back to the collective bliss and purity of the mythical and primeval origins. Hence, the Jacobins attempted to destroy not only the remnants of the *ancien regime*, but the fledgling modern society of Lockean individualism that was beginning to displace it. A revolutionary Messiah is needed to take us there – Robespierre, Lenin, Stalin, Hitler, Mao, Pol Pot, Khomeini, Al Baghdadi; to lead a corrupt and fallen world, against its will if need be, into this shining new day. His absolute tyrannical power in the present is justified as being necessary to end all tyranny and inequality forever.

It's true that these allegedly egalitarian movements often have an inner core of revolutionary cadres who follow the Leader and execute his will – the Jacobins with their Citizens' Tribunals, the Bolsheviks with the KGB, the Nazis with the SS, the shadowy "Higher Organization" of the Khmer Rouge (all middle-class Francophone intellectuals). As the revolution is being carried out to create a totalitarian state, these men certainly do form an elite set apart from the rank and file cadres. But it's not a traditional aristocracy with its restraints of liberal education, gentlemanliness, deference to custom, and a sense of responsibility (*noblesse oblige*) for the well-being of the common people. The revolution's cadres are often coarse and violent thugs, even psychopaths who, in ordinary times, would hide their impulses or end up in prison or a mental hospital. One definition of fascism is that it's where the elite meets the gutter; where the utopian fantasies spun by malcontent graduate students, unemployed journalists, crankish cafe intellectuals, threadbare lawyers, and failed artists meet the literal violence of the skinheads, the bullyboys, the sadists who form the shock troops for utopian genocide. It has been true of every millenarian revolution from the Jacobin sadist Fouche to the young Canadian killing for ISIS in Syria who boasted in a video that this murder spree was "the real Disney World." The cadres' ruthlessness in the present is justified by the collectivist egalitarian society of permanent peace and harmony to be brought about tomorrow.

Another way in which millenarian tyranny differs from even the most brutal of previous tyrannies, whether reforming or garden variety, is the sheer scale of the violence needed to bring about the apocalyptic passage from today to the shining future, and its methodical application. History was no stranger before 1789 to war, violence, civil strife, bloodshed, torture, and mass murder. But not until now is murder used in a dispassionate and methodical way to surgically remove entire designated classes and races from existence, the forces who embody all vice and evil and who, therefore, stand in the way of the coming collectivist Golden Age. As we have seen, as early as the Jacobins, the use of firing squads and cannons to mow down men and women into execution pits was already established, anticipating the Nazis' *Einsatzgruppen* or the recent mass killings in the self-proclaimed Caliphate of ISIS. The numbers liquidated mounted from upward of two hundred and fifty thousand across France during the Jacobin Terror to tens of millions under the twentieth- century's millenarian dictatorships with their vastly improved technology for "industrialized murder" in the Gulag and Auschwitz, in Mao's and the Khmer Rouge's reeducation camps. During the final years of Tsarism in Russia, the number of political prisoners executed peaked at 1144 after the failed Revolution of 1905. Immediately following the Bolshevik Revolution of 1917, Lenin had upward of hundred thousand "enemies of the revolution" liquidated, and by the time of his incapacitation in 1922, an estimated five million lost their lives due to starvation. The worst, of course, was yet to come.

Whereas past tyrannies had killed people for challenging their power through uprisings or military opposition, millenarian tyrannies commit genocide collectively against entire classes and races whether they oppose them or not. They must be annihilated to the last member before nirvana can come about. It was nothing personal. Moreover, this large-scale violence is not merely necessary to bring about utopia, but a therapeutic experience for the revolutionaries. The shedding of the class or race enemy's blood is a violent catharsis that purifies their own inner resolve, enabling them to throw off bourgeois or religious scruples that prevent the masses, still clinging to their outmoded religious faith or deference to tradition, from grasping the new world to come.

Even belonging to the classes or national communities who are to benefit from the coming new world order counts for nothing if one is seen as in any way resistant or clinging to old traditions. Most of the Jacobin Terror's victims were not the "aristos" but the ordinary folk they claimed to be liberating, who stubbornly clung to their loyalties to church, king, nobility, and their local soil. Being Russian or German did not save you from liquidation if you in any way opposed the Bolshevik and Nazi revolutions, or even simply made your objections known without daring to act on them. The fact that most Russian factory workers would have preferred some form of British or German trade unionism made no impact on Lenin at all – again, that was merely the "empirical" proletariat, whose backward and selfish views would have to be uprooted and transformed by the Bolshevik cadres who, while most often from middle-class, nonproletarian backgrounds themselves, nevertheless were animated by true "proletarian consciousness." Nor did Lenin have the slightest interest in improving the workers' material lot. They had to be forged by collectivization into a New Man, totally submerged in the collective and able to labor for the state without compensation. Similarly now, being a Muslim does not guarantee one's safety from revolutionary Jihadist movements. If you are the wrong kind of Muslim, or resistant to the absolute collectivization and the moralistic fanaticism of the emerging self-professed Caliphate, or even hoping to just lie low and avoid conflict, you are every bit as deserving of death as Israel, America, and the infidels.

Millenarian revolutionaries have no interest in partial or gradual reform of the Burkean sort, or the tangible aims of a liberal revolution like the Glorious Revolution or American Revolution for establishing individual rights and enabling every citizen to improve their lot. For the millenarians, individual rights are a part of society's disease, every bit as much as the feudal hierarchy they replaced. Both are corrupt and selfish, and both must be purged to create a pure collective in which every individual is interchangeable with every other and submerged in a monolith ruled by the revolutionaries themselves, former terrorists now victorious as godlike masters. It's all or nothing – as Lenin put it, "the worse, the better." The more oppressive or stubborn the revolution's enemies are in the present, the more necessary it will be to sweep them away through annihilating violence. True millenarian revolutionaries do not *want* things to improve, do not *want* concrete concessions like higher wages, economic development or social services. Such reforms only threaten to corrupt "the people" further by turning them into *petites bourgeois*. The Revolution needs to portray itself as incessantly "surrounded by enemies" in order to create the sense of peril necessary to galvanize violent action and vigilance. Hitler and Stalin both had to depict their respective nations as constantly on the brink of destruction by a secret conspiracy of evil people who on the face of it couldn't possibly (and in reality didn't) pose such a threat – the mythical "kulaks" of Bolshevik demonology and the mythical "Jewish world conspiracy" of National Socialism.

The progress of history had been seen by Gibbon, Burke, and friends of the modern world of individual liberty and representative self-government as a largely benevolent process, unfolding in slow but steady stages toward greater freedom for all, a peaceable evolution if sometimes marked by regrettable lapses into violence and war. By contrast, millenarian revolutionaries see the progress of history as entirely oppressive, unjust, and exploitive until now, but about to yield, through a final spasm of revolutionary violence, a world of perfect harmony tomorrow. The progress of history is needed as a violent dynamo of social, cultural, and economic strife to destroy corruption and complacency in the present and clear the stage for the future, a conviction common in varying ways to the philosophies of Karl Marx, Friedrich Nietzsche, Mikhail Bakhunin, and Martin Heidegger. Moreover, millenarian revolution is inevitably imperialistic, for it must culminate in war to spread the blessings of the future to all by force – a trend consistent from the Jacobins to ISIS. Whatever state the revolution may inhabit for the moment is no more than an outpost for the next phase of conquest, which is why revolutionary movements have no interest in "ordinary politics," the tasks of concrete improvement for their peoples. As Trotsky wrote, the Russian Revolution was "a bivouac life," a temporary encampment where "everything is extraordinary, temporary, transitory" because it was only a way station to world communism.

Millenarian revolutions seem to be more violent when they erupt in societies where the claim of premodern tradition and authority is still very strong. The values of the Enlightenment begin to erode the power of premodern authority before managing to establish individual liberties and self-government firmly, leading to a nostalgia for the mythical memory of a "lost" communal wholeness before the benefits of the modern age have been fully experienced. This trend also began with the French Revolution. The Glorious and American Revolutions took place in societies where the values of economic self-interest, freedom of worship, and self-government had already become widely influential – the political culmination in the establishment of representative democracy was merely the final outcome of this long period of gestation in which the feudal order had steadily been eroded. It required civil war and revolution, but not the killing of hundreds of thousands. By contrast, when the Revolution broke out in France, it was faced by the fierce opposition of an aristocratic and ecclesiastical establishment still extremely powerful and deeply hostile to the entire modern era. That old order could only be blasted away by the political equivalent of dynamite.

This combustible moment of a stalled or only partially successful conversion to Enlightenment values that produces the longing for a "lost" community of the past, and requiring massive violence in order to reverse the still very limited gains of the modern age while seeking a purer community of the distant primordial origins, is a recurrent trend throughout the great revolutions to come in Russia, China, Cambodia, and Iran. The way forward is the way behind the modern age of individual liberty to the communal bliss of the origins. Germany might not quite fit this pattern, because before the rise of National Socialism, Germany already had a long tradition of self-government, Enlightenment values of tolerance and freedom of thought and conscience spread by figures like Goethe and Schiller, and one of the world's most productive economies. But as we'll consider at greater length, National Socialism was in a way always a South German or Austrian ideal of romantic Wagnerian nationalism – "anticapitalist nostalgia" as one of its early leaders termed it – bred in Catholic Bavaria and the Tyrol, an intensely antimodern vision of life, which then managed to capture the great Prussian military and industrial power state of the Protestant North.

To stress an earlier observation, millenarian revolutions frequently erupt not when the old autocracy is at its most repressive, but when the autocrat introduces modern reforms without being willing to share absolute power. A liberal revolution for the rights of man occurs with the autocrat's inconsistent or reluctant acquiescence, but the expectations of reform already unleashed sweep the liberals away and bring the collectivists to the fore. Hence, Louis XVI's attempts to encourage market forces and a degree of legislative self-government brought about the liberal phase of the French Revolution, soon swept aside by the Jacobins. Tsar Nicholas II's veering between liberalization and repression sparked a revolution for liberal rights led by Kerensky, then swept aside by Lenin. Shah Reza Pahlevi's fitful efforts at modernizing Iran without yielding absolute power sparked the Iranian revolution, initially led by technocrats and socialists, soon swept aside by the Khomeinists. Mubarak had brought Egypt a degree of economic prosperity, but his and his cronies' monopoly on power sparked a peaceful revolution of secular liberals for rights and self-government, soon hijacked by the Muslim Brotherhood bent on establishing a theocratic republic and ending the peace with Israel.

It's sometimes suggested that modern millenarian revolutions beginning with the Jacobins were an attempt to "secularize" the apocalyptic strain in medieval Christianity – that they were modern continuations of breakaway religious movements such as the Cathars and Anabaptists that, anticipating the Reformation, had attempted to live in their own communities of devout fellow believers, with little or no private possessions, reaching their own vision of God free of priestly interference and ecclesiastical control.

It's a fair comparison as far as it goes. There was definitely a revolutionary side to the Reformation. As historian Paul Rahe has pointed out, the Puritans at their most radical foresaw a revolution spreading from England to all of Europe to rid men of both "priests and kings." As we saw in Part Two, it wasn't always easy to determine whether Oliver Cromwell and his Puritan followers were primarily religious or political revolutionaries. Robespierre and the Jacobins, according to historian Crane Brinton, "must be labeled Puritans in morals," and they stoked emotions of zeal and fanaticism akin to those of apocalyptic religious sects and their persecutors – Belloc, we recall, likened Robespierre to both a Puritan and the Holy Inquisition. But the comparison between medieval and modern millenarianism doesn't go very far. The millenarian religious movements of the Middle Ages were rapidly crushed. They were naive pacifists who thought they could actually live outside the feudal authority of Church and King. Moreover, they had very few aspirations of their own to form states, much less dominate other countries. They wanted to be left alone with their spiritual exercises in their own little communities.

By sharp contrast, revolutionary regimes beginning with the Jacobins also aimed to become great and powerful states to spread the blessings of their revolution by force of arms. The old European powers were astonished at how the rag-tag armies of the Revolution, initially commanded by men with no military experience, quickly achieved major victories, culminating in the martial glory of Napoleon. Radical Puritans had wanted to purify men and their corrupt institutions so as to open the way for them to Heaven. In doing so, as we saw in Part Two, the Reformation at its worst was capable of barbaric acts of destruction and oppression. But the Jacobins and their successors left them in the shade. That's because there is all the difference in the world between purging men's vices so as to make them worthy of salvation in the afterlife and purging their vices to actually *create* heaven on earth here and now, without God's help. It's the difference between teaching men to aspire to be less greedy and forcibly expropriating their possessions. Moreover, while apocalyptic movements in the Middle Ages probably contained budding Robespierres eager to pit themselves against established authority, precisely because those movements were aiming at a holy community of believers living peaceably on their own, such men were afforded no scope for massive bloodshed. On the contrary, it was they who were ruthlessly suppressed by royal and papal power. The millenarian revolutions beginning in 1793 did not so much imitate medieval apocalypticism, therefore, as release its more nihilistic impulses from their previous religious constraint. For those medieval movements to have been the true ancestors of modern millenarian revolution would be a little as if the Quakers had been equipped with the *Wehrmacht* or the Anabaptists with ICBMs.

Before we explore some major examples of millenarian tyrants such as Lenin, Stalin, and Hitler, I want to make it clear that I'm not arguing that millenarian tyranny has been the only source of large-scale violence and exploitation in the modern world. We should bear in mind that the opening of the New World by England, Portugal, Spain, France, and America had its dark side as well. The New World was only a "blank slate" from a European perspective, in the sense that there were a limited number of competing European powers and lots of room to expand into. In fleeing the feudal aristocracy of Britain, the settlers of America soon clashed with the original inhabitants, whose tribes, ironically, formed a kind of warrior aristocracy themselves. Their communal longhouses and endless chivalrous combat with one another hearkened back to the Bronze Age warrior chiefs we considered in Part One. They had something in common as well with the Vikings, who had also lived according to a code of honor requiring endless, inconclusive battles so that the warrior nobility could display their personal courage in combat (a parallel suggested with great effectiveness in the TV series *Vikings*, especially in the opening credits that seem to blend Nordic music and imagery with those of the North American tribes). The longhouses of the Iroquois with their warrior brotherhoods bore some resemblance to the early city-states of the Greeks. Except for the great Shawnee chief Tecumseh, in some ways an aspiring aboriginal Napoleon who wanted to unite the tribes against the encroaching white man, they, too, like the early Greeks, were stubbornly resistant to any form of universal authority.

The colonial Sons of Liberty, in other words, had a homegrown feudal nobility to vie with for possession of the land, and because of greatly superior numbers and weaponry, did so successfully, often with great brutality toward the natives. But it was not lost on observers that, in conquering the native culture, the Americans were acting toward the natives much as the Romans had acted toward the natives of Gaul and Germany – and, just as Roman observers like Tacitus could not help but admire the vanquished tribesmen for defending their ancient liberties as the Romans themselves had once done, some Americans steeped in the history of Republican Rome and disapproving of the Empire of the Caesars, felt a similar moral qualm about the treatment of the natives: that it was a kind of tyranny.

Finally, when the economic development of the New World led to slavery and the horrors of the Middle Passage, Atlanticist Republicanism ceases being merely about doughty yeoman farmers living on free soil and passes into the realm of genocide. We are in troubled waters indeed when we try to distinguish between the totalitarian genocide of millenarian revolutionary movements beginning in Europe with the Jacobins as the deliberate attempt to exterminate a race or class and the genocide of African slavery. Although it was meant for economic exploitation and not bent, like millenarian tyranny, on removing entire classes and races from the face of the earth, it nevertheless included horrors of cruelty that would not be approached until the Bolsheviks and Nazis themselves. It has not been my purpose in this book to deny that modern democracies are capable of tyranny, whether at home or abroad. What makes all the difference, though, is that, however long it may take, they can be shamed by their own moral principles into recognizing that tyranny and eventually reversing it. American Protestantism, which regarded the New World as its own sacred plot, also led the battle of conscience to remove the moral stain of slavery, culminating in Lincoln's presidency and the Civil War.

THE TIME OF THE GREAT NOON: MILLENARIAN REVOLUTION GOES UNDERGROUND

After the fall of Robespierre in 1794, a victim of the guillotine to which he had sent so many others, millenarian tyranny and terror go underground in Europe, to gestate beneath the surface for a century before, aided by an ever-mounting hatred of nineteenth-century civilization on both the extreme Left and Right, it explodes with renewed savagery in 1917.

The man who interred the Revolution was one of its own offspring. Napoleon Bonaparte was a unique figure – in part a reforming tyrant of the modern age but also the last gasp of the tyrannical splendor of the ancient world. As a young artillery officer he got his start after the fall of Robespierre by crushing a royalist uprising, firing his cannons into the streets of Paris, killing 1400 people. He charted his own imitation of ancient politics when he engineered a coup to become "first consul," Roman-style, of the Republic, in effect a dictatorship, reminding one of the rise of Julius Caesar to one-man rule. His Egyptian campaign in 1798, of dubious military value, imitated Caesar as well by combining glory in war with capturing a trove of ancient cultural treasures to enrich the homeland. Using his military genius, often placed on a par with Alexander the Great and Caesar, he extended through conquest and enormous bloodshed the original and more moderate *Girondiste* version of the French Revolution to the rest of Europe. He used the need to suppress continual plots by both the royalists and the Jacobins to have himself proclaimed Emperor in 1804, thus rolling a reenactment of Julius Caesar's rise into that of Augustus. He created a revived imperial cult with shades of Augustus and Charlemagne centering on his own godlike magnificence. He was said to have a mesmerizing effect in conversation, winning over rapt followers to his cause.

After defeating Austria, Napoleon created the Confederation of the Rhine, a collection of German states that laid the basis for the later unification of Germany. Stunning victories against Prussia and Russia followed. At the height of its extent, his Empire rivaled that of Rome and embraced some seventy million subjects. As a liberalizing autocrat, he in effect brought to a close the entire enterprise of modern state-building stretching back to the Tudors and the benevolent despots by abolishing the remains of feudalism in Europe. The Napoleonic Code, which aimed to make the law clear and available to all, was adopted by countries around the world. Napoleon dismantled the Holy Roman Empire and the Inquisition, established religious toleration and the right to divorce; he ended feudal tithes, closed the ghettos and made Jews equal citizens. As historian Andrew Roberts sums it up: "The ideas that underpin our modern world – meritocracy, equality before the law, property rights, religious toleration, modern secular education, sound finances and so on – were championed, consolidated, codified and geographically extended by Napoleon."

Yet these things could only be accomplished by a decade of war that, put together with the earlier wars fought by the Revolution against the royalist powers, cost upward of eight hundred thousand battlefield deaths on the French side. Like Henry VIII and the other reforming tyrants we have examined, debate still rages about whether Napoleon was a benevolent liberator or a bloodthirsty egomaniac. In the tradition of the reforming tyrant and universal monarchies we first discussed in Part One, Napoleon was capable of great good works, the promotion of law, art, and learning as the filigree for his blood-soaked wars of aggression. The conflicting emotions he provoked are perhaps best caught by French historian Francois Guizot, who wrote a generation later about "the page of universal history which General Bonaparte claims for his own, and which he has succeeded in covering with glory and crime."

Like reforming tyrants and universal monarchs going back to Cyrus the Great, Napoleon promoted natural ability. His original followers, often of middle-class or more humble origins, rose through their merit to create a glittering new (some would say parvenu) Napoleonic aristocracy that vied with what remained of the old one from the *ancien regime*. As a Corsican outsider whose family, later grafted onto various European royal and ducal lines, was like something out of *The Godfather,* Napoleon sensed the old aristocracy's hidden resentment of him as an upstart, summed up in his telling Talleyrand to his face that he was "a shit in a silk stocking." (Talleyrand's joke to the Russian ambassador that, whereas Russia was a nation of barbarians ruled by a civilized man, the case was exactly the opposite in France, had gotten back to him). Europe's thinking classes careened between admiration for his attempts to spread the Enlightenment to their own backward autocracies and loathing his attempt to annihilate their national independence. Tolstoy catches this ambivalence in the character of Pierre Bezhukov in *War and Peace* – as a sincere liberal, he wants Russia to become a modern country, but through its own efforts, not through foreign imposition.

The final defeat in 1815 of Napoleon by the Duke of Wellington at Waterloo brings together a number of themes we have talked about in this book going back to ancient times. Wellington's victory was cast as the defense of proud English traditions of self-government within the benign class hierarchy praised by Burke. Wellington, a member of the Anglo-Irish nobility, was the perfect foil for Napoleon, a Corsican outsider and an entirely self-made man. Wellington conceded Napoleon's brilliance as a general, saying that his mere presence on the battlefield was "worth forty thousand men." But he did not regard him as a gentleman. Whereas Napoleon was charismatic and seductive, Wellington was notoriously aloof toward his social inferiors. He disapproved of his soldiers cheering him – it was, he said, "too nearly an expression of opinion," as if their approval could possibly matter. Napoleon, still a revolutionary behind his title of Emperor, dismissed Wellington as an "oligarch." The defeat of Napoleon came to be seen as a new installment in the epic struggle of liberty against tyranny, of a free people repulsing a universal tyrant, stretching back to Salamis and Marathon, Elizabeth I versus the Armada, the Roundheads versus the Stuarts, the American colonists versus King George III, and forward to Churchill and the Dunkirk flotilla standing up to the new tyrannical bullyboy Hitler. We inheritors of the Cold War between the Soviet Empire and the West stand in this same direct line of inheritance, and it provides a moral compass for resisting ISIS and the Taliban today. It is not always perfectly accurate history – it would be hard to say whether the stolid and conservative Wellington was a greater human being than the reforming if blood-soaked Emperor – but the contours of this ongoing tradition of the resistance to tyranny by free peoples are sharp, clear, and still utterly relevant.

Between the Battle of Waterloo and the outbreak of World War I, Europe enjoyed an extraordinary era of peace and prosperity interrupted by occasional short-lived outbreaks like the revolutions of 1848, the Paris Commune of 1870 and the brief Franco-Prussian War. Observers like Ortega y Gassett and Stefan Zweig, looking back at the late nineteenth century from the other side of the catastrophes of World War I and Fascism, saw it as one of mankind's happiest eras since the Good Emperors of the Antonine Age. And yet, throughout this largely benevolent age, the intellectual and creative classes that stood at its pinnacle conceived an ever deeper hatred and contempt for the Enlightenment values behind that success, and expressed in art, literature, and philosophy an ever more drastic longing for a new era that would trample it all underfoot, reviving and extending Rousseau's original *cri de coeur* against "bourgeois" existence. Whether their solutions culminated in the Far Left of emerging Communism or the Far Right of tribalistic "blood and soil" nationalism, at the end of the day they both longed for that pure millenarian collective that would purge "the people" of their materialistic corruption.

Right and Left joined hands in this loathing for modern bourgeois Europe, such that figures from across the spectrum including Edmund Burke, the Marquis de Rivarol, Karl Marx, Hyppolite Taine, and others wrote denunciations of the shallowness and vulgarity of the modern world that are almost interchangeable with each other. Consider the following passage from Marx's

Communist Manifesto on the destructive effects of modern liberal individualism and self-interest on Europe's traditional social cohesiveness, much of which could have come from Burke's *Reflections on the Revolution in France*:

The bourgeoisie, wherever it has got the upper hand, has put an end to all feudal, patriarchal, idyllic relations. It has pitilessly torn asunder the motley feudal ties that bound man to his 'natural superiors,' and has left remaining no other nexus between man and man than naked self-interest, that callous 'cash payment.' It has drowned the most heavenly ecstasies of religious fervor, of chivalrous enthusiasm, of philistine sentimentalism, in the icy water of egotistic calculation. It has resolved personal worth into exchange value ... In one word, for exploitation, veiled by religion and political illusions, it has substituted naked, shameless, direct, brutal exploitation. The bourgeoisie has stripped of its halo every occupation hitherto honored and looked up to with reverent awe ... The bourgeoisie has torn away from the family its sentimental veil and has reduced the family relation to a mere money relation.

Burke, too, we recall, had lamented how the Enlightenment had "rudely torn off ... all the decent drapery of life." Marx welcomes the power of capitalism ("the most revolutionary force in history" to date) to sweep away the remnants of the old feudal and Christian order, but at the same time regrets its passing and hates its shabby and debased replacement. The same destructive revolutionary power that built capitalism, Marx fervently believed, must now be harnessed to vault us past the bourgeois age into a restored community of the future. This combination of nostalgia for a vanished communal harmony and a longing for unparalleled destruction so as to restore it is, as we have seen, the psychological hallmark of the millenarian revolutionary.

All in all, then, in the nineteenth century the Jacobin project for the achievement of mankind's future happiness through genocide in the present survives Napoleon and the era of conservative reaction inaugurated after his defeat by Metternich and the Congress of Vienna by going underground to gather new strength, becoming what Marx famously termed "the specter that haunts Europe." Meanwhile, the career of tyranny largely reverted to garden-variety autocracy – narrowly nationalistic, deeply traditional and pious, caught for the European imagination in Puccini's portrayal in *Tosca* of the sinister Scarpia, head of the Vatican Police who, in an age-old motif pitting the tyrant's erotic passion against the struggle for liberty that we first encountered in Part One, uses his dark powers to try to ravish the heroine Tosca against the backdrop of Napoleon's impending liberation of Savoy. Dangerous as such men could be, they were mere comic opera martinets compared to what was coming in the twentieth century. Moreover, most of Europe, especially the middle and upper classes, basked in the sunny uplands of increasing prosperity and individual freedom.

The extremism of the French Revolution had sometimes led to a disillusionment with all expectations from politics, certainly from revolutionary politics – Wordsworth and the German writer Friedrich Schiller being cases in point. But it also led to an ever more extravagant longing for a millenarian world to come that would destroy the modern bourgeois world altogether, led by a vanguard of the fanatically pure (Marx's proletariat, Nietzsche's Superman, Heidegger's summons in 1927 for "the people" to "choose its hero," soon revealed to be Hitler). European novelists often took the lead in capturing the psychological profile of the revolutionary, and not always in flattering terms. For instance, Flaubert's character Senecal in *Sentimental Education* is a prototype of the millenarian revolutionary who both recalls Robespierre and anticipates Stalin, Hitler, and their top aides. He dreams of ruling over an "American Sparta," a collectivized and industrialized totalitarian state, to revenge himself for his failure to rise in bourgeois society. An aspiring mathematician like Robespierre who also wants to "plane off" social inequality and rank as if resolving an equation, he is also a prude who fantasizes about the austere collectivism of feudal society. He is both a modernizer and a Romantic, a blend, Flaubert writes, of "the pedant and the priest."

Novelists like Flaubert and Turgenev cast a jaundiced eye on the revolutionaries of their day – the would-be anarchist Bazarov in *Fathers and Sons* despises all traditional attachments of family affection, faith, patriotism, and good breeding, regarding human beings as proven by modern science to be nothing but mechanisms for producing and consuming commodities, and whose materialistic sloth must be purged in a coming new order. But many political activists and ideologues tried to make revolution an aesthetic enterprise, akin to a great work of art fashioned out of human clay. Their critique of the bourgeoisie was at least as much on aesthetic grounds as it was a protest against their injustice – their spiritual deformity, ugliness, crass materialism, and bad taste (one thinks of Dickens' Uriah Heap) could only be corrected by their eradication in the beautiful world to come. Marx in effect takes the experience of human wholeness – of a bond between man and the world that Schiller had maintained in his *Letters on the Aesthetic Education of Man* could only be experienced through contemplating great art, never in politics with its unavoidable divisiveness, crass partisanship, and devotion to economic profit – and maintains that the coming world of socialism will achieve this same experience of wholeness and unity for all of mankind, not through the contemplation of art but by quite literally submerging the individual in the bliss of the collective.

This vision of the beautification of the coming age that will transcend all mere political disputation was accompanied by the beautification of revolutionary violence as a heroic act. Nineteenth century German philosophy and social thought as a whole contributed greatly to the disenchantment of the educated elites with the modern age and their preparation for millenarian upheaval. The great exception was Hegel, guardian of the center whose emphasis on historical precedent and the accumulation of custom was an attempt to rescue the modern era from revolutionary attacks from the extremes of both Left and Right. In his defense of moderate progressivism, he was a kindred spirit with Tocqueville, Burke, and J. S. Mill. But his successors, Marx, Nietzsche, and Heidegger, shattered this middle ground as the nineteenth century unfolded into the twentieth and insisted that true human wholeness could only be achieved through millenarian violence. Ever more intense calls from the Left for a super-Jacobin monolithic socialist state are paralleled on the Right by the call for "the people" to shatter the grip of Enlightenment rationalism and return to the "blood and soil" of its collective destiny.

Allies of moderate progressive liberalism continued to come to its defense and sound a warning about the dark clouds on the horizon as the nineteenth century moved forward. Consider the Jewish-born German poet Heinrich Heine's prescient warning (which provides the title for this part of the book) in 1834 that the powerful anti-Enlightenment trends in German culture will produce a German Revolution in the next century that will shake the world: "Then know at last the German thunderbolt has fallen. At this commotion the eagles will drop dead from the skies ... There will be played in Germany a drama compared to which the French Revolution looks like an innocent idyll." Alexis de Tocqueville, evolving from the precociously brilliant early observer of America to a seasoned moderate and trimmer in the turbulent politics of mid-century France, had warned in *Democracy in America* that the materialism, apathy, and self-absorption of democratic citizenries may lead to the emergence of a "democratic despot" who will rob them of their liberties by promising them ever greater equality and prosperity in exchange for giving him total power. This new kind of despot, he warned, will continue the Jacobin project of creating a monolithic, all-encompassing state as the artificial replacement for the sense of social harmony and unity that the Old World of feudal hierarchy and religious faith had provided before being assaulted by the individualistic creed of the Enlightenment.

Tocqueville lived to see the realization of his fears not in America, but in France with Napoleon III, who came to power through a military putsch followed by a plebiscite in which the French people could "vote" only for him (a device used routinely since then by despots down to Hitler's plebiscite in the annexed Sudetenland and Putin's "referendum" in the annexed Crimea). He was supported by the Right, who wanted social and economic stability after the revolutions of 1848, and by the Left, who thought he would curtail the power of the rich. Flaubert's character, Senecal, migrates throughout the course of *Sentimental Education* from being a latter-day Jacobin to a secret police agent and political murderer for Napoleon III, illustrating perfectly how the extremes of Left and Right merged in the longing for dictatorship.

Some of the early analysts of twentieth-century fascism rightly saw in Napoleon III an antecedent for the populist demagoguery of Mussolini and Hitler. For Konrad Heiden, Napoleon III was a "master of the modern mass and its state of mind ... Conspirator, usurper ... at once nationalist and socialist, democrat and tyrant, pacifist and conqueror, dictator by virtue of bayonets and plebiscites, applauded by the masses whom he had politically raped." All very true, but it should be added that Napoleon III was not driven by a millenarian vision requiring utopian genocide. Although he anticipated some of the tactics of the Bolshevik and Fascist seizures of power, he was more in the reforming-tyrant category. Like his vastly more successful uncle, Napoleon I, and earlier reforming tyrants like Caesar, he beautified Paris, adding to the great boulevards. Once firmly in control, his rule was affable and left people to enjoy themselves. He also imitated the first Napoleon's imperial aspirations which, given the nephew's complete lack of military ability and general mediocrity, led to his shattering defeat by the forces of Bismarck's Prussia at Sedan and his hasty abdication.

If there were some defenders of political moderation such as Heine and Tocqueville among Europe's intellectual classes, they were not among the most admired and influential thinkers. Along with the detestation for what Nietzsche called the "herd man" of "leveling" democratic morality went a longing among the educated elites for a return to the heroism of the archaic world, the emergence of new Homeric heroes who would lead the struggle to smash the contemptible bourgeois present and restore a sense of rank, greatness, and honor. Schliemann's famous excavations at Mycenae with which we began Part One galvanized the European imagination with visions of a new race of Achilles. In Germany, the name *Herman,* the modern version of the name of the Germanic warrior Arminius who had fought off conquest by Rome, became widely popular. The gradual displacement of Christianity as an intellectual and moral authority in nineteenth century Europe by Marxism and Darwinism popularized a worldview that saw all species as being driven by an insuperable urge to conquer and dominate their competitors. It undermined remaining religious restraints on revolutionary violence and led to a new paganism in which the drive for mastery and domination by individual states and by "Great Men" became widely admired in elite culture.

In all these ways, the great composer Richard Wagner was the embodiment of his century. His life also completely refutes those who persist in seeing a sharp distinction between the far Left and the far Right – usually accompanied by the view that leftist extremism was an unwitting excess or betrayal by a few people of its humane values, while violence on the far right was entirely characteristic of its immoral outlook. In fact, they are mirror image opposites of each other, as we'll see in more detail when we turn to Bolshevism and Nazism. Wagner began as a firebrand of the revolution of 1848 before migrating to the "folkish" Right as he created a new millenarian mythology through his breathtaking operas. But this migration from Left to Right was not a change of mind or heart, only a more effective means for what he wanted to do all along. The *Ring Cycle* embodies the whole revolutionary psychodrama originating with Rousseau – the summons back to a magic, primeval Golden Age that fuels the impulse forward to destroy the modern bourgeois world in the coming twentieth century's "politics of greatness," the struggle (as his sometime friend Nietzsche put it) between the "herd man" of democratic morality and the new "lords of the earth."

The vilest anti-Semitism combined in Wagner with a deep Romantic nationalism that he nurtured under the patronage of the King of Bavaria, later the cradle of the National Socialist movement. Wagner was also very much influenced by Marx's inspiration, Feuerbach, who had argued against Hegel's benign view of gradual historical progress guided by precedent, proclaiming that man must assert his will against nature and reshape it in whatever way he saw fit, tearing down all precedents, shattering all traditions, finally understanding that what we call God is merely the furthest limit of our *own* aspirations to complete creative freedom. Wagner's mythological depiction of world destruction in *Götterdämmerung* reflected his very real taste for anarchism. Consider his conflicted but starstruck description of his encounter with the notorious anarchist Bakunin, a portion of which I quoted earlier: "In this remarkable man the purest humanitarian idealism was combined with a savagery utterly inimical to all culture, and thus my relationship with him fluctuated between instinctive horror and irresistible attraction." (Wagner could have been describing Hitler as many of his early admirers saw him, including Wagner's daughter-in-law Winifred Wagner, often with the same mixture of revulsion and fascination). "The annihilation of all civilization was the objective on which (Bakunin) had set his heart," Wagner recalled. "It was necessary, he said, to picture the whole European world, with Petersburg, Paris, and London transformed into a pile of rubble." He would get his wish.

Friedrich Nietzsche, who late in life became Germany's most famous thinker, contributed to the mounting sense of impending doom and destruction that will yield a new world. "This is the time," he wrote in the 1880s, "of *the great noon of the most terrible* clearing up ... " The coming "lords of the earth," the "supermen," would face enormous spiritual tests of self-overcoming in order to be able to carry out their mission without bourgeois scruples: "To gain that tremendous energy of greatness in order to shape the man of the future through breeding and, on the other hand, the annihilation of millions of failures, and not to perish of the suffering one creates, though nothing like it has ever existed!" As he put it in the *Genealogy of Morals*, "the sick are the great danger of man, not the evil, not the 'beasts of prey.' They who are from the outset botched, oppressed, broken, those are they, the weakest are they, who most undermine the life beneath the feet of man."

As for communism, Nietzsche welcomed the attempt to create it, precisely because he foresaw what a disaster it would be: "The earth is large enough and man still sufficiently unexhausted; hence such a practical instruction and demonstration *ad absurdum* would not strike me as undesirable, even if it were gained and paid for with a tremendous expenditure of human lives." The violent struggle, he continues, to create such an absurdity as a classless society "will be able to be something useful and therapeutic: it delays 'peace on earth' and the total mollification of the democratic herd animal; it forces the

Europeans to retain spirit, namely cunning and cautious care, not to abjure manly and warlike virtues altogether, and to retain some remnant of spirit, of clarity, sobriety, and coldness of the spirit ... "

Later, the Nazis would consciously borrow Nietzsche's concepts of the "superman" and "the triumph of the will" for their own propaganda. Nietzsche's sister, Elisabeth Forster-Nietzsche, told Hitler that he was the superman her brother had been waiting for. Did Nietzsche intend his writings to contribute to a millenarian revolution? The issue here is very similar to the question of Rousseau's contribution to the French Revolution. Nietzsche's defenders maintain that his calls for a superman exercising the will to power were entirely metaphorical – that he was calling for an inner struggle to purify one's own spirit, not a literal war of destruction on the "herd man" and the creation of a new world. It's possible they are right in part, although one would have to read Nietzsche's books with blinkers on so as to avoid the many passages dealing with real-world events and the need for a new and terrible tyranny of the emerging "masters" so as to focus only on one's personal, inner self-development. But whether they are right or not, Nietzsche's rhetoric is so extravagant, so violent, so exhilarating in its celebration of struggle and mastery that, just as with Rousseau's influence on Robespierre, it's hardly surprising that someone like Hitler would take him literally, just as he saw in Wagner's operas a summons to create the National Socialist *Götterdämmerung*.

As Europe careened unwittingly toward World War I, Germany's educated classes devoured books by *Volkish* authors like Paul de Lagarde who called for the expulsion of all Enlightenment and liberal values from Germany so as to promote "the growth of what will sprout out of the old soil once it has been cleansed of rubbish: the roots of our being are still alive." The outlines of the coming "Third Reich" began to take shape in the German imagination, a term that deliberately transferred to violent revolutionary war and struggle the Biblical motif of the return of the Messiah and his establishment of the Kingdom of God on earth. "The Third Reich," wrote Arthur Moeller van den Bruck, "is a spiritual goal and simultaneously embraces a political task." A supreme leader would be needed to take us to this new world.

Herman Hesse in his 1919 novel *Demian* entertained the notion that the First World War would inaugurate the apocalyptic struggle for the New Order. These revolutionary fantasies only intensified after Germany's defeat. The war's unprecedented carnage and destruction, to most people a source of woe and horror, struck others as precisely the spiritual forge Nietzsche had seen as necessary for the strength of will needed to shape the "new man." As Ernst Junger, whose tract *The Worker* foresaw a new breed of worker-warriors anticipating both Bolshevik and Nazi poster art of muscled brutes, wrote of the World War I generation hardened by total war into a steely ruthlessness: "Never before has a race of men like ours stridden into the arena of the world to decide who is to wield power over the epoch." For Hitler and the other veterans who made up the core of the Nazi movement, the war had never ended. Five years before Hitler's seizure of power, the *Volkish* poet Stefan Georg was already envisioning the Führer:

> "He places the true symbol of the people's banner,
> He leads the band of loyal followers through the storm/
> and fearsome harbingers of dawn, to the work/
> of broad daylight/
> and plants the New Reich."

NO SECOND THERMIDOR: MILLENARIAN TYRANNY RETURNS

Out of the tremendous political and cultural ferment of the nineteenth century in its search for an escape from the modern bourgeois world, two fundamental revolutionary paths to utopia open up in the twentieth century – the Bolshevik reconstruction of society "from above" and the National Socialist revolution of "the people's destiny" from below. The Bolsheviks attempt to carry out, with renewed focus and on a much larger scale, the Jacobin project for creating a monolithic, totalistic, industrialized state (Senecal's "American Sparta."). Tocqueville's original formulation of the thesis of the revolution of rising expectations points to some broad historical similarities between the French and Russian revolutions that help explain why Russia was ripe for this explosion. For, just as the cautiously reformist monarchy of Louis XVI and the original liberal revolution of Lafayette gave way to the far more radical Jacobins, so was the fitful reformism of the last Czar and the liberal Kerensky government swept away by the brute force of the Bolsheviks.

The theories of Karl Marx gave the Bolsheviks a veneer of pseudo-rationality through his claim that history was unfolding in inevitable stages according to the principles of "scientific socialism." Equally important, however, was Marx's own ambivalence about whether to prefer violent revolution or gradual evolution in moving history forward, and how his waffling over the prospects for socialism in Russia invited Lenin and Trotsky to give history a sharp push and seize the state through a *coup d'etat*. At bottom, the real core of Bolshevism, typified by Lenin and Stalin, was sheer Promethean destruction, unlimited by any considerations of prudence or theoretical consistency. Indeed, while Lenin certainly viewed himself as a Marxist, there is reason to believe that the Bolsheviks' most direct spiritual and psychological forbears were not European Marxists at all, but millenarian and mystical Russian sects like the "god builders," inspired by Nietzsche's writings about the Superman to create a new world from the ground up on the ruins of the old. Dostoevsky and Slavophilic nationalism, the Russian parallel of the search by German writers and thinkers for a "rooted" tribal nationalism, also colored the Bolshevik vision of a future classless society purged of vice and selfish individualism, the Russian Orthodox Church's ancient sense of mission as the avatar of an apocalyptic "third age" redeeming all mankind now transferred from religious yearning to the goal of revolutionary action.

Crucial to the dynamism of what Trotsky called "permanent revolution" was Lenin's famous maxim, "the worse, the better." This maxim provided a building block for all subsequent millenarian revolutionary movements. It characterizes any opposition to a collectivist utopia as irredeemably hostile and corrupt, whose annihilation is, therefore, mandatory and unavoidable. Accordingly, real revolutionaries (as opposed to mere bourgeois reformers or labor unions) not only do not believe that liberal states and societies can reform, they do not want them to. The worse the revolutionary classes are oppressed, the more they will be driven by hopelessness, despair, and hatred to lash back in violent struggle. Lenin detested ordinary social democrats and liberal progressives because, by extracting better conditions from the capitalists for the workers, they prevented a real revolution from breaking out. Every brutal Tsarist crackdown and firing squad was eagerly welcomed because it a made liberal reformism an impossible option.

These potent historical, ideological, and cultural currents culminated in Stalin's "revolution from above," the bloody campaigns of forced collectivization and industrialization that claimed some sixty millions lives. But its features were already in place under Lenin. The Bolsheviks' drive to force Russia overnight from an agrarian society into a fully industrialized modern state, while simultaneously preventing the emergence of individual rights and private property, required a project of state-directed genocide whose eventual death toll is in the tens of millions, including mass extermination, slave labor camps, and artificially created state famines (a technique for reconstructing society later imitated in Ethiopia by self-proclaimed Marxist-Leninist ruler Colonel Mengistu). There was no important difference between the genocidal aims of Lenin, Trotsky, or Stalin. The "reform" communism of the Mensheviks and Bukharin – prepared to cooperate to a degree with market forces – was incompatible with Bolshevism's core vision of genocidal destruction and the creation of a "new man" purged of selfish individualism. Just as the Jacobins had invented the category of the "counterrevolutionary" – the single force whose obliteration would shatter the grip of vice and alienation on mankind and usher in the brave new world ahead – the Bolsheviks now invented the fictitious category of "the kulak," the imaginary "wealthy peasant" who becomes the sinister embodiment of all greed, deceit, and disloyalty, standing in the way of total collectivism.

Another trend originating with the Jacobins, but now expanding exponentially under the impetus of the nineteenth-century's fascination with the revolutionary Superman, the epoch-making builder of new worlds, was the growth of the Bolshevik secret police, the NKVD, as an elite vanguard entrusted with the spiritual mission of methodical mass murder, a state within the state like the SS was later to become. As early as 1917, the Bolsheviks' first year in power, the NKVD's poised and cold-blooded Felix Dzerzshinksy shocked a more moderate Menshevik leader who argued that Russian society would evolve gradually through "economic and political development" by calmly asking why this transformation couldn't be achieved more rapidly "through the subjection or extermination of some classes of society." Utopian genocide was already on the agenda.

As a high school student, I remember reading that the makers of the Russian Revolution swore there would be no second Thermidor like the first Thermidor during the French Revolution. I naively supposed this meant that they would not allow the idealism of their revolution to be betrayed by another bloodthirsty Robespierre. Only later did I discover that Thermidor was when Robespierre *fell*. The Bolsheviks weren't promising to *prevent* another Terror – they were promising to *continue* it on a much vaster scale. Terror was their ideal, and they were not going to allow any bourgeois liberals or mere reformers to obstruct its mission to reconstruct society from top to bottom. Millenarian tyranny, having taken a hiatus since 1793, now came roaring back.

In Lenin's version of Marxism, before the revolution, tactical compromise with other political groups was possible, but there could be no compromise on the strategic goal of a collective society without property. Like Robespierre, Lenin aimed to impose a geometrical purity on corrupt human fodder. As we mentioned in the Introduction, this cold-blooded lust for destruction was originally born out of outrage over a brother being executed for treason and the family's resulting disgrace, eventually projected as revenge on the entire world. Lenin never believed that socialism could triumph in Russia alone and would never have been content with such small stakes ("I spit on Russia," as he once put it. "This is merely one phase through which we must pass on the way to a world revolution"). He thought the Russian Revolution would act as a spur to a European revolution, which would then help the development of Russia's backward agrarian society with its far more advanced industrial economy. Seizing power in a *coup d'etat* as the Romanov dynasty crumbled, the Bolsheviks used the empty husk of the now vacant Caesaropapist absolute state of the Czars to begin imposing communism by force. From the very outset, though, as we've observed, Bolshevik savagery left the Czars at their most autocratic in the shade. As Lenin remarked, "a revolution without firing squads is meaningless ... The purpose of terror is to terrorize."

Although Lenin claimed to be an orthodox Marxist (and may even have believed it), he was really a *putschist* and would-be dictator. As mentioned, the real predecessors for the Bolsheviks included a Nietzschean sect called the "God builders," who envisioned creating a new world on the rubble of the old, as well as the "People's Will" movement, driven by Rousseauan and Tolstoyan nostalgia for an allegedly lost golden age of peasant wholeness. As Robert Conquest observed, "the communist party leadership was not a group of rational economists ... though they sometimes thought of themselves as such, and represented their actions as such to observers in the west. They were a group which had accepted a millenarian doctrine, and their rationale for holding power was that they would translate this into practice to produce a new and superior society." When Czarist Russia was shaken to its foundations by World War I, millions of casualties in the trenches and a collapsing economy sparking unrest at home, Trotsky egged Lenin on to seize control amidst the chaos. Despite his later pose in exile in the West as a sensitive intellectual, Trotsky was a complete nihilist and mass murderer (hundreds were mowed down by his traveling armored train for no other crime than being successful, something he had never achieved in normal times). He was Senecal brought to life, the revenge of the armed bohemian against his exclusion from social acceptability. "Whatever moral eunuchs and Pharisees might say," he enthused, "the feeling of revenge has its right ... We [must] direct all our strengths toward a collective struggle against this class structure. That is the method by which the burning desire for revenge can achieve its greatest moral satisfaction."

Lenin and his henchmen were devoid of patriotism, since their revolution was to be but the first stage in a coming international Communist order. While Kerensky tried desperately to continue the war effort after the Czar's abdication, Lenin – who had been sent back from exile into Russia by the German Kaiser like, as Churchill put it, a "plague bacillus" to undermine the regime – gave up huge chunks of the country in order to make peace so that the "dictatorship of the proletariat" could entrench itself in what remained. Any illusions people might have had that Lenin stood for electoral democracy were lost when the 1921 Kronstadt rebellion against emerging Soviet dictatorship was ruthlessly put down. On a personal level, Lenin was as cold as ice and intolerant of all debate. He was no more of a "theorist" than Hitler, his dreary tracts mainly vicious diatribes against rivals. Ransacked bits of Marxism served his purpose of seizing absolute power and crushing society, just as Hitler did later in invoking Nietzsche. He couldn't speak inspirationally in public, although his famous call for "Peace, Land, All Power to the Soviets" on arriving at the Finland Station in the Kaiser's sealed car had an impressive simplicity.

In *Lenin in Zurich*, Solzhenitsyn tells the story of how Lenin's wife Krupskaya had her very ill mother living with them while they were in exile. She would sit up with her mother at night, and needing a few hours' sleep herself, once asked Lenin, who always stayed up late reading, to wake her up if her mother needed her. Next morning, Krupskaya woke up to find her mother had been dead in her room for several hours. When, very distraught, she asked Lenin, still at his desk, why he had not wakened her, he calmly replied: "You asked me to wake you if your mother needed you. She's dead – so she obviously didn't need you." Do we need to know more?

It was Lenin's old comrade Pyatakov who left the image favored by the Bolsheviks of Lenin as an earth-shaking, monumental figure, one who, as Mussolini admiringly remarked, was a sculptor of human souls. Lenin's actions were not guided by analyzing social and economic conditions, as Marxism taught. Instead, he *created* those conditions, like Rousseau's Legislator or Nietzsche's Superman: "The real Lenin," Pyatakov wrote, "was the man who had the courage to make a proletarian revolution first, and then to set about creating the objective conditions theoretically necessary as a preliminary to such a revolution. What was the October revolution, what indeed is the Communist Party, but a miracle?" He went on: "According to Lenin, the Communist Party is based on the principle of coercion which doesn't recognize any limitations or inhibitions. And the central idea of this principle of boundless coercion is not coercion by itself, but the absence of any limitation whatsoever – moral, political and even physical, as far as that goes." It was the complete identification of revolutionary political action with an omnipotence formerly reserved for God: "Such a party is capable of achieving miracles and doing things which no other collective of men could achieve ... A real communist ... becomes himself in a way a miracle man."

THE NUMBER-ONE LENINIST

Stalin was misunderstood for a long time in the West because of Trotsky's self-serving portrait of him as an obscure "grey blur" who took power through controlling the Party bureaucracy and driving out Trotsky, Lenin's heir and the sensitive and sincere social democrat, betraying the Revolution by ruling like a modern-day Genghis Khan. All of this was false. Unlike many of the pince-nezed cafe ranters, bohemian pamphleteers, and failed students around Lenin, Stalin really did come from a peasant background. As a Georgian – like Alexander the Great, Napoleon, and later Hitler, an outsider from a somewhat looked-down-upon hinterland – he may have nurtured a resentment against proper Russians. His upbringing by a brutal drunkard of a father apparently gave him a lasting taste for brutality and revenge projected onto the world of privilege. His understanding of Marxism was akin to a catechism, as were his speeches, dry and thin-voiced, reflecting his stint as a seminarian, perhaps an early outlet for his fanaticism. But he really did believe in communism as it had been created by Lenin, and carried out Lenin's genuine policies to the letter –rapid industrialization and collectivization at a cost of tens of millions of lives. In reality, Lenin favored him from very early on, admiring his ruthlessness and taste for physical violence. He was one of the party's leading fundraisers through bank robberies. Lenin gave him his position as General Secretary of the Communist Party not because he was a mere bureaucrat, but because he trusted him. Lenin had no time at all for intellectuals – if this is the proper term for a rabble-rousing putschist and killer like Trotsky – other than himself. Although conventional and apologetic histories depict the extreme measures of slave labor during the 1918–1921 period of "war communism" (eagerly orchestrated by Trotsky) as a temporary response to the desperate threat of the Soviet government's defeat by the White Russians, distracting Lenin from the constructive tasks of building a modern economy, in truth, "war communism" was what Lenin wanted all the time. Lenin's so-called new economic policy (NEP) of the 1920s, when collectivization was temporarily slowed and a limited degree of land ownership and small business was allowed, was a concession to stave off complete starvation, especially for Party members, meant to be shelved as soon as possible so that the Party could return to its mission of complete collectivization. In other words, "war communism" *was* communism.

Stalin's triumph over Trotsky after Lenin's death and his rise to supreme power was a brilliant maneuver that left the vain and verbose Trotsky, who thought that ranting for three hours meant that everyone agreed with him, in the dust. First, Stalin patronized Bukharin and the NEP so as to rout Trotsky for being too far to the left. Having driven his main opponent into exile, he then veered to the far left himself and routed Bukharin and the reformers. The horrors of full collectivization followed, just as Lenin had wanted, a task that Trostky, as demonstrated by his earlier role in organizing slave labor and the mass liquidation of "class enemies," would have carried out if he had been given the chance. In returning to Lenin's utopian vision of rapid collectivization, Stalin correctly sensed the psychological orientation of the Party, especially the young – they wanted the excitement and idealism of what Lenin, the "miracle man," had envisioned, and they wanted to become miracle men themselves through the limitless exercise of willpower against the Revolution's enemies.

The NKVD, later KGB, Stalin's favorite people (unlike the tweedy, cafe intellectuals of the Bolshevik Old Guard whom he despised), became a state within a state as they spearheaded this genocidal mission, a power grab later imitated by the Nazi SS. Relentless terror was justified by the Soviet economic doctrine of "primitive socialist accumulation." In other words, every ounce of wealth had to be squeezed from the people in order to finance overnight the building of factories and a huge modern military. After all, the Bolsheviks reasoned, hadn't capitalism done this itself over the centuries in creating modern industrial productivity? Marx called it the extraction of "surplus value" from what the workers produced, paying them a pittance of its actual worth and confiscating the rest for profit and for building new factories. It was just a matter of speeding that process up, but this time, economic strength would serve a selfless ideal, not bourgeois luxury and greed. A modern industrial state had to be built overnight, from above, in the midst of a thoroughly agrarian culture. But no one must be allowed to profit from it – all labor would be organized by the state. This had been Lenin's mission, and Stalin was determined to see it through. As unforgettably diagnosed by Solzhenitsyn, the Gulag system was not merely a means for procuring slave labor, but also the prototype of the ideal world to come, the "New Soviet Man" himself, stripped of all attachments to soil, faith, family, and private possessions, loyal only to the crushing monolith of the Stalinist state. At bottom, this process of the total subordination of the individual to the collective was even more important to Bolshevism than building an industrial economy. As Stalin himself put it, he was less interested in producing more factories than in being "the engineer of human souls."

The Terror Famine of 1932–1933 in the Ukraine, deliberately engineered by Stalin to extract every ounce of agricultural production for sale abroad to finance new factories while Ukrainians starved was, as Robert Conquest wrote, "one vast Belsen" in which parents were driven to cannibalize their own children or sell their body parts as food. The Politburo had resolved that "the time is ripe for the question of the elimination of the kulak to be posed in a specific form" – the same sort of bureaucratese later used by Heydrich and Eichmann to discuss the "question" of the extermination of the Jews. There must be no hesitation, no bourgeois moral scruples, about destroying the class of so-called rich peasants. As Zinoviev put it, "We must carry along with us ninety million of the one hundred million Soviet population. As for the rest, we have nothing to say to them. They must be annihilated." Actually, the number of deaths through execution, starvation, collectivization, and slave labor was closer to twenty million, according to Roy Medvedev, not counting the twenty million deaths from World War II that were also Stalin's fault, as we'll discuss shortly. (Historian Norman Davies puts the death toll at fifty million, not counting wartime casualties). Stalin himself reasoned, "it is ridiculous and fatuous to expatiate today on the expropriation of the kulaks. You do not lament the loss of hair of one who has been beheaded." The young Party cadres who went into the countryside to supervise the genocide did so with enthusiasm and harsh dedication. As one organizer lectured, "you must assume your duties with a feeling of the strictest Party responsibility, without whimpering, without any rotten liberalism." A young woman "activist" recalled: "In order to massacre them, it was necessary to proclaim that kulaks are not human beings. Just as the Germans proclaimed that Jews are not human beings. Thus did Lenin and Stalin proclaim, kulaks are not human beings." Another official remarked, "We know that millions are dying. That is unfortunate, but the glorious future of the Soviet Union will justify that." If you were to replace "kulak" with "Jew" in these accounts, you could be quoting the Nazis, the SS, and Himmler.

Unlike Lenin, Stalin believed that communism could be fully achieved in Russia. But then its blessings must be spread to the entire world – as he observed in his 1937 speech *Mastering Bolshevism*, so far "the Soviet power" only covered one sixth of the globe: There was much left to be done. As a millenarian revolutionary, he was necessarily an imperialist. Through his 1939 pact with Hitler – the one man, as Solzhenitsyn mordantly remarks, Stalin ever really trusted – no single person was more responsible, after Hitler himself, for World War II and the death, destruction, and suffering it unleashed than Stalin. For without that pact, Hitler could never have taken out France and (as he believed) Britain, then turned on central Europe, inaugurating the Holocaust. Yes, the Russian people suffered incredibly – a fact hauled out relentlessly by Soviet and Russian leaders ever since, including Putin, as if that past suffering in some vague way justified his conquest of other peoples today. But that suffering, too, was the result of Stalin's actions, including his persistence in ignoring the signs of an impending Nazi betrayal and invasion. When Hitler invaded, Russian armies were driven against the Germans at gunpoint, including women, children, mental patients, and prisoners who were forced to precede the troops into suspected minefields so as to set the mines off. After the defeat of Germany, Stalin was bent on keeping every scrap of territory that he and Hitler had agreed upon originally, especially Poland – that was why his promise at Yalta to hold free elections in territory occupied by the Red Army was a lie from the outset, making the Cold War inevitable.

Personally, Stalin was by all accounts smart, well-read, and inquisitive. He was capable of a bearish charm with his subordinates, but could not stand having his views challenged and never forgot the offense. He also could not stand being shown up. During the victory parade in Red Square after Germany's defeat, Russia's most successful commander Marshall Zhukov, said to have "never lost a battle," rode a dashing white stallion. Stalin had planned to do the same, but fell while trying to mount the horse. After the war, Zhukov was demoted to a minor regional post. (Rare among Stalin's subordinates for openly disagreeing with Stalin over the conduct of the war, he had earned Stalin's respect, which may have saved him from a far worse fate). Stalin seemed to believe his own propaganda about being a genius in all spheres of human activity, and he intervened frequently in the arts. He cautioned Pasternak about how to write Soviet fiction and gave Shostakovich advice on composing music that was truly Bolshevik (no modernist influences, which Stalin regarded as anti-Communist). He distrusted anyone of upper-class origins, and almost lost the war to Hitler because he had purged much of the officer class. But his massive purges of the Party enabled young people to rise rapidly into the vacated positions, which, along with being worshipped for the godlike scope of his power, was a source of his authority with the younger generation. Another "miracle man" like Lenin, he tapped the true Nietzschean core of the Bolshevik ethos. No act of brutality, cruelty, or sadism later committed by the Nazis had not been trail-blazed by Stalin and the Bolsheviks. Little wonder that when German Foreign Minister Von Ribbentrop visited Moscow to seal the Hitler-Stalin pact, he later enthused to the Führer that meeting Stalin and his paladins had been "just like being among our old Party comrades!"

The death of his first wife, Stalin claimed, had removed any trace of pity from his heart. But did he ever have any? Solzhenitsyn remarked that his one true talent was to sense precisely where every man's soul intersects with the mud, that point where our best aspirations to do good are subverted by our fear and greed, and to take advantage of it. He enjoyed toying with his victims, tormenting Bukharin by having the NKVD call him in for questioning, then purporting to save him from arrest – all the while knowing he would order the arrest soon. He told Dzherzinsky in a revealing moment: "To choose one's victims, to prepare one's plans minutely, to slake an implacable vengeance, and then to go to bed ... There is nothing sweeter in the world." He claimed (like Saddam Hussein, one of his admirers, later) that he could see treason in a man's eyes. His humor was sardonic, as in his description of Communist sympathizers in the West as "useful idiots," or his habit of summoning some expert from the hell of the Gulag to be given a favored assignment and beaming at the frightened wraith saying, "Yuri, where on earth have you been? I've been looking for you all over the place! We need you!" His close associate, KGB chief Beria, indulged in sadistic excesses on the scale of Klaus Barbie, with a dungeon in his house for the torture of enemies and the rape of kidnapped schoolgirls.

While many Party bigwigs lived lavishly, Stalins's way of life was not opulent. He enjoyed power, not the enjoyment of the riches it brought. His biographer Simon Sebag Montefiore compares the scale and furnishings of his apartment in the Kremlin to that of an Oxford don. His tastes were coarse – huge portions of meat swilled down with gallons of sweet wine. He spent months on end in the Crimea because of its climate, as had the Czars. Like a tyrant of ancient times, his personal household was hard to distinguish from the government – he ran the entire country from his dinner table, often at raucous binges that went on all night. He pursued Lenin's utopian vision with what Montefiore describes as a "quasi-Islamic fanaticism," but at the end of the day the entire experiment was a vast, pointless tragedy. Prior to 1917, Russia had one of the fastest-growing economies in Europe – all Lenin and Stalin accomplished, after tens of millions had died, was to damage it almost beyond recovery.

This is why I think that Machiavelli, who as we saw in Part Two laid down the principles of modern state building, would not have counted Lenin or Stalin in the category of the "outstanding prince" who exerts his will to "master Fortuna." Machiavelli had no objection to the use of force, but only if it resulted in prosperity and security for the prince's subjects. That was "well-used cruelty," and as it was mainly preventive and pre-emptive, Machiavelli argued, its scale and duration need not be immense. Killing millions to pursue some fantasy of a world "beyond politics," a "classless society" of complete happiness and unity forever would have struck Machiavelli as completely pointless. Once again, millenarian tyranny differs in the scale of its violence and the fantasy of its aims from the reforming tyrant even at his most ruthless.

War and imperial aggression made up for the Soviet Union's economic failures, from Stalin's occupation of eastern Europe and Kruschev's flirtation with provoking nuclear war through his proxy Castro during the Cuban missile crisis to Brezhnev's invasion of Afghanistan. Contrary to a view still inexplicably widespread in the West, the Cold War was entirely Stalin's fault for breaking every promise he made at Yalta, even menacing Greece before the United States, then the sole nuclear power, warned him off. Of all the uncomfortable decisions about choosing the lesser of evils that we've been discussing in this book, surely none was more sickening than the necessity of allying with the faithless and cynical Stalin against the greater evil Hitler, a moral grey zone symbolized by the presence on the Nuremberg Tribunal of Soviet officials who had committed some of the same atrocities of which the Nazis in the dock stood accused – Iona Nikitchenko, who had orchestrated the notorious "show trials" during Stalin's Great Purge, and Roman Rudenko, who later commanded an NKVD camp in which 12,500 prisoners died of starvation and disease.

The kind of ally we took on with the Soviet Union is captured by an eye-witness account of a scene left behind by the NKVD when they fled from the German advance into Poland, methods of ruling they had exported from Russia to the territories newly acquired through the Hitler-Stalin pact. The floor was covered in eight inches of blood. "Men had had their sexual organs and women their breasts ripped or cut off. Eyes had been gouged out, bodies were beaten or crushed into unrecognizable masses of bones and flesh ... (They) bore on their faces distorted expressions of unimaginable agony ... the dead body of a small girl, aged about eight years, hanging from the ceiling lamp."

These atrocities may not have been widely known, but they were certainly known to some, including in official Washington. Viktor Kravchenko, who had escaped from the Gulag, chronicled in his 1946 book *I Chose Freedom* many of the same horrors later given wider exposure by Solzhenitsyn. To his astonishment, he met a brick wall of self-willed ignorance among the "useful idiots" (Stalin's phrase) in the United States. "I saw men and women who themselves called President Roosevelt a dictator grow furious when Stalin was called one ... Great chunks of the Communist reality – like slave labor, police dictatorship, the massive periodic purges, the fantastically low standards of living, the Great Famine of 32–33, the horrors of collectivization, the state-organized child labor – [W]hen I ventured to mention such things ... Americans looked at me incredulously and some even hastened to enter cocksure denials ... To my amazement, I discovered that they thought Russia a country in which 'the workers ruled,' in which the farmers 'lived in a cooperative society,' in which 'everyone was equal'!" The explanation for these delusions about Soviet rule may be nothing more sophisticated than that the Soviet Union claimed it stood for equality (while the Nazis openly proclaimed that they did not) coupled with a now centuries-old tradition of individual liberty, tolerance, and the rule of law in the West that, having resulted in such prosperous and peaceable societies, made it difficult for people to fathom how fellow human-beings could sink to being such depraved beasts.

THE NATIONAL SOCIALIST WORLD BLESSING

Walking through the remains of the Auschwitz-Birkenau death camp in Poland, one is struck that it is a vast battery cell of death, shunting and distributing across a grid of forty square kilometers the energy of mass murder. It's comparable to an abattoir for human beings, or to a stationary version of the slave ships that transported human cargo from Africa. The prisoner barracks are very much like drawings you have seen of those slave ship holds, stables for human beings stacked like logs, except that real animals would never have been treated so badly. The ruins of the gas chambers made me feel eerily as if I were touring the ruins of some vanished and brutal ancient culture, like the Mayan pyramids where endless human sacrifices were carried out. There is a strange peacefulness, and this was noticed by eye-witnesses even when the camp was in operation: "What impressed us," one of the SS doctors later recalled, "was the fact that Auschwitz was a collective effort ... and the disturbing thing was that it was not something passionate ... It was something calm. There was nothing emotional about Auschwitz." As Reinhard Heydrich, architect of the Final Solution under Himmler – once described as a "young god of death" – commented macabrely about the means of extermination developed to perfection there: "I must admit this gassing had a calming effect on me. I was always horrified at the executions by firing squad."

Even today, one is struck by the vast symmetry and flawless planning of the site, essentially two long avenues intersecting near the platform where the prisoners were unloaded from cattle cars. If the SS doctor waved you to the left, you went straight to the gas chambers. If he waved you to the right, you went to the barracks for slave laborers. Viewing the entire camp from atop the entrance tower where the trains passed under the famous *Arbeit Macht Frei* sign ("Work Will Make You Free") in its sinisterly elegant wrought-iron pattern, the whole huge complex with its two enormous avenues and thousands of perfectly spaced barracks interspersed with hundreds of perfectly spaced guard towers made one think, once again, of an enormous battery cell of death.

It's one thing to read about the Final Solution, as I had for years. To see its remains up close is quite another, because you see for yourself the unbelievably methodical way, brick by brick and plank by plank, in which these perfectly functioning, perfectly symmetrical death factories were created – how much ingenuity, talent, imagination and, above all, deep conviction and enthusiasm were invested in their creation by dedicated men like Adolf Eichmann and Heydrich. As Treblinka survivor Richard Glazer said after the war: "This is something, you know, the world has never understood, how perfect this machine was. It was only lack of transport because of [the war] that prevented them from dealing with far vaster numbers than they did. Treblinka alone could have dealt with six million Jews and more besides. Given adequate rail transport, the German extermination camps ... could have killed all the Poles, Russians and other east Europeans that the Nazis planned to kill."

Historian Ian Kershaw, in posing the question of why Nazi Germany fought until the bitter end, without civil authority collapsing into civil strife as it had at the end of World War I, suggested the answer was "ultimately, a deeply inculcated and utterly warped sense of duty ... " The "underlying mentalities ... are the most fundamental ... [A]ll the other factors were ultimately subordinate to the way the charismatic Führer regime was structured." In other words, what sustained the regime even in the face of certain defeat was the millenarian utopian vision of National Socialism, very different from the mere Great Power militarism that motivated the Kaiser in WW I. As Propaganda Minister Joseph Goebbels had put it years before: "National Socialism is a religion. One day soon (it) will be the religion of all Germans ... That is my gospel." The central rite of that religion, its chief sacrament, was the removal of the Jewish people from the face of the earth so as to usher in the 1,000 year "National Socialist world blessing."

In his classic 1937 study, early Party member and later defector Herman Rauschning called Nazism "the revolution of nihilism." More important than any specific ideological doctrine, he wrote, was its primary drive for sheer destruction and annihilation and the rebuilding of the world as a monolithic collective based on racial purity. It took Bakhunin's and the Anarchists' vision of burning European civilization to the ground and harnessed it in service of the New Order to come – a consistency of purpose and a utopian blueprint for the future that explains why the German Anarchist movement was early on rolled into the Nazi storm troopers. As Herman Goering revealingly put it, "I joined the Party to become a revolutionary, not because of any ideological nonsense!" In other words, it was about action and adventure, not dull policy debates. Summoning the spontaneous violence of "the people" to shatter the grip on Germany of the Enlightenment and liberalism led to a constant emphasis on youthful passion – Nazism was widely known simply as "the youth movement."

For Rauschning, the revolution of nihilism was "a philosophical system (amounting) to the belief that the use of violence in a supreme effort liberates creative moral forces in human society, which lead to social and national renewal." Precisely the tendency fostered by the Enlightenment to be skeptical about absolutes, about traditions of deference and restraint, over time fed an atmosphere that undermined *all* authority, even that of democracy and rights, and instead worshipped sheer instinctive force of will. "When all other standards have been unmasked by the skepticism toward all doctrines, reason itself is robbed of its force. The anti-intellectual intellectual attitude of 'dynamism' is not mere chance but the necessary outcome of an entire absence of standards. Man, it holds, is not a logical being, but a creature following his instincts and impulses ... The barbaric element of violence, which reformist Socialism and moderate Marxism would place in safe custody under lock and key, is the one element that can change a social order." In other words, through the Nazi revolution of nihilism, Nietzsche's *Will to Power* meets the gutter of the jack-boot and truncheon. "These young people," Rauschning goes on, "already see the one essential common element in the revolutionary processes in their destructive character, and they no longer attach any importance to the doctrines that divide them ... They see life's meaning in its perils, life's purpose is domination, the means as violence, and the goal as the world-wide totalitarian empire." Replace that final phrase with "world-wide Caliphate," and the entire last passage could be a description of what animates the young fighters in ISIS.

The following passage from the official journal of the SS might also have been written to court today's potential Jihadists: "When we speak of young Europe and its young nations, we contrast them to the senile world of dying liberalism ... We offer the youth the freedom to develop ... room for creative fantasy, the opportunity to transform great thoughts to reality outside the lecture hall. We offer the realization of dreams on a world scale." That dream turned out to be the Holocaust, and here is what it looked like: "At the fourth transport, a small baby wrapped in a pillow was thrown out of the lorry. It began to cry. The SS men laughed. They machine-gunned the baby and tossed it into the ditch."

There were other contemporary observers who, like Rauschning, saw Nazism and fascism generally for the revolutionary movements they truly were, completely at odds with traditional conservatism just as they were with liberalism. Ortega y Gassett viewed fascism as modern democratic mass man's rebellion against the elevated culture, gentlemanly politics, and demanding educational standards of the high bourgeois civilization of late-nineteenth-century Europe, which democratic man wanted to cast aside to embrace the brutality of "direct action." Ortega believed that fascist leaders like Mussolini and Hitler appealed to a hidden longing in ordinary people for a master to relieve them of the responsibilities and burdens of self-government, fulfilling Tocqueville's earlier warning about the emergence of a "democratic despot." In some ways, Hitler was indeed something of a throwback to the demagogues of ancient times and their courting of the mob. He claimed that Wagner's *Rienzi*, about how a *condottieri* switches allegiance from the despot who is paying him to the common people the despot is trying to repress, was "the beginning of it all" in his own desire to become the German people's tribune. But the utopian project that animated National Socialism, culminating in the Holocaust, and whose main visionary was Hitler, made him something very different from those ancient demagogues or a cynical authoritarian passing himself off as the people's friend like Napoleon III.

Leni Riefenstahl's propaganda masterpiece, *The Triumph of the Will* (a title with deliberately Nietzschean overtones), crystallized the brave new world the Nazis, led by Hitler, fervently believed they were creating, and why it would prove a "world blessing" for all mankind once its main impediment, the Jews, had been removed forever. Hitler participated actively in shaping the film at every stage – he understood the potential of the film medium for manipulating political imagery and mass emotion. The millenarian rapture and youthful, communal joy captured in this film inspired the energies that led directly to the Holocaust, the necessary means to bring about its ecstatic vision of national and eventually world-wide renewal, the convictions that also motivated all of Hitler's foreign policy and war aims. Central to the National Socialist world-view was the use of modern technology at its most advanced to destroy the modern age and return to the primeval destiny of the German people. Accordingly, the Nazis were both ultra-traditionalists (but hearkening to a primordial destiny far back behind the conventional conservatism of received tradition) and ultra-modernists. Riefenstahl's film opens with Hitler in an airplane sleekly circling over Nuremberg, sailing through the clouds like a Valkyrie to Wagnerian-sounding strains, while the city's ancient Gothic spires are festooned with swastika banners below. He is both the man of the future and the restorer of the mythic past.

National Socialism achieved political victory in 1933 when, having won the largest (but not a majority) bloc of deputies in the Reichstag, Hitler was invited to become Chancellor (much against the personal preferences of the crusty old nobleman and World War I Field Marshall, President Paul von Hindenburg, who despised Hitler as a parvenu) by cynical conservatives who thought they could "contain" Hitler while using his popularity to combat the far Left. Hitler quickly used his powers to create a one-Party state with all authority concentrated in his hands, ending elections altogether. When Hindenburg died, the office of president was allowed to lapse, and the army swore a personal oath of loyalty to the supreme Leader. Hitler's popularity soared.

This victory cannot be understood without reference to the long-gestating and potent culture of revulsion for the Enlightenment that we discussed earlier. The way to power for Nazism was prepared by at least half a century of steadily accumulating fantasies about Germany's destiny lying in "the East," the archaic realm of Teutonic myth and soil, and not in the corrupt Enlightenment "West" of effete France and money-grubbing England. As we observed, popular intellectuals like Paul de la Garde and Moeller van den Brucke made this theme respectable among the educated reading public. It was intensified by the growing popularity, amounting to deification, of Wagner's music, which summoned modern man to throw off the shallow bourgeois materialism of the modern age and return to primeval fantasies of Nordic knighthood and world-shattering struggle. That is why, in his way, Hitler was one of Wagner's truest disciples. Wagner's *Götterdämmerung* revels in the vision of world cataclysm, inspiring the young Hitler to envision a future Germany either as master of the world or going down in flames. The end of the Third Reich in Hitler's bunker with Berlin in flaming ruins all around fulfilled Wagner's exultant prophecies of catastrophe.

National Socialism was often misunderstood in America and Britain as a return to the Great Power militarism of Bismarck, Von Moltke, and the General Staff of WWI, "the Hun." In reality, it was above all a millenarian revolutionary movement like Bolshevism. Most of us in our schooling were – and still are – subjected to the falsehood that Nazism was also a form of "radical" or "late" capitalism," that it existed to protect the capitalist order. This distortion was concocted by the Left in the 1940s and persists to this day. European and American observers with any insight grew increasingly aware of the similarities between Bolshevism and Nazism. Thinking people recognized that they were two variants of the same movement, "the revolution of nihilism" to use Rauschning's term, and people in both movements also recognized this about each other. (Recall Von Ribbentrop's feeling right at home among Stalin's henchmen). But many people on the Left were embarrassed by this similarity, just as they were embarrassed by the Hitler-Stalin Pact. Their response was to convince themselves (who can say with what degree of sincerity?) that there was no resemblance whatever between these two in fact closely kindred movements, claiming instead that Nazism equaled the naked face of capitalism stripped of its pretensions to democracy. That way, they could paint the Hitler-Stalin Pact as the Soviet Union's morally justified need to fend off the Nazi threat so as to safeguard the gains of socialism, instead of what it really was – two wolves agreeing to devour the sheep before turning on each other for the final show-down between their two totalitarian world-views. In reality, the Nazis detested capitalism every bit as much as they did Bolshevism, equating both with the "Jewish world conspiracy" that could don either hat at its convenience in its mission to destroy the wholeness of the people with its materialistic values. As Gregor Strasser, a founding member of the Nazi party who later left the movement described it, Hitler and the Nazis were heavily motivated by "anticapitalist nostalgia," the longing for a bucolic Golden Age of communal bliss and the obliteration of the modern era's materialistic selfishness.

The Nazis regarded Bolshevism as a false version of socialism, which they believed should be nationalistic and patriotic, not international. But they themselves believed in a "classless society" (as Hitler's speeches in *The Triumph of the Will* stress repeatedly) and central planning (aping Soviet vocabulary, they had their own "five-year plan"). Their anthem, the Horst Wessel song, thundered against both "Bolshevism and the Reaction," the latter meaning traditional, old-fashioned Throne-and-Altar aristocratic and religious conservatives, but also big capitalism, high finance, plutocrats, "the men in top hats" – all the forces many in America and Britain mistakenly believed they represented. The Nazis believed that capitalism, along with the other individualistic values of the Enlightenment, had led to hopeless corruption and spiritual degradation, including the scandal of Germany having dozens of squabbling political parties. They called themselves the "anti-Party" because, more important than any specific policy, they believed they embodied the will and destiny of the entire German people. Like the Bolsheviks' dedication to spreading world revolution, they believed in the need for world war and genocide to usher in what they called "the National Socialist World Blessing" for all mankind. The war between Germany and Russia in the east, unlike Germany's conquests in the west, had the qualities of a holy war of apocalyptic extermination – in effect, these two close-as-could-be revolutionary and nihilistic cousins were battling it out for the future lordship of the earth.

Nazism's mission was based on the mobilization of mass hatred and the destruction of all traditional social, religious, and cultural bonds. In its drive to complete the collectivization of all social forces within "the community of destiny" – a process they called "coordination" (*Gleichschaltung*) – National Socialism's true forbear was the Jacobin Terror and its true counterpart was Bolshevism's similar agenda for destruction in Russia. Just as Stalin invented "the kulaks" as the enemies of happiness and peace whose extermination would bring about utopia, so Hitler invented "the Jews." In one case, the extermination of an imaginary class leads to nirvana, in the other, the extermination of an imaginary race (Jews bore no more resemblance to Hitler's fantasies about them than had the kulaks to their depiction by Stalin). The structural similarities between Bolshevism and Nazism, and the scale of their genocide and violence, are far more important for explaining Nazism than any incidental connections to the German past, which, up until WW I, was, despite instances of anti-Semitism and some anti-Semitic parties on the local level, rightly admired as one of the most advanced and humane cultures in Europe, and one in which Jews proudly participated in its cultural, professional, and economic elites. In attempting to exterminate the Jews as Lenin and Stalin had attempted to exterminate the Kulaks, the Third Reich trod a path already cleared by the Soviet Union – expropriation, death marches, concentration camps, slave labor, starvation, torture, mass executions – and added refinements that only the superiority of German technology could provide, the "industrialized murder" of the death camps with their gas chambers and crematoria. Although happy to benefit from spontaneous local outbursts of anti-Semitism, the Nazis disapproved of their messiness. A methodical plan was needed.

In understanding the evolution of Nazism, it's important to stress that it was shaped by coming *after* Bolshevism and was in part a reaction against its claims to rationalism (the doctrine of Marxism-Leninism) and its soulless emphasis on economic productivity. Anticipating Third World Socialism and Jihadism, the Nazis were equally opposed to Soviet-style communism *and* capitalism (against "Bolshevism and the Reaction," as the Party anthem had it). Nazism burrowed deeper into the sheer populist spontaneity of the Jacobins' return to the Year One, whereas, they believed, Bolshevism had aped the Enlightenment's claims to universality, cosmopolitanism, and reason. That had made Bolshevism an equal opportunity oppressor that rooted out *Volkish* or what the Soviet Union termed "chauvinistic" signs of tribal or ethnic nationalism across the board. Thus, whereas Hitler was a pseudoartist and bohemian who spoke with existential passion, reflecting the demonic upsurge of revolutionary energy being conjured from below, Stalin was a pseudoscientist with a dry scholastic style, reflecting the state-driven revolution being constructed from above according to "scientific socialism." The contrast between Stalin's catechistic speaking style and Hitler's emotional and demagogic intensity is caught in this 1936 speech, where Hitler casts his intimate bond with the German people in pseudo-Biblical language: "You once heard the voice of a man and it struck your hearts. It awakened you and you followed this voice, without even having seen the owner of the voice, you merely heard a voice and followed it … Not everyone of you sees me, and I do not see everyone of you. but I feel you, and you feel me! Now we are together, and we are Germany!"

In the end, though, their shared vision of a utopian society purged of individualism gave the Bolshevik and National Socialist revolutions much more in common than their differences. That included the scale and intensity of their genocidal missions and the growth of an elite state within the state of dedicated ideological murderers (the NKVD and the SS) to carry them out. Although Nazism was fundamentally nationalistic, it also envisioned its own "International" of racially pure Aryan peoples around the world, prefigured by the SS International brigades, as well as cultivating Arab nationalists and anti-Semites incensed by the emigration of Zionist Jews to Palestine, along with the "axis" of other fascist powers including Italy, Spain, and Japan. More than material self-interest united this constellation of forces. Hitler frequently expressed admiration for Stalin's revolutionary ruthlessness and contempt for bourgeois scruples, saying late in the war as defeat loomed that he wished the Nazis had been as rigorous as Stalin's purges by liquidating the old officer classes and the *Junker* aristocracy, whom he suspected of disloyalty. Common to both millenarian movements was the belief that the only objection to genocide was not the victims' suffering, but the psychological toll taken on the delicate emotions of the *murderers,* who had to repress all normal human qualms in order to carry out their duty to mankind and the future. As Himmler put it in a secret speech to the top SS leadership in 1943, "Most of you know what it means to see a hundred corpses lay side by side, or five hundred, or a thousand. To have stuck to this and, excepting in cases of human weakness to have kept our integrity, this is what has made us hard. In our history, this is an unwritten and never-to-be-written page of glory." Numerous statements by Bolshevik leaders can be found expressing the exact same sentiment, like this one by Bukharin praising the mass execution operations of the NKVD: "Do not let us forget how many of those who remain are wrecks, and sometimes hopelessly ill. For their work was such torture, it demanded such gigantic concentration, it was such hellish work, that a truly iron character was required."

More important than any differences between them was the common underlying longing for an apocalyptic struggle culminating in genocide and world war to bring about a future of communal bliss. The main distinction between them was this: In the dynamic of a leap into an unknown future in order to recover a mystical past, the Bolsheviks stressed the leap ahead into the technological mastery of the world, whereas the Nazis stressed a leap backward to the primordial will of the people. But even that distinction was not absolute – as we have seen, the Bolsheviks' also invoked "the people's will," and the Nazis avidly developed new technology. For both, the war in the east with its tens of millions of casualties was the final struggle between these two rival paths to utopia.

THE FÜHRER

Many factors explain the rise of the Nazis and the outbreak of WWII – the Depression, humiliation over defeat in WW I and the search for a scapegoat to blame for "the stab in the back." But a central vision was required (what Ian Kershaw describes as the "underlying mentalities") – insane but internally coherent – to bring these grievances together into a program for revolutionary upheaval. This was Adolf Hitler's contribution – he was, as his biographer Joachim Fest put it, "National Socialist Number 1," the most fervent believer in the Third Reich over which he had absolute power.

By all accounts, Hitler was something of a spoiled mama's boy who never had to work hard as a child, and from early on was monstrously vain, lazy, and full of pretensions based on no measurable achievement. When he was turned down as a student at the Vienna Academy of Fine Arts, he believed the world had conspired to deny his genius, nurturing that burning inner sense of grievance common to so many millenarian tyrants: "He saw everywhere only obstacles and hostility," his boyhood friend from Linz, Auguste Kubizek, recalled. "He was always up against something and at odds with the world ... I never saw him take anything lightly." His limitless hatred of Jews as the source of his own and everyone else's misery seemed to be constructed out of a fantasy world, since he had little actual contact with them. The first and only real success he ever had in life was as a political leader, and at bottom it was because he embodied the life experiences and values of his followers – a common soldier, decorated for bravery, who could not believe Germany had lost WWI, and that it must have been betrayed on the home front by a Jewish-led conspiracy that brought the hated Weimar Republic to power, crammed with pacifists and communists.

Millions of Germans shared these views, but he distilled them into two or three basic points that all could grasp. Hitler didn't have to hypnotize people. Even Thomas Mann, an ornament of high culture, who left Germany rather than live under Nazi rule, spurning the lavish patronage the regime dangled before him, admitted that the young Hitler reminded him of himself. Hitler formed his worldview in the early 1920s as an agitator for far-Right generals and nationalist politicians bent on subverting the Weimar regime, and it never changed. He made many tactical shifts to gain power, but the strategic goal was always the same. He would wage a war of life and death with "Jewish Bolshevism" in the east to achieve "living space" for Germans and bring the National Socialist world blessing to Germany and the world by exterminating the source of all evil, greed, and injustice – "World Jewry." As there were only two hundred thousand Jews in Germany at the outbreak of the war, the Nazis *needed* to conquer the east in order to find the greatest number of Jews to exterminate. Even the hardened killers of the SS murder squads, the *Einsatzgruppen*, sent into Poland with the *Wehrmacht* to begin liquidating the "Jewish Commissars," quickly realized that the poor and frightened people they were massacring rarely occupied any position of power, least of all in the Communist Party. It didn't matter – they were a metaphysical specter in human disguise that had to be eradicated.

If Bolshevism had been a top-down revolution carried out from the height of the hijacked Tsarist autocracy, the Nazis, partly to win elections, but also partly out of conviction, were more of a bottom-up revolution, a genuine mass movement whose talents and enthusiasm were welcome so long as they were coupled with total obedience to the Leader. Hitler's purge of his right-hand man Ernst Rohm, head of the Party's paramilitary formations, the Sturmabteilung (SA, "storm troopers"), was in part driven by the need to throttle back on the Party's populist and Anarchist roots once state power had been secured and more discipline was called for, as well as to secure the support of the professional military, which feared the SA as a competitor. But taking the initiative in serving the Reich, whether with your fists or brains, was still encouraged. Hitler was not lying when he proclaimed at the Nuremberg Rally in 1935, "the state does not order the National Socialist movement. The National Socialist movement orders the state." Party members were drilled to ask themselves in any situation "What would the Führer do?" and to "work toward the Führer," by, for example, figuring out how to kill more Jews more quickly with gas as opposed to bullets. Hitler let his broad aims be known and others competed to please him by bringing them about. This reflected his Social Darwinist belief that the best men rise through struggle with one another for predominance. Promotion and prestige rewarded such success. Not jealous of others' ability like Stalin, Hitler promoted talent, favoring daring young officers over cautious old-school professionals. Whereas Colonel Charles de Gaulle was completely ignored by the French military establishment when he argued in 1934 for the use of massed tank formations in war, Hitler backed General Heinz Guderian for promoting the same policy, leading to the stunning early German *Blitzkrieg* victories in Poland and France. Hitler had read De Gaulle's book! Again unlike Stalin, after the fall of Rohm, Hitler did not conduct large-scale purges of the Party. Failure didn't guarantee death – defeated or timid generals were usually just transferred or eased into retirement. A few people, including Albert Speer, could even cautiously take issue with Hitler's views and be heard out.

Hitler gave Walter Schacht, the world's leading monetarist, carte blanche to bring Germany out of the Depression through huge public works projects of a kind later imitated by FDR, and without regard for the grumblings of the private sector. Although he affected the artistic temperament of someone who relied on impulse and instinct, Hitler was capable of great self-control. His famous frenzies when speaking for an audience were not the man people knew in private, one of whom reported, "I never saw Hitler be anything but totally courteous ... He had a very quiet voice, shy and appealing to Germans with his soft Austrian accent." Lord Boothby described his "soft, hesitant and thoughtful voice."

Like Stalin, he did little disciplined work in a day. Major domestic and foreign policy victories alternated with long bouts of idling at his summer house at Berchtesgaden in the Bavarian Alps, where hours of movie-watching alternated with Hitler's interminable monologues on every conceivable subject from ancient archeology to diet. Just as the Villa Jovis with which we began this book presented the Emperor Tiberius as the earthly counterpart of

Jupiter, Hitler made his summer house into a kind of Wagnerian stage set for his historic mission. Visitors gazed from its terrace at the looming Untersberg, where according to legend Charlemagne was sleeping until he was summoned back to lead a final battle between good and evil (Hitler once told frequent visitor Albert Speer, "Look at the Untersberg over there. It is not by chance that I have my seat across from it"). Even more reminiscent of the Villa Jovis is Hitler's Tea House, which survived Allied bombing and sits perched on a high mountain peak, to be reached by an enormous brass elevator like nothing so much as Superman's Fortress of Solitude. Like Stalin and many ancient garden-variety tyrants, Hitler ruled the state from his private household and dinner table.

But utopian genocide remained his central mission, even more important than victory in war. (During the final year of impending defeat, trains indispensable for the war effort were diverted from transporting weaponry and troops for use as transports to the death camps). According to Himmler, Hitler knew every detail of what was going on in the Holocaust. But while his vision was insane, there is no proof that he was. We want there to be something out of whack with Hitler because it's less disturbing to believe that a complete nutter representative of a tiny out-group among human beings could do such things than someone who is otherwise like the rest of us. But by every indication, his private life was completely ordinary, including his sweet-natured airhead of a girlfriend.

To understand Hitler's foreign and military policies, we have to grasp that the genocidal project for the destruction of "Jewish Bolshevism" guided it from the outset, down to its most pragmatic details. Hitler outlined this project in *Mien Kampf* in 1927 and followed it unwaveringly until his suicide in the bunker in 1945. Hitler didn't launch the Holocaust out of bitterness or frustration because he was losing the war. On the contrary, he waged the war in the way that he did so that he could launch the Holocaust. The plan was always to knock out France and Britain in the west while the pact with Stalin avoided the danger of a two-front war – whatever Stalin may have thought, it was never meant to be permanent – then wheel around and hit the Soviet Union with devastating force to carry out the final Armageddon against the most important foe. When Hitler became convinced that Germany's military advantage was waning with time, he made his great riverboat gamble of invading Russia ahead of schedule while Britain still held firm. It may not have been sound military strategy because it left Germany fighting on two fronts, but it was consistent with Hitler's life-long mission.

Hitler's foreign policy, therefore, bore little resemblance to that of Bismarck or earlier Great Power militarism including the Kaiser's aggression in World War I. It was entirely directed by the mission of confronting the Jews embodied as Bolshevism and destroying them. Goering, at heart a throwback to an Italian *condottieri* who wanted nothing more than to enjoy his new-found riches, fell out of favor when he hinted that perhaps they should be content with having created the largest European empire since Charlemagne and leave off invading Russia. Hitler could not possibly have *not* gone through with Operation Barbarossa. To say that he overextended German forces misses the point. The strength of will that enabled him to achieve the earlier lightening victories in Poland and France was always at the service of this main aim. Hitler linked the coming Holocaust with the war from the very start, addressing the Reichstag in 1939: "Today I will once more be a prophet. If the international Jewish financiers inside and outside Europe should again succeed in plunging the nations into a world war, the result will not be the Bolshevization of the world and thus the victory of Jewry, but the annihilation of the Jewish race throughout Europe." He repeated this prophecy many times, including in his "Political Testament" before killing himself in the bunker. As its pseudobiblical language implies, the war in the east was to be a holy war: "Harshness is kindness toward the future," he instructed his commanders on the eve of Operation Barbarossa. "The leaders must demand of themselves the sacrifice of overcoming their scruples." As the faithful Goebbels, Nazi propaganda minister, recorded in his diary: "The Führer realizes the full implications of the great opportunities offered by this war. He is conscious that he is fighting a battle of gigantic dimensions, and that the fate of the entire civilized world depends on its issue ... (T)he Jewish race is the most dangerous one that inhabits the globe .... This riffraff must be eliminated and destroyed. Otherwise, it won't be possible to bring peace to the world."

As the war went badly, the Holocaust intensified – since it was the core of the utopian vision, it had to be carried out at all costs. Like earlier millenarian movements going back to the Jacobins, this one attracted sadists, psychopaths, brawlers, and brigands. But it also attracted students (one of the earliest social groups to go over en masse to the Nazis) and others who believed in the perverse "idealism" that genocide would make the world a better place – a similar mixture of brutes and true believers to what we saw in Stalin's Terror Famine. Of the fifteen high officials who attended the Wansee Conference in which Heydrich and Eichmann outlined the plan to exterminate European Jewry, six had doctorates. Jonathan Littell's novel *The Kindly Ones* chronicles how the initially victorious Wehrmacht divisions in eastern Europe and Russia were followed by detachments of ethnographers, archaeologists, and anthropologists sent from the finest universities in Germany by nationalist professors to conduct research on inferior races and find remnants of "Aryan" blood. As Robert J. Lifton wrote in his masterful account of the SS doctors in the death camps, "Genocide becomes a difficult but necessary form of *personal ideal*." Heinrich Himmler told his staff that "a man has to sacrifice himself" for "the Germanic world as a whole ... even though it is often very hard for him; he oughtn't to think of himself." As for the doctors, Lifton continues: "Precisely because they were convinced of the justness ... of the National Socialist 'world-blessing' and that the Jews are the root evil of the world ... did they believe ... that the Jews, even existentially, had to be absolutely exterminated."

One of the paradoxes of National Socialism was its development of the most advanced modern technology – the most lethal new weaponry as well as the machinery of the death camp – in order to bring about the millenarian vision of an antitechnological world of "blood and soil" belonging. The Nazis did not exterminate millions of Jews because they possessed the technology to do so. They developed the technology because they wanted to exterminate millions of Jews. Technology was not an end in itself, but a means for recovering the people's destiny and ushering in an Arcadian collective of peace and wholeness. That is why the National Socialist utopia required a powerful modern state. In *Hitler's Willing Executioners*, Daniel Goldhagen argues, in opposition to Hannah Arendt, that the Holocaust was largely a spontaneous local phenomenon taken advantage of by the Nazis. I would argue that it was, on the contrary, a project conceived and methodically undertaken at the highest levels of the regime; the SS disliked the unruliness and messiness of local outbursts. Arendt was correct that there was a master plan carried out by the state. But she was wrong about the motivation and entirely missed the utopian vision that made the Holocaust so exhilarating to its designers, including Adolf Eichmann.

Viewed against the backdrop of the Nazis' millenarian project, figures like Eichmann were the very opposite of the bloodless bureaucrat "just following orders" made famous by Arendt in *Eichmann in Jerusalem*. Eichmann was passionately dedicated to his role in the Holocaust and, far from being a mere cog in the wheel, he participated in it at the very highest level of authority, only a few rungs away from Himmler and Hitler, and with self-conscious relish and excitement. His last reported words as he faced the gallows, once he had given up on the faceless bureaucrat charade with which he had tried to deceive the Israeli court, revealed his true self: "I will leap into my grave laughing knowing that I helped kill six million Jews!" He also said: "I didn't just take orders ... I was a part of the thinking process. I was an idealist." His only regret was that "we didn't do our job properly. We could have done more." Rudolf Hoess, commandant of Auschwitz, felt ashamed at his "weakness" in occasionally regretting the gassing of children "after I talked to Eichmann," who explained that "the children have to be killed first, because where was the logic in killing a generation of older people and leaving alive a generation of young people who can be possible avengers of their parents?" Franz Staengl, commandant of Treblinka, had no scruples about executing this "logic." After all, as he observed, the victims "were cargo ... It had nothing to do with humanity. It was a mass – a mass of rotting flesh."

With the gas chambers and crematoria going full blast as Germany's cities lay in ruins, the Wehrmacht in full retreat, Hitler, Goebbels, and the inner core of the movement, far from despairing over Germany's destruction, exulted in the final act of the Wagnerian drama. For Hitler, it proved that the German people had shown itself to be inferior to its enemies, and so according to Darwin's law of the survival of the fittest, deserved to be annihilated. Reveling in the orgy of destruction they had unleashed, the Old Party Comrades who had been with Hitler since the 1920s reverted to the underlying dynamic of "the revolution of nihilism" – the destruction of all civilization. Echoing the Anarchists, including the quote from Bakhunin we looked at earlier that Wagner found so thrilling, Goebbels wrote near the end: "Under the ruins of our devastated cities the last so-called achievements of the bourgeois nineteenth century have finally been buried ... Now, when everything lies in ruins, we are forced to reconstruct Europe ... [without] bourgeois constraint ... [The bombing of German cities has] only razed the walls of the prisons that incarcerated them ... the enemy who strove to annihilate Europe's future has succeeded only in annihilating the past, and consequently everything old and worn out is gone." Bakhunin's dream had at last come true – but all it brought about was misery.

Did the "Thousand-Year Reich," toppled after only twelve years, leave a legacy? One of the paradoxes of National Socialism was that, like the Russian Revolution, it did advance the modernization of Germany in some ways – but at the catastrophic and unnecessary cost of genocide and war. To a degree, it blended some ingredients of reforming tyranny with its much more important millenarian mission. The Nazi movement was often simply referred to as "the German Revolution," implying that it was the continuation of other great national revolutions such as the Glorious, American, and French. On one level, this was true. The Nazis forged a truly pan-Germanic national identity in a country that, in spite of its impressive level of industrialization, remained fragmented into numerous small traditional former duchies and principalities that often inspired more direct loyalty than Germany as a whole. Under the Wilhelmine Empire, much of Germany's national unity was imposed from above by the cult of the Kaiser, and especially his exclusive command over military affairs, part of the legacy of Frederick the Great. (Significantly, when Japan set about to modernize itself, the top-down model of Wilhemine Germany appealed to it more than the full representative democracies of the UK and America – in effect, the *Mikado* was transformed from a sacerdotal god-king into a constitutional monarch whose continuing divinity nonetheless commanded total obedience). That top-down imperial unity was ended by Germany's defeat in WW I, and the Nazis had to rebuild Germany's national identity, this time in a genuinely populist, bottom-up fashion.

Riefenstahl's film *The Triumph of the Will* shows the dexterous way in which the Nazis played upon a nostalgia for the premodern past – milkmaids in period dress presenting flowers to the Führer – while rolling those parochial loyalties into a steely new sense of collective unity, as in the scene where thousands of identically uniformed members of the Labor Service shout out their different regional origins in a way that clearly symbolizes how those ties have now been superseded by the new pan-German nationalism. Hitler's 1933 campaign slogan, "Hitler Over Germany," not only forecast his coming supremacy in a democratic election that would do away with the need for further elections and get rid of the corrupt squabbling of "rotten parliamentarism," but was a pun on the fact that Hitler was the first politician to make election visits throughout the entire country by airplane, another paradoxical reliance on cutting-edge technology to restore a sense of the "lost" premodern community. It also pointed to air travel, film and radio (along with the new highways) as ways of uniting "the community of destiny." *The Triumph of the Will* was shown throughout Germany, since even the humblest hamlet was sure to have a movie theater. The film's emphasis on the Hitler Youth, living in their comradely tent communities, cooking communal meals, also spoke about a new generation for whom duty to Germany came first. They entered the army – especially the elite Waffen SS units – in droves when the war broke out, and were among the regime's most tenacious defenders until the last breath.

The terms fascist and Nazi are often used interchangeably, and they have some common roots. Both grew out of the nineteenth century's hatred of liberalism on the far Left and Right. In place of liberalism's humane and tolerant values, they wanted strength, honor, manliness, and heroism. Oswald Spengler in *The Decline of the West* envisioned a new "Caesar" who would trample underfoot democratic political squabbling and its mercenary politicians, a role that had been partly fulfilled by the "democratic despot" Napoleon III. Fascism was against both capitalism and socialism, but was more like socialism in its longing for a collective society. Like Flaubert's fictional revolutionary, Senecal (and like Wagner), Benito Mussolini began on the far Left and moved to the far Right. A student of the teachings of Georges Sorel, who praised violence as man's most creative impulse, he admired Lenin (as I observed earlier) as a "sculptor" of the masses, confirming the unimportance of Marxist doctrine in comparison with the longing for "direct action" to smash the world of tradition and build Senecal's "American Sparta." Mussolini used the Italian fascist state to introduce some of the same redistributionist economic policies that Schacht designed for the Nazis, crush the Mafia, and "make the trains run on time." Extensive excavations of the Roman Forum sponsored by *Il Duce* (their origins delicately avoided on today's signage except for the date) were meant to show that Fascist Italy was the inheritor of Rome's glories, although its only military success came from the use of massive airstrikes and poison gas against a primitive Abyssinian army equipped with rifles and spears.

Mussolini's switch from the Socialist Left to the Fascist Right shouldn't surprise us, because both wanted to use the modern state to bring relief to the masses through public works and social welfare. In their early years, both Italian Fascism and National Socialism displayed a genuinely populist dimension. During the height of the Depression, Hitler often urged his followers to feed their fellow Germans at common meals even if they did not support the Movement, a method used to great effect by the Muslim Brotherhood more recently to win over "the Arab street" at the expense of their corrupt fat-cat Baathist or Arab nationalist rulers. But Italian Fascism was not a truly revolutionary movement – Nazism was a much closer cousin of Bolshevism than it was of the other fascist regimes. Italian and Spanish Fascism had no millenarian project for worldwide revolution and the ushering in of utopia through genocide. Fascist Italy cooperated with Germany over anti-Jewish regulations and round-ups, but balked at the full-scale Holocaust. Like Franco's fascism in Spain, Italian fascism was rooted in old-fashioned authoritarian and religious corporatism and class hierarchy. The Catholic Church supported both regimes – even though Italian fascism in particular had a strong anti-clericalist streak – because they all agreed on the notion that people needed to be part of a larger social whole, that greed and self-interest should be curtailed and moral decency promoted. Because the Italian Fascists were more cooperative with conventional Throne and Altar conservatism than were the Nazis, Mussolini, unlike Hitler, never achieved supreme dictatorial power. He remained formally the appointee of the King, who dismissed him when things went south. Hitler began as Mussolini's junior partner in the Fascist constellation, but that ended with Germany's stunning early military victories. Increasingly, Hitler, Goebbels, and the Nazi leadership viewed Mussolini and Franco as mere reactionaries and conservatives, not true revolutionaries, and lacking the stomach for radical action.

In short, while all Nazis and Bolsheviks were fascists, not all fascists were millenarian revolutionaries. Fascism was a blend of garden-variety and reforming tyranny. Its descendants, more kleptocratic than reforming, included Salazar of Portugal, Latin American dictators like the Somozas of Nicaragua, Arab nationalist rulers including Mubarak and Assad, and the Soviet Union in its final phase as a *nomenklatura* state where revolutionary fervor had long since given way to a frozen hierarchy of Party privileges, not unlike Byzantium. With his swaggering machismo, Mussolini was also a model for a populist *caudillo* like Juan Peron. His contemporary, Governor Hughie Long of Louisiana (described by H. L. Mencken as "a backwoods Mussolini") had a similar recipe for helping the "little man" with social-welfare schemes and public works, and stirred up a thuggish populist resentment for the "good government" blue-stockings who looked down on "the hicks" of which he proudly boasted he was one. When FDR rolled the Progressives and Prairie Populists into his great coalition, he took on some of Long's redistributive economic policies.

The cronyism characteristic of garden-variety tyranny even when it boasts a program of reform to help the common people was rampant under Mussolini, who never seemed to run out of relatives to appoint to high positions. While the Third Reich did not lack for corrupt and depraved hedonists (think of Goering) among the leadership (not Hitler, who shared Stalin's lack of interest in pronounced personal luxury and was a teetotaler and vegetarian to boot), outwardly it presented an image of steely dedication to duty and honor. The Fascist regime in Italy, by contrast, wore its hedonism on its sleeve, rather like Vichy France, and its shabby climax when Mussolini and his mistress, having drunk themselves into a daily stupor for weeks as they evaded capture, were finally strung up by their heels in front of a howling mob, recalled both the erotic criminality of ancient tyrannies and a Mafia hit.

As we have seen throughout this book, tyrannies with some sort of claim or pretension to creating a new universal culture often try to put their stamp on society through architecture. But whereas the Caesars beautified Rome, and Napoleon's wish to restore Imperial Roman grandeur under his reign produced some architectural gems, the Bolsheviks' and Nazis' anarchistic urge to destroy all past civilization combined with their contradictory nostalgia for a premodern sense of "heroic" greatness to produce a generally ghastly pastiche with no distinctive qualities except its gargantuan scale. For Stalin, this took the form of stupendously ugly skyscrapers combining brutalism with fitful Art Deco and Gothic dabs, like something from the subconscious mind of Ayn Rand on sodium pentothal. Hitler's chief architect Albert Speer began as a modernist influenced by the functionalism of Bauhaus, which he wanted to merge with traditional neoclassical Palladian articulations, a respectable ambition. But under Hitler's influence, his attempt to graft those Palladian touches onto the Pharaonic proportions demanded by Hitler in his fantasies of a totally rebuilt Berlin (whose grand dome was to be six times larger than Rome's Pantheon) produced a flop, evidenced in Speer's surviving Air Ministry building in Berlin, which, despite its flimsy efforts at restrained Palladian orders dabbed incongruously on top of square miles of grim granite, looks like nothing so much as an enormous prison.

Indeed, the extraordinary Topography of Terror site in today's Berlin provides nothing less than an enormous burial mound, in layers like the excavation of Troy, for the two failed totalitarian empires where they met in a head-on clash – the first departing the stage of history in 1945, the second in 1989. The lowest layer is the excavation of the SS-SD-Gestapo complex in Berlin. Until I saw it, I had not realized how close this complex (including interrogation cells) was to the very heart of the government quarter, near the Foreign Ministry and kitty corner to Hitler's Reichschancellory. One wonders whether they could almost hear the screams. Above that complex runs a fully intact section of the Berlin Wall. Looming above both is Speer's Aviation Ministry, every brick of which survived the Allied bombing. Walking along the lowest level, you can gaze up and contemplate three layers of almost incomprehensible human woe and terror.

There is no doubting the Machiavellian brilliance of Hitler's early triumphs – the bloodless coup in the Sudetenland (a combination of bullying and the alleged defense of "minority rights" recently imitated by Putin in Ukraine), the lightening victory over France. He correctly saw at the Munich Conference that the western democracies, who handed over Czechoslovakia for dismemberment, had no stomach for war, and exploited it to the hilt until they woke up. But these pragmatic victories of *Realpolitik* were all for the sake of the final, catastrophic war in the east fought over the fantasy of "Jewish

Bolshevism," which brought the Third Reich crashing down. This is where Machiavelli would have seen Hitler as a fool, sacrificing his and his people's "security and well-being" to a delusion, to what Machiavelli would have called an "imagined republic."

For Machiavelli, we recall from Part Two, a prince should combine the calculation of the fox with the passion of the lion. While Hitler was too much of a lion, relying too much on his "artistic" instincts, Stalin displayed more of the qualities of the fox. He played a longer game, surviving Hitler's invasion by allying with the West, and then holding onto everything he and Hitler had originally agreed to share. As military historian B. H. Liddell-Hart summed it up, the war ultimately "proved of profit only to Stalin ... by opening the way to communist domination of central Europe." It would be another 44 years before the Soviet Empire, all revolutionary conviction long since spent and crippled by its own economic backwardness, joined its Nazi cousin in history's grave.

FROM NATIONAL SOCIALISM TO THIRD-WORLD
SOCIALISM TO THE INTERNATIONAL JIHAD

Now the strange career of tyranny moves from the ruins of Berlin to liberated Paris, where the fateful postwar marriage between Marxism and existentialism gives birth to Third-World Socialism, whose rejection of both the American and Soviet models of economic and social development was also deeply influential on the rise of the International Jihad.

In a bold transformation of the earlier currents of millenarian tyranny we have examined in Part Three, the fantasy of "the people" now moves from the collectivist far Right of National Socialism to the collectivist far Left of Marxism. The catalyst for this transition was the founding philosopher of existentialism, Martin Heidegger, "the hidden king" of twentieth-century thought as Hannah Arendt had dubbed him years earlier. The most fervent philosophical disciple of Nazism now became the hero of French Marxists and existentialists led by Jean-Paul Sartre. Already in his 1927 magnum opus, *Being and Time*, Heidegger had tied his existentialist code of passionate risk, daring, resoluteness, and commitment to the German people's return to its collective "destiny" in a life and death struggle against the spiritually debased forces of modern materialism and individualism, thereby envisioning the National Socialist "community of destiny" that came to power in 1933. As George Steiner put it, Heidegger was already looking for Hitler when he wrote in 1927 that the German people must "choose its hero." In 1935, Heidegger wrote of "the inner truth and greatness of National socialism" in its struggle to "build a new world," praise he never retracted throughout his long life.

Through Heidegger's influence on French intellectuals and their disciples including aspiring revolutionaries such as Pol Pot and the intellectual godfather of the Iranian Revolution Ali Shariati, National Socialism's *Volkish* vision of "the people" recovering its primordial origins from the alienating influences of the Enlightenment, liberal democracy, and capitalism morphs into "the people" of Third-World Socialism recovering its destiny through the violent struggle of "national liberation movements" aimed at the colonizing powers of the West. In this way, "the people" replaces "the proletariat" in the revolutionary psychodrama, and the focus of revolutionary struggle shifts from the class struggle *within* advanced industrial democracies to the struggle *between* the colonialized East and its Western oppressors – between what Maoist ideologue Lin Piao called "the rural areas of the world" and the values of liberal individualism and the Enlightenment, now embodied by America (and, soon enough, Israel). Why did it happen? Because, after World War II, the "proletariat" of Europe and North America no longer existed or had any potential for a workers' revolution. The workers themselves had become part of the bourgeoisie, more interested in summer vacations and new cars than in revolution. Those who continued to hate the West needed to find a new force for its destruction, and they believed they had found it in the Third World.

Continuing the apocalyptic theme we traced throughout previous millenarian revolutionary movements, the single oppressive force that must be shattered in order to bring about utopia is now transferred from "the bourgeoisie" as an international class to the capitalistic nation-states of the West. The world to come will not be a universal society such as Marx had envisioned, but a flowering of unique and distinct "peoples." At the same time, a revolutionary maxim of Lenin's – "the worse, the better" – is retained. For in the third-world socialist view, there can be no evolution or peaceful progress in relations between East and West, no gradual extension of the benefits of economic modernization and liberal pluralism. The oppression of the colonialist powers – their rapacious corporations, armies, police, and torture squads – is actively welcomed so as to free the colonized peoples from any illusions about becoming modern capitalistic democracies themselves.

Frantz Fanon, the Sorbonne-educated Algerian intellectual and protégé of Sartre, was the chief visionary of third-world socialism because he wed Heidegger's *Volkish* philosophy of the radical Right to the revived Marxism of the radical Left. "The people," Fanon wrote in *The Wretched of the Earth*, must experience the oppressors' violence and lash back violently to win its freedom. Violence is not merely a means to freedom, but a "catharsis," a spiritual purification through the "life and death" struggle with the colonial master. And, just as in Heidegger's invocation of a mystical German destiny, a past far behind any ordinary received traditions about the past, Fanon calls on "the people" to "recover its destiny" by shattering its own native social and religious traditions because these "masks" are hopelessly tainted by centuries of collaboration with the colonial master. Gungha Din and Uncle Tom must give up their craven loyalty to their masters and reach for a Kalashnikov. Throw out *The Jungle Book* – reach for Mao's Little Red Book.

Many of these new currents were put into practice by one of the era's most ruthless dictators, Chairman Mao Tse Tung. (The death toll from his rule has been estimated at seventy million, resulting from execution, the incitement of mob justice, suicide, starvation, and labor camps). His "cultural revolution" (three million dead) was a deliberate attempt to smash the very limited economic modernization achieved under Chinese communism so as to purify the people of any latent or reviving bourgeois materialism or traditional Confucian values, forcing them back into a more primitive collective, his version of the Jacobins' original return to the Year One. He didn't want economic progress of even the meager kind the Soviet Union under Kruschev had achieved, which he contemptuously referred to as "goulash socialism" because it actually tried to feed people, thereby corrupting their collectivist purity with a despicable selfish motive. The Cultural Revolution called on the most fanatical among the young to terrorize and torture their elders for their pathetic gains in status and comfort. Mao gleefully watched his feral young warriors make their elder teachers and parents parade in dunce caps and confess their counterrevolutionary sins, and he encouraged them to dynamite ancient Chinese architecture. The "discovery" of the famous terra cotta army now touring the world actually resulted from a Red Guard attempt to blow up the burial mound containing them, halted when Mao declared the Cultural Revolution over. Mao himself had overseen the razing of most of the Forbidden City to make room for modern highways for cars that didn't yet exist. Just as Stalin had done during his revolution from above, Mao called on the young to supply the cadres for institutionalized terror as a way of preventing anyone else, especially among the older generation, from gaining enough independent status to make the dictator share his absolute power. Mao's Red Guards were the lineal descendants of the Hitler Youth and the idealistic young German students whom Heidegger called on to sweep away the bourgeois world of their parents and march behind the Führer.

Maoism extended the scope and drive of revolutionary terror. The purpose of Stalin's terror had been to reduce people to human integers interchangeable with every other integer in the collective, stripped of all individual liberty, loyalty, and attachments. Mao and third world socialism took this a step further. Now the state deliberately reduces its people to a Stone Age of barbarous deprivation and primitivism, not only to maximize control over them, but driven by a Rousseauan sentimental fantasy about how this will enable the people to enjoy a spiritually more pure existence, relieved of the burden of materialistic corruption (not including the leaders, of course, who lived in walled compounds of immense luxury). Stalin had wanted to build a productive modern economy without private property or profit. Beginning with Mao, the state's goal under Third-World Socialism was to crush the economy altogether.

This seemingly idealistic drive for fanatical purification, for the redemption of the people from bourgeois corruption, attracted young people in the West who viewed it from afar through a haze of endless, seemingly joyous parades and festivals. A pattern that went back to the French Revolution is repeated. As we saw, foreign observers of the French Revolution at the beginning of the

Terror – and later of the opening days of the Russian Revolution and the Third Reich – often admired what seemed to them a more virtuous, purposeful and comradely way of life than what bourgeois society could offer. In the same way, many young people in America and Europe identified with the Red Guards, wearing their red scarves and riding bikes in imitation of them, sympathizing with the perceived need to purge the older generation of its bloated selfishness and apathy. The same trend continued with the romanticization of the Viet Cong, the PLO, and the Sandinistas. Palestinian nationalism had always been attracted to Nazism, as an inspiration both for nationalism and the destruction of the Jews. Muslim Brotherhood founder Hassan al Banna was an admirer of Hitler, and the Grand Mufti of Jerusalem organized a Muslim SS unit. But sensing the *Zeitgeist* of the 1960s, Yasser Arafat donned the green fatigues of Castro and other "national liberation movements" and began parroting Marxist slogans. He knew that young people in America and Europe would romanticize the PLO's struggle with Israel as akin to that of the Vietcong against America.

The fusion of Heidegger's and Fanon's political existentialism with Marxism to produce third world socialism was terrifyingly summed up by the horrors of the Khmer Rouge regime in Cambodia. Pol Pot and Khieu Shampan had studied in Paris in the 1950s and they were influenced by Sartre and Fanon. They drew up their blueprint then for what they would later do when they seized power back home. When applied in practice by the Khmer Rouge, this led to the bloodbath of 1975–1979 in which the cities of Cambodia were forcibly evacuated and the Cambodian people were purified of the taint of Western corruption by being reduced to a primitive collective of slave labor. Their project was nothing less than the deliberate, cold-blooded torture and slaughter of every remnant of Cambodian society in any way tainted by old-fashioned religious and class loyalties, or by any exposure to Westernization, liberal democracy, modern education, and individual rights. Upward of six million Cambodians were systematically exterminated in labor and death camps recalling those of the Bolsheviks and Nazis. At one camp, guards had a favorite tree which they swung babies by their feet against (in front of their mothers) in order to smash their skulls, hurling the tiny corpses into a pit.

The Khmer Rouge's leaders, the "Higher Organization" (a small group of middle-class Francophone intellectuals including five teachers, one professor, a civil servant, and an economist) were determined to turn their own people overnight into Stone Age savages whose only function was to labor as slaves without reward or productive purpose and to be murdered at will. The mountains of skulls recovered from their death camps showed the conscious descent by Parisian-educated intellectuals from the most privileged stratum of society to the savagery of the most primitive past they could imagine, the most single-minded and determined attempt to carry out the original Jacobin project of returning to the Year One – or as they termed it, going Robespierre one better, the Year Zero – in the fanatical conviction that their enslaved, starving, and terrified people would experience Rousseauan bliss in returning to the "state of nature," saved from the psychological agony of bourgeois materialism. It was to *stay* the Year Zero forever.

THE TYRANNICAL PERSONALITY

Time and again since the beginning of the modern age and the Enlightenment, its optimists have argued that tyranny and unjust wars will soon be disbanded as people come to taste the benefits of a lasting peace, prosperity, and rights. Edward Gibbon's *The Decline and Fall of the Roman Empire*, for example, displayed brilliant insights into the psychology and practice of ancient tyranny Yet as we've seen, Gibbon, writing in the 1750s, did not believe that modern Europe's progress could ever regress back into the barbarism of Rome's decline into the Dark Ages – let alone something worse. German philosopher Immanuel Kant predicted in 1795 that, as modern states achieved greater and more widespread prosperity, they would not risk it by going to war, an argument revived on the eve of World War I in a best-selling book by Norman Angell. World War I was widely proclaimed "the war to end all wars" because, it was believed, its catastrophic carnage and destruction would finally teach one and all the folly of war and imperialism. Yet 1914 was merely the prelude for a series of tyrannies and revolutions unparalleled in history for their levels of genocidal carnage and devastation. Even that, though, did not prevent the same hopes in the progress of history from being raised once more after WW II, and again after the defeat of the "Evil Empire" in the Cold War, when it was said that we had reached "the end of history" and the inevitable spread of liberal democracy around the world. Then came 9/11. More recently, when Vladimir Putin tried to reverse the outcome of the Cold War through the invasion and annexation of Crimea and menacing the rest of Ukraine, the American secretary of state expressed bewilderment that someone so "nineteenth century" had somehow popped back up – the quote with which we began this book.

My reason for writing this book about the strange career of tyranny is to suggest that, however many times decent people express the decent hope that mankind has learned its lesson, the drive to tyrannize is a permanent passion in human psychology. It's never going away. We will always have to be on guard against it, prepared to resist it, if need be to fight it. I've also maintained that, throughout its many varieties, tyranny has always been both a form of government and a type of human being. Before turning to the final installment in tyranny's career to date – Islamist terrorism – let's make some broad observations about the psychological characteristics of millenarian tyranny.

The biographies of millenarian tyrants including Robespierre, Lenin, Hitler, Mao, Pol Pot, and Bin Laden (all from middle class or more affluent backgrounds) confirm that economic deprivation is not the "root cause" of terrorism, but a fanatical passion for justice and revenge. They want a revolution now in order to build a collectivist future that will enshrine their absolute power, avenge past perceived slights and injustices to themselves, and force everyone else into a grim straitjacket of submersion in the mass so as to purge them of selfish modern materialism and individualism. An excessive and unforgiving passion for justice as part of one's overriding lust for power, influence, and fame is a characteristic trait of a certain kind of young man, and, not surprisingly, therefore, tyranny in general has always been something of a youth employment opportunity. Alexander the Great, Julius Caesar, Octavian, Robespierre, Stalin, Hitler, Mao – all began their rise to power at a fairly early age.

Although I've argued that millenarian tyranny does not appear until the French Revolution, millenarian tyrants do share some psychological traits with the ancient tyrants we considered in Part One – the capacity diagnosed by ancient thinkers led by Plato for excessively righteous zeal, anger, bellicosity, jealousy of rivals, suspicion, and possessiveness. (Plato called it the "spirited" part of the soul, in contrast both with reason and the desire for mere survival). On the lowest level of base conniving thuggery, the rise of a Saddam Hussein through treachery and murder could have come out of the annals of past tyrants and political adventurers including Hiero of Syracuse or Cesare Borgia, and Plato and Aristotle would have no trouble recognizing in Bashar al Assad a typical tyrannical kleptocrat fighting to control an entire country as if it were his personal property. But overall, millenarian tyrants have much less in common with ancient examples of excessive erotic passion and a lust for glory (like Alcibiades or, depending on your viewpoint, Caesar) and more in common with Torquemada and the Inquisition. They are secular fanatics, abstemious and ascetic, or at least not prone to public displays of luxurious personal grandeur, ornamentation, architectural splendor, and robes of state characteristic of traditional universal monarchs going back to Cyrus the Great. (Napoleon's imperial ceremonial, meant to sheath the modernization of Europe through conquest in a revived Roman splendor, was the exception that proves the rule).

It was Robespierre – "the Incorruptible" – who launched the ideal that, in contrast with the splendid, charming, and hedonistic rulers of antiquity, the modern ruler must be "disinterested" (free of self-interest), a kind of "secular saint" (to use Michael Walzer's term) who disdains frivolous pleasures and entertainment. Robespierre wore a plain frock coat, while Stalin, Hitler, and Castro favored the unadorned military tunic or greatcoat of the private soldier. The conspicuous absence of gorgeous medals, sashes, and braid, seemingly a sign of modesty, was meant to show that their rank vastly exceeded that of any mere general. As the source of all such honors for others, they stood above them for themselves. Hitler's Iron Cross and small Party badge and Stalin's similarly inconspicuous Order of Lenin pinned to their otherwise plain uniforms confirmed the unique and total scope of their personal authority. Mao and his comrades favored a similarly unadorned field jacket, the famous "Mao jacket" (although for the highest ranks they were tailor-made). Napoleon, despite his pretensions to imperial magnificence at his court, had made a similar point on the battlefield by wearing a plain greatcoat while surrounded by his dazzlingly plumed and braided peacocks of Marshals. His habit of pinching their cheeks in public as he bestowed yet another honor was meant to show that their rank meant nothing without his personal favor, to be revoked at will.

In contrast with the vivid and urbane tyrants of the ancient world, millenarian tyrants have a public image that is titanic, omnipresent, and beyond human scale (reflected in the industrialized genocide and architectural brutalism of Stalin and Hitler) and in their personal lives a kind of self-effacement, crankishness, banality, or awkwardness. Whereas the lives of the ancient tyrants are seamlessly interwoven with the patrimonial character of their regimes, so that their political predominance is merged with the possessiveness, but also at times the generosity, charm, or flamboyance of a lover (think of Alcibiades or Caesar), we are astounded at the kind of "grey blur" (to use Trotsky's famous if self-serving description of Stalin) who stands behind the levers of the totalitarian state's superhuman might. While having millions killed, Hitler showed an elaborate Austrian courtesy toward his secretaries, like that of a bourgeois banker, teasing them that they were fattening him up with too much cake. Himmler suffered from chronic stomach pains and, while supervising the Holocaust, thoughtfully remembered his secretaries' birthdays. These rulers do not seem to seek public glory – at least not in the traditionally recognizable splendor of past emperors or kings – avoiding the public for years at a time in their bunkers or walled compounds. Hitler's summer retreat has been compared to that of a relatively prosperous businessman. Osama bin Laden, once the aspiring revolutionary leader of the Muslim world, was killed in a near-empty bedroom. The point is not that these leaders were actually incorruptible or did not have secret vices and purloined wealth. The point is that their personal lives were disconnected from their monumental public image, whereas past despots lived on a scale and in a way (think of Nero's Golden House or Louis XIV's Versailles) that merged their taste for luxury, adornment, and refinement with their public identities as rulers. From Cyrus the Great to the Sun King, they were emblems of an orderly and beneficent world.

Reclusive in their "Spartan quarters," modern millenarian tyrants have aimed to purge and recreate human existence on a vast scale, through the destruction and transportation of millions of people, in the service of doctrines that proclaim an ideal, beyond compromise, of equality, virtue, classlessness, and communal or racial purity. Although capable of setting in motion prodigies of terror that in the past one can only find in descriptions of the most vengeful deities – and which the Enlightenment believed would vanish with the end of Europe's religious wars – in person our tyrants tend to be gray, mild, lacking in vanity of dress or manner, studious, gluttonous, and fussy. Sometimes they are histrionic in the manner of an overwrought professor or cafe intellectual, eager to lay out their crankish opinions on all facets of life from the cycles of empire to music, diet, and grooming.

A brief illustration from ancient and modern literature will crystallize this contrast. In Aristotle's depiction in the *Politics*, the tyrant is a monster of desires who outrages his subjects by plundering or ravishing them. Citizens are driven to tyrannicide by the need to rid society of this bloated exploiter. We considered some examples of the tyrant as a monster of erotic excess in Part One with the stories of Harmodius and Aristogeiton and the overthrow of the Tarquins. This condemnation, repeated and embellished by humanist commentators both religious and secular, still animates many denunciations of oppressive regimes, like the 2011 uprisings in Tunisia, Egypt, and Syria against corrupt kleptocrats and their idle, spoiled families and hangers-on. In striking contrast, however, as we saw earlier in Sergey Nechaev's classic modern statement of the terrorist's creed, *Catechism of the Revolutionist*, the terrorist's violence is aimed at purging society's *own* bloated desires and corruption. Tyrannical methods are used for ascetic aims by ascetics who want to force everyone else to be ascetics. Nechaev's very use of the term *catechism* suggests that terrorism aims to create a politicized, secularized version of a community of religious penitents with its absolute monastic discipline, forced to renounce their pleasures and luxuries for the sake of the collective. Even pity for the oppressed themselves, the poor and disadvantaged, cannot stand in the way of striking at those among them who, through foolishness or venality, prop up the established order. As we have observed, the majority of the guillotine's victims under Robespierre were from the middle and lower orders. The terrorist's creed calls for an idealistic and disinterested tyrant, murderous and pure of spirit, something difficult to recognize in the ancient understanding of the tyrant's hedonistic personality. "Hard toward himself," Nechaev writes in language at once ruthless and principled, "he must be hard toward others also ... He must not be what the promptings of his personal inclinations would have him be, but what the general interest of the revolution prescribes."

Just as these actual or aspiring terroristic tyrants promote the image that they are not hedonistic, vain, or flamboyant in their desire for pubic adulation, they do not attract their followings due to the fact that, as Plato had argued, tyrants pander to the masses' own hedonism and moral laxness, so that, for Plato, tyranny emerges directly from the basest traits of democracy. On the contrary, millenarian tyrants often inspire a kind of selfless zeal on their followers' parts as well. The followers participate in the leader's sense of having a "historic mission" whose scope and intensity of destruction were formerly approached only by the most savage religious wars and persecutions, a mission that requires of all its participants that they renounce not only an easy life of pleasure and relaxation, but the luxury of ordinary moral scruples and decent sentiments of tolerance and compassion, as we saw in Himmler's infamous Posen speech to the SS leadership. What distinguishes millenarian revolutionary movements in their own minds from the selfish interests of both bourgeois democratic and traditional conservative politics is precisely the lack of venality or personal passion that characterizes the elite cadres who carry out the surgical reconstruction of society through genocide. The "greatness" of the revolutionaries in their own minds stems from their ability to feel nothing toward their victims, not even an ugly spasm of envy, cruelty, or triumph. They aspire to a purely disinterested murderousness.

Striving for this ideal of impersonal destruction protects the purity of the revolutionary movement not only from moral objections based on traditional and customary notions of shame, pity, and decency, but from the temptation to perform one's duty to kill out of any sense of personal gratification, let alone profit. The point is not that the murderers actually or even frequently attained this state of inner purity, but that the movements understood and presented themselves this way as an ideal to which they should aspire. Himmler was appalled at any instance of unorganized violence or spontaneous sadism toward the victims of the Holocaust that might taint the will to annihilate the Jews with corrupt personal motives, and he was scandalized by, and sought to punish, the widespread theft of the victims' belongings by the camp guards and officers. The German Volk must take everything from the conquered with a clear conscience, but the SS man must aim for a higher standard: to liquidate the German people's enemies without personal greed or malice toward individuals.

That ideal of utopian genocide lives on in today's Terrorist International, as we'll now see.

MILLENARIAN TYRANNY TODAY

Now we reach the final installment in the strange career of tyranny bringing us back to the present – Jihadist terrorism. In the wake of the Al Qaeda attack of 9/11, many Western observers began to ask, in the words of Bernard Lewis, "what went wrong" with Islam? How had it happened that men claiming to be Muslims, one of the three great monotheistic religions that shaped our history, were apparently bent on destroying the West, including Israel, and other Muslims, through mass murder? I'm going to argue that Jihadist terrorism is best understood as the direct heir of Third-World Socialism and the other millenarian revolutionary movements we've looked at so far. Before tracing that pedigree, however, let's look at the broader context.

The debate about "what went wrong" continues as Al Qaeda has been succeeded by ISIS, and there are many possible answers. I don't believe that Islam is inherently more inclined to terrorism and violence than the other two Abrahamic faiths. All three speak with mixed voices. As Rezla Aslan observes: "The same Bible that commands Jews to 'love your neighbor as yourself' also exhorts them to 'kill every man and woman, child, and infant, ox and sheep, camel and donkey' who worship any other God. The same Jesus Christ who told his disciples to 'turn the other cheek' also told them he had 'not come to bring peace but the sword' ... The same Quran that warns believers 'if you kill one person it is as though you have killed all humanity' also commands them to 'slay the idolaters wherever you find them.' "

Many wars of conquest were carried out under the banner of Christianity, including, as we saw in Part Two, barbarous acts of murder and destruction against both nonbelievers and Christian minorities. Mind you, just as it would be self-serving to pretend that only Islam is inherently bent on violent conquest while acting as if Christian tyranny was a betrayal of the faith's high moral standards by men who had no claim to be its representatives, it is equally hypocritical for Muslims to pretend that Christian Europe's attempt to reconquer its traditional heartland in the Middle East, let alone Spain, was some kind of unbelievable "catastrophe" such that the very word "crusade" is deeply offensive. Muslim armies took by force what had once belonged to the Roman Empire, including the cradle of Christianity, and tried to conquer Europe, too. Then the Europeans tried to take those territories back. Neither side was morally superior to the other.

Several interpretations of "what went wrong" are especially relevant to our theme of tyranny's career. Like its Roman and Byzantine predecessors, the Ottoman Empire gradually declined from vibrancy and innovation into corruption, stagnation, and clinging to the past. For five hundred years, the Ottoman Sultans had embodied their claim to be Caliphs in a solid record of institutional and legal stability, tolerance (relatively speaking) for other faiths, and the promotion of education and economic enterprise. When the Ottoman Empire fell, the longing for the Caliphate entered a realm of fanatical fantasy divorced from any conception of stable and lawful government, and it remains there today, as witness the murderous attempts of the Taliban and ISIS to apply the most severe version of Sharia law over those whom they rule. They display no interest in or knowledge of the actual record of the Ottoman Caliphate or any successful Muslim precedent for orderly government, preferring – like all millenarian revolutionaries since Robespierre – to return to a past behind the past, a mythical collective of total purity, allegedly the first Muslim community founded by the Prophet himself. Invoking this precedent conveniently allows today's Jihadists to jettison twelve hundred years of historical experience, along with the need to educate themselves about it (leaving more time for computer games and planning murder).

It has been suggested that, unlike the Christian West, Islam underwent neither a religious Reformation nor a secular Renaissance. The twin principles of religious and political (including economic) individualism – the key, as we saw in Part Two, to the rise of liberal democracy – did not take root. As early as the Middle Ages in Europe, Thomism recognized a division between the claims of divine authority and those of the secular realm of politics and economic life that laid the basis for the eventual separation of church and state, but no such transformation took place in Islam. While Thomism won the battle over Christian fundamentalists who wanted all human affairs directly governed by religious revelation and theocracy, in the Muslim world, the initial brilliant period of philosophical enlightenment sparked by Al-farabi and Avicenna in their attempt to reconcile ancient Greek philosophy with Islamic revelation was snuffed out by the all-embracing fundamentalism of Ibn Tamiyya, who believed that the claims of reason must be entirely set aside in the name of Sharia law. He was one of the originators of the Wahabbists' severe interpretation of Sharia embraced by Islamic fundamentalists today.

Add to this that when the Ottoman Empire finally collapsed in the wake of World War I, the triumphant European powers seized its former satrapies and, suiting their own self-interest, cobbled together a number of ersatz new "nations" including Syria and Iraq. When modernization finally reached these often fragile entities, significantly, they chose the Soviet rather than the European model. The nationalist movement that swept the Arab world under the "young colonels" like Nasser and Gaddafi initially had high hopes that their peoples could be brought into the modern age. But, perhaps because of an inherent conservative distrust of popular government and a preference for political hierarchy, they preferred the Soviet model of development "from above" under a one-party state. They also bought the Soviet claim that backward nations could "skip" the stage of capitalist development and, through central planning, build modern industrial economies overnight. That went hand in hand with their admiration of Stalin for his brutal wielding of absolute power to transform society so rapidly. According to V. S. Naipaul, many Arab men including Saddam Hussein sported a bushy mustache in imitation of the Father of Peoples.

In time, these hopes for reform withered along with the Soviet experiment itself, and the Baathist and nationalist regimes became what they were on the eve of the Arab Spring – one-party states or dictatorships where the meager economy, its development paralyzed by the absence of genuine market forces and entrepreneurialism, was carved up and given away by the dictators to their families and cronies. Assad, Mubarak, Saddam, and the old survivor Gaddafi were all this variety of failed reforming tyrant, their claims to be modernizers eventually exposed as a tired, worn-out husk as the Soviet Union had long since collapsed under its own economic mediocrity. Their naked greed was an open invitation to the Muslim Brotherhood's work in providing charity relief to the masses.

The twin aim of Jihadist terrorism going back to Al Qaeda's declaration of war on America, Israel, and the West has always been to overthrow these corrupt, reactionary nationalist regimes and colonially imposed monarchies (while happily accepting their funding) while simultaneously pursuing the destruction of the "Great Satan," America, and its local "little Satan" proxy, Israel. The ultimate goal is the creation of a worldwide Caliphate, in this sense departing from Third World Socialism's vision of a future flowering of autonomous "peoples" and embracing a more Leninist conception of a worldwide collectivist state. Even terrorist groups like Al Fatah that initially claimed to be "secular socialist" freedom fighters against colonialism inspired by Ho Chi Minh and Che Guevara eventually Islamicized their doctrines as Jihadism spread a new revolutionary fervor among the young and the dispossessed. Among his last desperate gambits, Saddam recast himself as "the Sword of Islam," even though Stalin had been his hero. Although the tactics have varied about which aim took priority – battling America or overthrowing corrupt Arab states – the overall structure of revolutionary belief has remained consistent down to ISIS as I write these words. But of central importance to the evolution of Jihadism is the extent to which Islamist extremism draws on long-standing *European* currents of revolutionary nihilism going back to the Jacobins, Bolsheviks, Nazis, and Third-World Socialist movements.

Before turning to that pedigree, let's pause to consider one of the relatively more successful examples of despotic state building from above in the Muslim world that took place amidst the ruins of the great Ottoman Empire itself. With Kemal Ataturk, one feels in the presence of our other great modernizers including Henry VIII, Peter the Great, and Frederick the Great – "great," as we earlier observed, not necessarily meaning morally great, but an unusual combination of intelligence, far-sightedness, an insight into human psychology, toughness, and perseverance. Unlike later movements for modernization in the Arab world, Ataturk understood that simply building factories or buying weapons from the West without an accompanying cultural transformation would have no long-term success. He and the other "Young Turks," Western-oriented modernizing army officers, believed that the influence of Islam had to be tamed by the secular state, exactly as had happened to the Church in Europe. (While the other Young Turks tried to convert the Ottoman state into a constitutional monarchy, Ataturk spear-headed its replacement by a republic in 1922, including the abolition of the Caliphate.) Ataturk also wanted to end Turks' sense of dependence on Arab and Iranian culture, replacing the use of Arabic in the mosque and Farsi in the political and cultural elites with a wholly modernized Turkish language whose reconstruction anticipated a similar linguistic miracle later with modern Hebrew (and, linguistically speaking, recalled Peter the Great's command that the Boyars shave off their beards).

Like our other state-building despots, Ataturk was capable of calculated violence and brutality in his effort to create a new sense of Turkish ethnic nationhood. During the dying days of the Ottoman regime, as many as half a million, possibly a million, Armenians lost their lives in a campaign often described as genocidal. Some accuse the Young Turks as having been complicit. While Ataturk, stationed at the time in the Dardanelles, was not likely involved, his opinion of what went on in Armenia remained unclear. During the Turkish War of Independence in which, after the collapse of the Ottoman state, the Kemalists fought the Western powers and their proxies including Armenia and Greece, upward of twelve thousand Armenians were killed during the Battle of Marash and two hundred and sixty-four thousand Greeks lost their lives The population exchange in 1923 between Turkey and Greece forced millions of Anatolian Greeks to go to Greece and Greek Muslims to come to Turkey under often very brutal conditions. Kemal's role in all of these events is still heatedly debated. Moreover, in the best tradition of Peter the Great, he did not believe that the Turkish people were "ready" for actual self-government. A one-party state backed by a Kemalist-dominated military must retain control until ordinary Turks shed their backward Muslim ways. Kemal was a model for liberalizing authoritarians such as Anwar Sadat and Pervez Musharraf (with decidedly mixed results). One wonders whether Egyptian President Morsi, with his call for an Islamic reformation, may be channeling him, too.

It has been argued that modernization has been *relatively* more successful, relatively more prosperous, creating societies that are relatively more open and political structures that, although not out-and-out elective democracies, are relatively reflective of society's major groups in countries like Turkey, Egypt, and Iran that were always great civilizational centers, even before Islam, and, therefore, had an unusual degree of cultural self-confidence and national cohesiveness. One can do no more than detect patterns, nothing like the "laws" or "paradigms" ever sought after like the Dulcinea of political science's Don Quixote. Iran and Turkey are currently ruled by Islamists, while the jury is still out in Egypt. But at least some form of complex civil society exists in those countries, as does the sense of a "lost" premodern greatness and rootedness that sparked Europe's own great revolutions since 1789. By contrast, modernization seems to have been far less successful in countries like Pakistan, Iraq, Libya, and Syria, along with many African nations, which were created out of nothing by the Great Powers of the West and then saddled with the need to erect modern states overnight.

A WORLDWIDE CALIPHATE: JIHADISM'S UTOPIAN VISION

The International Jihad is the twenty-first century's main heir to millenarian revolutionary movements stretching back through Third-World Socialism and National Socialism to the Jacobins. Whatever differences may exist among the Khomeinists, Al Qaeda, the Taliban, Hamas, Hezbollah, and ISIS, they share the same utopian aim – the establishment of a worldwide Caliphate – and they are united in their implacable hatred of the "Great Satan" America, and its local proxy, the "Little Satan" Israel.

Al Qaeda grew out of the struggle of the Mujahadeen in Afghanistan against the Soviet Union, the birth of their cult of honor and death in battle (As one of the Afghan Mujahadeen put it, "The Americans believe in Coca-Cola. We believe in death"). As proclaimed in Al Qaeda's 1996 *Declaration of War Against America*, Jihad became a rallying call for this-worldly, secular revolution against both the West and corrupt, self-professed Muslim regimes that, in the Jihadists' view, collaborated with the West and are tainted by its selfish materialism and hedonistic degradation. In the *Declaration*, Osama Bin Laden called on Muslims to put aside their differences so as to concentrate against the Western enemy, a movement he described two years later as the

"World Islamic Front." Al Qaeda blended many previous third-world socialist critiques of the West into its allegedly religious call to arms – its list of grievances included Western colonialism, economic exploitation, and the attempt to repress national liberation movements like the Vietcong.

Commentators including Bernard Lewis and this writer observed early on an affinity between the collectivist ideal of a pure Islamic state aimed for by Al Qaeda and the *Volkish* nationalism of Heidegger and European fascist movements of the 1920s and 30s. Lewis traces "the mood of anti-Westernism" in political Islamism to Heidegger, Ernst Junger, Rainer Maria Rilke, and the Nazis. As the appeal of Marxism-Leninism with its scenario of international class conflict waned, he argued, the strain in fascist ideology extolling "the spirituality and vitality of the rooted, human, national cultures of the Germans and other 'authentic peoples'" fed "the new mystique of Third Worldism emanating from Western Europe" among Muslim intellectuals.

Jihadism also borrowed from Third-World Socialism's belief in the existence of an authentically rooted "people" whose true past exists far behind the conventionally received orthodoxy about the meaning of tradition, a true past that can only be recovered by an act of revolutionary violence. As we observed earlier, Al Qaeda's and other Islamists' vision of a pure Islamic state bears little resemblance to the whole rich history of Muslim religious, political, and cultural values as they evolved gradually over the centuries. By predating the pure society to the earliest origins of Islam, Al Qaeda implied that its entire subsequent history is hopelessly tainted by Westernization and colonization, just as Fanon had maintained was the case with the received traditions ("masks") of third-world peoples. This vision of a restored pure community of the faithful comes down to little more than the vaguest generalizations about community, lack of selfishness, and lack of corruption. It is as much a leap into an unknowable future as it is a return to the past, sweeping aside every counsel of prudence, received wisdom, theological precedent and the rule of law – the true heir of millenarian tyranny going back to the Jacobins return to "the Year One."

Of special interest is Islamism's intellectual founder, the Egyptian Sayyd Qutb, and his critique of Western spiritual corruption, decadence, sexual depravity, and nihilism, based on observations he made while visiting the United States as a student. These criticisms contributed to a long pedigree of the excoriation of the secular Enlightenment and liberal democracy that began, as we have seen in Part Three, in the West itself, typified by Rousseau, Marx, Nietzsche, Heidegger, plus numerous promoters of fascism, and was exported to the non-Western world along with Western economic and cultural influence. Ironically, in finding these defects in the West, Qutb was contributing from the East to a lexicon originating in the anti-Enlightenment culture of the West itself as far back as Rousseau's *Discourse on the Arts and Sciences* in 1750.

All the hallmarks of millenarian revolution that we've looked at in Part Three stretching back to the Jacobins come together in the International Jihad.

*The return to the Year One, a grim collectivist utopia allegedly based on the earliest, purest version of Muslim society in the seventh century. *The identification of *one* force that stands in the way of nirvana for all mankind, and which must therefore be obliterated. For the Jihadists, that force is America – the embodiment of the Enlightenment, capitalism, globalization, bourgeois corruption – allied with Israel and the Jews. *Lenin's maxim "the worse, the better." Al Qaeda attacked the United States on 9/11 because it *wanted* America to respond with lethal force, thereby unmasking itself as a colonialist oppressor, galvanizing the Islamic masses, and removing any hope of accommodation. Revolutionary movements do not *want* peace, prosperity, or sound government for their peoples (and that's true of ISIS and Hamas today). *Finally, just as earlier millenarian tyrannies found "useful idiots," as Stalin termed them, who actually believed that the Enlightenment West was responsible for the revolutionaries' justified rage, numerous American intellectuals and pundits believed that America had brought 9/11 on itself because, as *The Nation* magazine put it within weeks of the attack, it had been a "rogue state" oppressing third-world peoples for decades.

THE NUCLEAR REPUBLIC OF GOD

That brings us to the Iranian Republic, where we're going to end our discussion of millenarian tyranny. Not only does it sum up the entire vision of Jihadist extremism including Al Qaeda, Hamas, the Taliban, and ISIS, but it has put into practice just about all the hallmarks of millenarian revolutions we have discussed in Part Three going back to the Jacobins.

The Iranian Republic has established a radical theocracy of harsh Islamic law over the territory of a major state – a major aim of all Jihadist movements, but otherwise so far unattained except for the shifting regional influence of the Taliban and ISIS and the Hamas statelet in Gaza – and is an important regional military power. It attempts to export terrorism and revolution through its proxies including Hezbollah and Hamas against what it regards as corrupt or pro-Western regimes (especially Israel). As with the Jacobins and Bolsheviks, the Iranian Revolution began as a reformist uprising against a fitfully liberalizing autocrat, Shah Reza Pahlevi, but then the original secular progressives, Marxists, and technocrats were quickly swept aside by the forces of the charismatic Ayatollah Khomeini, the revolution's equivalent of Lenin or Hitler, with his message of a complete transformation of human life. Like previous totalitarian regimes where terrorists came to power such as the Soviet Union and Third Reich, the Khomeinist "Republic of God" acts as a beacon for its revolutionary kindred everywhere.

Like the Bolsheviks' KGB and the Nazis' SS, the elite cadres of the Iranian Republican Guard have created a state within the state that not only guards the radical purity of the revolution and conducts terror against its own population and abroad, but controls whole swaths of the economy. Most significant of all, like the Jacobins, Bolsheviks, and National Socialists, the Iranian Republic has a utopian project to be brought about by genocide – a worldwide Islamist state ushered in by the destruction of Israel and ultimately America. But whereas past totalitarian imperialists could only hope to spread the blessings of their revolutions by means of conventional military force, Iran has added a new and truly terrifying ingredient – the bringing about of Armageddon through world-wide nuclear war.

This new version of utopian genocide was articulated by another charismatic Iranian leader, President Mahmoud Ahmadinejad. Although not an absolute dictator like Stalin or Hitler owing to the supreme authority of the Ayatollahs, he summed up the most extreme tenets of the Iranian Revolution. Little is known about him, except that he was an engineer by training and was supposedly chosen, when Mayor of Tehran, to be a more pliable president after Hahmed Khatamai's attempts at democratic reform (inconclusive, but to the Ayatollahs still intolerable). If that's true, he proved to be far more formidable than a mere tool. Although he is no longer president (but not necessarily powerless – we know very little about the murky world of tribal and political allegiances in Iranian politics), his vision of nuclear genocide still influences the top Iranian leadership.

Lucid and affable-seeming in interviews he gave in the West – yet, according to Iranian expatriate circles, a man who had killed prisoners with his bare hands – President Ahmadinejad always seemed to be smiling, as if he knew something we didn't, or at least not yet. It was tempting to view him as a madman (as if David Koresh ruled a country soon to be equipped with nuclear weapons, as Israeli prime minister Netanyahu put it). That way, when he spoke of wiping Israel off the face of the earth, we might have convinced ourselves that he was no more than a fanatical front man for the Iranian Republic's desire to possess nuclear weapons so as to assert itself in the manner of China or any other aspiring great power.

Unfortunately, whether mad or not, Ahmadinejad had a coherent ideological vision in which the call to wipe out Israel was no ordinary manifestation of anti-Semitism. Instead, it is the beckoning of an apocalyptic event that will usher in a millennium of bliss for all believers, indeed all mankind. Nuclear weapons are the indispensable means to this end since they are the most reliable way of exterminating the Jewish state. They are therefore not to be negotiated away in exchange for other economic or security benefits. The revolution needs nuclear weapons to carry out its utopian mission.

Ahmadinejad made his aims clear many times in public. At a "World Without Zionism" conference in Tehran in October 2005, at which he also called for "death to America," he said: "They ask, is it possible for us to witness a world without America and Zionism? But you had best know that this slogan and this goal are attainable, and surely can be achieved." At the same conference, he called for Israel to be "wiped off the map," adding that "very soon, this stain of disgrace will vanish from the center of the Islamic world. This is attainable."

Iran's senior-most Islamic leaders gave their full support to this genocidal aim. Ahmadinejad announced that he intended to return Iran to the purity of the revolution that brought the Ayatollah Khomeini to power in 1979. The annihilation of Israel, he claimed, was a goal first announced by Khomeini himself, thus a project endowed with the highest possible authority.

Like many millenarian tyrants including Hitler and Stalin, he professed a love for mankind, justice, and world peace while setting in place the mechanisms of mass murder needed to bring this world about. Ahmadinejad reflected the Iranian Revolution's assimilation of traditional Islamic categories of faith to a Marxist lexicon of violent revolution. (Unsurprisingly, he made common cause with secular Marxist dictators like Hugo Chavez and Robert Mugabe in denouncing American imperialism). The Iranian revolution's brand of jihadism has close structural similarities to – and an actual historical descent from – strains of European revolutionary nihilism including that of the Jacobins, the Bolsheviks, and the Nazis, and extending to later third-world offshoots like the Khmer Rouge.

As we've seen throughout Part Three, all these revolutionary movements have a common set of genocidal aims that reemerged in Ahmadinejad's lethal rhetoric. They all envision a return to a grimly repressive collectivist utopia in which individual freedom is obliterated in the name of the common good, and people are purged of their vices. Returning to a past so pure and distant requires the destruction of all received tradition, including religious traditions, extending back centuries, and so is, paradoxically, at the same time a radical leap into the future. That is why neither the allegedly Sunni faith of the Taliban nor the allegedly Shiite faith of the Iranian Revolution bears any close resemblance to the traditions and restraints imposed by those faiths, especially restraints on this-worldly political extremism, terrorism, and the slaughter of noncombatants.

As we have seen, the second aim that all these revolutionary movements share is the identification of one class or race enemy whose extermination is the crucial necessary step to bring about the utopian community where all alienation and vice will end forever. The class or race enemy becomes the embodiment of all human evil, whose destruction will cleanse the planet. In Ahmadinejhad's flirtation with nuclear Armageddon, the destruction of Israel plays the same apocalyptic role that the Nazis assigned to the destruction of European Jewry. Stalin assigned the identical role to the destruction of the "kulaks," the so-called rich peasants. Now it was the Jews' turn again. When Ahmadinejad promised Muslims "a world without Zionism," he meant it quite literally.

We have already stressed the connections between al Qaeda and European ideologies of revolutionary extremism. The Iranian Revolution's connections with these ideologies are, if anything, even better documented. The key figure here is the acknowledged intellectual godfather of the Iranian revolution, Ali Shariati. To understand Ahmadinejad's campaign to return to the purity of the original Khomeinist revolution and why it leads him to flirt with nuclear Armageddon, it is necessary to understand Ali Shariati.

Ali Shariati (1933–1977) was an Iranian intellectual who studied comparative literature in Paris in the early 1960s and was influenced by Jean-Paul Sartre and Frantz Fanon. He translated Sartre's major philosophical work, *Being and Nothingness*, into Farsi, and coauthored a translation of Fanon's famous revolutionary tract *The Wretched of the Earth*. As we've seen, Sartre and Fanon together were responsible for revitalizing Marxism by borrowing from Martin Heidegger's philosophy of existentialism, which stressed man's collective need to struggle against a purposeless bourgeois world in order to endow life with meaning through passionate commitment. By lionizing revolutionary violence for its own sake as a purifying catharsis that forces us to turn our backs on the bourgeois world, Sartre and Fanon hoped to rescue the downtrodden from the seduction of Western materialism. Fanon was even more important because he imported from Heidegger's philosophy a passionate commitment to the destiny of the people, the longing for the lost purity of the premodern collective that had drawn Heidegger to National Socialism.

This potent brew of violent struggle and passionate commitment to a utopian vision of a collectivist past reborn as the future deeply influenced Ali Shariati, just as it had influenced another student in Paris a few years earlier, the future Khmer Rouge leader Pol Pot. Ali Shariati aimed to politicize the Shiite faith of his fellow Iranians with this same existentialist creed of revolutionary violence and purification. His distinctive contribution to Jihadist millenarianism was rooted in a theological difference between Sunni and Iranian Shia Islam, a messianic strain in Shia that awaits the return of the Hidden Imam to establish justice on earth. Ali Shariati hitched Shia messianism to the service of creating a purely this-worldly revolution in which, no longer content to wait passively for the Hidden Imam's return, the masses will create a just society through political struggle – a fusion of Shia apocalypticism with the blend of Heidegger, Fanon, and Third-World Socialism that Ali Shariati had absorbed in Paris. He sought to turn Shiism from pious hopes for a better world to the creation of a political utopia in the here and now.

Although one cannot look into another man's heart and assess the sincerity of his religious beliefs, Ali Shariati's critics argue with some plausibility that Islam was in many ways no more than a religion of convenience for him. It was the most powerful social force in Iran, these critics contend, so Ali Shariati subverted its categories with a neo-Marxist agenda alien to true faith. Following Fanon, Ali Shariati believed that "the people" had to return to its most distant origins and so create what Fanon had termed a "new man" and a "new history." Like Fanon as well, Ali Shariati defined a people as sharing "a common pain" inflicted on them by Western oppression.

Frequently citing Sartre, he proclaimed existentialism superior to all other philosophies because, in it, "human beings are free and the architects as well as masters of their own essence." This assertion of man's absolute control over his own destiny violates all three Abrahamic faiths, which stress that human beings are servants of God and powerless to do good without Him. When Ali Shariati was criticized in 1972 by traditionalists among the Iranian clergy, he wrote to his father arguing that those who had fought French colonialism in Algeria were closer to the true revolutionary spirit of Shiism than traditionalists like the Ayatollah Milani who avoided all involvement in politics.

Throughout Ali Shariati's discussions of Shiism, religion is harnessed to revolutionary politics. He tried to transfer Shiites' hopes for a better world achieved through the return of the Hidden Imam, the Mahdi, to revolutionary agendas of armed struggle and historical progress. The return of the Mahdi, he proclaimed, will bring about a "classless society," a Marxist slogan. An unconventional Muslim at best, Ali Shariati was deeply interested in Sufi mysticism including the poetry of Rumi, and he loved Balzac and other European writers. Like Sartre and later Michel Foucault, Ali Shariati had a passion for literature that went hand in hand with a passion for revolution, a confusion of politics with art – the wish to shape the human mass into a harmonious whole – that, as we have seen, is a common theme in millenarian revolutionary movements. In his works, political struggle becomes a beautifying myth of heroic valor and the triumph of the will, the delusion that "the people" can achieve through revolutionary violence the aesthetic wholeness and unity of a work of art.

Returning to Iran in the early 1970s, during the rule of Shah Reza Pahlavi, Ali Shariati began to organize for the coming revolution. While he repudiated the formal doctrine of Marxism-Leninism because of its atheism and materialistic interpretation of history, he expressed admiration for the revolutionary fervor of Iranian Marxists and occasionally supported their protests against the regime. His lectures at the Ershad Institute in Tehran, which set forth his fusion of Shiism and revolutionary struggle, were wildly popular. He had several run-ins with the Shah's secret police, Savak, who monitored his classes.

He also tried to forge links with the Iranian religious establishment. Many of its most reputable theologians continued to regard his attempt to blend Shiism with third-world revolution as heretical. They maintained that Shia Islam had no sanction for the kind of secular revolutionary cause espoused by Shariati; that man could do nothing through his own actions, especially political action, to hasten the advent of the Last Days and the return of the Hidden Imam. One important figure, however, refused to condemn Ali Shariati when called upon to do so in 1970 by his fellow clerics: the Ayatollah Khomeini. He and Ali Shariati were not direct allies. But Khomeini – who once said that "Islam is politics" – was no traditionalist either, and he wanted to harness the popular energy Ali Shariati had stimulated among Iranian students to help fuel his own political movement for a theocratic dictatorship.

Ali Shariati died in 1977, two years before the Iranian Revolution, but largely thanks to his influence, the ideology brought to power by Khomeini's rule is an Islam distorted by European left-wing existentialism and the romanticization of violence. Shiism's strong messianic strain sets it apart from mainstream

Sunni Islam. Shiites rejected the institution of an earthly caliphate that was the source of both secular and religious authority, such as the Ottoman sultanate, in favor of the rule of the descendants of the Prophet. The last of these, the Hidden Imam, left the world in 874, and devout Shiites faithfully await his return. When he does return, he will lead the righteous in a war against the wicked and establish a kingdom of perfect justice on earth. In the meantime, since the only prospects for true justice reside with the Hidden Imam, in his absence the world is a sad and empty place, providing less of an institutionalized link between believers and God than is the case in Sunni Islam, with its more direct involvement in earthly government. The Caesaropapist fusion of absolute monarchy and supreme religious authority that we traced in Part Two from Byzantium to the Ottoman Sultans traditionally had no place in Shia. That all changed due to Shariati and Khomeini.

Ali Shariati took the messianic strain that distinguishes Shiism from mainstream Islam and secularized it, making it the vehicle for Heideggerian existentialist commitment, resolve, and willpower on behalf of the oppressed people. Messianism became the impetus for collective political struggle. The Last Days, which traditional believers can only await in faith, hope, and pious devotion, could be brought about in the here and now by human action, creating a regime capable of achieving the purity of the collective, the return to the Year One. In traditional Shiism, the blessings of the return of the Hidden Imam cannot be hastened by this-worldly political action. Because of the vast gap between the imperfect world of now and the perfect realm to come when the Hidden Imam returns, there can be no earthly government of mere men claiming to rule directly on behalf of God. That is why the very notion of a ruling mullocracy like today's Iranian Republic is a distortion of Shiism, which is even more skeptical toward a fusion of religious revelation with earthly political power than is Sunni Islam with its tradition of the caliphate. By secularizing that messianic strain, Shariati tried to transform Shia into a far *more* worldly and politically engaged version of the faith. The present Iranian theocracy, with its ceaseless drive for the centralization of power and regimentation of every aspect of life, is a departure from traditional Islam but bears a strong resemblance to the totalitarian Party of the Jacobins, Bolsheviks, Nazis, and Khmer Rouge. Like the vanished Communist Party of the Soviet Union, the Iranian theocracy claims exclusive possession of "the unity of theory and practice."

Since Ali Shariati died before the revolution, we cannot know for certain what his reaction would have been to the Ayatollah Khomeini's reign of terror. Would he have been appalled, disillusioned, or willing to hang on and give the revolution a chance? Some argue that, with his third-world socialist credo, Ali Shariati was not strictly speaking a Khomeinist or supporter of theocracy. But how much of a genuinely Islamic ruler was Khomeini himself? Before him, ayatollahs had never wielded the instruments of state power to execute thousands of ideologically defined enemies, drive hundreds of thousands into exile, confiscate property, and launch wars. As Bernard Lewis observed, "All this owes more to the examples of Robespierre and Stalin than those of Muhammed and Ali. These methods are deeply un-Islamic, but thoroughly revolutionary." Before Khomeini came to power, direct political authority in Iran had never been exercised by the men of religion. The Iranian mullahs did not restore an ancient order. Rather, following Ali Shariati and Fanon, they tried to create a "new man" and a "new history" through a dictatorship with no Islamic precedent.

In his murderous fantasy of destroying Israel, Ahmadinejad drew together all the strands of Ali Shariati's Islamist ideology and added his own sinister twist, one that made it far more dangerous. Although a utopian in his belief that a politicized Shiism might bring about a regime through which the dignity of the people could be rescued from the corrupting influences of the West and establish a classless society, Ali Shariati did not contemplate, as far as one can tell, actually bringing about the Last Days, the apocalyptic struggle between the righteous and the wicked, through a worldwide military cataclysm. Ahmadinejad did. "Our revolution's mission," he declared, "is to pave the way for the reappearance of the Twelfth Imam." A rumor denied by the government but widely believed in Iran held that Ahmadinejad and his cabinet signed a secret "contract" pledging themselves to work for the return of the Mahdi. Ahmadinejad believed that the apocalypse was imminent and Iran could accelerate the divine timetable. He was not content, as a traditional believer would be, to wait for the Hidden Imam to return. He planned to make the Last Days come on his own schedule, by using nuclear weapons to destroy the wicked as soon as possible. Ahmadinejad linked Iran's development of a nuclear capability with the coming apocalypse – the implied threat of a nuclear strike that would knowingly invite a nuclear response from Israel and America, thereby sparking a worldwide conflagration and the beginning of the Last Days. As with previous millenarian revolutions, one group was held to stand primarily in the way of mankind's future bliss – Israel. Nuclear annihilation offered a new method for utopian genocide, faster and more thorough than death camps.

And in this utopian blueprint – like Hitler's, insane but internally coherent – the cost to Iranians themselves is of no consequence. When Iran's Islamic leadership – including supreme religious leader Ayatollah Ali Khameini and Ayatollah Akbar Hashemi-Rafsanjani – hastened to support Ahmadinejad's call for Israel's annihilation, Rafsanjani, a former president of the Islamic Republic, added a mad detail: The Iranian leadership would be happy to see Iran devastated by an Israeli nuclear retaliatory strike if it meant they could wipe Israel off the map. "The application of an atomic bomb," he sanguinely remarked, "would not leave any thing in Israel, but the same thing would just produce damages in the Muslim world."

This willingness to see Iran absorb the "damages" of an Israeli nuclear response (surely millions of casualties) was reminiscent of Hitler's willingness to divert resources needed to win the Second World War and expose Germany to catastrophically destructive bombing and invasion in order to speed up the Holocaust, even if it meant Germany going down in flames – worth it for the chance to kill millions of Jews. Something akin to demented mirth sparkled in Ahmadinejad's eyes as he made his cryptic little jokes about coming "surprises."

Ahmadinejad did not represent all political forces in Iran, not even all radical forces. Doubtless, Iran's acquisition of nuclear weapons is, for many Iranians, a question of traditional national pride or a bid for great power status. But Ahmadinejad represented an important dimension of the Iranian revolution we cannot afford to ignore. Those who dismiss such views as mere sabre-rattling or rhetorical red meat to rally the movement should recall that many people believed this about Hitler's blueprint for genocidal war in *Mein Kampf*, before he took power and proceeded to systematically carry it out. To this day, the Iranian Republic has never disavowed Ahmadinejad's project of nuclear Armageddon. Indeed, just recently, Supreme Leader Ayatollah Khameini once again branded America as "the Great Satan" and predicted that Israel would not exist twenty-five years from now. As long as that is so, whatever tactical shifts may occur in Iran's relations with the West, it is extremely doubtful that the West can negotiate a reliable and verifiable agreement with Iran over nuclear weapons. Their commitment to the destruction of the Jews is a matter of principle, just as the implementation of the Holocaust was for the Nazis and the liquidation of the kulaks was for the Bolsheviks. Genocide through nuclear weapons is designed to bring about the happiness of the Year One for all of us. That's why Ahmadinejad was always smiling.

TERRORISM IS A MEANS TO AN END: REVOLUTIONARY UTOPIA

Wherever the International Jihad strikes today, it does so on behalf of the same goal – the establishment of a worldwide Islamic state. This is as true of Taliban units conducting terrorist operations in Pakistan as it is of the Iranian Republic, whose constitution proclaims this as the Revolution's ultimate goal. It is equally true of terrorist attempts carried out in America, Europe, Asia, and Africa, whether it be Fort Hood, London, Madrid, Mumbai, Detroit, Boston, Moore Oklahoma, Paris, Nairobi, or Copenhagen. And it makes no difference whether the terrorists are homegrown, come from somewhere else, or are Americans training in Al Qaeda camps in Yemen. Whatever regional issue may be advanced for rhetorical convenience by the Jihadist network – national dignity, expelling the foreign invader, ending social injustice – all these terrorist actors, whether statist or nonstatist, are united by a single revolutionary goal, a millenarian ideology calling for the destruction of the West and its code of Enlightenment values through violent struggle to usher in a new millennium of happiness for all mankind.

Despair about the economic future in non-Western countries has certainly been a recruiting ground for Islamist movements, just as it was for previous revolutionary movements like Third-World Socialism. Jihadists frequently weave the language of Marxist class struggle, national liberation movements, environmentalism, and anticapitalism into their allegedly religious call to armed struggle. But the "despair" explanation does not suffice for explaining the motives of the Jihadist leaders themselves, the actual designers and strategists of terrorist attacks, because it ignores the fact that people are capable of a principled, methodical hatred of liberal democracy and the political values of the Enlightenment, especially when they are seen as forces that taint the Muslim homeland with foreign invasion or corrupt values. Reducing the root causes of terrorism to poverty ignores the long-established if unedifying psychological possibility that a hatred born of wounded honor and moral outrage is independently rooted in the human character, and is, therefore, an independent variable in violent political extremism, an insight with a pedigree stretching back to Plato's consideration of the spirited part of the soul.

Terrorists are revolutionaries committed to utopian genocide to bring about their ideal of a better world for us all. To fit into this particular tribe, its members must carry out acts of large-scale political murder for the sake of a future society that they believe will end all alienation, vice, and unhappiness forever by submerging the individual in the bliss of the collective. Whether working in the United States or abroad, today's Jihadist revolutionaries are bent on the eventual overthrow of the American government and all other actual or aspiring liberal democracies and their replacement with a collectivist global dictatorship. While sometimes imitating the language of freedom and equality, revolutionary movements as far back as the Jacobins, and including the Bolsheviks, Nazis, Khmer Rouge, and today's Jihadists, originate in the conviction that representative government and the other values of the Enlightenment including the liberty of the individual have been disastrous for human dignity, spiritual distortions and a degradation of all that is truly virtuous.

Terrorism is the means required by the goal of creating the future collectivist utopia that will erase forever the blight of the Enlightenment, and it is but one means, albeit the most horrifying, among others including relentless propaganda, bribery, the intimidation of opponents, paralegal military organizations, conventional warfare, charitable good works among potential converts, tactical compromises with ordinary political processes, and the ceaseless psychological conditioning of young people to fight against that one oppressive force supposedly blocking the people's road to happiness, all integrated and directed by the blue-print for the coming new society. From Robespierre to Stalin, Hitler, Pol Pot, and today's Jihadists, they should be described for what they are – *revolutionaries* – whose violence today is the necessary means for their fervent belief in the world of tomorrow where they will rule.

Today's terrorists are aspiring tyrants, they kill in order to bring about a grim collective whose power over us all will be absolute, thereby making the rest of us "happy" by purging us of the corruption of individualism, economic well-being, freedom of choice, and rights. And wherever such idealists of death have come to power, they have built regimes that continue to terrorize their populations in order to build this "new man." Looking through the charters and pronouncements of groups like the Taliban or Hezbollah, never far beneath the pseudoreligious surface is the language of socialism (both national and international), the leveling of classes, and the eradication of individual liberty under a monolithic dictatorship. However they may understand themselves, the Jihadists, like their Bolshevik and Fascist predecessors, cannot be considered true men of faith, because all three of the Abrahamic faiths deny that man can save the world through secular political action, much less through mass violence. For truly pious people, only God can redeem the world. Moderate Muslim religious authorities have consistently denounced the Jihadists as irreligious. One such group in Jordan has written that "Islam does not countenance utopian ideology," and adds: "When one can justify any act in the name of a worldly utopia, then one has passed into pure utilitarianism."

That brings us to the end of our search for the strange career of tyranny from Achilles to Al Qaeda. I hope the dragons on that Mercator map I promised in the Introduction stand out more clearly now in the deep waters just beyond the edge of civilization. In the Conclusion, we'll look at the topography of tyranny and terror in the world of the twenty-first century and ponder further how Western democracies can defend the spirit of human liberty against its foes.

Conclusion: How Democracy Can Win

On the first page of this book, I suggested that you might not find it worth reading any further if you were confident that the progress of history was making tyranny a thing of the past – that, despite a few bumps in the road like ISIS or Putin, we were heading inevitably toward the spread of American-style democracy around the world. If you've made it this far, that means you're willing to entertain the possibility that the danger of tyranny is a permanent feature of the human and political landscape, as much now as ever. It's never going away, and neither is the need to defend free self-governing societies against it.

How does the world look when we remove our rose-colored "end of history" glasses and view it straight on? The world is what it has always been. But we will see it rather differently. Let's do a world tour with our three main varieties of tyranny as the guidebook.

ALL ABOARD FOR THE TYRANNY TOUR

Garden-variety kleptocratic tyrannies have been alive and well all along. Sometimes they are dressed up with the tired principle of belonging to "the developing world" (examples include much of Africa, the Arab Baathist dictatorships, Haiti's Duvaliers) as a lure for foreign aid to be filched (Malawi's former president Bakili Muluzi has been accused of embezzling twelve million dollars of foreign-aid money, one on a long list of such scandals), sometimes used to cobble together made-up countries (Jordan, for example, the original intended Palestinian state, with its British-backed Hashemite monarchy), sometimes masked with a pretense of piety (the Saudis, who hide in their luxurious compounds while their subjects are left to the tender mercies of the harshest Salaafist version of Sharia law). Fidel Castro is, as I write, the last of the club of satellite Soviet dictators. By allowing his brother to lift a few restrictions on business and travel in pursuit of normalizing relations with the U.S., he apparently hopes to stave off the fate of Ceausescu and other long-gone communist dictators while holding onto supreme control for his prosperous clan. After predictably ruining the Cuban economy by nationalizing it in accordance with Soviet Marxist doctrine which, combined with killing or driving into exile Cuba's best and brightest, reduced the island to harvesting sugar cane (dressed up with a pretense to be a Maoist-like "back to the country" campaign to rid Cubans of bourgeois corruption through farm labor), the Castros have long since become greedy kleptocrats and their "socialism" is an empty ruse for a massive police state. Aside from sending Cuban forces to meddle in Angola as a Soviet proxy while at home people barely had enough to eat, Castro's most notable achievement was bringing the world to the brink of World War III by goading Nikita Khrushchev to prove he was an *hombre* by placing Soviet missiles in Cuba.

The tour continues: Russia and China are oligarchical despotisms built on the remains of Marxist-Leninist totalitarian states. In a sense, they qualify as reforming tyrannies. To them, a free-market system simply meant that the Communist Party would immediately transition to being the owners of all major industry and business. Since communism had previously enslaved and broken the common people, they stood ready as easily manageable low-paid workers, with all political power still safely in the hands of their former Communist masters now recast as the wealthy titans of a mercantilist economy. Nevertheless, both states are attempting to raise the standard of living of the masses and thereby continue the tradition of benevolent despotism and universal monarchy. China, in particular, is spending billions a year on infrastructure, factories, and affordable housing. They are gambling that they can create widespread prosperity without true entrepreneurialism (China has been very sluggish at enabling business start-ups not heavily connected to the Party elite and government bureaucracy) or the full panoply of Western individual freedoms, particularly electoral representation. China's oligarchy has blended the former Maoist Communist concept of the one-party state into an alleged revival of traditional "Confucian" values of social harmony, which, in practice, means primarily that the masses must obey. China is also flexing its military muscle with a new ocean-going fleet. No longer having a revolutionary mission to export, its aims seem limited to a nineteenth-century Great Power militarist strategy of securing a zone of influence for itself in southeast Asia that is nevertheless rightly worrying to India, Japan, the Philippines, Australia, and the United States. Concern has been expressed about a global league of despotisms including China, Russia, and the oil emirates, which also control enormous amounts of capital ("sovereign wealth funds") in part from buying American debt. It is doubtful, however, that they could ever arrive at a unified political strategy to combat the democracies.

Our third variety, millenarian tyranny, is spearheaded in its purest form today by the International Jihad, heirs to Robespierre, Stalin, Hitler, and Pol

Pot. For them, terror is not a temporary tactic or occasional extreme, but the fundamental principle of the Return to the Year One. All states and political movements are capable of violent and unlawful acts, but these are usually seen as unfortunate but temporary means to a tangible security, economic, or foreign-policy aim, or recognized as a lapse from self-professed ethical principles during an emergency situation. But for genuinely revolutionary movements from the Jacobins to Al Qaeda, terror is the *only* principle, because after the enemy is defeated, the terror will have to be institutionalized and turned on human nature to purge and re-construct it. At bottom, the term *terrorism*, while useful, can be misleading, because it suggests something stateless or a random psychological aberration akin to "rampage killings." Terrorists do not have a random impulse to kill, then cast about for an ideology to justify it. Instead, they are already committed to a utopian vision of the future, which shapes and directs their murderous pathology toward utopia's enemies and inflames it with moralistic zeal. In reality, to stress once again, terrorists are tyrants in waiting, and tyrants are terrorists who have gained power. The real battle is not with *terrorism*, an abstract noun, but between two fully actualized regimes with their diametrically opposed principles – liberal democracy and tyranny.

As we saw in Part Three, all of today's Jihadist revolutionaries – Al Qaeda, ISIS, Hamas, Hezbollah, Boko Haram, Iran – share a common vision of the coming utopia. Sectarian religious differences, while real, are overcome by the common hatred of America and Israel. When they capture states, such as Iran and Gaza, jihadist regimes sometimes interweave with garden-variety kleptocracy, either to finance further terrorism and arms purchases or even out of simple greed (Iran's mullahs reportedly have billions stashed abroad). But little actual reform takes place, because these groups are not interested in the mundane responsibilities of day-to-day governing. Their hijacked states and subjects are nothing but springboards for the progress of the revolution toward world rule.

VLADIMIR PUTIN: REFORMER AND KLEPTOCRAT WITH A DASH OF THE MILLENARIAN

Russia under Vladimir Putin is a unique mixture of the three faces of tyranny – numbers one and two with a side order of three. Whereas Communist China seemed to flip overnight from a communist dictatorship to a mercantilist oligarchy – the absolute power of the Party preserved intact – Russia's transition was far rockier. In the classic pattern of the reforming despot who unleashes a revolution of rising expectations, Mikhail Gorbachev as the last Secretary-General of the CPSU invited Russian society to liberate itself, but under the continuing guidance of the Soviet state. (I once heard RAND scholar Jeremy Azrael sum up this paradox in a droll imitation of Gorbachev attempting to explain to the Communist Party his new policy of *Glasnost* or "openness": "Glasnost is about new ideas. Glasnost is about freedom of thought. And those comrades who do not accept this *will have to change their minds!*"). But once ordinary people tasted the freedom of expression and thought, and the chance to buy and sell for profit, they wanted it all, as did satellite countries like Poland and Hungary. The Soviet Empire imploded from within. The wreckage of the Soviet Union was swept away by the bumptious Boris Yeltsin, who pulled out all the stops – free elections, and opening the formerly state-controlled economy to international market forces. But that economic policy of "shock therapy" designed by Columbia University economist Jeffrey Sachs was too much too soon after fifty years of central planning. Once it was set free to float with world currencies, the ruble was gutted, leaving millions nearly destitute on fixed incomes and pensions. That cleared the way for Putin, who earned tremendous popularity by putting the breaks on "shock therapy" and restoring a degree of artificial currency control to prevent people's incomes from collapsing. While lamenting the Soviet Union's demise as a tragedy, he did not attempt to restore it. But he did revive Stalin's role as the *Vozhd,* the "master" as he had been informally known, itself an echo of tsarist autocracy, and ordinary people welcomed the new sense of order and stability Putin thereby created. Ironically, Putin won his dictatorial power by election, due to Yeltsin's democratic reforms. Because the path to free markets was rockier in Russia, and perhaps because its vast internal empire was inherently more ungovernable, Russia has not matched China's march to prosperity. While in China there is no distinction between its smoothly run businesses and the state, Russian business often seems like something out of the Roaring Twenties, headed by its chief mobster Bugsy Putin in a hail of bullets. But it's in the realm of foreign policy that Putin aspires to leave his real mark. In another classic pattern, he is dazzling his people with military invasion and muscle-flexing abroad in order to distract them from the country's continuing failure to attain the economic prosperity of the United States and Europe.

As I wrote in the Introduction, Putin's imperial aggression is from every century, not just the nineteenth. Time and again, the social sciences miss the boat on this because they assume, going back to Hobbes, that political actors are motivated solely by material self-interest. They'll try to grab as much as they can, but when checked (say with sanctions), will relent and accept a fair or at least a realistic share of the pie. The only problem is, it's not true, and never has been. Robespierre, Lenin, Stalin, Hitler, Mao, Pol Pot, Bin Laden – men such as these are driven by much more than material self-interest. Honor, ambition, glory, righteous anger, burning conviction, a passion for justice as they see justice, resentment, utopian ideology, all factor in. It took Western liberal democracy four centuries of character development, beginning in the Renaissance and Reformation, to enable us to look past such aggressive passions and embrace tolerance and a preference for the peaceful arts of commerce over the warrior's code of honor, and we are still far from having succeeded entirely in doing so – the West can be tyrannical too, and democracies cannot always avoid being warlike. But the rest of the world rolls on as it always has, not convinced that material gain trumps every other meaningful experience, passion, or commitment.

This is true even of tyrannical aggression that falls short of true millenarianism, such as Russia's attempt to reassert its hegemonic role in eastern Europe. But while recognizing that nineteenth century Great Power Bismarckian militarism (a continuation of the pedigree of reformist state-building despots including Frederick the Great) is alive and well in the twenty-first century would be the beginning of wisdom for those who trust in the progress of history to make tyranny a thing of the past, in reality, Putin's tyranny is a mixture of the kleptocratic and the reformist strains of tyranny with the millenarian. The millenarian dimension is by no means as extreme as in the Jacobin, Bolshevik, National Socialist, Third-World Socialist or Jihadist variations, but it is definitely there, and its chief exponent is Putin's close advisor Aleksandr Dugin. His writings are a throwback to the pro-fascist writings of Ernst Junger, Carl Schmitt, and Martin Heidegger in the 1930s. In them, Russia takes the place of Germany as the "people of destiny" that will lead a revolution on behalf of mankind against the debased values of the Enlightenment and liberal democracy, a mission to be spread not only spiritually but also through force of arms as Russia reasserts her imperial role.

Just as National Socialism drew upon previous decades of fascination with "the East" as the true Teutonic heartland of the Aryan race and an antidote to the effete bourgeois liberal West, Dugin argues that Russians are fundamentally an eastern, "Eurasian" people, including their Slavic brethren in the Balkans and Eastern Europe who must be reclaimed by the Motherland (including, to begin with, Ukraine and Belarus). He has revived the notion of Russia as the "third way" (notice the millenarian overtone of the Last Days preceding the Kingdom of God) between the West and the far East whose deep spirituality can redeem all mankind through an antimaterialistic "revolution of archaic values," marrying this Slavophilic motif from Dostoyevsky and Berdyaev with the *Volkish* ideology of the Third Reich. "In principle," he has written, "Eurasia and our space, the heartland of Russia, remains the staging area of a new anti-bourgeois, anti-American revolution … The new Eurasian empire will be constructed according to the fundamental principle of the common enemy, the rejection of Atlanticism, strategic control of the USA, and the refusal to allow liberal values to dominate us. This common civilizational impulse will be the basis of a political and strategic union."

Dugin's reinterpretation of the Soviet era as "National Bolshevism" strips away its pseudoscientific Marxist veneer and returns it to its origins in the revolutionary populism of the People's Will movement and the God builders that we discussed in Part Three. Marxism-Leninism, he argues, was only a superficial import from the West. The heart and soul of Bolshevism was a return to the true Slavic soul of agrarian Russia and a rejection of the Europhile leanings of Turgenev and other pro-European elitists. This recasting of Soviet communism as a form of Slavic nationalism fits well with Putin's long-term agenda to shut down the opening to the West that took place under Gorbachev and to gradually rehabilitate the Soviet era as a legitimate and proud part of Russian history. Dugin's "Eurasianist National Bolshevik Party" believes that a war to re-conquer the former Soviet empire will not only make Russia great again but, when that war is ultimately carried to the primary enemy, America, will redeem all mankind (including the American masses themselves, slaves to their plutocratic elites) from the soulless materialism and decadence of the West, which America sums up. Dugin wants to make common cause with Jihadism against the American foe, believing that Islamist and Eurasianist collectivism have more in common with each other than they do with Western Enlightenment individualism. He has Putin's powerful patronage, and we cannot exclude the possibility that, in annexing the Crimea and menacing Ukraine, Putin (who is known to favor Slavophilic authors like Berdyaev) is beginning to implement Dugin's millenarian agenda for the re-creation of the Soviet empire as the springboard to a world war with the United States – or, at the very least, finds it useful to his Great Power aspirations to whip up Slavophilic nationalism at home to provide popular fervor for these expansionist aims. The sense of a world-salvational mission lends a dash of millenarian fervor to Putin's expansionist agenda that, even if he does not literally believe in it himself, is certainly useful to his ambitions. Putin is a rational actor in international relations in the sense that, unlike Hitler or more recently Ahmadinejad, he does not contemplate himself and his country going down in flames as an acceptable price for attempting to bring about utopia. But by the same token, what he sees as Russia's need to recover her honor and greatness and avenge the humiliation inflicted on her by losing the Cold War means that he will risk a very great deal – certainly a severe blow to the Russian economy through sanctions, and possibly even active military opposition from the West – before he will be willing to compromise his sense of historic mission. When honor is more important to a leader than economic prosperity, bargaining becomes very hard indeed.

Moreover, the neo-Fascist Right in Europe looks increasingly to Putin and Dugin's "revolution of archaic values" for inspiration in their own hopes for revival. In their eyes, Russia is now to the European Union as National Socialism once was to the Weimar Republic – a bulwark of robust and aggressive collectivist populism that will shatter the corrupt materialism, urban decadence, elitism, and bourgeois politicking of liberal democracy. In proclaiming that Europeans have become a rootless mass of "consumers disconnected from their natural attachments – the family, the nation and the divine," French National Front leader Aymeric Chauprade could have been quoting from Dugin, or from Heidegger in the 1930s. If, as I suggested in Part Three, fascism can be described as a marriage between anti-Enlightenment intellectual revolutionaries and the skull-bashing thugs of the gutter who are fired by their ideas, then Europe's neo-Nazi skinheads, already riding a lurch to the right in Hungary and a resurgence of vituperative anti-Semitism, may find their way to Professor Dugin as the visionary they have been waiting for. American and European journalists who argue that, because Putin labels Ukrainians who oppose his conquest of them as "fascists," it is "puzzling" that he might form alliances with fascist groups in the rest of Europe, are being superficial. The Soviet Union's branding of anyone and anything that opposed it as "fascist" was one of its most tiresome and tired traits, stemming from their uncomfortable recognition that, at bottom, their "fascist" foes were the mirror image opposite of themselves. As a Soviet-era holdover, Putin (a former KGB officer) uses this term as well to defame his intended Ukrainian victims, and it's equally meaningless. At bottom, Putin can make common cause with Europe's far right because they share each other's values. He's courting them out of both ideological affinity and strategic self-interest.

THE TOUR CONTINUES: DEMOCRACY AND THE TYRANNICAL TEMPTATION

As for liberal democracy itself, it is still most strongly rooted in its original heartland of Western Europe and North America, seedbed of the Reformation and the Enlightenment. The defeat of the Third Reich and the Axis in World War II discredited all nondemocratic value codes for decades to come, such that the neofascist Right in today's Europe, although it bears careful watching, is not remotely close to a widespread resurgence. Meanwhile, the collapse of the Soviet Evil Empire in 1989 enabled the former Warsaw Pact countries enslaved by Stalin to reconnect with their own Enlightenment and religious heritages, still quite strong despite years of repression in the case of Poland, Hungary, East Germany, and the Czech lands. What Daniel Patrick Moynihan once called "the Party of Freedom" in the world, the established democracies led by America, Britain, Canada, Europe, and Israel, remains militarily insuperable by direct attack or invasion. They can only be defeated by the forces of tyranny through their own lack of resolve to take the necessary measures to preempt the dangers those forces pose. We can hope the Party of Freedom will grow. Many nations in the non-Western world, or at least significant movements within them, aspire to liberal democracy – in India it has taken root, if not without problems. In all nondemocratic regimes, a thin filigree of Western-oriented, secular professionals, intellectuals, artists, and students strive to maintain outposts of Enlightenment values against formidable despotic apparatuses and religious or tribal populism (Pakistan, Afghanistan, Russia, and China are cases in point). While that's encouraging, their prospects for becoming democracies remain profoundly uncertain.

In concluding our brief tour of tyrannical forces in the world today and their competition with the forces of freedom, we should remember that, for most of human history and in much of today's world, the view that the primary social unit is some kind of clan headed by a patriarchal chieftain – that's why we began this book with the Bronze Age warrior-chiefs chronicled by Homer – not only expresses itself at the level of entire regimes (Putin's Russia, the monarchy of Saudi Arabia) but is woven deeply into the social and cultural fabric of all societies, especially those that have not fully embraced modern liberal individualism or have actively turned against it (like large sections of the Muslim world), but even in regimes that do have a long track record of success as democracies. Whether it is organized crime in the United States and Europe, rogue corporations, gang violence, or the marginal but still disturbing resurgence of fascism in Hungary, a kind of private tyranny or warlordism is always threatening to erode the boundaries of the rule of law. The ancient notion going back to the Greeks and Romans that the father is the king of his family household may be most pronounced in the Muslim world, but it has a strong presence wherever pre-Enlightenment outlooks linger, including a strong residual presence in the West itself, where just about everyone recognizes the need for a certain degree of nonnegotiable authority of parents over children. Not only is this intermingling of absolute authority in some reaches of private life with our public equality as citizens impossible to expel from human nature, but it is to some degree, justifiable – sometimes children just have to be told no, for their own welfare. Who can't remember either saying or hearing the words: "Because I said so!"

As we assess the forces of tyranny in today's world, it is natural to wonder whether there's a danger that the American government itself might degenerate into a tyranny. The danger, although not inconceivable, is slight. To be sure, liberal democracies are capable of tyrannical actions, both against their own citizens and abroad. Look at American slavery, Jim Crow, the internment of the Japanese. Some would include the annexation of the Philippines and the war in Vietnam. But the fact that liberal democracies are capable of tyrannical actions does not mean that they are tyrannical *regimes*. As representative governments with power shared among the legislative, executive, and judicial branches, they are capable of self-reform. One branch can check another's overbearing actions or attempt to remedy its moral failings. One may even say the American Founders designed the U.S. Constitution with a view to preventing tyranny from arising. The crime against humanity of slavery provoked the election of Abraham Lincoln and the Civil War that brought about its end, and, eventually, the fruition of that moral victory in the Civil Rights Act of 1964. America's rise to a world power exposed, many felt, a troubling connection between the authority of the president as chief executive and as commander in chief, a residue of potentially tyrannical power that (as we saw in Part Two) can be traced back to Machiavelli's teaching on republican government and the need for recurrent princely "founders" acting outside the law, which many felt surfaced in Lincoln, FDR, LBJ, and Nixon. But presidential actions thought by many to be illegal – Lincoln's suspension of Habeas Corpus, LBJ's illegal wiretaps, Nixon's dirty tricks, Gitmo – were eventually checked by Congress, the courts, or both. At bottom, liberal democracies are capable of recognizing that they have not lived up to their own best principles and so must make the necessary changes. The framers of the American constitution had in mind the permanent possibility of tyranny (by the government or by electoral majorities) and aimed to forestall it before it gathered strength. By contrast, when tyrants like Assad or Saddam commit mass murder against their own populations, they are not falling beneath a moral standard that they might conceivably return to and mend their ways. Tyrannical oppression *is* their only standard. Nor does a truly independent legislature, judiciary, or media exist to check the tyrant's power.

If the American constitution provides fairly certain safeguards against the American regime becoming a tyranny, could America itself ever succumb to a homegrown revolution that would overthrow the government, abolish the constitution, and establish a millenarian tyranny of the Jacobin kind? That, too, is unlikely. Although America has had its brushes with millenarian revolution – those like Jefferson who thought the United States could use a dose of the more radical Jacobin version of the French Revolution; the worker unrest of the Dirty Thirties; the New Left and counterculture upheaval of the 1960s – no such revolution has come close to breaking out. I think the reason is that, as Louis Hartz famously put it, America has never had any tradition but a liberal tradition. There is no sense of the "lost community" we discussed in Part Three – the combustible moment where the people's premodern collectivist heritage is perceived as being eroded by Enlightenment individualism before the Enlightenment's benefits have become ingrained – that made the French, Russian, German, and Third World revolutions so extremely violent, continuing with today's International Jihad. America has always had political extremism on both the Left and Right (the KKK, Anarchists, Wobblies, Minutemen, Black Panthers, Weathermen, Aryan Nation, Unabomber), but never have they coalesced around a broad-based utopian vision for tomorrow based upon returning to the mystical "destiny" of the past that might enlist millions. Some would point to the Confederacy as hearkening back to such a past, but, aside from the taint of slavery, its planter gentry were simply a slightly older-fashioned, less capitalistic version of the American Founding – their ideal was Jefferson's "yeoman farmer," as opposed to what Stonewall Jackson called "the banks and the moneyed interest" of the smokestack belching North. They saw themselves as Jane Austen characters as opposed to Uriah Heap.

Insofar as libertarianism at its most extreme calls for the virtual complete dismantling of government, it's certainly a utopian vision. But precisely because it wants *no* government of *any* kind, it could never result in a tyrannical regime. It's another version of anarchism, although in favor of private property. The Oklahoma City bombing could be described as a kind of Libertarian Jihad, but that's precisely because its perpetrator Timothy McVeigh was already sympathetic to Islamic fundamentalism and its portrayal of America as an imperialistic oppressor. America certainly produces people – Charles Manson, David Koresh, Elliot Rogers – who would be *capable* of joining, maybe even leading, millenarian revolutions, seeking revenge on the world at large for their own perceived suffering and unjust treatment. Manson's belief, inspired by the Beatles' *Helter Skelter*, that his "family's" murders would ignite a race war and avenge his brutalized childhood and rejection as a great artist resembled in broad outline the revolutionary scripts of Lenin, Hitler, and Mao. Serial killer of women Elliot Rogers wrote that his "anger" brought him to the conviction that he had to "destroy" sex if he couldn't have it, making "the world a fair and just place." Substitute "sex" with "property" and you have a common revolutionary theme. Manson and Rogers could have found in the NKVD or SS a state-sanctioned outlet for their murderous rage. But again, because Americans in general do not feel nostalgia for a lost community of destiny whose recovery from the shrouds of myth requires genocide in the present, the pathologies of such men can never mesh with a larger utopian vision and mass movement – such malcontents gather at best a few other failures and misfits. The greatest danger of homegrown revolutionaries on American soil today does not stem from internal American politics but from young men who self-identify as converts to Jihad, working from within to bring about the worldwide Caliphate.

Someone might object that, in my distinction throughout this book between millenarian tyranny driven by utopian genocide and ordinary, kleptocratic, garden-variety tyranny – sometimes dressed up with pretensions to reform, or having degenerated into kleptocracy from an original program of reform – I am somehow suggesting that the abuses of these ordinary, garden-variety tyrants are morally less reprehensible than the actions of a Stalin, Hitler, or Pol Pot. Not at all. As an ethical matter, Bashar al Assad's destruction to date of some two hundred thousand Syrians opposing his tyranny is every bit as worthy of condemnation as the violence of Stalin's Famine Terror or the Nazi Holocaust. It makes no difference to a man forced to dig his own grave before being shot whether his killer has a utopian vision of the future or not. Some forms of genocide – ethnic cleansing in Kosovo, or Saddam's mass liquidation of Shiites – are more about exercising complete political domination than any sort of utopian vision of the future. But that does not make them less condemnable than true utopian genocide. The point is not that millenarian tyranny is ethically worse than ordinary tyranny, or that the latter is somehow less evil. It's simply that millenarian tyranny is *different* from the other kinds – and, given the historical record, more likely to result in wars of imperial aggression and the extermination of *millions*.

More than that – ordinary tyrants like Assad commit mass murder against their subjects because their subjects oppose their monopoly on power. Had the Syrian civil war not broken out, destruction on the current scale would not have occurred. Am I saying that to knuckle under to a tyrant and give up the hope of self-government in order to avoid death is an acceptable situation? No, it's not an acceptable situation – as long as it's possible to achieve freedom, human beings will try. But knuckling under to a tyrant to avoid a worse fate is surely a *less bad* situation than to be marked for death by a genocidal regime that is bent on the extermination of your entire race or class *regardless* of whether you want to rebel or not – even if you'd be willing to serve it loyally. A potential rebel can give in to an ordinary tyrant, refrain from rebelling, with some expectation of survival. Kulaks in the Soviet Union and Jews in Nazi Germany could not. They were killed not for rebelling but for existing.

Early modern political thinkers like Machiavelli and Hobbes argued that, in an extreme situation, you could not be faulted for accepting a tyrant's rule over you if the alternative was death for challenging his supreme power. The desire for political freedom shouldn't be a suicide mission. Using the example of Cesare Borgia's occupation of the Romagna, Machiavelli argued that, at times, a despot's ruthless suppression of civil strife can be to everyone's long-range advantage if their persons and property are thereby safe-guarded: "cruelty" toward a minority of malcontents results in "compassion" toward the majority. Hobbes took this further and argued that the rule of even the worst imaginable tyrant was preferable to the limitless dangers and destructiveness of civil war, because at least basic order would be maintained and you would be free to survive and even prosper in private life. The flip side of this was that Machiavelli and Hobbes assumed that tyrants were *also* motivated by material self-interest, and that, if they pursued their own selfish aims sensibly, they would want subjects living in peace and prosperity so as to swell their own wealth and power. Hobbes in particular urged monarchs to promote their subjects' freedom to prosper through trade and commerce in private life so as to compensate them for their lack of political freedom, and to refrain from violating their lives or property so as to prevent civil strife and the collapse of all order and safety in "the war of all against all." Machiavelli and Hobbes would both hope that a tyrant like Assad would realize that being at peace with his subjects instead of slaughtering them would be to everyone's material advantage. But Machiavelli and Hobbes never encountered millenarian tyrants like Stalin and Hitler, who *deliberately* set about to murder millions of their own subjects and destroy society and the economy motivated by the sheer fantasy of building a better world of tomorrow. This is the point at which the pragmatism of early modern state building as recommended by Machiavelli and Hobbes cannot comprehend the fantasy of the return to the Year One sparked by Rousseau. Millenarian rulers don't care whether their societies prosper or not, and no appeal to their own self-interest sets any limit on their destructiveness. With them, there can be no bargaining, no compromise – knuckling under won't be enough if you are slated for utopian genocide. Ask the survivors of the Azaris or Shia whose peoples have been massacred by ISIS.

WHAT SHOULD THE WEST DO?

It's not easy in a book to suggest practical approaches to international relations that won't end up debating headlines soon to be outmoded by the rush of events. But some broad principles can be suggested. My hope is that the strange career of tyranny can help us decide among the lesser of evils that present themselves in revolutionary situations in the present, guided by the old counsel of prudence: Don't let the perfect be the enemy of the good. Millenarian tyrannies like the Nazis and ISIS must be fought with every means at our disposal. But we might have to put up with the other two kinds of tyranny if their collapse would bring the millenarians in to fill the vacuum.

American foreign policy has always been guided by three not entirely harmonious aims. A strong isolationist streak going back to Washington and Jefferson wants to preserve America from any involvement in foreign wars: The "essential principles of our government," Jefferson proclaimed, are those of "peace, commerce, and honest friendship with all nations, entangling alliances with none." Another strain, emerging with President Woodrow Wilson, holds that, on the contrary, America has a moral responsibility to intervene abroad, militarily if need be, to protect and promote the spread of democracy. A third, most clearly articulated by Henry Kissinger, holds that America should take a morally neutral approach to world affairs, allying itself with regimes regardless of whether they are democratic or not if that helps American interests and combats a more dangerous foe. Segments of both the Democratic and Republican parties have embraced all three of these positions at various times throughout their history. The challenge is to steer foreign policy between the Scylla of withdrawal from the world and the Charybdis of excessive interventionism. A democratic populace can only be asked to fight wars for so long.

It is clear that a majority of Americans are worried about the threat posed by ISIS and other terrorist organizations, not only in the Middle East but in the United States itself. These concerns span both major political parties and all walks of life. What is less clear is what can and should be done about the threat. People who agree that terrorism must be combatted do not necessarily agree on the wisdom or possibility of massive military intervention. After so many years of war in Iraq and Afghanistan, Americans may not be ready for another major land war. And even if they were, people can reasonably disagree over where that effort is most usefully expended. Should America be helping Iraq fight ISIS in that country, which is uncomfortably close to a full-scale alliance with Iran, itself a sponsor of terrorism, threatening to gain nuclear weapons, and an implacable foe of America and Israel? It's not crystal clear where our real interests lie in that situation. What about Syria – should we be aiding other militias in the civil war there to fight off ISIS, when they commit some of the same atrocities as ISIS itself, and frequently differ only marginally from ISIS about the character of the Islamist theocracy they intend to impose on Syria once Assad is toppled? Confronted by the clash in today's world between secular dictatorships and millenarian Jihadists, we often search for a deluded middle ground, hoping that revolutions and civil wars can be won by teachers and bank clerks demonstrating peacefully for their rights, rather than by a fanatical inner core of radicals. We want to believe, against all evidence to the contrary, that so-called "secular rebels" exist in sufficient numbers among the armed opponents of dictatorships like that of Assad to stave off radical Islamism and make the transition to democracy. But what if no such middle ground exists?

A further thought about ISIS specifically: I personally believe, as I write these words in the summer of 2015, that ISIS shares every feature of the most dangerous and radical of millenarian tyrannies we have examined in this book reaching back to the Jacobins. It wants to impose a grimly repressive collective wherever it gains power, employing genocide to do so. It is inherently imperialistic, bent on extending the "blessing" of its Caliphate by terrorism and open warfare until it stretches around the globe – it boasts that its flag will one day fly over the White House. It is a threat to peace, security, and human rights in the Middle East wherever it has gained territory so far, and to North America and Europe, as it plans to export – or instigate – more and more acts of terrorism. Through its relentless and sophisticated propaganda, it attracts followers among the angry young men whose self-righteous rage provides millenarian revolutions with their cadres, some of them in the United States itself. But while the danger is apparent to just about everyone, no consensus on how precisely to deal with it, especially through military action, has as yet taken shape in American politics or in American society at large. As always, when and if it does, it will involve choices among the lesser of evils.

This is not the place to enter further into these geopolitical scenarios, none of which is fully satisfactory or straightforward, and which may well change even as this book is being written. My purpose is to contribute to our ability to *recognize* the threat posed by contemporary Jihadist terrorism by seeing how it flows from the long history of tyranny in its several varieties. Conservatives have criticized President Obama for refusing to brand terrorism as specifically Jihadist, a legitimate concern. But when the same critics go on to liken today's Jihadist terrorism to past totalitarian movements such as Bolshevism and Nazism, they are in a way conceding a part of his point – Jihadism is not intrinsically Muslim, but the perversion of a genuine religious faith by hitching it to an agenda for this-worldly revolutionary violence that is every bit as much repudiated by traditional Muslim teachings as it is by Judaism and Christianity. In my view, and as I've argued throughout this book, tracing the connection between Jihadist terrorism and its totalitarian predecessors stretching back to Robespierre is the path to true clarity about the nature of the foe we are facing. Connecting those dots also serves to remind us that the struggle we are facing will be a long one. The Islamists' quest for what I have called the "lost community" – formerly pursued by European and Third World collectivists – will, like those earlier struggles, go on for decades. For a comparison, just think of the twenty years of terror and war unleashed between 1793 and 1815 by the French Revolution and Napoleon's determination to spread its lessons throughout all of Europe by force.

I've argued in this book that we should not act against or undermine garden-variety or decayed reformist tyrannies when that would increase the chances of a millenarian tyranny swooping in. In other words, I'm reviving the maxim of Jeanne Kirkpatrick and the other founders of neoconservative foreign policy that we should not undermine authoritarian regimes when that increases the prospects of a totalitarian regime taking their place – and that, moreover, authoritarian regimes have some prospect of evolving toward democracy, whereas totalitarian regimes do not (unless toppled from without). I've set aside the terms "authoritarian" and "totalitarian" because they are too freighted with the attempt of the social sciences to remain value neutral in describing despotic political systems. Let's just call them for what they are – tyrannies, some kinds worse than others.

Kirkpatrick's main impetus was the Carter administration's deliberate undermining of the Shah of Iran because of his less-than-perfect human rights record and progress toward free elections, which brought the far worse tyranny of the Ayatollah Khomeini to power, creating a disaster for the Iranian people and a mortal foe for the West. We saw a similar pattern in the Arab Spring. By demanding that kleptocratic dictators like Mubarak and Gaddafi step down at the first sign of civil unrest, U.S. neoconservatives seem to have forgotten the pragmatic Kissingerian side of Kirkpatrick's original advice stressing the need to choose among the lesser of evils and rushed pell-mell into the undiluted Wilsonian fantasy that everyone on earth is a natural Jeffersonian democrat waiting only to be freed from their tyrants so that they can become liberal democrats just like us. As a consequence Egypt was delivered over to the Muslim Brotherhood, bent on breaking the peace treaty with Israel and creating an Islamic theocracy modeled on Iran. The coup conducted against Morsi by the military – headed by Al Sisi, an aspiring Ataturk who has called upon Islam to reform itself and establish equal rights for women and religious minorities – was a welcome reversal of the Brotherhood's plans, if at the unfortunate cost of a coup d'etat. (But coups d'etat are not always bad: Would anyone have preferred that the plots to assassinate democratically elected Adolf Hitler and overthrow his government by disaffected officers before the outbreak of World War II *not* have succeeded?) As for Libya, the removal of Gaddafi has plunged it into a war of rival Islamist militias.

Even choosing the lesser of evils, however, is no recipe for guaranteed success. While it is likely the case that garden-variety tyrannies have better prospects for evolving into democracies than the millenarian kind, it's not a certainty. Franco's Spain, Salazar's Portugal, and the Somozas' Nicaragua could be listed as comparative successes at this transition. Lee Kuan Yew, "prime minister" of Singapore for over thirty years, is widely credited with transforming that island into a financial powerhouse and a quasifunctioning democracy. (I met him once, and he struck me as a modern-day version of Xenophon's depiction of Hiero of Syracuse, whom the poet Simonides advises to win his people's loyalty by encouraging them to prosper economically). But sometimes, as in Chile's transition from the brutal dictatorship of General Pinochet to a self-governing society with a free market economy, a terrible price is paid in human rights abuses to fend off a collectivist threat that one can only speculate might otherwise have taken control. Gorbachev's dissolution of the Soviet Empire from within through democratizing reforms is an impressive example of how a millenarian revolution, having already degenerated into a frozen kleptocratic hierarchy of Party privilege, might make the transition to self-government. The Shah of Iran might have made the same transition eventually. But there are no certainties, only historical patterns, benchmarks, precedents, and probabilities. As Aristotle wrote, statecraft can't achieve the predictability of geometry, because political life is a realm of contingency and change – prudent judgment is the best we can hope for, and it's never infallible. There's no QED in the merry algebra of political strife.

Even in successful cases of the transition to democracy, outside military and economic pressures are often involved. South Korea would not be the flourishing economy it is today without America's enormous sacrifices in the Korean War, saving it from absorption into the Marxist insane asylum to the north. The war in Vietnam, although well intentioned, had more mixed results. In general, America's self-interest also serves the interests of democratic forces around the world – but not infallibly so. The annihilation of the Third Reich and the Japanese Empire in WW II as the necessary prelude to democratization in those countries demonstrates that, again, democracy may be natural, but not spontaneous. It won't necessarily happen on its own. And the scale of the military effort and sacrifice required of America and her allies – hundreds of thousands of casualties and billions of dollars – in bringing those tyrannies to their knees means that such efforts at massive military intervention on behalf of democracy can only be sustained on very rare occasion.

Democracy is not simply the absence of despotism. It took four hundred years for a civil society based on tolerance and rights to evolve in the West. As we saw in Part Two, the spread of the values of individual economic self-interest in North America and Europe preceded the establishment of full-blown representative government. Peruvian economist Hernando de Soto Polar has argued that this may be the best path for the non-Western world today; that the establishment of contract law enforced by the state as a neutral umpire – instead of, as in so many kleptocratic despotisms, swooping in on any successful business enterprise to steal its profits – is the indispensable prelude to the evolution of a democratic civil society, and that a nondemocratic regime that protected property rights might be preferable to one that proclaims a full-blown democracy on paper overnight before those rights have become entrenched in the political culture. There were signs Mubarak was headed in this direction. Again, though, the notion that creating a market economy can help smooth the transition to democracy won't always work. As we observed, the attempt to introduce market norms in Russia overnight led to a huge backlash and Putin's despotic ascendancy. Choices like this don't make for peaceful sleep.

Whatever prospects may exist for the spread of democracy, one thing is certain – we have to learn again how to identify the varieties of tyranny for what they are. Without that, no prudent judgment of any kind about the greater good or the lesser of evils is possible. Modern liberal democracy was based on the hardheaded assessment by writers like Machiavelli and Hobbes that human nature is governed by self-interest, and that states become prosperous and powerful by cooperating with that passion. But precisely the success of the West in creating such societies can, in their general peacefulness, comfort, and lack of violent political strife, lull us into thinking that the entire world is that way, or can become so simply by wishing for it. Machiavelli and Hobbes knew that societies had to guard their security and well-being from the tyrannically minded wolves prowling the dark perimeter around the well-lit compound of the social contract. We have a tendency to think the whole world is nothing but that bright compound, or soon will be once the wolves learn they will be fed. But wolves are predators – they kill whether they're hungry or not. To the realism of Machiavelli and Hobbes we should add Aristotle's even more fundamental reminder that tyrants value mastery and honor over material comforts. As he put it: "Men don't become tyrants to get in out of the cold."

THE FRONTIERS OF TWENTY-FIRST CENTURY REVOLUTION

Guarding against the wolves brings us back to where we began in the Introduction – the righteous anger of young men and the recruits it provides for terrorism both at home and abroad. Sometimes the motivation is largely nihilistic. I was particularly creeped out by the video of a young Canadian wreathed in a feral grin as he told the camera that joining ISIS was "like, man, the real Disney World." Presumably what he meant by this was that beheading, raping, and burying alive real people was way cooler than mere three-dimensional simulations and computer games based on endless violence like *Grand Theft Auto*. It reminds us of the plausible connection made between "gaming" and rampage killings like Columbine in 1999. In assessing that event, a former West Point psychology professor and Army Ranger, Lieutenant-Colonel Dave Grossman, argued that video games desensitized young men from seeing other people as real human beings in a way similar to the training that the military receive to enable them to kill the enemy: Whereas Marines learned to kill America's enemies in war, these "gamers" turned on their own fellow citizens. But however much the "self-radicalized" terrorists of the new century may resemble rampage killers, they are fundamentally different, because they are motivated by the ideology of Jihadist millenarian revolution. Whether recruits to an actual foreign terrorist operation (like the Underwear Bomber), responding on their own to an Internet summons to kill the infidels (like the beheading in Moore, Oklahoma), won over by Islamist imams on the Internet (the Boston Marathon shooter), or just convinced that the Jihadists are right (Major Hassan), they are revolutionaries motivated by a righteous zeal to destroy the corrupt West and bring it under the rule of the coming worldwide Caliphate. The attempt to portray them as "loners" who "snapped" out of marital frustration or employee dissatisfaction or racial hatred, even if true, is irrelevant to the main motivation for terrorism. Those who advance this interpretation think that they are somehow calling into question the sincere attachment of such killers to their version of Islam. But as we've seen throughout this book, the projection of personal anger over a perceived slight or injustice into the need to purge the entire world of its vices through revolutionary violence is at the very core of terroristic behavior. Lenin, Stalin, Hitler, Mao, were all in various ways "disgruntled loners" who "snapped" over what they felt was unjust treatment by leading movements of mass murder. The danger of Jihadism, like previous aspiring millenarian tyrannies, is precisely that it provides young men bent for whatever reason on violence, who might otherwise have worked it off in fights or ordinary crime, with a coherent utopian vision that convinces them their rage is sanctified by bringing about a just world.

As I said in the Introduction, I haven't discussed *every* force in the world that could be called tyrannical. If the meaning of "tyranny" can be stretched to include any power capable of destroying or degrading the human race, then nuclear weaponry and the devastation of the environment could be included as tyrannical forces. The danger posed by modern technology is especially dramatic in the case of totalitarian tyrants such as Hitler or Stalin because it enabled them to launch genocidal and military destruction unavailable on such a scale to past despots, just as the Iranian Ayatollahs' possession of nuclear weapons technology would equip them to threaten world annihilation today. The ever-more pervasive power of global communications technology is both a source among dissidents of potential liberation from oppressive regimes such as China or Syria but also of such despotic states' extension of their own capacity for monitoring all communication among their subjects. The old jesting reference to Stalin as "Genghis Khan with electricity" can now be updated to "Genghis Khan on Twitter." As for the conviction expressed in Lenin's maxim "the worse, the better," originating with Marx, that the tyrannically oppressive force of History itself, culminating in the horrors of capitalism, might bring about the utopian collective of the future through sparking revolutionary action, it remains active in a diluted way today. While "the Sixties" were more of a cultural ferment of alternative lifestyles than a conscious project for seizing revolutionary power, Jonathan Schell, for example, in his own Boomer version of "the worse, the better," argued in *The Fate of the Earth* that nuclear weapons technology and the threat of annihilation it posed might, like the Augustinian fear of God's damnation, terrify Western consumer societies into bringing about world peace and justice.

Today's protesters against "the One Percent" believe that "globalization" is the worst oppressor in history, with capitalist America as its spearhead. But they also believe – as had Marxists before them – that the overwhelming oppressiveness of capitalism can unite the "dispossessed" and "marginalized" and usher in a new utopia that will shatter globalization's grip, the coming "new global civil society" of the enviro-friendly and nonmaterialistic. It's an updated version of Marx's classic formula that bourgeois society will act as "its own grave-digger." However, while Marxists longed for violent revolution, most anti-One Percent protesters are peaceful. The self-proclaimed "anarchists" who trash businesses as they tour the world for economic summits are a tiny unrepresentative minority. As this example illustrates, while for reasons I discussed earlier the millenarian impulse in America in general is largely shorn of the desire for direct revolutionary violence aimed at creating a monolithic new state, the utopian impulse retains some of its familiar themes among the young as a continuing cultural and aesthetic protest against the alleged injustice and emptiness of bourgeois life whose origins we traced in Part Three.

Finally, as we continue looking for the frontiers of revolution in the new century, there is a sense in which some advances in medical technology pose a new danger of utopian extremism, whether it be the hopes placed in psychotropic drugs to reconstruct the human personality so as to rid it of all aggressiveness and anxiety or the more recent "transhumanist" movement that believes that all limitations on genetic manipulation should be lifted so as to create a new *Herrenvolk* of superior IQs and perfect health and looks. In effect, the longing for the bliss of a complete release from the limitations of our human self-hood, for a world nirvana of endless and ecstatic happiness, that began with Rousseau and sparked the great revolutions from the Jacobins onward is now removed from the sphere of political action to the realm of pharmacology and embryonic manipulation.

One final variety of global technology is worth mentioning, and that's global entertainment culture, mainly American. Does American pop culture itself encourage nihilistic fantasies about violence that may undermine civic morality at home and feed the longing for destruction in America's enemies abroad? The 9/11 attacks uncovered some disturbing nihilistic undercurrents in our own way of life in the West and our own subterranean dissatisfactions with the modern "bourgeois" way of life. Consider again, for instance, the now extremely eerie scene in the movie *Fight Club*, released just two years before 9/11, in which the fascistic "manly man" played by Brad Pitt as an alter-ego for the wimpy IKEA-furniture-buying Ed Norton serenely surveys his gang's destruction of the New York City skyline through a massively coordinated terrorist bombing. As we observed in the Introduction, after 9/11, and as if *reviewing* such a film instead of a real massacre, the German *avant-garde* composer Karlheinz Stockhausen pronounced the spectacle of the Twin Towers going down under Al Qaeda's onslaught as "the greatest work of art imaginable for the whole cosmos." Continuing terrorist plots around the world point to the attraction of native-born Europeans and Americans to the secret thrill of contemplating the West's destruction. We need to ponder further the vicarious identification of Western intellectuals with Jihadist movements, which they regard as spiritually more pure than ourselves and as the means by which we will be punished for our crimes of colonialist greed and exploitation, as exemplified by Michel Foucault calling the Ayatollah Khomeini "a mystic saint," and his romanticization of violent revolution as a "heroic" code. In this, he was inspired by Mussolini's favorite author, Georges Sorel, who had admired Lenin as a Nietzschean Superman. All of these questions prompt us to some necessary soul searching about the origins and temptations of political mass violence.

A HOMEOPATHIC CURE FOR THE TYRANNICAL TEMPTATION

If there is an antidote for the temptation to tyrannize – therapy for the rage of Achilles – it begins with a homeopathic cure. In other words, before young men can spot the temptation of tyranny, especially in themselves but in those around them as well, they have to have a sense of what that temptation *feels* like. Only then will they realize how powerful a narcotic passionate ambition, honor seeking and righteous wrath can be. And only then will they realize that terrorism and tyranny are not one big awful misunderstanding, as we are so often told now no matter how much proof exists to the contrary; that people will give up their violent and dominating passions when the "root cause" is addressed – first, when they get enough to eat, then when they get enough material comfort and entertainment to make their rage go away for good, perhaps assisted by medication, anger management, and a twelve-step program for self-esteem. It simply doesn't work with everyone, especially for the most dangerous predators. If America's historically unprecedented levels of personal liberty, wealth, equality, and leisure were able to sooth all such savage souls, why would terrorist attacks by her own citizens occur with increasing frequency on her own soil? As for terrorists in the non-Western world, the top leaders are often already rich and living in luxury (like Bin Ladin, who inherited millions, and Hamas' leader supervising human shield operations in Gaza from his five-star hotel in Qtr), even if the human tools they employ are sometimes wretchedly poor. They want to kill us because they hate and despise us as a matter of principled conviction.

Socrates was the originator of the homeopathic cure for tyranny when he argued in the *Republic* that, in reforming Homer's poetry in order to prevent it from inspiring future Achilles to narcissistic selfishness exploding in a towering rage, the statesmen of a just society must sample – in their imaginations – a *degree* of the vices they intend to forestall in the citizenry, especially young men, through the right kind of civic education. If you can't feel the attraction of a vice in your own imagination, Socrates is saying, it will be hard to come up with a convincing account of why it's the wrong way to go; why vigorous and virtuous citizenship in the service of the common good is better than tyranny, both for decent politics and for living a happy life. You can't feel (as opposed to merely think) that a moderate way of life devoted to an aspiration to moral excellence is happier than a life of tyrannical excess if you haven't at least imagined what it would be like to be a slave to your basest passions and how degrading a fate that would be. A purely intellectual exercise in choosing virtue over vice won't take hold throughout one's entire character without this psychological dimension. The homeopathic cure for tyranny lies in the canon of the Great Books with their breadth, depth, and psychological finesse about the best and worst in human nature, beginning with Plato and the ancient thinkers, and extending to profound and realistic diagnosticians of human desire and political passion including Machiavelli, Hobbes, Shakespeare, and great historians who demonstrate a knowledge of human nature's complexity and capacity for evil as well as good such as Gibbon. The list of Reading for Further Interest at the end of this book also features some standouts in more contemporary writing about tyranny, including some of the great scholarship of the Cold War and biographies and histories of the French Revolution, Bolshevism, Nazism, and their successors.

Only from this immersion in the very best of philosophy, history, and literature might young people learn in their hearts and minds to replace a zeal for domination with a zeal for the common good; to be able to distinguish a permissible ambition to excel in serving the common good from an impermissible ambition to dominate one's fellow citizens; to be mature enough to realize that there are few pure idealists in political life (and when there are, they tend to be dangerous), and that some of the darker, more aggressive qualities that drive the soul of a tyrant can also be found in the inner make-up of great statesmen, a paradox we considered going all the way back to Sophocles' *Oedipus Tyrannus*. Ambition cannot be removed from the human soul, no matter how much wealth, comfort, and entertainment we are offered. It can only be reshaped by liberal education, and redirected from unjust to just goals. No one better understood what he called "the tribe of the lion" – men like Alexander, Caesar, and Napoleon – than Abraham Lincoln, or the temptation he explored as a young man in the *Lyceum* speech for a statesman to achieve immortal fame by overthrowing the republic rather than by serving it. I believe that Lincoln made the right choices in his own rise more resolutely because he understood, and overcame inwardly, the appeal of the wrong ones. By saving the American republic – not only from disintegration but from the moral taint of slavery on its soul – through an ordeal that summoned to the last ounce his innermost qualities of ambition, justice, fortitude, and compassion, he achieved immortal glory in the service of civic honor.

This maturity about political motivation and honor seeking is especially necessary today, when the canon of the Great Books is so often undermined by the self-absorption of identity politics and the hopeless lack of realism in the social sciences, which persist in refusing to recognize that tyrannical ambition is a permanent motivation in political behavior. The belief in globalization, leading either to the elevation of economics as the chief field for the study of human affairs or to the utopian fantasy of a coming "global civil society," has also done great harm to liberal education by making young people unaware of the richness of the psychology of honor seeking in the canon of the Great

Books and the crucial distinction they make between just and unjust, better and worse regimes and political systems – which further robs young people of the ability to distinguish between tyranny and free self-government, and to reflect on why liberal democracy, even at its worst and most flawed, is preferable to tyranny even at its best.

This book's account of the strange career of tyranny – its varieties and their degrees of injustice – is my contribution to that homeopathic cure. I've argued that, from the pharaohs, Cyrus the Great, Alexander the Great, and Julius Caesar down to modern state-building autocrats like Henry VIII and Peter the Great, "enlightened despotism" can play an important role in laying the foundations for orderly, prosperous, and civilized societies. But that is the very *best* case scenario for what I call reforming tyranny. Few tyrannies that profess such reforms carry them out entirely successfully, and rarely to a degree that would trump their constant violation of human rights. Look at the disastrous attempts of the Third Reich and Soviet Union to create utopia through terror. Even the most successful reforming tyrannies quickly outlive their usefulness. If we are lucky, they will make a voluntary transition to a more free form of government, as happened with Franco and Gorbachev (with obviously mixed results). Sometimes, as we have observed, that transition to self-government can only be achieved by lethal military force from the outside – the democracies of Japan and West Germany rose on the ashes of their near annihilation by the Western Alliance. The West cannot impose democracy throughout the world by endless war – its own democratic culture would never tolerate being on a permanent war footing, even for the best of causes. At the same time, we have seen the perils of "nation-building" in societies not yet converted to the values of the Enlightenment, and riven by religious and ethnic strife where politics is seen as a way of smashing the other side. That is why it is better to coax the development of freedom by degrees wherever possible, even if it means tolerating the continued existence of less than democratic, or even openly non-democratic, governments if the likeliest alternative is millenarian dictatorship. Sometimes, though, war will be unavoidable. That is a terrible lesson of history, but the recurrent defeat of tyranny's attempts to enslave the world from Marathon and Salamis to Dunkirk and D-Day should be a source of hope as well as sober realism. After all, the as-yet unending career of tyranny is also the history of its as-yet unending defeat by freedom.

I have said that liberal democracy of the Western kind is not natural in the sense of being spontaneous. The mere removal of a tyrant does not guarantee that people will automatically embrace their inner Jeffersonian democrat. They may only want revenge, and triumph for their own clan, tribe, or sect. But liberal democracy definitely *is* natural in the ancient Platonic and Aristotelian meaning of human nature – not mere survival, but the cultivation of our greatest potential for moral virtue as free citizens of a self-governing republic, including tolerance, freedom of thought and expression, liberal education, and cultural excellence. Tyrannies at their best can sometimes protect people's lives against a greater threat posed by civil strife, or promote material prosperity. But they can never enable people to pursue happiness and self-fulfillment. As long as we remain vigilant against the wolves who prowl the perimeter, democracy is bound to defeat tyranny because it's simply a better idea.

Reading for Further Interest

This book is about how political ideas and human nature, culture, and history have interwoven to produce the career of tyranny. As far as primary sources go, my main references have been to Homer, Herodotus, Sophocles, Thucydides, Plato, Aristotle, Xenophon and Cicero (among ancient thinkers), St. Augustine, St. Thomas Aquinas, and Martin Luther (among Christian theologians), and Machiavelli, Hobbes, Locke, Burke, and Rousseau (among modern thinkers). Other ancient primary sources for the description and diagnosis of tyranny in contrast with sound statesmanship include Aeschylus, Virgil, Sallust, Suetonius, Plutarch, and Tacitus. Renaissance sources abound, but at a minimum we would have to mention Erasmus and Castiglione, to say nothing of Shakespeare.

As for millenarian revolution, I have made some observations about the influence of Marx, Nietzsche, and Heidegger on the extremist thinking of their times. Nineteenth-century European fiction also offers a rich trove of observations about terrorism and both the danger and attraction of tyranny, including (at a minimum) novels by Flaubert, Tolstoy, Turgenev, Balzac, Stendhal, and Dostoevsky, continuing in the twentieth century with Hesse, Solzhenitsyn, and Kundera.

Readers interested in a more scholarly discussion of tyranny as a theme in political philosophy are invited to consider my book *Tyranny: A New Interpretation*, which also contains an extensive bibliography and discusses current interpretive debates about how ancient and modern tyranny differ. The Platonic diagnosis of and therapy for potential tyrants is the theme of my earlier book *Ruling Passion: The Erotics of Statecraft in Platonic Political Philosophy*. Tyranny and the danger it poses to virtuous statesmanship also figures prominently in my anthology *What Is a Man? Three Thousand Years of Wisdom on the Art of Manly Virtue* and in my books *The Code of Man: Love, Courage, Pride, Family, Country*, and *The Soul of a Leader: Character, Conviction, and Ten Lessons in Political Greatness*.

What follows is a list of general-interest works for further reading – mainly histories, biographies, and anthologies, but also some fiction and social science. It's a list that is entirely personal to me, one might even say idiosyncratic, gleaned from a lifetime of thinking, teaching, reading, traveling, and conversation. Every item on it comes from my own library. Some of it is quite recent, some quite old. Some readers will doubtless find what strike them as gaps or missing works of importance. I've tried to be comprehensive, but if I haven't left every stone unturned, bear in mind that most of these books also contain extensive bibliographies inviting further exploration of their topics from other perspectives. No one was intentionally overlooked. My reliance on and debt to the pathbreaking efforts and superb scholarship of the writers mentioned here, as well as those with whom they have been engaged, is profound and, I trust, self-evident.

Ackroyd, Peter. *Tudors*. London: St. Martin's, 2012.
  Foundation: The History of England from Its Earliest Beginnings to the Tudors Rebellion. New York: St. Martin's Press, 2014.
Andress, David. *The Terror: The Merciless War for Freedom in Revolutionary France*. New York: Farrar, Strauss and Giroux, 2005.
Applebaum, Anne. *Gulag: A History*. New York: Anchor, 1994.
Arendt, Hannah. *Eichmann in Jerusalem*. New York: Penguin, 1963.
  On Revolution. New York: Viking, 1963.
Armstrong, Karen. *A History of God*. New York: Ballantine, 1993.
Baker, Simon. *Ancient Rome: The Rise and Fall of an Empire*. London: BBC Books, 2006.
Balot, Ryan. *Greed and Injustice in Classical Athens*. Princeton, NJ: Princeton University Press, 2001.
Barone, Michael. *Our First Revolution*. New York: Crown Forum, 2008.
Barrett, Anthony. *Caligula: The Corruption of Power*. New Haven: Yale University Press, 1998.
  Livia: First Lady of Imperial Rome. New Haven: Yale University Press, 2002.
Beevor, Anthony. *Stalingrad: The Fateful Siege 1942–43*. New York: Penguin, 2003.
  The Fall of Berlin 1945. New York: Penguin, 2006.
Belloc, Hilaire. *Robespierre: A Study*. London: Nisbet, 1927.
Billington, James. *Fire in the Minds of Men*. New York: Transaction, 1980.
Birley, Anthony. *Marcus Aurelius: A Biography*. New York: Barnes and Noble Books, 1993.
Bortoli, Georges. *The Death of Stalin*. London: Phaeton, 1973.
Brinton, Clarence Crane. *The Anatomy of Revolution*. New York: Vintage, 1973.
Bryce, James. *The Holy Roman Empire*. New York: Burt, 1886.
Bullock, Alan. *Hitler: A Study in Tyranny*. New York: Bantam, 1961.
Bury, J.R. *A History of Greece*. New York: Modern Library, 1927.
Cannadine, David. *Aspects of Aristocracy*. New York: Penguin, 1995.
Carcopino, Jerome. *Daily life in Ancient Rome*. New York: Penguin, 1960.
Chalidze, Valerii. *To Defend These Rights: Human Rights and the Soviet Union*. New York: Random House, 1974.
Charles-Picard, Gilbert. *Augustus and Nero: The Secret of Empire*. London: Phoenix, 1966.
Charnwood, Lord. *Abraham Lincoln*. New York: Garden City Publishers, 1917.
Cheng, Nien. *Life and Death in Shanghai*. London: Grafton, 1986.
Churchill, Winston. *Great Contemporaries*. New York: Putnam's, 1937.
Cobban, Alfred. *A History of Modern France*. London: Pelican, 1980.
Cohen, Stephen F. *Bukharin and the Bolshevik Revolution*. New York: Vintage, 1975.
Cohn, Norman. *The Pursuit of the Millennium*. Oxford: Oxford University Press, 1970.
Conquest, Robert. *Power and Policy in the U.S.S.R.* New York: Harper and Row, 1967.

The Great Terror: Stalin's Purge of the Thirties. New York: Collier, 1973.

The Harvest of Sorrow: Soviet Collectivization and the Terror-Famine. New York: Oxford University Press, 1986.

Cooper, Duff. *Talleyrand*. New York: Harper's, 1932.

Cornwell, John. *Hitler's Pope*. London: Penguin, 2008.

Crankshaw, Edward. *The Shadow of the Winter Palace*. New York: Penguin, 1978.

Dahrendorf, Ralf. *Society and Democracy in Germany*. Garden City, New York: Doubleday, 1967.

Dallin, T. and A. Larson, eds. *Soviet Politics since Kruhschev*. Englewood Cliffs, NJ: Prentice-Hall, 1968.

Davidowicz, Lucy S. *The War against the Jews· 1933 1945*. Toronto: Bantam, 1975.

Davies, Norman. *Europe: A History*. London: Pimlico, 1997.

Djilas, Milovan. *The New Class*. New York: Praeger, 1958.

Conversations with Stalin. New York: Harcourt Brace, 1963.

de Tocqueville, Alexis. *The Old Regime and the French Revolution*. Garden City, NY: Anchor, 1955.

Democracy in America. Mansfield and Winthrop trans. Chicago: University of Chicago Press, 2002.

Deutscher, Isaac. *The Prophet Unarmed*. London: Oxford University Press, 1959.

Heretics and Renegades. New York: Bobbs-Merrill, 1969.

Dolgun, Alexander. *Alexander Dolgun's Story: An American in the Gulag*. New York: Knopf, 1975.

Eckert, Allan W. *A Sorrow in Our Heart: The life of Tecumseh*. New York: Bantam, 1992.

Eliade, Mircea. *History of Religious Ideas*. Chicago: University of Chicago Press, 1981.

Elton, G. R. *The Tudor Revolution in Government*. Cambridge: Cambridge University Press, 1967.

Evans, Richard J. *The Coming of the Third Reich*. London: Penguin, 2005.

Everitt, Anthony. *Hadrian*. New York: Random House, 2004.

The Rise of Rome. New York: Random House, 2012.

Fanon, Frantz. *The Wretched of the Earth*. New York: Grove, 1968.

Fest, Joachim C. *The Face of the Third Reich: Portraits of Nazi Leadership*. Michael Bullock trans. New York: Ace Books, 1970.

Hitler. New York: Vintage, 1975.

The German Resistance to Hitler 1933–1945. London: Phoenix, 1996.

Finkelstein, Israel and Neil Asher Sherman. *The Bible Unearthed*. New York: Simon and Schuster, 2001.

Freeman, Charles. *AD 381: Heretics, Pagans and the Christian State*. London: Pimlico, 2008.

Friedlander, Saul. *Nazi Germany and the Jews 1933–1945: The Years of Extermination*. New York: Harper, 2007.

Friedrich, Otto. *Before the Deluge: A Portrait of Berlin in the 1920's*. New York: Fromm, 1986.

Fukuyama, Francis. *The Origins of Political Order*. New York: Farrar, Strauss and Giroux, 2012.

Gere, Cathy. *The Tomb of Agamemnon*. Cambridge, Massachusetts: Harvard University Press, 2008.

Gibbon, Edward. *The Decline and Fall of the Roman Empire*. New York: Fenlon, Collier and Son, 1900.

Gilbert, Martin C. *The Holocaust: The Jewish Tragedy*. Glasgow: Fontana/Collins, 1986.

Ginzburg, Ugenia. *Journey into the Whirlwind*. New York: Harcourt, Brace and World, 1967.

Goebbels, Joseph. *The Goebbels Diaries 1942–1943*. Garden City, NY: Doubleday, 1948.

The Diaries of Joseph Goebbels: Final Entries 1945. New York: Avon, 1979.

Goldhagen, Daniel. *Hitler's Willing Executioners: Ordinary Germans and the Holocaust*. New York: Knopf, 1996.

Goldhill, Simon. *The Temple in Jerusalem*. Cambridge, Massachusetts: Harvard University Press, 2005.

Goldsworthy, Adrian. *The Fall of the West*. London: Weidenfeld and Nicholson, 2004.

Caesar. London: Phoenix, 2008.

Augustus: First Emperor of Rome. New Haven: Yale University Press, 2014.

Goodman, Martin. *Rome and Jerusalem*. New York: Penguin, 2008.

Goodspeed, D.J. *The Conspirators: A Study of the Coup d'Etat*. Toronto: Macmillan, 1967.

Gray, John. *False Dawn: The Delusions of Global Capitalism*. London: Granta, 1998.

Griffin, Roger, ed. *Fascism*. New York: Oxford University Press, 1995.

Guizot, Francois. *France*. R. Black trans. New York: Fenelon, Collier and Son, 1900. Eight volumes.

Haing, Ngor, *Survival in the Killing Fields*. New York: Basic Books, 2003.

Hanson, Victor Davis. *A War Like No Other*. New York: Random House, 2006.

Hardt, Michael, Antonio Negri. *Empire*. Cambridge, Massachusetts: Harvard University Press, 2000.

Hartz, Louis. *The Liberal Tradition in America*. New York: Harcourt, Brace and World, 1955.

Heather, Peter. *The Fall of Rome*. London: Penguin, 2006.

Heiden, Konrad. *Der Fuhrer*. Boston: Houghton-Mifflin, 1947.

Heine, Heinrich. *Religion and Philosophy in Germany*. John Snodgrass, trans. Albany, NY: SUNY Press, 1986.

Herf, Jeffrey. *Reactionary Modernism: Technology, Culture, and Politics in Weimar and the Third Reich*. New York: Cambridge University Press, 1984.

Hibbert, Christopher. *The French Revolution*. New York: Penguin, 1986.

Hochschild, Adam. *King Leopold's Ghost: A Story of Greed, Terror and Heroism in Colonial Africa*. New York: Houghton Mifflin, 1998.

Hopkins, Keith and Mary Beard. *The Colosseum*. Cambridge, Massachusetts: Harvard University Press, 2005.

Hughes, Robert C. *The Shock of the New*. New York: Knopf, 1991.

Hutchinson, Robert. *The Last Days of Henry the Eighth*. London: Phoenix, 2005.

Thomas Cromwell. London: Phoenix, 2008.

Ignatieff, Michael. *The Warrior's Honor*. New York: Viking, 1998.

Jaeger, Werner. *Paideia: The Ideals of Greek culture*. New York: Oxford University Press, 1963.

Johnson, Paul. *The Birth of the Modern*. London: Weidenfeld and Nicholson, 1991.

Intellectuals. London: Phoenix, 1993.

Jo-hsi, Chen. *The Execution of Mayor Yin*. Bloomington, Indiana: Indiana University Press, 1978.

Judd, Denis. *Empire: The British Imperial Experience from 1765 to the Present.*

Kagan, Donald. *The Peloponnesian War.* New York: Viking, 2003.

Kapucinski, Ryszard. *The Emperor: Downfall of an Autocrat.* New York: Vintage, 1984.

Katz, Solomon. *The Decline of Rome and the Rise of Mediaeval Europe.* Ithaca, NY: Cornell University Press, 1963.

Kershaw, Ian. *Hitler.* London: Penguin, 2008.

   The End: The Defiance and Destruction of Hitler's Germany 1944–1945. Penguin: London, 2011.

Khrushchev, Nikita. *Khrushchev Remembers.* Crankshaw ed. New York: Bantam, 1971.

Kinross, Lord. *The Ottoman Centuries.* New York: Morrow Quill, 1977.

Kleiner, Diana E. E. *Roman Sculpture.* New Haven· Yale University Press, 1992.

Kohn, Hans. *The Mind of Germany.* New York: Harper Torchbook, 1965.

Kolakowski, Leszek. *Main Currents of Marxism.* New York: W.W. Norton, 2008.

Kornhauser, William. *The Politics of Mass Society.* New York: The Free Press, 1959.

Kravchenko, Victor. *I Chose Freedom.* Garden City, NY: Garden City Publishing, 1946.

Kriwaczek, Paul. *In Search of Zarathustra.* New York: Vintage, 2002.

Landes, Richard. *Heaven on Earth: The Varieties of the Millennial Experience.* Oxford: Oxford University Press, 2011.

Lane Fox, Robin. *Pagans and Christians.* New York: Harper and Row, 1988.

   Traveling Heroes. New York: Vintage, 2010.

   The Classical World: An Epic History of Greece and Rome. London: Penguin, 2014.

Laqueur, Walter ed. *Fascism: A Reader's Guide.* Berkeley: University of California Press, 1978.

Laqueur, Walter and Yonah Alexander, eds. *The Terrorism Reader.* New York: Penguin, 1987.

Leites, Nathan. *A Study of Bolshevism.* Glencoe, Illinois: Free Press, 1953.

Leonhard, Wolfgang. *The Three Faces of Marxism.* New York: Holt, Rinehart, Winston, 1974.

Levi, Primo. *Survival in Auschwitz.* New York: Collier, 1961.

Lewis, Bernard. *What Went Wrong?* Oxford: Oxford University Press, 2002.

   The Crisis of Islam. New York: Modern Library, 2004.

Leys, Simon. *Chinese Shadows.* New York: Penguin, 1978.

   The Chairman's New Clothes: Mao and the Cultural Revolution. London: Allison and Busby, 1981.

Liddell-Hart, B. H. *History of the Second World War.* New York: Putnam's, 1970.

Lifton, Robert Jay. *The Nazi Doctors: Medical Killing and the Psychology of Genocide.* New York: Basic, 1986.

Littell, Jonathan. *The Kindly Ones.* New York: Harper, 2010.

Luttwak, Edward. *The Grand Strategy of the Roman Empire.* Baltimore: Johns Hopkins University Press, 1976.

Lyons, Eugene. *Workers' Paradise Lost.* New York: Paperback Library, 1967.

MacCulloch, Diarmad. *Reformation: Europe's House Divided.* New York: Penguin, 2004.

MacMillan, Margaret. *Paris 1919.* New York: Random House, 2003.

Magee, Bryan. *The Tristan Chord: Wagner and Philosophy.* New York: Henry Holt, 2000.

Mandelstaum, Nadezhda. *Hope against Hope.* New York: Penguin, 1975.

Manuel, Frank E., ed. *The Enlightenment.* Englewood Cliffs, NY: Prentice-Hall, 1965.

Massie, Robert K. *Nicholas and Alexandra.* New York: Dell, 1967.

Peter the Great: His Life and World. New York: Ballantine, 1980.

McCullough, David. *1776*. New York: Simon and Schuster, 2005.

Miller, James. *The Passion of Michel Foucault*. New York: Doubleday, 1993.

Mitchell, Lynette. *The Heroic Rulers of Archaic and Classical Greece*. London: Bloomsbury, 2013.

Montefiore, Simon Sebag. *Stalin: The Court of the Red Tsar*. New York: Vintage, 2005.

Jerusalem. New York: Knopf, 2012.

Mosse, George L. *The Crisis of German Ideology: Intellectual Origins of the Third Reich*. New York: Grosset and Dunlop, 1964.

Naipaul, V. S. *Among the Believers*. New York: Vintage, 1982.

Nolte, Ernest. *The Three Faces of Fascism*. New York: Henry Holt, 1966.

Nyiszli, Miklos. *Auschwitz: A Doctor's Eyewitness Account*. New York: Arcade, 1960.

Ober, Joshua. *Political Dissent in Democratic Athens*. Princeton: Princeton University Press, 1998.

O'Brien, Conor Cruise. *On the Eve of the Millennium*. New York: The Free Press, 1995.

Ortega y Gassett, Jose. *The Revolt of the Masses*. New York: W. W. Norton, 1932.

Panin, Dmitri. *The Notebooks of Sologdin*. New York: Harcourt, Brace and Jovanovich, 1976.

Panné, Jean-Louis, Andrzej Paczkowski, Karel Bartosek, Jean-Louis Margolin, Nicolas Werth, Stéphane Courtois, Mark Kramer (Ed, Trans). *The Black Book of Communism*. Cambridge, Mass: Harvard University Press, 1999.

Pipes, Richard. *Russia under the Old Regime*. New York: Scribner's, 1974.

Polanyi, Karl. *The Great Transformation*. Boston: Beacon, 1944.

Rahe, Paul. *Against Throne and Altar: Machiavelli and Political Theory under the English Republic*. Cambridge: Cambridge University Press, 2008.

Rajaee, Farhang. *Islamism and Modernism*. Austin: University of Texas Press, 2007.

Rauschning, Herman. *The Revolution of Nihilism*. New York: Alliance, 1939.

Revel, Jean-Francois. *The Totalitarian Temptation*. New York: Penguin, 1978.

Ricciotti, Giuseppe. *Julian the Apostate*. Milwaukee: Bruce, 1959.

Roland, Paul. *The Nazi Files*. London: Arcturus, 2013.

Rubin, Barry. *Modern Dictators: Third World Coup Makers, Strongmen and Populist Tyrants*. New York: McGraw Hill, 1987.

Rubinstein, Richard. *When Jesus Became God*. New York: Harcourt, 1999.

Aristotle's Children. New York: Mariner Books, 2004.

Schama, Simon. *Citizens*. London: Vintage, 1990.

Schmidt-Hauer, Christian. *Gorbachev: The Path to Power*. London: Pan, 1986.

Scully, Vincent. *The Earth, the Temple, and the Gods*. New Haven: Yale University Press, 1979.

Sereny, Gita. *Into That Darkness: An Examination of Conscience*. New York: Vintage, 1983.

Albert Speer: His Battle with the Truth. New York: Vintage, 1996.

Shalamov, Varlam. *Kolyma Tales*. New York: W. W. Norton, 1982.

Shapiro, Leonard. *The Communist Party of the Soviet Union*. New York: Vintage, 1971.

Shawcross, William. *Sideshow: Kissinger, Nixon and the Destruction of Cambodia*. New York: Simon and Schuster, 1979.

Smith, Mark S. *The Early History of God*. Grand Rapids, MI: Erdmanns, 2002.

Snyder, Timothy. *Bloodlands: Europe between Hitler and Stalin*. New York: Basic, 2010.
Solzhenitsyn, Aleksandr I. *Cancer Ward*. London: Penguin, 1968.
  The Gulag Archipelago. New York: Harper and Row. 3 vols. 1973.
  First Circle. New York: Bantam, 1976.
  Lenin In Zurich. New York: Farrar, Strauss and Giroux, 1976.
Speer, Albert. *Inside the Third Reich*. New York: Avon, 1970.
  Spandau: The Secret Diaries. New York: Pocket Books, 1977.
Stalin, Joseph. *Mastering Bolshevism*. San Francisco: Proletarian Publishers, 1937.
Sterling, Claire. *The Terror Network*. New York: Holt, Rinehart, Winston. 1981.
Stern, Fritz. *The Politics of Cultural Despair: A Study in the Rise of the Germanic Ideology*
  Los Angeles: University of California Press, 1974.
Strauss, Barry. *The Trojan War*. New York: Simon and Schuster, 2007.
  Masters of Command. New York: Simon and Schuster, 2013.
Sukhanov, N. N. *The Russian Revolution 1917*. New York: Harper Torchbook, 1962.
Syme, Ronald. *The Roman Revolution*. New York: Oxford University Press, 2002.
Talmon, J. L. *The Origins of Totalitarian Democracy*. London: Penguin, 1986.
Tawny, R. H. *Religion and the Rise of Capitalism*. London: Peter Smith, 1950.
Taylor, A. J. P. *From Napoleon to Lenin*. New York: Harper Torchbook, 1966.
Thomas, Keith. *Religion and the Decline of Magic*. New York: Penguin, 1971.
Tolstoy, Nikolai. *Victims of Yalta*. London: Corgi, 1979.
  Stalin's Secret War. London: Pan Books, 1981.
Trevor-Roper, Hugh. *The Last Days of Hitler*. New York: Macmillan, 1947.
Tuchman, Barbara. *The Guns of August*. New York: Macmillan, 1962.
Tucker. *Stalin as Revolutionary*. New York: W.W. Norton, 1973.
von Lang, Jochen. *Top Nazi: General Karl Wolfe*. New York: Enigma, 2013.
Watkin, David. *The Roman Forum*. Cambridge, Massachusetts: Harvard University Press, 2009.
West, John Anthony. *The Traveller's Key to Ancient Egypt*. New York: Knopf, 1989.
Wildavsky, Aaron. *Moses as Political Leader*. New York: Shalem, 2005.
Woolf, Greg. *Rome: An Empire's Story*. Oxford: Oxford University Press, 2014.
Zweig, Stefan. *The World of Yesterday*. New York: Viking, 1943.
  Marie Antoinette. New York: Harmony Books, 1984.

Index